ANCIENT INDIAN TRADITION & MYTHOLOGY

TRANSLATED BY

A BOARD OF SCHOLARS

AND EDITED BY

Dr. G.P. BHATT

VOLUME 47

ANCIENT INDIAN TRADITION AND MYTHOLOGY SERIES

[PURĀṆAS IN TRANSLATION]

Volumes Released

ŚIVA 1-4
LIṄGA 5-6
BHĀGAVATA 7-11
GARUḌA 12-14
NĀRADA 15-19
KŪRMA 20-21
BRAHMĀṆḌA 22-26
AGNI 27-30
VARĀHA 33-36
VĀYU 37-38
PADMA 39-48
SKANDA, PARTS I-XXI, 49-69
VĀMANA 72-73

Volumes Under Preparation

SKANDA, PARTS XXII-XXIII, 70-71
BHAVIṢYA
BRAHMAVAIVARTA
DEVĪBHĀGAVATA
KĀLIKĀ
MĀRKAṆḌEYA
MATSYA
VIṢṆU
VIṢṆUDHARMOTTARA

THE PADMA-PURĀṆA

PART IX

Translated and Annotated by

DR. N.A. DESHPANDE

MOTILAL BANARSIDASS PUBLISHERS
PRIVATE LIMITED • DELHI

Reprint: Delhi, 2009
First Edition: Delhi, 1991

ISBN: 978-81-208-0881-2

MOTILAL BANARSIDASS
41 U.A. Bungalow Road, Jawahar Nagar, Delhi 110 007
8 Mahalaxmi Chamber, 22 Bhulabhai Desai Road, Mumbai 400 026
203 Royapettah High Road, Mylapore, Chennai 600 004
236, 9th Main III Block, Jayanagar, Bangalore 560 011
Sanas Plaza, 1302 Baji Rao Road, Pune 411 002
8 Camac Street, Kolkata 700 017
Ashok Rajpath, Patna 800 004
Chowk, Varanasi 221 001

UNESCO COLLECTION OF REPRESENTATIVE WORKS—*Indian Series*
This book has been accepted in the Indian Translation Series of the UNESCO Collection of Representative Works, jointly sponsored by the United Nations Educational, Scientific and Cultural Organization (UNESCO) and the Government of India

PRINTED IN INDIA

By Jainendra Prakash Jain at Shri Jainendra Press,
A-45 Naraina, Phase-I, New Delhi 110 028
and Published by Narendra Prakash Jain for
Motilal Banarsidass Publishers Private Limited,
Bungalow Road, Delhi 110 007

PUBLISHER'S NOTE

The purest gems lie hidden in the bottom of the ocean or in the depth of rocks. One has to dive into the ocean or delve into the rocks to find them out. Similarly, truth lies concealed in the language which with the passage of time has become obsolete. Man has to learn that language before he discovers that truth.

But he has neither the means nor the leisure to embark on that course. We have, therefore, planned to help him acquire knowledge by an easier course. We have started the series of Ancient Indian Tradition and Mythology in English Translation. Our goal is to universalize knowledge through the most popular international medium of expression. The publication of the Purāṇas in English Translation is a step towards that goal.

Acknowledgements

It is our pleasant duty to put on record our sincere thanks to Dr. R.N. Dandekar and the UNESCO authorities for their kind encouragement and valuable help in the publication of the volumes in this series.

EDITORIAL

We are happy to offer this forty-seventh *Āhuti* ('oblation') in the *Jñāna-Yajña* ('Knowledge-Sacrifice') that we have undertaken in the form of the *Ancient Indian Tradition and Mythology Series*. The concept of *yajña* has certain noble implications, the foremost one being that it is a selfless venture fraught with difficulties and motivated not by any selfish gain or profit but by universal good in view. In this present *yajña* dissemination of knowledge and popularization of the Purāṇas is our sole aim and this is our apology for calling it '*Jñāna-Yajña*'.

So far the *Padma Purāṇa*, of which this is Part IX in English, has been the biggest one and one still bigger is yet to follow. The last part of this Purāṇa, that is Part X, also is almost ready and thus the complete set of the Purāṇa will be made available to our readers within the next three months.

This part comprises chapters 185-245 of the sixth section, viz. Uttarakhaṇḍa, of the Padma Purāṇa. The reader will find here also, as usual, a rich variety of interesting themes.

The first eight chapters eulogize the saving power of the last eight chapters of the great Bhagavadgītā supported by illustrative stories. The next six chapters show the efficacy of reciting and listening to the Bhāgavata. It has been claimed that this Purāṇa is capable of removing misery, poverty, ill-luck and sins, of overcoming passions and anger in this Kali age. The listening to it is prescribed for seven days (*Saptāha*) at a time only on account of lack of self-control, disease, shortening of life and other blemishes characteristic of the present age. The *Bhāgavata Saptāha* has been praised as better than performing a sacrifice, observing a vow, practising penance, visiting a holy place etc. This is a form of devotion to Kṛṣṇa, which is said to be the only means of salvation fit to be resorted to in this age of unrighteousness. In an allegorical representation Bhakti (Devotion), Jñāna (Knowledge) and Vairāgya (Detachment) are depicted as a woman with two sons. She is said to have been born in the

Draviḍa country, brought up in Karṇāṭa, then to have lived in Mahārāṣṭra and become old along with her sons in Gurjara due to contact with heretics who persecuted them. This is just a figurative way of saying that the devotional movement originated in Tamil Nadu, reached its height of development in Telugu and Marathi speaking regions and declined in Gujarat, probably because of its proximity to the first entry points of Muslim raiders from the Arabian countries. It is further stated that she again became a beautiful young girl in Vṛndāvana, though Jñāna and Vairāgya remained grey-haired and old, thus showing their unpopularity and ineffectiveness in this age.

In our previous Editorials we have reiterated that in view of obviously corrupt readings, obscure passages and wrong words frequently encountered in the existing Purāṇa versions, there is a great need of bringing out thoroughly edited versions of the Purāṇa texts. A clear and convincing case is cited here. In a number of chapters of the text beginning with ch. 199 a name in the vocative case occurs very frequently as 'Śive' and sometimes as 'Śibe'. Now both the names 'Śivā' and 'Śibi' have broadly the same form in the vocative, except a difference of 'va' and 'ba' which is very likely to be ignored and has actually been ignored by some translators, though the person is different in the two cases, one being the consort of god Śiva and the other an ancient king, son of Uśīnara. The dialogue in which this occurs and that runs into several chapters is between Nārada and king Śibi but a reader who is not cautious enough may get the wrong idea that the dialogue is between Nārada and Pārvatī. It is learnt that All India Kashiraj Trust in Varanasi has been doing a laudable work in editing the Purāṇas but apparently the progress is very slow. One would wish that more bodies could come forward in the field.

One more confusing situation is found in chapters 200-209 and further up to ch. 222, where a number of holy places, viz. Prayāga, Kāśī, Śivakāñcī, Gokarṇa, Dvārakā, Kośalā, Madhuvana, Badarikāśrama, Haridvāra, Puṣkara and Naimiṣa which actually have a distance ranging from a few to hundreds of miles, are jumbled up together in a small place named Indraprastha! This obviously needs some researcher to come forward and clear this geographical mix-up.

In chapters 224 and 225 the characteristic sectarian marks are prescribed for the Vaiṣṇavas. One should compulsorily have a mark called *Ūrdhvapuṇḍra* on the forehead and imprint other parts of the body also with disc, conch and other emblems of Viṣṇu heated in fire. Viṣṇu's *Vibhūtis, Vibhavas* and *Vyūhas* are the topics of chapters 227-229.

Chapters 235 and 236 contain very interesting observations of the author of the Purāṇa on the birth of heretics, the measures adopted for bringing about their downfall and destruction and the grouping of the sages, doctrines and texts into *Sāttvika, Rājasa* and *Tāmasa.* In the list of heretics those who have on their body skulls, ash, bones and other inauspicious things are prominently included, thus casting aspersions on god Śiva himself. But in the case of Śiva it is justified as deliberately done to delude and destroy demons and heretics. Not only this but Śiva is also further said to have deliberately composed vicious scriptures like those of Pāśupatas and other Śaivite sects for the purpose. Preaching of the Buddhist doctrines and Śaṅkarite *Māyāvāda* etc. also is shown as part of the same divine conspiracy. Among the Purāṇas Matsya, Kūrma, Liṅga, Śiva, Skanda and Agni are condemned as Tāmasa (vicious). Ten vicious sages include names such as Durvāsas, Kaṇāda, Gautama etc.

In the last few chapters the incarnations of Viṣṇu in the forms of the Boar, Nṛsiṁha, Vāmana, Paraśurāma, Rāma and Kṛṣṇa are described.

—G.P. Bhatt

CONTENTS

PUBLISHER'S NOTE v

EDITORIAL vii

ABBREVIATIONS xv

PADMA-PURĀṆA: SECTION VI: UTTARAKHAṆḌA (CONTINUED)

185. The Greatness of the Eleventh Chapter: Sunanda's Story 2943
186. The Greatness of the Twelfth Chapter: Siddhasamādhi's Story 2950
187. The Thirteenth Chapter: Durācārā's Story 2954
188. The Fourteenth Chapter: Story of a Bitch and a Hare 2957
189. The Fifteenth Chapter: The Story of King Narasiṁha 2960
190. The Sixteenth Chapter: Khaḍgabāhu's Story 2963
191. The Seventeenth Chapter: Duḥśāsana's Story 2965
192. The Eighteenth Chapter: A Brāhmaṇa Becomes Indra 2967
193. The Greatness of the Bhāgavata 2971
194. Śrīmad Bhāgavata, the Destroyer of All Miseries 2976
195. The Rule of Reciting and Listening to the Bhāgavata for a Week 2981
196. Dhundhulī's Story 2987
197. The Seven-day Bhāgavata Recitation 2994
198. Procedure to be Followed during the Saptāha 3001
199. The Glory of Yamunā 3010
200. The Episode of a Bhilla and a Lion 3014
201. Śarabha's Story 3021
202. The Story of King Dilīpa 3028
203. Dilīpa Obtains a Son by Propitiating Nandinī 3033

204. The Story of a Merchant Śarabha and a Demon Vikaṭa 3038
205. The Efficacy of Nigamabodha 3047
206. A Woman Should Never Desert Her Husband 3051
207. The Story of Vimala 3055
208. The Greatness of Dvārakā 3060
209. The Story of Brāhmaṇa Mukunda 3065
210. Mukunda Goes to Heaven 3069
211. Caṇḍaka's Fate 3074
212. The Efficacy of Kośalā 3078
213. A Śrāddha at Madhuvana is More Meritorious 3082
214. The Greatness of Madhuvana 3087
215. Budha Infuriated and Appeased 3095
216. The Greatness of Badarikāśrama 3099
217. The Greatness of Haridvāra 3106
218. The Greatness of Puṣkara: Puṇḍarīka's Story 3109
219. The Greatness of Puṣkara: Puṇḍarīka Attains Absorption into Viṣṇu 3113
220. The Greatness of Prayāga: Mohinī's Story 3116
221. The Greatness of Prayāga: Hemāṅgī and Vīravarman Go to Vaikuṇṭha 3120
222. Kāśī, Gokarṇa, Śivakāñcī, Tīrthasaptaka and Bhīmakuṇḍa 3123
223. Gem of a Formula 3129
224. Bearing the Marks of a Disc etc. Essential for a Brāhmaṇa 3135
225. The Efficacy of Ūrdhvapuṇḍra 3140
226. The Meaning of the Mantra (Formula) 3144
227. The Description of the Vibhūti of Tripād 3150
228. Description of the Highest Heaven etc. 3156
229. A Description of Viṣṇu's Vyūhas 3163
230. The Fish Incarnation of Viṣṇu 3174
231. Durvāsas Cures Indra 3176
232. The Rise of Goddess Lakṣmī 3180
233. Ekādaśī as a Day of Fast 3184
234. How to Observe the Vow of Dvādaśī 3186
235. The Birth of Heretics 3189
236. Characterization of Various Texts and Doctrines as Sāttvika, Rājasa and Tāmasa 3193

237. The Boar Incarnation of Viṣṇu 3195
238. The Emergence of Nṛsiṁha 3198
239. The Rise of Bali and Kaśyapa's Penance 3208
240. Viṣṇu Incarnates as Vāmana 3211
241. Paraśurāma's Story 3215
242. The Story of Rāma 3221
243. Rāma's Consecration 3244
244. Rāma Goes to Heaven 3247
245. The Brave Deeds of Kṛṣṇa 3254

ABBREVIATIONS

Common and self-evident abbreviations such as Ch(s)—Chapter(s), p—page, pp—pages, v—verse, vv—verses, Ftn—Footnote, Hist. Ind. Philo.—History of Indian Philosophy are not included in this list.

ABORI	*Annals of the Bhandarkar Oriental Research Institute*, Poona
AGP	S.M. Ali's *The Geography of Purāṇas*, PPH, New Delhi, 1973
AIHT	*Ancient Indian Historical Tradition*, F.E. Pargiter, Motilal Banarsidass (MLBD), Delhi
AITM	*Ancient Indian Tradition and Mythology* Series, MLBD, Delhi
AP	*Agni Purāṇa*, Guru Mandal Edition (GM), Calcutta, 1957
Arch. S.Rep.	Archaeological Survey Report
AV	*Atharva Veda*, Svādhyāya Maṇḍal, Aundh
Bd. P.	*Brahmāṇḍa Purāṇa*, MLBD, Delhi 1973
BG	*Bhagavadgītā*
Bh. P.	*Bhāgavata Purāṇa*, Bhagavat Vidyapeeth, Ahmedabad
Br.	*Brāhmaṇa* (preceded by name such as Śatapatha)
BS. P.	*Bhaviṣya Purāṇa*, Vishnu Shastri Bapat, Wai
BV. P.	*Brahma Vaivarta Purāṇa*, GM, 1955-57
CC	*Caturvarga Cintāmaṇi* by Hemādri
CVS	*Caraṇa Vyūha Sūtra* by Śaunaka, Com. by Mahīdāsa
DB	*Devī Bhāgavata*, GM, 1960-61
De or GDAMI	*The Geographical Dictionary of Ancient and Mediaeval India*, N.L. De, Oriental Reprint, Delhi, 1971
Dh. S.	*Dharma Sūtra* (preceded by the author's name such as Gautama)
ERE	*Encyclopaedia of Religion and Ethics* by Hastings
GP	*Garuḍa Purāṇa*, ed. R.S. Bhattacharya, Chowkhamba, Varanasi, 1964

GS	*Gṛhya Sūtra* (preceded by the name of the author such as Āpastamba)
HD	*History of Dharma Śāstra*, P.V. Kane, G. O. S.
IA	*The Indian Antiquary*
IHQ	*The Indian Historical Quarterly*
JP	*Purāṇa* (Journal of the Kashiraj Trust), Varanasi
KA	*Kauṭilya Arthaśāstra*
KP	*Kūrma Purāṇa*, Veṅkaṭeśvara Press Edn., Bombay; also Kashiraj Trust Edn., Varanasi, 1971
LP	*Liṅga Purāṇa*, GM, 1960; also MLBD, Delhi, 1981
Manu.	*Manusmṛti*
Mbh.	*Mahābhārata*, Gītā Press, Gorakhpur, VS 2014
MkP	*Mārkaṇḍeya Purāṇa*
MN	*Mahābhārata Nāmānukramaṇī*, Gītā Press, Gorakhpur, VS 2016
MtP	*Matsya Purāṇa*, GM, 1954
MW	Monier Williams' *Sanskrit-English Dictionary*, MLBD, Delhi, 1976
NP	*Nāradīya* or *Nārada Purāṇa*, Veṅkaṭeśvara Press, Bombay
PCK	*Bhāratavarṣīya Prācīna Caritrakośa*, Siddheshwar Shastri, Poona, 1968
Pd. P.	*Padma Purāṇa*, GM, 1957-59
PE	*Purāṇic Encyclopaedia*, V. Mani, English version, MLBD, Delhi, 1975
PR or PRHRC	*Puranic Records on Hindu Rites and Customs*, R.C. Hazra, Calcutta, 1948
ṚV	*Ṛg-Veda*, Svādhyāya Maṇḍal, Aundh
Śat. Br.	*Śatapatha Brāhmaṇa*
SC or SMC	*Smṛti Candrikā* by Devanna Bhaṭṭa
SEP	*Studies in Epics and Purāṇas*, A.D. Pusalkar, Bharatiya Vidya Bhavan (BVB), Bombay

CHAPTER ONE HUNDRED EIGHTYFIVE

The Greatness of the Eleventh Chapter: *Sunanda's Story*

The goddess said:

1-2. O god, this history is a great means of accomplishing the good. O merciful one, my desire is further aroused on hearing it. O Virūpākṣa, O the first (i.e. greatest) one among speakers, explain to me the importance of the eleventh chapter (of the Gītā) supported by a story.

The lord said:

3-17. O dear one, listen to a story resting on the description of the Gītā. Even the greatness of the chapter (called) Viśvarūpa (-darśana) is purifying. O you of large eyes, (the greatness of) the chapter cannot be told. There are thousands of stories. One of them will be told by me. On the bank of the river Pragītā there was a city known as Meghaṅkara. It had a heavily laid foundation, lofty ramparts and gates. It had big (sacrificial) halls of hermitages adorned with golden pillars. Rich, happy, calm, well-behaved men with their senses controlled and speedy in their actions lived there. It was charming with the places where four roads met. It was adorned with markets and quadrangulars where gold in the jewelled pillars was shining. In it the sweet and indistinct sound of the multitude of (moving) banners and jingling bells was (heard). The atmosphere was shaken with the loud noise of Vedic recitation. The vast sky was full of the loud sounds of musical instruments. It won battles with the breezes due to flags and foliage (*obscure*). It appeared splendid with the jingling sounds of the anklets of women on the royal path and at the excellent gates, and with (sounds of) lutes, flutes, songs and the neighings of excellent horses. It constantly appeared to be equal to the cities of the regents of the quarters. There the lord of the world, Śārṅgapāṇi, shone. He was the embodiment of the highest Brahman, and the life of the sight of the world. His great form was worshipped by the lotus-eyes of Lakṣmī (*obscure*). His body was that of Trivikrama; he was dark like a cloud. His lustre was mild; he had Śrīvatsa (mark) on his chest; and was adorned with lotuses and garland of wood-flowers. He was having (i.e. had put on) many ornaments and was, as it were, the ocean full of jewels. His lustre was like that of a cloud with the flashing of the streak of lightning. On his (?) crown dwelt the highest soul Śārṅgapāṇi himself. On seeing him a living being is freed from the bondage of the worldly existence. In that city there was a great holy place called Mekhalā. By bathing there men always obtained the position of Viṣṇu. Having seen Narasiṁha, the lord of the world, the ocean of pity there, a man is free from a terrible sin committed during seven existences.

18-27. A man who sees the lord of gaṇas at Mekhalā always overcomes dangers, even though they are difficult to be overcome. In that Meghaṅkara (city) there lived an excellent brāhmaṇa who practised celibacy and self-control, who was free from the feeling of mineness and from egotism. He was well-known as Sunanda, and was proficient in the Vedas and in (other) holy texts. He had subjugated the group of his senses; he was highly devoted to Vāsudeva. O dear one, by the side of god Śārṅgin he recited this eleventh chapter (of the Gītā called) Manifestation of the Cosmic Form. The ascetic obtained knowledge of Brahman due to the power of the chapter. The meditating saint, enjoying liberation (even) while alive, desiring to reach a steady condition, always remained in profound intellectual meditation, praiseworthy due to the mass of great joy. Once that great meditating saint set out on a pilgrimage to Godāvarī when Jupiter was in the Zodiacal sign Leo. Having, on the first day, come to the excellent holy place Viraja, and having begun with the centre among the holy places, he bathed again and again, and saw Kamalā (i.e. Lakṣmī), the prop of the world. Having worshipped her, the great divine power, giving the fruit of all desires and then bathing at Tārātīrtha, then at the confluence of Kapilā, he visited the eight holy places. Then having offered oblations to the dead ancestors, having bowed to the lord of Kumārī, Śiva, he came to Kapilādvāra.

28-40. Having bathed there, and washed off the sins of former existences, having worshipped, saluted and heard (about) god Viṣṇu and having lived there for that night, he went with the brāhmaṇas from it in the morning. In the forest Narasiṁha there is at the holy place a well sacred to Rāma. Narasiṁha worshipped by Prahlāda himself dwells there. Having seen that lord of gods, having devoutly worshipped him, and having passed the day there, he went to the city of Ambikā. Ambikā, showering grace on her devotees, dwells there. She fulfils all the desires of men. Having devoutly worshipped Ambikā with flowers and unguents, with various hymns, and salutations also, the brāhmaṇa then reached the city called Kaṇṭhasthāna in olden times. There the great power, Mahālakṣmī, of great lustre, dwells. Having seen her, having the orb of the brightness of nectar and the sun, the river of the nectar from lotuses cutting off the torment of the worldly existence, and served by royal swans of the lotuses of the hearts of best meditating saints, full of the sound produced without beating, and of the form having no second, having worshipped with a devout heart that revered Mahālakṣmī, giving desired objects, the lord of sages reached along with the brāhmaṇas, the city called Vivāhamaṇḍapa. In every house in the city he asked for taking shelter. The brāhmaṇa could not get lodging in any house. The head of the village showed to him a big temple to stay in. The brāhmaṇa entering it with his companions stayed there. Then when it was bright morning he saw from his place of lodging his body, where by chance all travellers were produced. When he was going, the village-head saw him coming (to him).

41-50a. The village-head said to him: "You are by all means a long-lived one. You are (the best) among the lucky, and (most) auspicious among the auspicious also. O child, you have some extraordinary power. Where have your companions gone? How did they get out of that house? See that, O best sage, I shall tell you. But I do not see here any other ascetic comparable to you. Do you know a great spell? Which science do you practise? Due to the kindness of which god have you this uncommon power? O best brāhmaṇa, then please stay in this village. O revered one, I shall render you every service." Speaking like this, he made the best sage stay in the village. He devoutly served him day and night. When seven or eight days passed, he came (to him). Having come to him in the morning, he, much grieved, wept before him. "The devout son of me who am luckless today, was eaten at night by a demon having bright fangs." When the protector (of the village) said like this, the restrained one asked him: "Where is the demon? Tell me how your son was devoured."

The village-head said:

50b-59. In the city there is a terrible demon eating human beings. Everyday he comes and eats men frequenting the city. All the citizens formerly requested him: "O demon, protect us all. We shall arrange for your food. O demon, eat those travellers who sleep (here) at night." For protecting his life, he devoured the travellers that were ushered into this house by the village-head. You had slept in this house accompanied by other unlucky persons. They were eaten by him, and you were abandoned, O best brāhmaṇa. O best brāhmaṇa, you know your own power. Today a friend of my son has come. I, being ignorant, (i.e. unknowingly) put that dear (friend) of my son in the (same) house along with other travellers. Hearing that he was put into it, my son went to bring him at night. He too was eaten by the demon. I who was afflicted, said to the demon in the morning: "O wicked-minded one, at night you ate my son also. O demon, tell me if there is a means by which my son gone down into your belly will be revived."

The demon said:

60-63a. Through ignorance I devoured your son that has gone into (my belly). This your son was eaten by me through ignorance along with the travellers. Brahmā has also laid down (the way) in which he who has entered my belly, will be revived. By the power of the brāhmaṇa who constantly recites the eleventh chapter, I shall get salvation and the dead will be revived.

The village-head said:

63b-73. "How does the eleventh chapter have such wonderful power?" O brāhmaṇa, thus asked by me, the demon said: "Formerly some vulture going along the aerial path dropped from its beak a piece of bone somewhere in the water. Someone, best among the wise, having come to that lake, and taking it to be a great holy place, had offered oblations to the dead ancestors. All people said to him: 'Tell (us) how this is a holy place'. The restrained one muttered the eleventh chapter thrice a day.

The brāhmaṇa who had observed silence, was killed by thieves on the way. A piece of his bone fell from the vulture's beak into water. Due to that this has become a divine holy place destroying sins. Then all those men bathed there in that lake. Due to their being free from sins, they obtained the highest position. Owing to the power of the eleventh chapter, I too will get salvation, and the travellers will again come back to life. The brāhmaṇa spat out by me, will stay here only. If he constantly muttered the eleventh chapter, and if that best brāhmaṇa throws on me the water that is consecrated by the hymn of the eleventh chapter, then, undoubtedly I shall be free from the curse." Thus told by him, I have come to you.

The brāhmaṇa said:

74-89a. O protector (of the village), tell (me) due to what sin he had become a demon, eating men in the house at night.

The village-head said:

Formerly in this village there was a brāhmaṇa farmer. Once he was busy with the protection of the paddy-field. Not far from him, a great vulture devoured a traveller. An ascetic at a distance took pity on him to free him. Just then the bird ate up the traveller and went by the aerial path. Then the ascetic, through anger, said to the farmer: "O you wicked-minded, harsh-hearted, cruel ploughman, fie upon you who are selfish, averse to protecting others, and of an accursed life. One who though capable, ignores men being struck by thieves, wild boars, serpents, enemies, poisoned water, vultures, demons, evil spirits, goblins etc., would obtain the fruit of their murder. He who being capable, does not free a brāhmaṇa seized by thieves etc. goes to a horrible hell, and is again born as a wolf. He who (seeing one) being killed (or) harassed by a vulture or a tiger in a forest, says 'Leave (him), leave (him)', goes to the highest position. Those also who are killed while (protecting) cows by tigers, hunters or wicked kings, go to Viṣṇu's position, difficult to be obtained even by meditating saints. Thousands of horse-sacrifices and hundreds of Vājapeya sacrifices are not worth even a sixteenth part of the protection of one seeking shelter. Even a meritorious person, by ignoring a helpless and a frightened person, is roasted in the Kumbhīpāka (hell) after (some) time. Since you were unkind, as you on seeing the traveller (being) eaten by the wicked vulture, did not ward off (the vulture) though you were capable of warding it off, you will be (born as) a demon." Having heard this curse of the sage, the ploughman, with his body trembling, saluted the brāhmaṇa and said (these) piteous words: "With my eyes cast on protecting the field here, I did not notice this man being killed by the vulture. Therefore, please favour me who am helpless."

The brāhmaṇa said:

89b-91. When the water consecrated by him who knows the eleventh chapter (of the Gītā) and mutters it everyday, falls on your head, then you will be free from the curse.

Speaking like this the ascetic left, and the ploughman became a demon. Therefore, O brāhmaṇa, come on; consecrate him with (the recitation of) that chapter. Drop with your (own) hand the holy water on his head.

Mahādeva said:

92-108b. Having heard this request of him, the sage, full of pity, saying 'All right' went with the head of the village near the demon. The brāhmaṇa, the meditating saint, dropped on his head the water consecrated with (the recitation of) the eleventh chapter (called) Viśvarūpa (-darśana). By the power of the chapter of the Gītā, he obtained freedom from the curse. Abandoning the body of the demon he became one having four arms. Those men, the travellers who were ejected, were in thousands. They became four-armed ones holding conches, discs and maces. They got into aeroplanes. At that time he said to the demon: "O demon, which is my son. Show him (to me)." Thus addressed by the village-head, the demon of divine intellect said: "Know your son to be four-armed like these and having dark lustre like the tamāla tree and having a crown of rubies, and adorned with divine, jewelled ear-rings, with great shoulders charming due to a necklace, and adorned with a golden armlet, having lotus-like eyes, affectionate, and holding a lotus in his hand, having got into a divine aeroplane, and having obtained godhead." Hearing these words of him, and seeing his son like that, he started taking him home. Then the son laughed (and said): "O protector (of the village), for how many times have you become my son? Formerly I was your son, (but) now I am a god. Due to the brāhmaṇa's favour I shall go to Viṣṇu's abode. See this demon also has secured a four-armed body. Due to the greatness of the eleventh (chapter) he will go to heaven with (these) people. Learn the chapter from this brāhmaṇa and constantly mutter it. There is no doubt that you will obtain the same position. Therefore, O father, the company of the good is always difficult to be had by men. That too has come up for you today. Accomplish your desired object. What is the use of wealth, enjoyment, gifts, sacrifices, penance, acts of pious liberality? Final bliss is obtained by the recital of the (chapter called) Viśvarūpa(-darśana). By hearing the chapter (men see) that form of Viṣṇu which is the highest, which came out of the mouth of Kṛṣṇa, the Brahman, the mass of complete joy, which—the nectar of salvation—was spoken by him to his friend Arjuna on Kurukṣetra, which removes maladies, diseases and fears of men afraid of the mundane existence, which destroys the misery of many existences. I do not see any other (hymn) like that. Remember it."

Śiva said:

108c-110. Speaking like this, he went to Viṣṇu's highest position with them. The village-head learnt that chapter from the brāhmaṇa. Due to its greatness both of them went to Viṣṇu's position. Thus I have told you the account of the eleventh chapter, by merely hearing which great sins perish.

CHAPTER ONE HUNDRED EIGHTYSIX

The Greatness of the Twelfth Chapter: Siddhasamādhi's Story

Mahādeva said:

1-11. In the southern country there is a city named Kolhāpura. O good one, it is the abode of pleasures, and the source of accomplishment of superhuman powers for the good ones. It is a great seat of the Parāśakti (Supreme Power), and is resorted to by all gods. It is well-known in the Purāṇas as giving enjoyments and salvation. There are crores of holy places there, and crores of phalluses of Śiva. There is Rudragayā. It is large and well-known in the world. The ramparts are like high mountains, and the banners on the gates are shining. On the top of the palace there is a high golden banner. The city is adorned with a row of high mansions and topmost of the houses resembling the moon. The quarters were made fragrant with the smoke of the incense coming out of the holes of windows. It has a great shadow due to the moving banners. It is endowed with temples. It is inhabited by clever, handsome, affectionate, rich, pure men, of good conduct and having many ornaments. Women live there, whose eyes are like those of deer, whose faces resemble the moon, whose hair is curly, who resemble the blooming campaka, whose breasts are stout and high, who are adorned with deep navels and three folds (on their bellies), whose hips are large, whose pairs of shanks are charming, whose feet are excellent, whose girdles are making sounds, whose jewelled anklets are jingling, whose lotus-like hands have bracelets that are tinkling, and the rays from whose nails are flashing, and that fascinate even sages. The city is endowed with all objects, and full of all enjoyments. It possesses all auspicious things, and has Mahālakṣmī (living in it).

12-33. There came some young, fair man of charming eyes. His neck was conch-like; his shoulders were broad; his chest was large; his arms were long. He was endowed with all (good) marks; was fair and handsome in all limbs. Entering the city he saw the beauty in all the high mansions. His mind was eager to see Mahālakṣmī, the chief goddess. He bathed in Maṇikuṇḍa and offered oblations to his dead ancestors. Having seen Mahālakṣmī, Mahāmāyā, he devoutly praised her. "The mother of the world, the protector, having infinite pity, brings about by her glance the existence and protection of the world. Lord Brahmā ordered by that Power creates (the world). Viṣṇu depending upon that Power, maintains the world. Śiva being entered by that Power destroys everything. I worship that great Power, mighty due to her creating, maintaining and destroying (the world). O you whose lotus-like feet are meditated upon by meditating ascetics, O Kamalā, O you having a lotus as your abode, You grasp all our innate properties within the range of the senses. You alone are the mass of thoughts. You make the mind fit for that. You are of the form of desires, knowledge and acts. You are of the form of the highest consciousness. You desire no fruit; you are spotless; you are eternal; you are formless; you are unstained. You are constant; you are free from agony; you are independent; you are free from disease. Who is capable of describing your greatness like this? I salute you, moving in the twelve (months) after disclosing the collection of the six (seasons). You are of the nature of anāhata śabda* (sound produced without beating); you are of the nature of nāda*, bindu* and kalā*. O mother, you are the river of the nectar oozing from the full moon. O affectionate one, you nourish children like Sanaka etc. who are naked. You are auspicious, consciousness attached to (the states of) waking, dream and deep sleep. You are in the fourth state; you are in the combination of pity and courteous language. To all living beings the entire wealth of Brahman is given by you who are beyond the fourth state after having withdrawn the group of all the reals. By you who are indeterminate, identity with bimba (?) is granted to the yogins. I salute the Parā, Paśyantī, Madhyamā and Vaikharī (the four kinds of vāc—speech) also. O goddess, for the proper protection of the world you take up (various) forms. You are Brāhmī, Vaiṣṇavī, Māheśī, O mother. O Vārāhī, you are Mahālakṣmī, Nārasiṁhī and Aindrikā. You are Kaumārī, Caṇḍikā, Lakṣmī, the purifier of everything; you are Sāvitrī, the mother of the world, Śaśinī and Rohiṇī. You are Svāhā, Svadhā; you are the divine nectar. You are Durgā; you are adorned

*These terms are highly technical in Tantra.

with a mass of clubs and staff-like arms. O you with your eyes reeling due to drinking blood dropping from the body of Raktabīja (a demon), O you having the strong pair of arms taken out from the neck of an intoxicated he-buffalo, O you who put in great valour in tearing the great demon called Śumbha, O you having unlimited acts, O you mother of the three worlds, I salute you. O you wish-fulfilling tree to your devotees, O you goddess, favour me." Thus praised by him goddess Mahālakṣmī then took up her own form and spoke to that man.

Śrī Lakṣmī said:

34a. O prince, I am pleased, ask for an excellent boon.

The prince said:

34b-40a. My father, a king, while performing a great horse-sacrifice, was unfortunately overcome by a disease and died. Having dried his body with heated oil, I have kept it. The sacrifice continued as before. The horse that had wandered over the earth, (was tied) to a post. Someone at night cut off the bond and took him somewhere. When (my) men after not finding him, came back, I, addressing all priests, have sought your refuge. O goddess, if you are pleased, then may my horse of the sacrifice be seen, so that the sacrifice will be completed and my father, the king, will be free from debt. O mother of the world, O you who love those who seek your refuge, do like that.

The goddess said:

40b-42. A brāhmaṇa, known as Siddhasamādhi, is at my door. By my order he will accomplish all your work.

Thus addressed by Śrī Mahālakṣmī, the prince then came to the place where the sage Siddhasamādhi was. Having saluted his lotus-like feet, he stood there with his palms joined.

43-60. Then the brāhmaṇa said to him: "You are sent by Ambā. See, I shall accomplish all that is desired by you." Speaking like this, the māntrika (knower of spells) drew (to his presence) all gods. The son of the king then saw the gods having joined their palms and with their bodies trembling. Then the best brāhmaṇa spoke to all the gods: "This prince's horse meant for a sacrifice was snatched and taken away at night by the lord of gods. O gods, bring (back) his horse, do not delay." Having heard the sage's words, the gods gave him (back) the horse. He allowed the gods (to go). Having seen the gods drawn (by him), and having received the lost horse, the king's son bowed to the sage, and said to him: "O best sage, this your power is a wonder. You have done a marvel by drawing on the gods in a moment. Having drawn the horse give me (back) my horse meant for the sacrifice. There is nothing else which is difficult to be done even by gods. You alone, and none else, will be capable of doing it. O brāhmaṇa, listen. My father was king Bṛhadratha. He commenced a horse-sacrifice, but died through (bad) luck. Even now his body lies, dried with heated oil. O best one, please bring him back to life again." "We shall go there where (the body of) your father is, and where your sacrificial hall is." Having come (there) along with that Siddhasamādhi, he consecrated water and threw it on the head of the dead body. Then the king got (back) consciousness, and saw (the people there). The king asked him: "O Dharma (i.e. pious one), who are you?" Then the prince told everything to the king. The king saluted the brāhmaṇa who had given (back) his life again. He said: "Due to which religious merit have you this uncommon power by means of which you gave (back) my life and called the gods, and also by means of which (power) you rescued the sacrifice? Tell (me) that". Being thus addressed, the brāhmaṇa spoke in soft words. "I carefully mutter the twelfth chapter of the Gītā. Due to that (I have) this power by means of which you (re-)gained life."

61-62. Hearing these words the king learnt the excellent twelfth chapter from that brāhmaṇa sage along with brāhmaṇas. Due to the greatness of that chapter all of them obtained good position. Other living beings also, after having recited it, obtained great salvation.

CHAPTER ONE HUNDRED EIGHTYSEVEN

The Thirteenth Chapter: *Durācārā's Story*

The goddess said:

1. You told me the greatness of the twelfth chapter. Tell me the very beautiful greatness of the thirteenth chapter.

The lord said:

2-22. O Pārvatī, listen to the greatness—a treasure—of the thirteenth chapter, by merely hearing which you will get great joy. In the southern country there is the great river Tuṅgabhadrā. On her bank is a charming city named Harihara, where, O goddess, revered god Harihara himself dwells. By seeing him (a man) gets great happiness. In that city lived a brāhmaṇa named Hari Dīkṣita. He was engrossed in penance and sacred study. He was learned and had mastered the Vedas. His wife was Durācārā (literally 'of bad conduct') both in name and deeds. She who used abusive language, never slept with her husband. She, wandering wantonly, did not remain in her house even for a moment. At the door of the brāhmaṇa she drank liquor (filling her belly up) to her throat (i.e. too much). She repeatedly threatened her husband's relatives. Always intoxicated, she constantly dallied with her paramours. Sometime seeing the city full of citizens here and there, she herself made a rendezvous in a forest. The clever one, proud of her youth, passed a long time there only dallying with her paramours. When she was (thus) living in the city wantonly, the spring season, the friend of Cupid, set in. It was full of foliage from roots (of trees); it had brought back to life Cupid by means of the cooings of the cuckoos in the fifth note (of the Indian gamut) due to the mango tree liable to change(?). It had tossed the forest-trees with breezes coming from the Malaya (mountain) carrying the fragrance of campaka flowers and blowing very gently. It was beautified all around by sound due to hummings of the swarms of bees breaking their fast with the fragrant spirituous liquor of the blooming jasmine flowers. It was smiling with the pleasing, charming, fragrant lakes. It was manifested by lakes with hosts of swans collected (there). In it the earth was beautified with trees having dense foliage and having (under them) young ones of deer seated comfortably in their dense shade. In that spring season that lady going to meet her lover (*Abhisārikā*), being delighted, saw, at night the moonlight, giving joy to the world. It had thin drops of nectar dropping from the ends of the beaks of the moving cakoras. It was full of springs of nectar oozing from the melting moon-stone. In it the mass of hail was clustering together in the expanding middle parts of the flowers; the billows of the mass of water that were flashing, embraced the sky. It was a knife cutting the throats of unchaste women of the great lion of Cupid. It was clever in tearing off the mass of dense darkness. It was full of snow (or coolness) for others like the Himālaya mountain that had whitened Satī. It gave joy to the young people, due to the closing of withered lotuses. It was the witness to the piteous wailings of the female cakravākas. It had brightened the atmosphere with pure rays like a row of pearls.

23-33. When the moonlight became profuse and filled the ten quarters, the lustful woman became blind with passion, and she, amusing herself in the high mansion, not seeing her paramours on the way at night, and breaking the bolt of (the door of) the house, went out of the city, to the place of appointment. She, with her mind deluded by passion of love, looking for one of her lovers, did not see any (lover) in any bower or under any tree. At every step she heard the gentle words of her lover. Then she playfully went to that place where there was a destructive sound. Having heard the notes of the cakravākas, she, misunderstanding them for the words of her lover, again and again moved to all lakes. Through error (that it was) her lover, she awakened the flocks of deer asleep at the root of a tree, saying, with encouragement, 'I have come'. Taking a branchless trunk for the lord of her life she embraced it, and kissed a blooming lotus mistaking it for his face. Everywhere her exertion was futile. She did not see her lover. Swooning, she lamented in the grove with various words. 'O you of a charming fortune, O you treasure of fortune and handsomeness, O you having a face like the full moon, O you having eyes like lotuses, O dear one, O you full of virtues, O you who are a celestial tree where fulness relaxes, if, through anger, you are remaining somewhere in disguise, I propitiate you, O dear one, even by offering my dear life.' Thus through separation (from her lover) she lamented in all directions.

34-49. Having heard her words, a tiger, who was asleep, awoke. He growled, and angrily looked in every direction along the path. Striking the ground with his nails and roaring in the sky-cavern, he speedily raised his tail suspended from the back. The tiger jumped and went where the abhisārikā was. She too, mistaking him, who was coming (to her), for her lord (i.e. paramour) went with her mind full of love to stand by him. Then blinded by the cruel sport of his nails, she gave up the idea of his being her lover on hearing his loud roar. Even though the woman was (reduced to a condition) like that, she quickly gave up her wrong notion (and said): "O tiger, for what purpose have you come here to kill me? Tell me all this for which you wish to kill me." Hearing these words of her, the tiger of violent strides, for a moment left the food (in the form) of her, laughed and said: "In the southern country there is a river named Malāpahā. On her bank is a city called Muniparṇā. There Maheśvara Pañcaliṅga actually dwells. In that city, I, being the son of a brāhmaṇa, lived. I acted as a priest for those not entitled to performing a sacrifice. On the bank of the river I ate (food) at a śrāddha performed for one definite individual. With a desire for (obtaining) wealth, I always sold the fruit of the recital of the Veda. Through greed I condemned other mendicants with bad words. I always accepted wealth not fit to be given and that was not given. Through the desire to seize the opportunity, I deceived all people. Then after some time I became old. I had wrinkles (on my body), grey hair, and being blind, stumbled and fell. My teeth had fallen, (but) again I was absorbed in accepting gifts. Through greed of getting wealth, I, wandering on the parvan days, and with darbhas in my hands, went near a holy place. Then I, with my limbs having become loose, went to the house of a brāhmaṇa to ask for food, but in the middle (i.e. while on my way) I was bitten on my leg by a dog. Fainting I fell on the ground in a moment. Then losing my life, I went to the stock of a tiger.

50-61. Remembering my former sin I live in this forest. I do not eat religious sages and good men and chaste women. But

I devour sinners, wicked ones, and unchaste women. Therefore, I shall really eat you, O unchaste woman." Saying so, he, cutting her limbs into pieces with his cruel nails, devoured her who had resorted to a sinful body. Yama's servants took her to Yama's city, and there by Yama's order quickly dropped her many times into the fierce yellow pools full of feces, urine and blood for crores of kalpas; and again and again bringing her from there, they put her into Raurava hell for a period of hundreds of periods of Manu. Even after dragging her from there, they threw her, fully helpless, weeping, with her hair loose, limbs broken, into fire. Thus, having experienced the fierce torment in the hell, wholly sinful, she was again born on the earth in the stock of cāṇḍāla. Then, in the cāṇḍāla-house also, she growing day by day, was as before due to (the effect of) her former deeds. Then after some time she went to her house, where, goddess Jṛmbhakā of Śiva, the goddess of the city, was. There she saw a pure brāhmaṇa, Vāsudeva by name, constantly reciting the thirteenth chapter of the Gītā. Then merely on hearing it, she was free from the body of cāṇḍāla, and getting a divine body, she went to heaven.

CHAPTER ONE HUNDRED EIGHTYEIGHT

The Fourteenth Chapter: Story of a Bitch and a Hare

The lord said:

1-9. O Bhavānī, for freedom from the worldly existence, I shall hereafter narrate (the importance of) the fourteenth chapter of the Gītā. O you of a pleasing smile, listen to it. On the earth there is a large region of Kāśmīra; it is the charming capital of goddess Sarasvatī. After staying there the goddess of speech goes to Brahmā's world after mounting her swan. There the quarter attains importance after serving Sarasvatī's lotus-like feet with saffron sent by Sāvitrī and rising from the folds of the wings of the swan. Due to having no interruption the language of gods is in a moment got by men who speak Sanskrit. In the morning the orbs of the moon and of the sun have a tawny tinge due to saffron rising from the courtyard of the house. There was king Śauryavarman, a heap of lustre, who had cut off the circle of his enemies with volleys of bright arrows that were ready. In Siṁhaladvīpa there was a king, brave like a lion, named Vikramavetāla, also a treasure of arts. Gradually they increased the friendship of each other by means of heaps (of) excellent (presents) produced in their respective countries.

10-17. Once, king Vikramavetāla saw a perfect pair of bitches sent with love by Śauryavarman. He sent to his friend Śauryavarman intoxicated excellent elephants, horses, jewelled ornaments and chowries. Once, the king, eager for hunting having got into a palanquin, being fanned by charming chowries, taking the pair of the bitches tied with golden chain, and with a collection of musical instruments and small drums went with the princes to a forest. A hare was taken as a prey for the wager. There was a great noise made by the princes. Then the king laying a high-priced wager with a prince of his age sported with eagerness. Then the king, having taken down the bitch from the palanquin, set her after the hare, running fast. The prince, of great arms, also released his object of love. Having loudly repeated the panegyric or laudatory poem he stopped the bitch.

18-28. While all the kings were witnessing, the pair of the bitches was running with a speed that could not be perceived and was jumping. Due to great exertion the hare fell into a great ditch. Though fallen the hare could not be overpowered by the bitch. Then the hare, slowly getting up, vomitting foam, was angrily overpowered and seized by the king's bitch. Then the hare who somehow jumped and was going, tumbled and was seized at the neck by the king's bitch. In the din of the people, talking 'We have won' the hare got out of the mouth of the bitch that was frightened. Then the hare, having blood (on his body) that was dropping and that was caused by the line of the wounds (made) by the teeth (of the bitch), hid in a place rustling (with leaves etc.) and remained (there). He who, being just seen by the king's bitch, smelling that part of the land with great anger, was frightened, and went (from there to a distance) of just a cubit, to a place where the wind coming from the camphor and plantain trees and the bottom of the tiger's caves and kissing the cheeks of the Cola-ladies, blew. There the deer, with their eyes partially closed due to the pollen from the cups of the ketakī flowers that had opened up, confidently resorted to the shade. There the monkeys also, satisfied with the ripe mangoes, fell down along with the coconuts. There even lions played with the young elephants; serpents entered fearlessly into the peacocks' tails.

29-36. There in a hermitage a brāhmaṇa named Vatsa, who had curbed his senses and was tranquil, lived, constantly muttering the fourteenth chapter. (The hare) going here, with his life just sustained and repeatedly panting, fell into the mud caused by the water (poured) by his disciple while washing his lotus-like feet. The hare, having crossed the mundane existence just due to the contact with that mud, got into a divine aeroplane and went to heaven. Then that bitch also, with her body besmeared with a few drops of mud and free from hunger and thirst, abandoned her canine form, got into a celestial aeroplane charming with divine ladies and adorned with gandharvas, went to heaven. Then his intelligent disciple named Svakandhara, amazed after thinking about the cause of the enmity in the former existence, laughed. The king, an ocean of modesty alone, with his eyes smiling, also saluted him with great devotion and asked him, "O brāhmaṇa, tell me the story, how the two ignorant ones, the bitch and the young hare, that had resorted to a mean stock, went to heaven."

The disciple said:

37-39. In this forest there is a brāhmaṇa named Vatsa, with his senses curbed. He always mutters the fourteenth chapter. O king, I am his disciple, proficient in every (branch of) knowledge. Everyday I mutter the fourteenth chapter, O king. O king, the hare along with the bitch, rolling in the water (used) for washing my feet, went to heaven.

The king said:

40. O best brāhmaṇa, with what intention did you, thinking carefully that it has some meaning, laugh?

The disciple said:

41-45. There was a great city named Pratyudaka in Mahārāṣṭra. There was a brāhmaṇa named Keśava, a leader of gamblers. His wife was Vilobhanā, a wanton woman. He through anger, and remembering the enmity of the (former) birth, killed her. Then due to the sin of the murder of a woman, the brāhmaṇa was born as a hare, and she due to her birth (full) of deceit, was born as a bitch. They, taking different births, never forgot the enmity practised in the former birth, and each other also.

The king, full of faith, having understood all this, studied the entire Gītā, and got the highest position.

CHAPTER ONE HUNDRED EIGHTYNINE

The Fifteenth Chapter: *The Story of King Narasiṁsha*

The lord said:

1-11. O you large-eyed one, O you daughter of the Himālaya mountain, I shall tell (you) the importance of the fifteenth chapter of the Gītā. Listen to it. In the Gauḍa country there was a kind king named Narasiṁha. In the war by the edge of his sword the divine groups were killed. The earth could bear the agony due to the heat of the sun, even in summer, by means of the water of the stream of rut of his intoxicated elephants. Intoxicated elephants, frightened due to being challenged and seeking his refuge, shone like moving mountains. The mountains respectfully echoed the trumpets of the intoxicated elephants of him, the kind protector. It was a wonder how the earth was not reduced to pieces, when it was shattered with the multitudes of (the strokes of) the hoofs of his running horses. When he, a friend of Indra, emancipated the earth, Phaṇīśvara (Śeṣa; Patañjali) again brightened Mahābhāṣya. He had an intelligent soldier named Sarabhabheruṇḍa, who was an abode of weapons, holy texts and arts, and had large round arms. By means of his treasure, horses, brave soldiers, and very inaccessible forts he was equal to the king. Some time the sinful one made up his mind to rule over the kingdom after having forcibly killed the king together with the princes. With a desire to do like this he was determined (to kill the king with the princes). Due to the disease of cholera he died.

12-26. O you of a thin belly, after death the sinful one was born, due to that act, as a bright horse in Sindhu country. A certain vaiśya-son, knowing the facts about horses, bought him at a great price and took him (to his place) with great effort. After his death the king got old in course of time and looked after his kingdom with (the help of) his grandsons. The vaiśya-son came to give the horse to the king. He remained at the king's door waiting to meet him. Though the vaiśya was already known, he was presented (before the king) by the doorkeeper. "Speak why (you have come)." Thus asked by the king, he told (everything) clearly. "Thinking that this horse is a gem of the three worlds, I (bought) this horse of auspicious marks at a price of a million coins." Then looking at the faces of those seated by his side, the king ordered the vaiśya: "Bring the horse here." The great horse made the heads of those knowing the marks of a horse, nod, and exciting the minds of the brave, ejecting hisvery bright fame earned by many speedy runs across, the entire earth, as it were, in the form of saliva and foam, he actually became comparable to Uccaiḥśravas by means of the similarity in virtues (with him). The very bright one bent his neck, as it were, through bashfulness. Constantly being fanned by chowries, white like the moon, he was like Uccaiḥśravas, unsteady like the Milky Ocean. Like the beauty of the clouds he had a pair of blue umbrellas, and the beauty of the peak of the Himālaya, with clouds touching it. Repeatedly raising his handsome neck, he was, as it were, turned into fire by the contact with the earth. He tore all the enemies; he brought prosperity in the form of victory with his loud neighing; he declared glory in (all) quarters. He was a very high heap of vitality; was, as it were, the treasure of gaits. He was actually the abode of beauty; he was the ocean of (auspicious) marks.

27-40. The vaiśya brought the horse; and the king saw him. The ministers knowing the (auspicious) marks described him in various ways. Giving the merchant as much gold as desired and aked for by him, the king, full of extreme joy, quickly took the horse. Then having called the horsegroom, and carefully instructing him the king dismissed the assembly and went into his house after being taken leave of in many ways by (the members of) the assembly. He (took) the king, having the ornaments in the form of rows of scars of wounds made in battle, and resembling sattva (energy?). Once, the king, full of curiosity, having the sport of hunting (in mind), mounted him, and entered a forest. Leaving his soldiers behind, all of whom were running around, the king, being attracted by deer, was oppressed with thirst. Then the king got down from the horse, and looking for water, tied the horse to the branch of a tree, and ascended a rock. He saw half the verse from the fifteenth chapter of the Gītā written, and fallen where he looked into a fissure. When the king was reading the line of letters, the horse, hearing it, obtained salvation, and quickly fell. Then having cut off the knot, and dropping the saddle, he, being lifted by the king did not get up, (but) was dead. Then Sarabhabheruṇḍa, talking to the king in a sweet tone, got into a celestial aeroplane, and went to heaven. Then going up the mountain, he saw an excellent hermitage. It was full of the trees of punnāga, plantain, mango and coconut. It had groves of grapes and sugarcanes, and trees like nuts, nāgakesara and campaka. It had young elephants and deer playing in it. It had the flocks of peacocks dancing. The king, being free from the desire for worldly existence, saluted the brāhmaṇa who was in the hut, and asked him with great devotion:

41-46. "(Please) tell me, with what purpose the horse went to heaven." Having heard these words of the king, the brāhmaṇa said: "Due to his sin, he became a horse after a long time. Having heard half a verse from the fifteenth chapter of the Gītā written somewhere, when you read it, the horse went to heaven." Then the king, surrounded by his attendants who had come there, with horripilation due to joy, saluted the brāhmaṇa and left. The king, with his eyes dilating due to joy, read that writing having (half the verse from) the fifteenth (chapter) of the Gītā and he, along with the ministers, the counsellors, consecrated his son powerful like a lion, on the throne, and he of a pure mind, obtained salvation.

CHAPTER ONE HUNDRED NINETY

The Sixteenth Chapter: Khaḍgabāhu's Story

The lord said:

1-9. Hereafter I shall narrate the greatness of the sixteenth chapter. Hear it, O fawn-eyed one, O you showering joy and eagerness. In the Gurjara country there was a city by name Saurāṣṭrika. There lived a king Khaḍgabāhu by name. He was, as it were, another moon. The ocean is made fragrant by the string of the fragrance of his flowers and Viṣṇu with Lakṣmī sleeps comfortably in it. The particles of the camphor of his fame shine in the sky, under the pretext of stars, after they were scattered there by the sighs of his enemies. Kings among his enemies who had bathed in the holy place of the edge of his sword, (though) fascinated by the words of divine women, even now turn back from heaven. He had an elephant named Arimardana. He was unrestrained due to rut. He had swarms of bees (hovering round and) humming in the water of the flowing ichor. It shone like mount Añjana with the springs rising, turbid due to being the water in the form of the stream of ichor crossing his large temples. In the interior of the forest the chowries bright like the moonlight shone on his limbs like the rays of the moon falling on them. He looked splendid with his temples shining with the cover of the particles of red lead. He was like a portion of the sky pervaded with the evening clouds.

10-22. Once, at night, he freed himself from the chains and fetters and forcibly broke the iron pillar (to which he was tied) and went out. Angrily ignoring all the hosts of drivers flashing the goads by his side, he broke his abode, though he was being struck in various ways with bamboo sticks to which goads were fixed, and though the drivers frightened him much. Then on hearing this wonder came there the king with those adept in the art of (the marks of) elephants and with princes. Having come (there) the king saw the mighty elephant stupefying the pride of brave heroes and taking away rows of lofty mansions. The citizens, turning away from any other curiosity and through fear guarding their children, looked at the very fierce elephant by keeping themselves at a distance. The paths were made fragrant by the drops of his rut and blocked by people intent on fleeing. Then a brāhmaṇa, after having bathed and muttering certain verses from the sixteenth chapter of the Gītā, came along the path, though he was prohibited in many ways by the citizens and the drivers of elephants. Not caring for those who were scared of the elephant, he walked on. The elephant covered the people with hissings and crushed them. The brāhmaṇa touched his ichor and went happily. Even when the citizens were watching, there arose a great wonder in the mind of the king which cannot be grasped by words. Then getting down from his horse, saluting the brāhmaṇa. the king asked him:

The king said:

23-24. O brāhmaṇa, today you have done a great, uncommon thing. How did you pass by the elephant resembling Death? Which god do you worship? Which hymn do you mutter, O lord? Which divine power do you possess? Tell it, O brāhmaṇa.

The brāhmaṇa said:

25-34. O king, everyday I mutter a few verses from the sixteenth chapter of the Gītā. All these divine powers are due to that.

Then leaving the elephant, the interesting object of curiosity, the king, taking the brāhmaṇa with him, came home. Having pleased the best brāhmaṇa at an auspicious time with golden coins numbering a lakh, he received from him the Gītā-hymn. The curious king also studied with reverence, a few verses from the sixteenth chapter of the Gītā. Once, with his soldiers, he went out of the city. Clearly not caring for the pleasures of the kingdom, he let loose the intoxicated elephant from his driver. The king offered his life like grass before the elephant. The king, the leader of the daring ones, took him, of large temples and unrestrained due to the line of the rut, and due to his confidence in his ministers came there. The king got away from the elephant as the moon would come out of Rāhu's mouth or a righteous person from the mouth of Death or a good one from that of a wicked one. Having come to the city, the king consecrated his son (on the throne), and due to the muttering of the sixteenth chapter, obtained the best position.

CHAPTER ONE HUNDRED NINETYONE

The Seventeenth Chapter: Duḥśāsana's Story

The lord said:

1-9. I told you the power of the sixteenth chapter. Now listen clearly, O Śiva, to the greatness of the seventeenth chapter. Duḥśāsana was a servant of Khaḍgabāhu's son. He came to seize that elephant and was killed by the elephant. With his mind fixed on that desire, he obtained the stock of the elephant, (but)obtained the highest position on listening to the seventeenth chapter of the Gītā.

The goddess said:

I have heard that Duḥśāsana became an elephant and was released. O auspicious lord, tell me that only in detail.

The lord said:

There was a certain wicked-minded man. He laid a high-priced wager with the feudal princes and then mounted upon an elephant. The fool named Duḥśāsana, having gone a few steps only, (though) warded off by people, uttered audacious words. Then the elephant, hearing them, was blind with fury. With the princes trembling, he, with his steps stumbling, fell down. Then the elephant, unrestrained like death, angrily uprooted something panting and fallen. The mad elephant separating his bones, even though he was already dead, scattered them.

10-17. Then having died in course of time, he obtained the stock of elephant. He passed a long time (like that). The king of Siṁhaladvīpa had a close friendship with king Khaḍgabāhu. Then the honoured elephant was sent by the water-route by Jayadeva to Khaḍgabāhu. That king also took him with joy. Remembering his previous existence, and seeing his kinsmen and his brothers, he passed a few days with great grief. Not showing (any recognition) he quietly lived in Khaḍgabāhu's house. He, some time being pleased by the completing of an incomplete stanza (in a contest) (by a poet) gave the poet the elephant as a present. The poet, being afraid of a harm from a disease, sold the temple-elephant to the Mālava king for a hundred (coins). After some time had passed, the elephant suffering from fever due to old age difficult to be enjoyed, was on the point of dying. The elephant did not smell cold water, nor did he take a morsel; he did not sleep comfortably, but shed tears only.

18-27. Then hearing the account told by the elephant-driver, the king came where the elephant suffering from fever, lay. The elephant too, seeing the king, gave up the agony due to the fever, and spoke in a voice causing wonder to the world. "O king, O you who know all sacred texts, O you ocean of the science of politics, O you who have vanquished the host of your enemies, O you to whom Viṣṇu's feet are dear, what is the use of medicines, shoots, and mutterings of hymns? Bring a brāhmaṇa who would mutter the seventeenth chapter of the Gītā. There is no doubt that my disease will end due to that." The king did as was told by the elephant. Then Duḥśāsana gave up his state as an elephant, and got release. When the brāhmaṇa had thrown consecrated water on the excellent one, the king saw that Duḥśāsana, lustrous like Indra, got into a divine aeroplane.

The king said:

Tell me what your caste is, who you are, what your livelihood is. Due to what act did you become an elephant? How did you come here?

Asked by the king, Duḥśāsana who was freed, remaining in the aeroplane, told in definite words his account. Then the lord of Mālava, muttering the seventeenth chapter of the Gītā, was released after a short time.

CHAPTER ONE HUNDRED NINETYTWO

The Eighteenth Chapter: A Brāhmaṇa Becomes Indra

Pārvatī said:

1. O Śiva, you have told me the greatness of the seventeenth chapter. (Now) tell me the importance of the eighteenth chapter.

The lord said:

2-15a. O you daughter of the (Himālaya) Mountain, listen to the greatness of the eighteenth chapter which is holy, which is the essence of all holy texts, which is the elixir that has come to the ears, which is intent on tearing off the mass of pangs in the worldly existence, which is the great secret of the siddhas, which is capable of uprooting ignorance, which is vitality, which is the best, the highest position of Kaiṭabha's enemy (i.e. Viṣṇu), which is the root of the creeper of discretion, which removes the dirt of passion and anger, which gave repose to the hearts of gods like Indra, which amused the minds of the great meditating saints like Sanaka, which has given a setback to the roars of Yama merely by its being recited, which is the cause of uprooting the roots of one hundred and eight diseases. O you whose gait is like that of an elephant, there is no greater secret than this. It removes the three (kinds of) torments and destroys major sins. As I am eternal among times, as the desire-yielding cow is among the beasts, as Vyāsa is among the best sages, or as he who knows Brahman is among the Vyāsas, as Indra is among gods, as Guru (i.e. Bṛhaspati) is superior to Śukra, as among the liquids nectar is the best and well-known in the world, as Kailāsa is among mountains, and as Indra is among gods, as Puṣkara is among the holy places, as lotus is among flowers, as in the worlds Arundhatī is among the chaste and virtuous wives, as the horse-sacrifice is among the sacrifices, as Paradise is among the gardens, as among all Rudras is my follower Vīrabhadra, as a gift of land is among gifts, as Godāvarī is among rivers, as Harikṣetra is recommended for all religious rites, so is the greatness of the eighteenth chapter excellent in the world. About it, O Pārvatī, listen devoutly to this auspicious account, so that by merely listening to it a being is free from sins.

15b-28. On the peak of Meru there was a beautiful city (named) Amarāvatī. It was formerly fashioned for my amusement by Viśvakarman. It is always full of virtues, and resorted to by crores of gods. There, palaces giving desired objects and built with desire-yielding stones, excel. It (spread) up to the city of Brahmā. It possessed a mass of lustre, and is well-known like the knowledge of the Supreme Spirit. There happily sitting under the shade of the desire-yielding tree Śacī enjoyed the song sung by gandharva women. The divine river there turned bloody due to the billows of the blood of the demons whose lives were crushed by gods. There the gods, repeatedly remembering the ancient sweet ambrosia, and being emaciated with hunger, everyday drank the digit of the moon. In it, resembling final beatitude, formerly lived Indra. The prosperous one was accompanied by Śacī, and was waited upon by all gods. When once he was seated comfortably he saw a great man having a thousand eyes, waited upon by Viṣṇu's messengers, coming (to him). Then due to his lustre Indra was overpowered. He quickly fell into the hall from his jewelled throne. When he went away from the throne, Viṣṇu's soldiers tied him with the strap of the sovereignty over the gods. Pulomajā quickly sat on the left lap of that great Indra who was consecrated to the accompaniment of sounds of drums. Then gods along with their wives sang divine songs. The celestial ladies waved lights before him. Then sages gave him blessings with (hymns from) the Vedas. The bands of celestial nymphs like Rambhā danced before him. Gandharvas sang charming songs with auspicious desires.

29-44. Thus they served the new Indra who had not performed a hundred sacrifices. Seeing that old Indra was amazed. "By me (him?) lakes were never fashioned on the path; trees giving rest to travellers were never planted. God Tripurabhairava (i.e. Śiva) was never seen. Goddess Madālasā living in the place of treasure was never worshipped. Śārṅgadhara residing at Meghaṅkara was never seen. A bath was never taken at Viraja. The city of Kāśī was never visited. Narahari himself residing at the divine grove was never seen. Eraṇḍa Viṣṇu Heramba(?) was never contemplated upon. Mother Reṇukā living in the city was never seen. The goddess living at Dānāpura was never devoutly worshipped. Tryambaka with three phalluses was not devoutly seen at Tripura. Somanātha living at the Śārdūla lake was never seen. Ghuśṛṇeśa living at Revāpura was never seen. Nāganātha, well known in the city of Nāgadanta, was never seen. Great Amṛteśvara residing at Parṇagrāma was never seen. Harihara himself living on the bank of Tuṅgabhadrā was never seen. Śrīnivāsa residing on Veṅkaṭādri was not properly seen. Śrīraṅga residing at Kāverī Karṇikā was not at all seen. Poor and helpless and wailing people were not released from gaol. Beings were not honoured with (i.e. by giving them) food during a famine. On no night a water-fountain was erected at a place without water. A bath was not taken in Godāvarī. Hariṇeśvara was not seen. A bath was not taken in Kṛṣṇaveṇī, when Jupiter was in the Zodiacal sign Libra. Not a piece of land was given. Poets were not at all honoured. A sacrificial session was never performed at the holy places. Sacrifices also were not performed in villages. Water places containing much water were never made on the path. At no place temples of Brahmā, Viṣṇu and Śiva were built. Those that were overcome with fear and sought my shelter were never protected. Due to one act of religious merit how such a divine gift was got?"

45-46. Being full of thought like this, Indra, being dejected, hastily went to ask Viṣṇu to the cave in the Milky Ocean. Having entered there that Indra saw Viṣṇu who was asleep. All of a sudden he told him of his being deprived of sovereignty.

Indra said:

47-49. O Viṣṇu, in order to please you I formerly performed a hundred sacrifices. Due to that religious merit I obtained the position of Indra. Now some new person has become Indra in heaven. He has not done religious acts, nor has he performed sacrifices. O Acyuta, how is my throne ascended by him?

Mahādeva said:

50. Having heard the words of him who was speaking like this, Viṣṇu, with his eyes dilating due to smile, spoke sweet words.

The lord said:

51. What is the use of gifts, giving small fruits? What is the use of austerities or sacrifices? Remaining on the earth, he formerly pleased me.

Indra said:

52. O lord, by means of which act, did the brāhmaṇa please you, due to which being pleased you gave him Indra's position?

The lord said:

53-63. He mutters five verses from the eighteenth chapter of the Gītā. Due to that religious merit, the crown gem of all (kinds of) religious merit, he obtained your excellent sovereign empire. Be steady.

Hearing these words of Viṣṇu, Indra, who had (thus) known the means, took the guise of a brāhmaṇa and went to the bank of Godāvarī. There he saw the very auspicious and excellent Kālikāgrāma. There god Kāleśvara, crushing Death, resides. There on the bank of Godāvarī, he saw a very religious, kind brāhmaṇa who had mastered the Vedas, who everyday muttered the eighteenth chapter and whose mind was controlled. Then having rolled at his feet with great joy, he recited the eighteenth chapter taught by him. Then due to that religious merit he secured union with Viṣṇu. And knowing the position of gods like Indra to be small, he abandoned it, and went to Viṣṇu's city. Therefore, only this is a great truth for the sages. I have told you the divine importance of the eighteenth chapter, by just hearing which one is free from all sins. Thus I have told you the importance of the Gītā, which destroys sins, which is meritorious, purifying, which gives (long) life, which leads (one) to heaven, and which is a great means of securing prosperity. O noble one, a man who devoutly listens to it, obtains the fruit of all sacrifices and would obtain absorption into Viṣṇu.

CHAPTER ONE HUNDRED NINETYTHREE

The Greatness of the Bhāgavata

Pārvatī said:

1-3. O Mahādeva, O god of gods, O omniscient one, O you giving all (kinds of) wealth, showing great compassion for me, tell me what I ask you. I heard the greatness of the Gītā, containing many wonderful tales. Therefore, an eagerness to listen to the great account of Kṛṣṇa has arisen in me. Among all the Purāṇas, Bhāgavata is the best, in what by every word Kṛṣṇa is sung in various ways by the sages. Now tell me its greatness properly and along with the historical accounts.

The lord said:

4. Śaunaka, adept in tasting the sweetness of the nectar of a story, said to the highly intelligent Sūta seated in the Naimiṣa (forest), after having saluted him:

Śaunaka said:

5-10: Narrate (to us) the account of Śrīmad Bhāgavata which is an elixir, which destroys the darkness of ignorance and the sins of a crore of (past) existences, O Sūta. How does discrimination rich with devotion, knowledge and detachment grow? How do Viṣṇu's devotees remove illusion and delusion? Here in this Kali-age a being has almost attained demonhood. What is the elixir to purify him who is overcome with affliction? Now tell (us) that which is the (highest) felicity of (all) felicities, which is the most purifying of (all) purifying objects, and which is the means to please Kṛṣṇa. A preceptor who is pleased gives (to his disciple) the desire-yielding gem, happiness in the world, the wealth of the position of the lord of gods, and also Vaikuṇṭha, which is extremely difficult to obtain.

Sūta said:

11-21. O best brāhmaṇas, I am pleased with you. (Therefore) I shall tell you that as I have heard it which is better than the best, which destroys the fear of the mundane existence, which increases devotion, which is the cause of pleasing Kṛṣṇa. Listen attentively when I am telling it. In the Kali-age Kṛṣṇa has told the holy text of Śrīmad Bhāgavata, which brings about the protection of the world which is held in the mouth of the tiger of Death. There is nothing superior to this that would purify the mind. It is obtained by good men by means of religious merit earned in many (previous) existences. Knowing the salvation of king Parīkṣit, the lotus-born one compared the holy texts and the great Purāṇas. Among them Śrīmad Bhāgavata came to be greater on the earth. The talk of Bhāgavata is difficult to be had even by gods. Thinking like this many good, pure sages looked upon Śrīmad Bhāgavata as a form of lord (Viṣṇu). By reciting and listening to it a man goes to Viṣṇu's position. Listening to it for a year gives great happiness. O best brāhmaṇa, devotion to it for a month earns splendour. Listening to it for a week gives salvation at all times. O good one, what is the use of talking too much? The good men should everyday drink the nectar of Śrīmad Bhāgavata which records the sports of Kṛṣṇa. Sanaka and others, full of compassion, formerly told it to Nārada who had (already) heard it from Brahmā. The manner of listening to it for a week (was also told).

Śaunaka said:

22-23. Having obtained excellent knowledge called Śrīmad Bhāgavata from his father, Nārada who knows the facts about the worlds, always roams over the earth. Where did Nārada meet those noble ones from whom the divine sage heard the manner of listening to it for a week?

Sūta said:

24-26. About this I shall tell you an account full of devotion, which formerly kind Śukra told me. Once the sages Sanaka and others saw at (the bank of) Viśālā, Nārada with his mind dejected. The sages, given to thinking about the Supreme Spirit and full of amazement, seeing their brother, the divine sage, thinking (like that) asked him.

Kumāras said:

27. O brāhmaṇa, what are you, very much helpless and afflict-

ed, thinking about? This is not proper for you who are associated with bliss. Tell (us) its cause.

Nārada said:

28-42. Knowing the earth to be the best of all the best, having various kinds of holy places, of an auspicious nature due to these auspicious places, I wandered here and there, at these holy places like Puṣkara, Prayāga, Kāśī, the bank of Godāvarī, Harikṣetra, Kurukṣetra, Śrīraṅga, Setubandhana, (but) nowhere did I find happiness, giving delight to my mind. Now the earth is afflicted by Kali, the friend of unrighteousness. On the earth truth, purity, pity, charity exist nowhere. People are selfish, miserable and are false witnesses. They are lethargic, dull-witted, and resort to highly heretical men. Householders attach importance to women; religious students are without (i.e. do not observe) vows. Anchorites are living in cities; those who have renounced the worldly ties are given to enjoyment. Through greed they sell their daughters; they are engaged in agriculture; they have fallen from (good) behaviour; they are hypocrites; they show wanton (behaviour). The hermitages, holy places, rivers, pools are besieged by Yavanas. The temples at other places are destroyed by the wicked. A meditating saint, a siddha or a wise man doing good deeds is not seen. Today fulfilment (of vows) is reduced to ash due to the wild fire in the form of Kali. Communities are everywhere seen to sell food; brāhmaṇas to use an auspicious object as a commodity; and beautiful ladies to use their hair as commodities. Once I reached the auspicious bank of Yamunā. There I saw Vṛndāvana where Viṣṇu had sported. O best sages, listen to the wonder that I saw there. A young lady, with her mind dejected, was seated there. Two old men, breathing and senseless, lay by her side. Weeping before the two, she was nursing and waking them up. I saw her looking into the directions, as it were, looking for her protector. Repeatedly she was fanned and advised by many women. Seeing her from a distance, I approached her through curiosity. Seeing me, the young lady got up and spoke these words:

The young lady said:

43-44a. O good man, stay here for a moment; remove my

anxiety. O good one, the sight of (good) men completely destroys streams of sins. I have had your sight due to my deeds in former existences. Therefore, O you who respect others, please remove my mental agony.

Nārada said:

44b-46. Thus addressed by her, I with my heart affectionate through pity, and full of curiosity, asked the beautiful lady: "O good one, who are you? Who are these two? Who are these lotus-eyed ones? Tell me the entire cause of your grief." Thus asked by me, that young lady, with her mind afflicted, told me her entire agony (and) the cause of the agony.

The young lady said:

47-52. I am known as 'Bhakti' (Devotion). These two are my excellent sons named 'Jñāna' (Knowledge) and 'Vairāgya' (Detachment). They are hurt due to contact with destiny. These rivers like Gaṅgā have come (here) to serve me. O Nārada, by these I am everyday served with respect. I am not getting any felicity; I am emaciated all round, O sage. O best brāhmaṇa, listen to my former account, due to which I became unhappy and am getting happiness nowhere. I was born in the Draviḍa country and brought up in Karṇāṭa. For a little (time) I lived in Mahārāṣṭra, and became old in Gurjara. There due to contact with heretics, I got my limbs cut. For a long time I have become weak, and become dull along with my sons.

53-66a. O Nārada, through luck I have reached this Vṛndāvana: I have, as it were, again become a beautiful young girl. Here these two sons have their minds greatly afflicted. Now I am unable to go leaving them who are very old. How have I become a young girl? Why have my sons become old? Due to what is this difference among us who were of the same condition? The old mother exerts herself when the sons are young. So I, with my mind full of wonder, am worried. O you who know religious practices, O kind one, O protector of the helpless, tell me truly the cause that might be there.

Thus asked by her, I, having thought for a moment, again spoke to Bhakti who was emaciated for a long time: "O sinless one, through my wisdom I see all your account. Do not be sad, O wise one; Viṣṇu will make you happy. O child, this is Kali age, fearful and destroying all goodness. Due to it good conduct, the path of Yoga and penance are violated. Sinful men, doing dishonest and bad acts, become deities in this (age), and the good are much afflicted with grief, and the bad are delighted at heart. No strong-minded, or wise man is seen. This earth having the burden of the groups of the wicked is not fit to be touched or seen. This is the order every year; everyday auspiciousness is given up. O beautiful lady, no one will either see you or these your sons. Men, full of great attachment, have abandoned you; (therefore) you have become infirm. Due to your contact with Vṛndāvana you have again become young. This Vṛndāvana where Bhakti has become young, is blessed. These two, for want of receivers, have not become young. It appears that they are asleep here due to a little joy to them."

Bhakti said:

66b-81. How did king Parīkṣit install this impure Kali? Why did Viṣṇu, given to kindness, ignore impiety? Remove this doubt of me. I am happy with your words.

O brāhamaṇa, having heard her words, I spoke again. "O girl, if you have asked affectionately, then listen. Since the day Viṣṇu, leaving the earth, went to his own place, Kali, obstructor of the truth, has proceeded. A king saw him in his conquest of the world, and he yielded like a helpless person. The seer of His virtues is not killed. This is common to all. In the Kali age an intelligent man gets that fruit by narrating the account of Viṣṇu, which he does not by means of penance, abstract meditation or concentration. Seeing Kali like this, giving substantial fruit from the unsubstantial, Viṣṇu established this for the good of those born in the Kali age. Due to bad actions, now all excellence has gone away from every place. Objects lie on the ground like husk without seeds. The brāhmaṇas have told the Bhāgavata story in every house out of greed for wealth. Therefore, the excellence has gone. Men doing very cruel deeds, atheists, and hypocrites stay at all holy places. So the excellence has gone. With their minds overtaken by passion, anger, great greed, desire they commence (religious) acts. Therefore, the excellence of the acts has gone. The fruit of abstract meditation has gone because of non-restraint of mind, greed, hypocrisy, resorting to heretics, want of the study of holy texts. The wise dally with their wives like he-buffaloes. They are expert in producing sons and not in accomplishing salvation. Devotion to Viṣṇu is (found) nowhere. All are led by tradition. All are given to censuring gods; all are fond of condemning the good. This is the practice of the age. Who should be blamed? Therefore, remembering the lotus-eyed (Viṣṇu) you will get happiness." Hearing these words uttered by me, she was amazed. O best brāhmaṇas, having praised me, she spoke again:

Bhakti said:

82-84. O divine sage, you are blessed. Due to my (good) luck you have come (here). The sight of the good gives all prosperity in the world. Now advise me in such a way that I will have a means for my happiness. O brāhmaṇa, in this world there is nothing to be accomplished by you. I salute Brahmā's son, having heard whose one sentence (Prahlāda) the son of Kayādhū (wife of Hiraṇyakaśipu) subdued the Māyā of (Viṣṇu) the unborn one, and due to whose grace Dhruva attained to an undecaying eternal position.

CHAPTER ONE HUNDRED NINETYFOUR

Śrīmad Bhāgavata, the Destroyer of All Miseries

Sūta said:

1. O kind sages, listen to what was told by Nārada when he was thus requested by that extremely helpless Bhakti.

Nārada said:

2-10. O girl, do not be sad in vain. Having placed your mind in your heart, remember Śrīkṛṣṇa's lotus-like feet. (By that) you will obtain happiness. That Kṛṣṇa who protected Draupadī from ignominy from the Kauravas, who looked after the beautiful cowherdesses, has not gone anywhere (else). O Bhakti, you are dear to him, (cared for) even more than his own life. Called by you, the lord will come to even mean houses. In the three ages like Satya knowledge and detachment accomplished salvation. In the Kali age Bhakti (devotion) alone brings about absorption into Brahman. Deciding like this he, of the nature of consciousness, of the form of highest bliss and consciousness, delighted in mind, produced you from his own body. With your palms joined you then asked Hari: "What do I do (now)?" Kṛṣṇa then ordered you: "Nourish my devotees." You accepted to do so. Hari was then pleased. He gave you Salvation as your maid, and Knowledge and Detachment as your sons. Remaining in Vaikuṇṭha you always nourished your devotees. To nourish your devotees you resorted to the form of your shadow (i.e. semblance). Salvation, Knowledge and Detachment came here (i.e. to the earth) with you. From the Kṛta (age) to the Dvāpara age, Mukti (salvation) stayed (here).

11-22a. But in the Kali age, she became emaciated, and suffered from the disease due to the heretics. By your order she again went (back) to Vaikuṇṭha. On merely being remembered by you, she quickly comes (to this world). Looking upon these two as your sons, you have protected them by your side. Due to being ignored in the Kali age both these your sons have become dull and old. Yet you give up anxiety. I shall think of a means. O you beautiful lady, there is no (other) age like the Kali age. In it I shall make you known in every house. If by obscuring other practices and putting forward great festivals, I shall not (be able to) promote you, then I am not Hari's servant. Those living beings, even though sinful, who are endowed with you in the Kali age, will, being fearless, go to Hari's abode. Those of pure forms, who are devoted to you, always of the form of love, will not see Yama even in a dream. An evil spirit, a goblin, a demon or an asura is not capable of touching or seeing those whose minds are full of devotion. Hari is not obtained by means of austerities, Vedas, knowledge or (religious) acts. He is obtained by devotion (only). The proof thereof are the cowherdesses. Men of righteous act might have devotion after a thousand existences. In the Kali age devotion alone (excels). By means of devotion Kṛṣṇa stands before (the devotee). Those who offend Bhakti, perish in the three worlds. Formerly Durvāsas who condemned Bhakti, suffered misery. Enough of virtuous conduct; enough of (visiting) holy places; enough of abstract meditations; enough of sacrifices; enough of narrations of wise tales; Bhakti alone always gives salvation.

22b-30. Thus addressed by me, and having heard her own greatness, she, with her entire body full of joy, again said these words (to me): "O Nārada, you are blessed. You have a steady affection for me. I shall never let go your attention to me. O good one, by you, kind (to me), my suffering is destroyed in a moment. My two sons do not have understanding. Rouse these two." Hearing those words of her, I, having pity, touching (them) with my hand, proceeded to rouse (them). Bringing my mouth near their ears, I loudly uttered the words: "Jñāna, rise quickly. O Vairāgya, awake." Though repeatedly being roused by the sounds of the Vedas, by the recitals of the Gītā, they did not somehow get roused. Not seeing (anything) with their eyes, and languidly yawning, both were grey-haired like cranes, and had their bodies mostly dry like wood. The two, emaciated with hunger, having observed (me), again went to sleep. Then I was full of thought: 'What should I do (now)? Oh, how will their sleep go (away)? Their old age is severe.'

31-42. O best brāhmaṇas, thinking like this, I constantly remembered Govinda. Just then there was heard a divine voice: "O sage, do not be dejected. Your exertion will be fruitful. There is no doubt. For this purpose, O divine sage, do a good deed. Good men, ornaments of the virtuous, will tell you that good deed. When that good deed is done, the sleep and the old age of these two will disappear in a moment. Bhakti (devotion) will spread everywhere." O brāhmaṇas, even after having distinctly heard this divine voice, I could not make out as to what was told by the voice in a secretive manner. What is that deed due to which the two would be endowed with understanding? Where would be the good ones? How will they tell that good deed to me? Now what should I do (about) what the divine voice told me? Then, O brāhmaṇas, having placed them there, I went out of Vṛndāraṇya, and asked the best brāhmaṇas here and there.

Having heard the entire account and with their minds amazed, they, not understanding the divine voice, did not give a reply. Some said: "It cannot be comprehended". Others said: "It cannot be understood." Others, thinking again and again, kept mum. The triad, though being roused with the sounds of the Vedas, and Vedāntas, and also by repeated recitations of the Gītā, did not rise. 'Oh, (how cruel) is fate! How can other human beings do that which the meditating saint Nārada himself could not understand?' Then being thoughtful I came to Badarivana. I determined to practise penance for that purpose. Just then I saw the best sages, Sanaka and others, bright like a crore of suns. I spoke to those best sages:

43-48. "I saw you due to great luck. Therefore, O noble ones, with your minds pleased, you may (please) tell me the means. You are the greatest among the meditating saints. You are intelligent. You are very learned; you, Kumāras, five years old, are the ancestors of the ancient people. You always live in Vaikuṇṭha; you are always engaged in narrating (the glory of) Viṣṇu. You are intoxicated by the account—the nectar—of (Viṣṇu's) sports. You are devoted to remembering Viṣṇu. Therefore, (old age,) the Daughter of Time does not trouble you. Due just to the knitting of your eye-brows, formerly the two door-keepers of Viṣṇu became demons for three existences, and again came back to their places. (Please) tell the means which is told by the heavenly voice. O kind ones, (please) tell me what should be done and in what way in this matter. The wise ones should well tell (me) how Bhakti, Jñāna and Vairāgya would secure happiness, and how they would attain fame in all the worlds".

Kumāras said:

49-57. O divine sage, do not be anxious. Have delight in your mind. There is a means in this matter, which can be easily had, and which gives happiness to the world. O Nārada, you are blessed. You are the crest-jewel of the detached ones. You are the foremost among those who are fit for Śrīkṛṣṇa's love. You are the best among speakers. O divine sage, it is no wonder for you, engrossed in the means of devotion, to spread devotion properly on the earth. For (securing) divine faculties the sages have designed various means. They could be secured with exertion; and all of them mostly give heaven as their fruit. The path leading to Vaikuṇṭha is hidden in the worlds. A good man, teaching it, is generally not found. O best sage, that good act which the divine voice indicated to you, is known by the ancients to be jñānayajña (knowledge-sacrifice). We feel that the talk (i.e. the recitation) of Śrīmad Bhāgavata is a knowledge-sacrifice, told by Śuka, and would give happiness to Bhakti, Jñāna and Virāga. All these sins of Kali, afraid of the sound of Śrīmad Bhāgavata, run away like wolves at the roar of lion. Bhakti, along with Jñāna and Vairāgya, producing the feeling of joy in each house, in each person, will sport happily.

Sūta said:

58. Having heard Kumāras' words, revered Nārada, with his mind delighted, looking to their prosperity, spoke again.

Nārada said:

59-62. The triad, covered by Kali's noxious qualities, is not rising (though) roused by sounds of Vedas and Vedāṅgas, and recitations of the Gītā. How (then) will it rise now by the recitation of Bhāgavata? You, whose sight is fruitful should (please) remove this doubt. O you who are affectionate to those who seek your shelter, (please) do not tarry in this matter.

Then Sanaka and others, detached and living in perpetual celibacy, the ancient brāhmaṇas, who had supernatural faculties, respectfully said to Nārada:

Kumāras said:

63-71. The Bhāgavata-account has risen from the quintessence of the Vedas and the Upaniṣads. Therefore, it appears to be the best, and the rise of fruit is different. As the taste is present in a mango fruit from the bottom to the top, but is different when separated and drunk, and delights all, as ghee present in milk is not thought to be pleasant, but when separated is divine, and increases the joy of gods, as sugar remains pervading the bottom, the middle and the end (i.e. the top) of a sugarcane, and is sweet when separated, so is Bhāgavata-story. The Purāṇa named Śrīmad Bhāgavata is relish itself; it is manifested for the happiness of Bhakti, Jñāna and Vairāgya to Brahmā, remaining in the lotus born from his navel, by Kṛṣṇa. The four-versed (summary) of it appears to be the entire Brahman. That account was narrated to you by Brahmā. You also narrated it to Vyāsadeva, to destroy torment. By remembering it Bādarāyaṇa (Vyāsa) instantly became depressed; and in a manner delighting the soul, composed (the work of) the great name. Due to what are you amazed, that you are asking again and again? The holy text of Śrīmad Bhāgavata is capable of attracting Kṛṣṇa.

Sūta said:

72. Having heard these desired words spoken by the foremost ones like Sanaka, the best meditating saints, Nārada devoutly seized their feet, and saluting them by bowing his head, said to them who destroy the misery of the world.

Nārada said:

73-74. Your sight destroys the stream of sins. It gives bliss to those who are afflicted by the wild fire in the form of the misery of the mundane existence, by drinking it when fully sung by Śeṣa's mouth. I have sought your shelter for the manifestation of love. If due to the rise of religious merit earned in many existences a lucky person gets the company of the good, his great darkness of delusion caused by ignorance would perish, and great discrimination springs (in him).

CHAPTER ONE HUNDRED NINETYFIVE

The Rule of Reciting and Listening to the Bhāgavata for a Week

Sūta said:

1. Then the divine sage, having asked for leave of the Kumāras, and bending down, showing respect for knowledge-sacrifice, said:

Nārada said:

2-4. With care I shall perform knowledge-sacrifice, highlighted by the narrative of the holy Śuka-text for establishing Bhakti, Jñāna and Virāga. O brāhmaṇas, tell me the place where I should perform the sacrifice. I have chosen you four only as the conductors of the sacrifice. O you proficient in knowledge-sacrifice, for how many days should the Bhāgavata-story be heard? What rite should be performed at that time?

Kumāras said:

5-12. O Nārada, listen. We shall tell you the place, being heard at which the story would destroy the heaps of sins of men, and increase their religious merit. Near Gaṅgādvāra there is a great city called Kāmada. To the north of the divine river there is a bank called Ānanda. It is resorted to by many hosts of sages and deities and siddhas. It is full of many trees and creepers, clean, soft sand. It is charming, is in a lonely region, and is adorned with golden lotuses. In the minds of the beings living near it and having in their minds love for one another, there was no enmity due to the power of this place only. You should carefully perform there knowledge-sacrifice. The story (of Bhāgavata) recited there will give unprecedented delight. Bhakti will come there followed by her two sons remaining on the street of Vṛndāvana and with their bodies worn out due to old age. Bhakti with her sons will become a young lady after drinking the nectar of Kṛṣṇa's glory at the place where there will be recitation of Bhāgavata.

Sūta said:

13-20. Having spoken like this, the Kumāras, along with Nārada, went quickly to Gaṅgādvāra for (performing) the knowledge-sacrifice. O best among Bhārgavas, when they reached the bank of Gaṅgā, there was a great din in the seven worlds like Bhū. The residents of the seven worlds, desirous of (enjoying) the flavour of Bhāgavata came there running, so also the devotees of Viṣṇu like Bhṛgu, Vasiṣṭha, Cyavana, Gautama, Medhātithi, Devala, Devarāta, Rāma, Viśvāmitra, Śākala, sons of Mṛkaṇḍa, of Atri, and Pippalāda, masters of abstract meditation, Vyāsa, Parāśara, Śuka and others, the chief among the followers of

Viṣṇu, who were accompanied by their disciples, who knew many holy texts, who were chief among those relishing Kṛṣṇa's account. The Upaniṣads, the Vedas, the hymns, the religious treatises teaching magical formulas for the worship of the deities, the digests, the ten and seven Purāṇas, the six Śāstras (philosophical treatises) also came there. So also rivers like Gaṅgā, lakes like Puṣkara, all holy places, all quarters, forests like Daṇḍaka, mountains like Himālaya, gods, gandharvas, kinnaras, islands, seas, regents of quarters, and residents of the nether world came there.

21-25. Nārada gave an excellent seat at the time of the initiation. All the Kumāras, highly devoted to Kṛṣṇa, who were saluted, sat (there). Devotees of Viṣṇu, those who were very much detached and had renounced the world, celibates, were the chief; they remained at the fore; and Nārada sat before them. On his left were the hosts of sages, on his right were the residents of heaven. O descendant of Bhṛgu, Vedas, Upaniṣads, so also the Holy Places were (seated) elsewhere. Echoing in the ten quarters the shouts of victory, words of salutation and the sound of conches touched the sky. The residents of heaven, being pleased, got into aeroplanes and showered flowers of desire-yielding trees over the assembly.

Sūta said:

26. When those Bhṛgu and others were seated as they deserved, they narrated the importance of Bhāgavata to Nārada.

Kumāras said:

27-48. O Nārada, listen. We shall, according to the rule, tell you the wonderful greatness of the holy text called Śrīmad Bhāgavata. Righteous people should always resort (i.e. listen) to the Bhāgavata-story, by hearing which they become contented. The treatise called Śrīmad Bhāgavata comprises eighteen thousand verses and twelve skandhas(sections), and is (in the form of) a dialogue between Parīkṣit and Śuka. As long as the text of (i.e. narrated by) Śuka does not reach the ears of a man, he, being deluded by ignorance, moves in the circle of the mundane existence. If men purified by devotion have not listened to Bhāgavata, what is the use of their having listened to many holy texts,

Purāṇas, digests and scriptures? The houses of those men, in which the Bhāgavata-story is always (narrated), are of the nature of holy places and destroy sins. Thousands of horse-sacrifices and hundreds of Rājasūya sacrifices are not worth even a sixteenth part of the Bhāgavata-story. O best sage, sins remain in this body as long as Bhāgavata is not properly listened to by a man. In the meritorious fruit, Gaṅgā, Gayā, Kāśī, or Puṣkara is not equal to the Bhāgavata-story. If you desire the destruction of the mundane existence, then recite everyday with your own mouth a half or a quarter verse from Bhāgavata. Bhāgavata is the origin of the Vedas, the mother of the Vedas, so also of the Puruṣa-sūkta. The triad of the Vedas is Bhāgavata; so also the two formulas—twelve-syllabled and eight-syllabled. The Sun, Prayāga, Time of the form of years, brāhmaṇas maintaining sacred fire, (the desire-yielding cow) Surabhi, the twelfth day (of a month), Tulasī, spring season, Puruṣottama (i.e. Viṣṇu)—among these, O best sage, there is actually no difference. O Nārada, the sin of that brāhmaṇa, committed during crores of existences, who would everyday expound Bhāgavata, perishes. To men, the listening to, reciting or thinking about Bhāgavata and waiting upon Tulasī and fire, give salvation and devotion. He who, being full of devotion, free from pride, eating limited (food), with his senses restrained, gives Śrīmad Bhāgavata along with a golden throne on the full-moon day of Bhādrapada to the best brāhmaṇa and listens to it from the beginning would obtain the world where absorption into Kṛṣṇa is had. He who, when his time of death has approached, abandoning fear far away, would devoutly listen to Bhāgavata, obtains salvation. He, the wicked one, who, right from his birth, has not, after properly controlling his mind, drunk (i.e. listened to) the account of Kṛṣṇa, has in vain led his life like a cāṇḍāla or a beast on the earth, and has very much tormented his mother. The life of those men who have not listened to Bhāgavata, have not worshipped the Ancient Man (Viṣṇu), have not offered oblations into the mouths of brāhmaṇas has become fruitless. The sages, the ancient siddhas, say: "Fie upon that man resembling a beast, a burden on the earth, whose mind, wicked due to the contact with the bad, does not take delight in the story of Bhāgavata." The story of Bhāgavata is quite difficult to be had (i.e. heard) on the earth. It is had by means of the religious merit due to crores of existences.

49-56. Therefore, O treasure of abstract meditation, O good man, the story of Viṣṇu should be heard everyday. O brāhmaṇa, there is really no rule about it (i.e. about listening to it). Since listening to it is believed to be done with truthfulness and celibacy, therefore, in the Kali age there is a special rule about it of the nature of (its being listened to for) seven days. The listening to it is prescribed for seven days on account of the lack of the control of a man's mind, a disease, or shortening of his life, and due to many blemishes of Kali. It is possible to control the mind and follow a prescribed course for seven days (only). Therefore, this rule is formed. That fruit which is had by devoutly listening (to it) everyday from the beginning to the end for seven days is laid down by Śuka. That fruit which is not had by means of penance, abstract meditation or concentration, is easily had by listening to it for seven days. The rule of (reciting or listening to) Bhāgavata for seven days is said to be better than performing a sacrifice, observing a vow, practising penance and meditation, acquiring knowledge and visiting a holy place. When Kṛṣṇa was ready to go to his own place after having left the earth, intelligent Uddhava, knowing it, said (these) words to Govinda:

Uddhava said:

57-63. O revered one, after having accomplished the entire mission of the gods, you now desire to go to your own place, beyond darkness. Therefore, O lord, worry due to fear of separation from you has arisen in me. O lord of gods, remove it. I have sought your refuge. This terrible Kali age has come. In it all people will be wicked. Therefore, O lord, tell (me) what should be done. Whose shelter will this earth, full of burden, seek? O Yadunandana, no other protector like you is seen here. Therefore, O treasure of compassion, showing pity on us, stay here only. O lord, you have manifested (yourself) only for the protection of the good. Even though you are qualityless, formless, and only of the form of the good, consciousness and bliss, your devotees will not remain on the earth in separation from you. There is difficulty in worshipping the qualityless. Therefore, do what is good for us.

Sūta said:

64-68. Having heard these words of Uddhava, Viṣṇu thought for a moment and being full of great compassion, gave him Bhāgavata, after having deposited his own lustre into it, O brāhmaṇa. Having given it to Uddhava, the lord entered his own place. Due to that this image of Viṣṇu in the form of words is here (in the world). By constantly resorting to it the sin of men would perish in a moment. Therefore, listening to it for seven days is said to be the best. O brāhmaṇa, its listeners, speaker or questioner become one with him. Bhāgavata is capable of removing misery, poverty, ill luck and sins, of overcoming passion and anger in the Kali age. Otherwise, how can, Viṣṇu's Māyā, difficult to be overcome even by gods, turn away from men without (the help of) Bhāgavata?

Sūta said:

69-73. Having thus told the greatness of Bhāgavata, they commenced narrating the divine story of Bhāgavata. When (the narration of) Bhāgavata, the essence of the Vedas and the Upaniṣads, was commenced by the brāhmaṇas, Bhakti in a moment manifested herself there only. She was full of love, of a charming body, and had held her two sons, full of joy, by her hands; and was uttering the names (like) Śrīkṛṣṇa, Govinda, Hari, Murāri, Nātha (lord). The members of the assembly saw her, the ornament of Bhāgavata and of a very fine dress; and with wonder in their eyes all of them thought: 'How (has she come)? Wherefrom (has she come)? Who is she?' Then the blessed Kumāras said: "Now she has come out from the contents of the story." Having heard words like this, she, along with her sons, politely said to the sons of Brahmā:

Bhakti said:

74. Though perished in the Kali age, you have today nourished me with the elegance of the (Bhāgavata) story. Where shall I sit with these two? Show me a favourite seat.

Sūta said:

75. Having heard these words, Brahmā's sons having thought and properly reflected in their minds, spoke to Bhakti, who

removes the disease in the form of the mundane existence, who gives love alone to those who have devotion for Viṣṇu.

Kumāras said:

76-78. When there are good devotees, having controlled their mind from going astray and having concentrated it on the lotus-like feet of Viṣṇu, after being devoted to Viṣṇu, these blemishes due to Kali, though powerful in the world, will not be able to see you. Led by Nārada, you alone will bring about the welfare of the world. In the entire world, those poor people in whose heart remains devotion to Viṣṇu alone, are, extremely blessed. Even Viṣṇu, tied by the bond of love, leaves his own world quickly and enters their heart.

CHAPTER ONE HUNDRED NINETYSIX

Dhundhulī's Story

Sūta said:

1-7. Seeing extra-ordinary devotion in the minds of Viṣṇu's devotees, Viṣṇu left his world, and went to the earth. He was having a garland of wood flowers; was dark like a cloud; had put on yellow garments; was wearing a crown; his group of girdles was dishevelled; his ear-rings in the shape of crocodiles were shining. He was charming due to three folds; was adorned with the beautiful Kaustubha; he was handsome like a crore of Cupids; he was besmeared with (the yellow sandal called) haricandana. He was the image of great joy and consciousness; he was sweet; and had held a flute. He entered the pure hearts of his devotees. Those followers of Viṣṇu, who lived in Vaikuṇṭha and were of tranquil minds, and of concealed forms, came to listen to Viṣṇu's tale. Then there was a shout of victory mixed with the sound of conches, due to which (everything) inauspicious, very fierce due to Kali, perished. Seeing that the people there had forgotten their houses and themselves, Nārada knowing the truth about the Supreme Soul said to the Kumāras:

Nārada said:

8-11a. O best sages, this greatness due to the seven days' (reading of or listening to the Bhāgavata) which I saw is uncommon. Even the fools, the wicked, so also the beasts and birds do reach the position known to be the highest. No other holy text so pure is laid down for the purification of the heart in the world of men. O Kumāras, in the Kali age, the abode of blemishes, it destroys the stream of sins, and brings about blessedness. (Please) tell me who are not purified by the devotional act (of reading of or listening to the Bhāgavata) for seven days, full of the stories (from it). You, the kind ones, have shown a new path for the good of the people.

Kumāras said:

11b-15. Those men who are sinners, very wicked, engaged in doing bad acts, are jealous, burnt by fire in the form of anger, crooked, passionate, go to Viṣṇu by means of the devotional act for seven days. Those who are without truth (i.e. are not truthful), who censure their father and mother, who are full of thirst (i.e. desire), who are out (of the fold) of the (four) stages of human life and castes, who are hypocrites, who are hurtful, go to Viṣṇu by means of the devotional act (of reading or listening to the Bhāgavata) for seven days. Those, who have committed the five terrible sins, who are deceitful, cruel, who are pityless like goblins, who have fed themselves with others' wealth, who are adulterous, go to Viṣṇu by means of the devotional act extending over seven days. Those wicked ones who violently always commit sins with their body, words or mind, who are mean, ungrateful, impure, wicked-hearted, go to Viṣṇu by means of the devotional act extending over seven days.

Sūta said:

16. Then, when Nārada, honoured by gods, was thus pleased in heart, the Kumāras who were pleased, again said to Nārada:

Kumāras said:

17-31. About this I shall tell you an old historical account, by merely hearing which, destruction of sins takes place. Formerly in the city called Kohala, full of the practices (proper) for the castes and the stages of human life, and of wealth and grains, (situated) on the bank of Tuṅgabhadrā, there was the best brāhmaṇa known as Ātmadeva, who was proficient in Vedic learning and rites, and engaged in daily duties. His dear wife was Dhundhulī by name. She was always engaged in her own welfare. She regulated (everything) with her words; she was beautiful, and was born in good family. Generally she talked much as a result of her former acts. She was valiant in domestic duties, cruel, and was quarrelsome. When the couple, having no child, was staying there, they crossed the age of the measure of fifty years. They, being childless, lived unhappily in their house. For the birth of a child they gave wealth etc. (to brāhmaṇas). So also they gave many cows, (pieces of) land, (coins of) gold and garments. (But) due to (the effect of) their former deeds, neither a son nor a daughter was born (to them). And once that best brāhmaṇa Ātmadeva, dejected and unhappy due to not having a child, left his house and went to a forest. With his mind overcome by grief, he, emaciated by hunger, and encompassed by thirst, wandering here and there, luckily reached a lake. That best brāhmaṇa, having drunk water in (i.e. from) that lake, sat after resorting to the shade of a tree, O Nārada. By chance, just then, a siddha, roaming over the earth, came (there); he too, drinking the water in (i.e. from) the lake, came there only. Having seen that tranquil anchorite, the noble-minded Ātmadeva honoured him and touched his feet as of his own preceptor. The two who were seated (there), being of very affectionate minds, asked questions to each other like a preceptor and his disciple in a hermitage. That anchorite, the ocean of pity, seeing him of an afflicted heart and sighing, asked that Ātmadeva, seated before him:

The siddha said:

32-33. O best brāhmaṇa, what great worry is there in your heart causing grief? O you who know religious practices, tell me that, tormenting you.

Hearing those words of that very noble siddha, Ātmadeva then told him the cause of his grief.

Ātmadeva said:

34-37. O sage, what should I tell you about the grief accumulated due to former deeds? My ancestors are drinking tepid water. My ancestors, so also deities, are not at all accepting the offerings made by me. Dejected due to that grief, I have come here to cast my life. Fie upon my life, my house without progeny, my wealth and family! Even the cow protected by me becomes barren. Even the tree planted by me becomes barren. What is the use of the life of me who am luckless and childless?

Kumāras said:

38-39. Speaking like this when he, oppressed by grief, wept loudly before him, great compassion arose in the heart of the sage. The wise one seeing the line of letters on his forehead and understanding it, spoke again in detail to the brāhmaṇa Ātmadeva:

The siddha said:

40-42. O brāhmaṇa, listen. Today I have read your fate. Your having a son is not seen till the seventh existence. Give up your persistence for a child. The course of fate is most powerful. Taking to right knowledge, be happy, O very intelligent one.

Hearing these words of the siddha, the best brāhmaṇa, with his heart fixed on having a child, and being very unhappy spoke to the siddha:

The brāhmaṇa said:

43-50. What would happen with right knowledge? Give me a son even by force. Otherwise, I, filled with grief, will cast my life before you.

Seeing this persistence of the brāhmaṇa, the ascetic said: "Sagara, king of Aṅga, obtained misery. Citraketu became miserable due to wiping out the writing of fate. Therefore, O you who know religious practices, you will not be happy with a son, for fate is very powerful." Saying so, that siddha, honoured by the good, gave a fruit to the best brāhmaṇa, who persisted for a son. "O brāhmaṇa, I have given this fruit to you for obtaining a son. Give it to your wife. By that a son will undoubtedly be born to you. The wife should, for a year, resort to truthfulness, purity, kindness, charity, eating once a day only. The son would be pure due to that." Speaking like this the meditating saint left, (and) the brāhmaṇa came home. Having given the fruit to his wife, he told her what the siddha had said. Then that cruel Dhundhulī was always eager to have her say.

51-59. She told her friend all that the siddha had said: "If I would eat the fruit given by the siddha, then I would be pregnant. How shall I be able to bear it? I shall have little food, and will not have strength to move or for domestic work. If the foetus would be slanting, then it would be my death. How can I, so delicate, bear the pangs of delivery? When I shall be dull my sister-in-law would take away all my possessions. I am worried. O you of bright smile, what do (i.e. should) I do?" She, O brāhmaṇa, for fear of breaking the friendship, with her face smiling affectionately said: "It is just so." Due to this wrong reasoning she did not eat the fruit at all. When her husband asked her: "Have you eaten the fruit?", she told him, "I have eaten it." Once her sister came to her house of her own accord. She told all that to her (saying): "This is my great anxiety. By being pregnant what shall I do? Tell me what is proper." She said: "I am carrying. After delivery I shall give my foetus (i.e. child) to you. Till that time live happily in your house, as if you are pregnant, concealing (the fact). I shall always nourish the child in your house only. O you of an auspicious face, today give the fruit to the cow to test (the siddha's words)."

60-69. Speaking like this, she went home with a pleased mind. Dhundhulī also did as her sister had told her. She, after having delivered a child, quickly gave it to Dhundhulī. She too told her husband: "The son is comfortably born." Due to a child born to Ātmadeva, people became happy. He gave gifts to best brāhmaṇas, and performed the ceremony at the birth of the child. In his house there was the auspicious sound of songs and musical instruments. Ātmadeva, the very intelligent one, was joyful. Then she said to her husband: "There is no milk in my breasts. How shall I now nourish the child born recently, O lord? My sister also has delivered; but soon her child died. Bring her and keep her in (our) house. She will nourish the child." Hearing the words of that Dhundhulī, the confused Ātmadeva, the best brāhmaṇa, full of joy, did just like that. The mother significantly named him Dhundhukārī. The boy obtained nourishment from the milk of his mother's sister. After three months had passed, the cow gave birth to a child. He was handsome in all limbs, was divine, spotless and had lustre like gold. Having seen him, the brāhmaṇa was pleased, and himself performed the sacraments. All people that had come with a desire to see him were very much amazed.

70-78a. (They said:) "Due to the rise of great good luck of the brāhmaṇa Ātmadeva a boy, of a divine form, is born of the cow. It is a great wonder." Due to destiny nobody knew the secret. Seeing the boy to have ears like those of a cow, he called him Gokarṇa only. After some time both of them attained youth. Gokarṇa was learned and wise. Dhundhukārin was very wicked. He was without a bath or purity or rites, ate prohibited food, and was full of anger. He was a thief, hated all people, and kept the company of wicked cāṇḍālas. He forcibly seized the children that were playing and threw them into a well. In the same way, being addicted to prostitutes, he diminished (i.e. squandered) his father's money. Like a helpless person, his poor father wept. "A childless person is happy. A bad son causes grief. Now I have experienced that the siddha's words are true. Where should I go? Where should I stay? Who would remove my misery? I shall cast my life in water or fire; or I would fall from a precipice." To him, his father who was thinking like this and whose face was hung down, the wise Gokarṇa came and properly advised him.

Gokarṇa said:

78b-84. O father, the mundane existence is worthless; it causes misery and delusion to men. O father, who is a son? What is wealth? Who is whose wife? Who is the husband? The helpless world, tied by delusion, suffers, and not due to any other cause. Indra does not have any happiness; a sovereign emperor has no happiness. O father, only a detached sage, given to seclusion, has happiness. Give up your ignorance, the delusion of the form of progeny, the cause of hell. Being free from the couples (of opposite qualities) and from pride, and giving up everything, go to a forest.

Hearing these words of him, the brāhmaṇa said to Gokarṇa:

The brāhmaṇa said:

O good one, tell me in detail what should be done in the forest. O you treasure of pity, emancipate me who am tied down by the chains of delusion, who am wicked and of a mean mind, and who am fallen in the ditch of the worldly existence.

Hearing these words of his father Gokarṇa, learned due to knowledge and with his mind pleased, spoke to his helpless, dejected father:

Gokarṇa said:

85-86. Quickly give up the feeling of mineness for this (your) body which is a collection of flesh and bones, and for (your) wife, sons etc. Note that this world is momentary. Be a wise man, taking interest in detachment, and be firm in devotion. Always resort to religious practices. Give up the practices of (common) people. Serve good men. Give up desire for pleasures. Quickly give up thinking about the faults and virtues of others, and drink deep the juice of the stories of Viṣṇu.

Kumāras said:

87. Having thus known the experience told by his son, he who was of a firm mind and free from desire, and who had crossed sixty years, abandoned his house; and the magnanimous one, always followed by people dear to Viṣṇu, and living in a forest, obtained Viṣṇu's position.

CHAPTER ONE HUNDRED NINETYSEVEN

The Seven-day Bhāgavata Recitation

Kumāras said:

1-10a. O Nārada, when the father had thus gone to the forest, the very wicked Dhundhukārin came and threatened his mother. O Nārada, (he said) to his mother: "Tell me where the wealth is. If you do not tell me about the grains, by all means I shall kill you. She, frightened by his words, and with her mind afflicted, fell at night in a well and died. After knowing it people took her out. Gokarṇa took out the dead body with the help of brāhmaṇas, her relatives. O sage, the wise one, to whom pleasure and pain were alike, went on a pilgrimage. Dhundhukārin lived in his house, and was surrounded by harlots. Due to his practice of very fierce deeds, he did not know how to feed them. The harlots, desiring ornaments, said to him: "O dear one, all of us have been associated with you, our protector, and have stayed (with you). O you who respect others, here there is no other giver of wealth. Therefore, give us fine garments and bright ornaments. Otherwise, we shall go to another man from (i.e. leaving) you." Hearing these words of them, he thought for a moment, and then he, blind due to desire for sensual enjoyment, and not being aware of death, went out of his house at night, stole from someone's house garments and ornaments, and O Nārada, he, full of joy, gave those to them to please them.

10b-22. Seeing those priceless garments and ornaments, the women thought: 'He has brought these by stealing them'. Deciding like this, they consulted one another. Everyday he commits thefts. The king will arrest him. Having snatched his wealth, he will certainly beat him. Then, why should we not secretly kill him committing thefts, and collecting much wealth go to another place? (Deliberating) like this, those wicked ones were intent on killing him, when asleep, binding him at the neck with very strong cords. When he did not die even after his neck was pressed, they threw many burning charcoals on his face. Being oppressed by the great affliction due to the flames of fire, he died. The almost rash women threw his body in a ditch. O best sage, nobody knew his whereabouts. When asked by people, they said, "Our lord has gone away. After getting wealth he will come (back) after a long time." Therefore, the best learned men should not trust women. They always hurt the one that trusts them, and go to newer and newer (men). Their words are full of nectar, increasing the interest of the passionate; (but) their heart is like the edge of a razor. Who indeed is dear to women? Then those prostitutes, taking the large wealth, much perturbed by the fear of the king, quickly went to another village. Dhundhukārin, doing bad deeds, became a big evil spirit. Taking up the form of a storm, he everyday ran (away) into the directions away from wicked death. He was troubled by cold and heat, was without food, and thirsty.

23-29. Repeatedly crying loudly "Ha! ha!" he did not get happiness anywhere. Knowing, after some time, that he was dead, Gokarṇa performed a śrāddha at Gayā during his pilgrimage. After completing his pilgrimage, he came (back) to his village. The villagers, his kinsmen and relatives honoured him. The brāhmaṇa stayed at home for a few days. Knowing that Gokarṇa was asleep in the yard of his house at night, wicked Dhundhukārin showed him his fierce form. For a moment he became an elephant; in a moment he became a camel; in a moment he became a buffalo; in a moment he became fire; in a moment he became a serpent; and a man in a moment. Seeing this inauspiciousness, the intelligent Gokarṇa, very much amazed, mustered courage and thought: 'What is this? This is some mean man, reduced to a miserable condition.' Deciding like this to his mind, he, full of pity, said:

Gokarṇa said:

30-36. Who are you so fierce, that have come at night to frighten me? Are you an evil spirit or a goblin? Due to what are you reduced to this condition? O glorious one, tell me what I should do for you now, since you, of a fierce form, have approached me at night.

Hearing these words of his brother, that very wicked Dhundhukārin who was reduced to the condition of an evil spirit, and who was very much afflicted, wept. Confused by his condition of an evil spirit, he was not able to speak with words. Being thirsty, he indicated with signs (that he wanted) to drink water. Then that highly virtuous Gokarṇa, esteemed by the good, took water in the hollow of his hands, and raising it, threw it (on him). That water thrown by the noble Gokarṇa, his brother, came to satisfy the evil spirit, Dhundhukārin. Then having obtained consciousness due to the water given by his virtuous brother, Gokarṇa, he spoke, O Nārada:

The evil spirit said:

37-47a. I am your brother named Dhundhukārin. Due to the fault of my deeds, I have been reduced to the condition of an evil spirit. My mother, terrified by me in many ways, died through grief. Then eager to feed the prostitutes, I, for getting money, committed prohibited acts like stealing, through greed of money. Once they asked me for excellent ornaments. Stealing them from a rich man's house at night, I brought them. Then through greed of wealth, O you who give respect (to others), they forcibly tied me at the neck, and killed me by throwing fire on me. Taking that abundant wealth, all of them, having given up the goodness of heart, ran away from this town through the fear of the king. I was reduced to the condition of an evil spirit. O brother, today being sprinkled by you, the kind one, with water due to (my) religious merit, I regained consciousness. I live on air. Due to my luck, the desired thing has come up. I saw you, my brother, asleep in the yard of your house. Then I suddenly exerted to attack you who did not know me. O good one, now I have been recognised by you. O my brother, O brother of the helpless, O ocean of pity, quickly free me from this condition of an evil spirit. There is no doubt that you are blessed.

Hearing these words of his brother, the wise, very intelligent Gokarṇa, with his mind dejected, spoke to his brother Dhundhukārin, who was afflicted:

Gokarṇa said:

47b-51. Hearing from the people's mouths that you were dead, I offered you a piṇḍa at Gayā. How have you been reduced to the condition of an evil spirit, O brother? Even one reduced to a miserable condition secures an auspicious course by means of a piṇḍa offered to him at Gayā. There is no doubt about this. How is it that you did not go to heaven?

Hearing these words of Gokarṇa, the noble one, Dhundhukārin who was in front of him and whose mind was afflicted, said: "Even by the śrāddha at Gayā I shall not be liberated. You should think of a means for my emancipation." Hearing these words of him Gokarṇa was amazed.

52-57a. He said: "If by means of śrāddhas you are not getting liberation, then your reaching heaven is impossible. O evil spirit, now, being fearless, resort to your own place. After having thought I shall adopt a means for your liberation." Having heard these words, Dhundhukārin went from there to his place, the bibhītaka tree in the cremation ground. Then, O Nārada, the remaining night Gokarṇa remained there thinking about his liberation. He did not find a means for that. In the morning that Gokarṇa told the account of the night to his relatives and members of his family, so also to brāhmaṇas who knew sacred treatises. When after having pondered over the matter (consulting) sacred treatises, they did not find the means, they eulogized the Sun.

The brāhmaṇas said:

57b-70a. Salutation to you, O Bhāskara, Āditya, Tamohantā (Dispeller of darkness), Gabhastimat (Possesser of rays), Lokasākṣin (Observer of the world), Jagaddhāman (Resort of the world), to you who are saluted by gods and demons, O Dvādaśātman, Harihayabhāsvan (Shining with bay horses), Lokaprabodhaka (Awakener of the world), you always are the resort of the people of pious nature. You are Brahmā; you are Viṣṇu; you are Śiva—the authors of creation, maintenance and destruction. O lord, except you there is no refuge of the living beings in the world. You are Śarva, of the form of the earth, and Bhava, taking up the form of water. You are of the form of fire; you are Rudra; you are air, taking up a fierce form. You are fearful, having the sky as your body. You are the sacrificer, and the lord of beings. You are Mahādeva, Īśāna, the form of the moon, so also the sun. Eight divine images of you pervading the three worlds are offered oblations by the teachers of the Vedas for accomplishing all desires.

You are the Fish, holding the Vedas. You are the excellent Tortoise, supporting the mountain. You are Varāha, supporting the earth; you hold the three worlds; you are Trivikrama (i.e. Viṣṇu); you are Bhārgava (i.e. Paraśurāma) destroying the harmers of brāhmaṇas. You are Rāghava killing those who harm the world. You are Kṛṣṇa removing the burden of the earth. You are Buddha deluding the demons. You are Kalki, the killer of the Mlecchas in every age when piety is declining. You, taking up the form of Brahman, are the creator of gods, demons, men, beasts and birds, of beings moving in the water, of beings of many kinds. O Lord of the host of senses, you are Indra, Dharmarāja (i.e. Yama), Varuṇa, Kubera. You live in the form of the regent of a quarter. You are of three forms; you are to be offered oblations three times (a day); you are having three abodes; you are of the nature of three constituents. You, the Sun, separated in three ways, are alone worshipped by people. O lord of the world, you alone cause the lotuses to bloom.

O best sage, when, having spoken like this, the best brāhmaṇas stood (there), (the Sun) moving in the sky spoke distinctly when they were listening:

Śrī Sūrya said:

70b-84. O best brāhmaṇas, since you extolled me for pacifying the major sin of Dhundhuli's son, listen. This Gokarṇa, a calf, will emancipate him by means of (the reading of) the Bhāgavata for seven days, due to the religious merit of Ātmadeva. By eulogizing (me) with the hymn composed by you, and describing my glory, a man will obtain a divine vehicle, O brāhmaṇas. A man desiring sons, wealth, piety, salvation, will obtain it surely by reciting the Vāñchācintāmaṇi hymn.

Saying so, god Bhāskara, remaining in the sky, ceased (speaking). The brāhmaṇas, with their minds delighted, said 'Well (done)' to Gokarṇa. Then to the assembly of the brāhmaṇas on the auspicious bank of Tuṅgabhadrā, the citizens went to see the very great wonder. Gokarṇa, who had known the truth, who was the reciter, was seated on a high seat. Having saluted Nārāyaṇa and others, he commenced (the reading of the Bhāgavata for) seven days. 'If the holy text, the word of Viṣṇu is truly a holy place, springing from his lotus like feet, then may the son of Dhundhulī obtain heaven.' Mentally resolving like this, he recited (the Purāṇa) called Bhāgavata, beginning with *Janmādyasya yataḥ* and ending with *Dhīmahi*. Then the evil spirit, having come there, and looking for a seat here and there, took up the form of air and entered a bamboo having seven knots. O Nārada, while the brāhmaṇas, the foremost among the best brāhmaṇas were listening, the son of Dhundhulī, remaining in the hole of the knot everyday listened (to the Purāṇa). When, O Nārada, on the first day the narration came to an end, one knot of the bamboo bursted. It was a great wonder. On the second and other days also the knots bursted like this. When the seventh (knot) bursted he instantly abandoned his condition of an evil spirit. Being one having a divine form, and being adorned with a garland of Tulasī (leaves), wearing yellow garments, dark like a cloud, and full of ornaments, he shone. Saluting his brother Gokarṇa, he, seeing the entire truth, said:

85-95. "O brother, you have kindly freed me from the foulness of an evil spirit. The account of the lord is indeed blessed, which is known to remove the condition of an evil spirit. The (recitation of the Bhāgavata for a) week is also blessed, leading one to Viṣṇu's world. Due to its power, I who was much afflicted, am freed from the condition of an evil spirit. The (recitation of the Bhāgavata for a) week would reduce to ash deliberate, non-deliberate, minor or major sins of speech, mind or act, as fire reduces the fuel to ash. Listen to the holy text of the Bhāgavata in this Bhārata liked even by gods. (Your) position (thereby) would be excellent. The body is said to be an aggregate of sinews, bones, marrow, flesh, blood. It is said to be pure due to relishing the Bhāgavata; and impure otherwise. The body, polluted due to the blemishes of acts, is the recipient of hell. To remove the blemish due to that, it alone is the means. Those (who live) without (reading or listening to) the divine holy text, are born to die only like bubbles in water or gnats among beings. The knot of the heart is broken. All doubts are cut off (i.e. removed). The (effects of his) deeds diminish, when the Bhāgavata is listened to, O brāhmaṇas." When he was speaking like this, an excellent aeroplane came there from Vaikuṇṭha; getting into it, he went to

Viṣṇu's abode. When he went to Viṣṇu's heaven, the minds of all were amazed, and they asked Gokarṇa, the best brāhmaṇa:

The brāhmaṇas said:

O glorious one, all of us, that have gathered here, have listened to the Bhāgavata. For what reason has your brother alone gone to Viṣṇu?

Gokarṇa said:

96-104. Listen. I shall tell (you) the reason for the good course of my brother, hearing which you will also go to Goloka. For a week (the Bhāgavata) should be heard (by you) intent on (observing) a fast, and with (your) minds concentrated upon Kṛṣṇa. That gives an access to Goloka. O brāhmaṇas, again listen to the Bhāgavata for a week, with concentrated minds. It always gives the nectar in the form of Kṛṣṇa's love.

Hearing these words of that Gokarṇa, the best brāhmaṇas settled to listen to the Bhāgavata for a week. O Nārada, with restraint, and with their minds concentrated on Kṛṣṇa, all the brāhmaṇas again listened to the Bhāgavata. At the end (of the narration) of the story, O best sage, lord Kṛṣṇa appeared there. He was lotus-eyed; he held a conch, a disc, a mace and a lotus. He had put on a crown and ear-rings; he was adorned with a garland of wood-flowers. He had put on yellow garments; he was dark like a cloud. He was adorned with bracelets and armlets. Seeing him accompanied by the excellent companions like Viṣvaksena, the sages, gathered on the earth, being delighted, saluted him. O sage, at that the shouts of victory and salutation prevailed everywhere. Then, Viṣṇu, delighting the brāhmaṇas made the sound of (i.e. blew) his conch.

105-114. Then, when the brāhmaṇas were looking on, many aeroplanes, with excellent attendants, came there from Vaikuṇṭha. (Viṣṇu) having embraced Gokarṇa, gave him similarity of his form. At that moment only, he made other listeners dark like clouds wearing yellow, silken garments and crowns and ear-rings; (made them) charming, and wearing garlands of wood-flowers. There was a great wonder also. By Kṛṣṇa's order all the people up to (i.e. including) the cāṇḍālas got into the aeroplanes and went to heaven. Kṛṣṇa, dear to the cowherds and the cowherdesses, went, along with Gokarṇa, to Goloka, situated above all (other) worlds. There is the charming Vṛndāvana, covered with a hundred peaks. Outside it shines a very wonderful forest covered with hemp. There are many pavilions, wells like Acchoda and pools. There are desire-yielding cows, resorting to the shades of the celestial trees; the son of Nanda, surrounded by young cowherds, with their minds intent upon sporting, plays there. In the midstof this excellent groveis fixed a great fig tree, brightening the charming rampart, decked with masses of gems and gold according to the desire of the Lord of Vṛndāvana. Then shines Śrī Gokula of a wonderful form, resorted to by cowherdesses and adorned by calves in every direction. In it the bright house resided in by Hari (i.e. Kṛṣṇa) shines, in which house of Nanda, they, the lofty ones, are propitiated by Rādhā. The great fortune of the child of a charming figure, meditated upon by (gods) led by (Śiva) the lord of Umā, with their minds, shines more by means of the rays of the lustre of the worlds. By means of the commencement of the seven-day rite called (Bhāgavata) Saptāha, he (i.e. Gokarṇa), born of a cow, obtained the world impossible to be got by means of subsisting on air, water, leaves, parching up one's body, severe austerities, mutterings and sacrificial rites. He who would read or listen to this holy account, goes to Goloka. Then what to say of (him who would read or listent to) Śrī Bhāgavata!

CHAPTER ONE HUNDRED NINETYEIGHT

Procedure to be Followed during the Saptāha

Kumāras said:

1-7. Now we shall tell you the manner of listening to the (Bhāgavata recitation during a) week, by which Bhāgavata would accomplish success for those men who have dedicated their minds to Kṛṣṇa. A devout man, after having called an astrologer, and after having honoured him with wealth and garments, should first ask him about the auspicious time. The commencement (of narrating the Bhāgavata) should be made at the auspicious time which he would tell. The months of Śrāvaṇa, Bhādrapada, Āśvina, Kārtika, Mārgaśīrṣa, Jyeṣṭha (and Āṣāḍha) are best for the commencement of the narration; so also the Pūrṇā tithi (i.e. 5th, 10th, 15th lunar days) is auspicious. Tuesdays and Saturdays shall be excluded and the constellations Dhruva and weak ones. The commencement is always recommended on an auspicious conjunction (of planets) and an auspicious lagna (i.e. the moment of the Sun's entrance into a Zodiacal sign). O best sage, when stories from the Purāṇas are (to be read) daily, a wise man should avoid Dvādaśī (the twelfth day) due to the impurity caused to Sūta. For the (reading of) Śrīmad Bhāgavata for a week there is no prohibition. Thus said those who know the past, O divine sage. The wise ones have said that (the reading of) Bhāgavata for a week is a great sacrifice.

8-16. Therefore, invitation should be extended to devotees of Viṣṇu all round: 'There will be a gathering during the week, O best devotees of Viṣṇu. Devotees of Viṣṇu desiring to listen (to the Bhāgavata) should come for it.' For those who come he should carefully make arrangement for their lodging at a holy place, in a grove, or in the village. He should erect a pavilion on the land that is purified. The pavilion should have four pillars with plantain trees, and should have banners in the four directions. A raised seat at its front is recommended for the speaker (i.e. the reader), O sage. The seats of the listeners are to be arranged on both the sides of him. The speaker, the most learned one, should face the north in the gathering. A speaker who knows the meaning and essential nature of the Vedas and holy texts, who is an excellent brāhmaṇa and a devotee of Viṣṇu, who is proficient in (telling) illustrative stories, who is patient, eloquent, free from desire, should be appointed. One removing all doubts should not be appointed. By the side of the speaker there should be another learned wise man. He should remove the doubts of the listeners and should enlighten the ignorant. To avoid any obstacle in (the narration of) the story, he should first worship Gaṇeśa. Then having, in the proper manner, worshipped Durgā, Śiva, Viṣṇu, Brahmā, the Sun and the brāhmaṇas, he should devoutly gratify the deities and the dead ancestors.

17-29. Then the chief listener should worship Viṣṇu represented in the book. Then having gone round, and having held in the hollow of his hands money, garments and fruits he should, O sage, request Viṣṇu (represented) in the book: "O divine one, you, Kṛṣṇa, have established yourself in this world. O lord, I have resorted to you for freedom from the ocean of the mundane existence. You should by all means make my desire fulfilled without any obstacle. O Keśava, I am your servant." Speaking like this and putting the money before the book, he should also, with his palms folded, salute and request the speaker (i.e. the reader): "O you best brāhmaṇa, of the form of Śuka, O you proficient in all holy texts, remove my ignorance by means of explaining the Bhāgavata." Having thus requested the speaker, he should select five brāhmaṇas for the recitation of the twelve-syllabled formula, O best sage. Having honoured those knowing the rules about singing and instrumental music with money, garments etc., he should at the end of the narration of the story appoint them for the recital (i.e. singing) of the glory of the lord. He who, having given up the anxiety about his wife, wealth, house, sons, listens with a concentrated mind, would obtain the entire fruit. For three watches and a half, beginning from sunrise, it—a sentence or a chapter, should be read and its meaning explained. O Nārada, he should take rest even for a ghaṭikā at mid-day. At the end of the (narration) of the story, the glory of Viṣṇu should be sung. A fast should be observed by the listeners desiring its fruit. A man incapable of doing it, should eat the food fit to be eaten during fast or should a little once (only). The body should be sustained without difficulty with water, or fruit, or milk or ghee only. O Nārada, listen to the rules to be observed by those who take the vow for seven days.

30-44. Those who are not initiated into (worship of) Viṣṇu, are said to have no right for this vow. O best sage, during the week one should observe celibacy, should sleep on the bare ground, and eat from a plate made of leaves everyday. He who is observing the vow, should avoid pulses, honey, oil, others' food, sugarcane juice, food polluted by thought, polluted by act, and stale food, so also onion, garlic, asafoetida, radish and gṛñjana (a kind of garlic). So also a man observing the vow of (reading or listening to the Bhāgavata) story should not eat lotus stalks and pumpkin gourd. He should not indulge in sexual pleasure, anger, pride, greed, hypocrisy, and jeolousy, so also infatuation, hatred and harm. He who is observing the vow of (reading or listening to the Bhāgavata) story, should avoid censuring Vedas, Viṣṇu's devotees, brāhmaṇas, preceptors, those observing the vow of (serving) a cow, so also women, kings and great men. The wise one who is observing the vow of (reading or listening to the Bhāgavata) should practise truthfulness, purity, kindness, silence, straightforwardness, politeness, and graciousness of mind. A man desiring wealth, desiring a son, desiring victory, or thinking of salvation, should listen to the Bhāgavata. He, having no desire, would obtain Śrī Hari. For its completion, he should fast on the seventh day. He should honour the reader with a cow, land, gold, garments etc. He should cause to give remnants of the food offered to the deity, garlands of Tulasī (leaves) to the listeners. So also with the (help of) those skilled in singing and playing upon musical instruments a festival should be celebrated. The wise one should also listen to the meaning of the Gītā on the next day. Or after every verse with the Gāyatrī hymn, he should make offerings (to Viṣṇu) according to the rules. He should also offer sweetened milk, honey, ghee, sesamum-seeds, rice, barley grains, sugar, priyāla, grapes, dates, lotuses, camphor, sandal, agaru (a kind of sandal), cloves, a thousand leaves of bilva separately. He should recite the (hymn called) Viṣṇu-sahasra-nāma for removing obstacles, removing deficiencies and excesses, and for purifying himself. He should devoutly offer sweetened milk to twelve, eighteen or more brāhmaṇas, and (should give them) gold or a cow as a present.

45-52. On this day or the day of Pūrvā Bhādrapadā or Uttarā Bhādrapadā (constellations) he should fashion (the) golden (image of a) lion, should place the Bhāgavata (text) on its back, and writing on it (his name etc.) should give it to the reader. When this is done according to the rule, the Bhāgavata that is listened to would remove all the sins of the listener and would give him good fruit, be the means of religious merit, of the fulfilment of the desire for sensual enjoyments, acquisition of worldly objects and salvation, and would give (i.e. produces) devotion. There is no object in the world that is not secured by this. Therefore, in the world, the Bhāgavata is regarded as superior to (other) Purāṇas. The reader is said to be free from eighteen blemishes, and the listener is supposed to be free from thirty-two faults by the wise. The Purāṇa named Śrī Bhāgavata gives men their desired objects. Yet listening to it produces devotion only in a person free from desires. The divine tree called Śrīmad Bhāgavata has starlike shoots; has a good origin; it shines with twelve large boughs (i.e. sections); it grows in the basin of devotion;it has three hundred and thirty-two bright branches (i.e. chapters); it has eighteen thousand leaves (i.e. verses); it gives desired objects; it is easily accessible; and it stands above all. Thus I have told you everything and have done what was desired by you. The youth of Jñāna, Vairāgya and Bhakti gives salvation to people.

Sūta said:

53-54. Having spoken like this, the Kumāras, inundated with the nectar (flowing) from Kṛṣṇa's feet, devotees of the lord, and intent on emancipating the helpless, ceased (speaking). Hearing their words, Nārada, dear to the lord, and with his palms joined, said to them in a voice faltering due to love:

Nārada said:

55-62. I am blessed; I am favoured by you highly devoted to compassion, since at the end of the Bhāgavata-saptāha (i.e. reciting or listening to the Bhāgavata for a week), you have presented Viṣṇu near me.

While Nārada, the best devotee of Viṣṇu, was speaking like this, Śuka, the chief among the meditating saints, (while) roaming, came there. His form was that of a youth of sixteen years; he was lotus-eyed; he was Vyāsa's son; he was the moon to the ocean of knowledge; he was content at heart with whatever (given) at the end of (the narration of) the story, and constantly recited Bhāgavata. The members of the assembly, seeing him of a great lustre, got up and gave him an excellent seat. When he comfortably sat on the seat, lotus-eyed Viṣṇu appeared (there). Śiva with Pārvatī and Brahmā with his sons came there to glorify and see him. Gods among whom Indra was the chief, came there in aeroplanes. The sky was covered by them. Prahlāda did the beating of time with a quick speed; Uddhava took the cymbals; the divine sage (Nārada) took the lute; Arjuna, through his skill in tunes, formed the musical modes. Indra played upon the tabor; the Kumāras uttered the loud shouts of victory. Vyāsa's son, of unsurpassed virtues, was a (versatile) speaker and of good sentiments. The triad of Jñāna etc. having new forms, just danced in the middle. Seeing the extraordinary glorification Viṣṇu, with his mind pleased, spoke as follows: "O devotees of Viṣṇu, ask for a boon from me who am very much pleased with the narration of the story." Hearing those words, they who were pleased, and with their heart flowing with love, said:

Kumāras said:

63-67. O Murāri (i.e. O Viṣṇu), you will be instantly pleased with the worship (in the form of reading or listening to the Bhāgavata) continued for a week in the very fierce Kali age by men having a short life and overcome by hundreds of obstacles. From you, the soul of everything and the creator, sustainer and destroyer of the universe, we, resorting to your lotus-like feet, ask for this boon and not any other (boon).

Saying, "Let it be so", Viṣṇu vanished there only. Nārada with his mind pleased, saluted Kumāras. Then those Sanaka and others, Bhṛgu and others and Śuka and others, delighted by drinking the nectar of the story went to their own hermitages. O Śaunaka, since then, Nārada propagated Bhakti along with her two sons over the entire earth.

Śiva said:

68. O dear one, having heard the great story, Śaunaka whose heart was pleased, again asked Sūta who removed all doubts:

Śaunaka said:

69. O you respecting (others), tell me when Śuka told it to the king, when Gokarṇa told it, and Brahmā's sons to the divine sage (Nārada).

Sūta said:

70-72. Śuka commenced (the narration of) the story on the ninth of the bright fortnight of Bhādrapada when the period of three hundred years of Kali after the departure of Śrīkṛṣṇa had passed. Gokarṇa told the story on the 9th day of the bright half of Jyeṣṭha (or Āṣāḍha), after two hundred years had passed from the time Parīkṣit had heard it. O brāhmaṇa, now a thousand years of the Kali age have passed from the time of Parīkṣit. (So) conclude the sacrifice.

The lord said:

73-81a. Hearing these words of him, the best sage Śaunaka completed the sacrifice that continued for a thousand years. These Purāṇas: Brāhma, Pādma, Vaiṣṇava, Kaurma, Matsya, Vāmana, Varāha, Brahmavaivarta, Nāradīya, Bhaviṣyaka, and half of Āgneya were formerly heard by excellent sages like Śaunaka from Sūta Lomaharṣaṇa up to the end of the Dvāpara age. When Baladeva came on a pilgrimage to (the forest) called Naimiṣa Miśrikā, he was called by the best sages. There seeing Sūta seated on an excellent seat, revered (Bala-)Rāma was agitated like the great ocean on a parvan day. O Pārvatī, on the Dvādaśī day of the bright half of Āṣāḍha, at the time of its earlier half, he, Rāma, being stupefied due to what was decided by Kṛṣṇa's Māyā, having darbhas in his hand, struck Lomaharṣaṇa. Then all the hosts of the sages did loud wailing, and their hearts were overcome by sorrow and grief, O daughter of the (Himālaya) Mountain. Then they, full of forgiveness, said humbly to Rāma, the lord of the world:

The sages said:

81b-87a. O Rāma, Rāma, O you of great arms, you, the author of the world, have ignorantly committed harm greater than that due to the murder of a brāhmaṇa. This is actually Vyāsa's disciple, an ancient sage, having a great penance (to his credit). We who had invited him, the narrator of the eighteen Purāṇas, gave him an excellent seat at this sacrificial rite. On (hearing) the story of the lord of the world one obtains long life, O you who honour (others). Therefore, you who promoted the bridge of piety, who are capable of curbing and favouring, who are the lord of the world, have manifested yourself for the protection of the world.

Speaking like this to Baladeva, O dear one, the sages, remembering the force of destiny, suddenly became silent. Then revered Rāma, killer of his enemies, following the path of the world and the Vedas, pleasing those brāhmaṇas, said:

Śrī Rāma said:

87b-89. O brāhmaṇas, may well-being come to you; listen after casting far away your anger. I know what you like and what gives success to your undertaking. Due to my blessing his son will be very wise. He will narrate to you the holy text desired by you. Tell me the work for which you have invited me.

The lord said:

90-100. Hearing these words of the very noble Rāma, they prompted the lord to murder Balvala. Then, having killed Balvala and pleased the pre-eminent sages and saluting them, he went on a pilgrimage after being permitted by them. O daughter of the (Himālaya) Mountain, when Rāma left for the pilgrimage, the chief sages like Śaunaka called Laumaharṣaṇi, and after honouring him placed him in his position for the narration of the remaining (part). With their minds delighted, they listened to seven Purāṇas and a half (beginning with) the greatness of the later part of Āgneya up to Bhāgavata. O you beautiful lady, Satyavatī's son (Vyāsa) was not mentally pleased after having composed seventeen Purāṇas and Bhārata also. Knowing that his heart was sad, revered Nārada, looking like a god, came to the excellent hermitage of Vyāsa. Seeing him, the son of Vāsavī (i.e. Vyāsa) hospitably received Nārada, offered him a seat, and honoured him with a rite according to the rules. Then Nārada said to him: "Tell me fully the cause of your doubt. What do you, with an afflicted mind, think of?" Thus asked by the sage, (Vyāsa) the son of Parāśara, said: "I really do not know the cause of the disturbance of my mind. You are proficient in knowledge. Understand it (i.e. the cause) and tell it to me." Thus requested by him, Nārada, proficient in the knowledge of the

Supreme Spirit, told him the highest truth obtained by him from Brahmā.

Nārada said:

101-110. O son of Parāśara, hear from me the cause due to which the mind of you, the master and the origin of holy texts, has become miserable. O innocent one, having descended on the earth, you have divided the Vedas into parts. You have also composed the Purāṇas along with the Itihāsa, in which, having observed in course of time the practices of the castes and of those living in the four stages of life, you have told them from the three Vedas. All women, śūdras, the twice-born fraternity, those prone to the company of the good, are entitled to listening to it. Religious practices, as are lasting, have been described in them by you. But you have not at all prominently described therein the greatness of Viṣṇu. O sage, in the Kali age, void of all religious practices and rites, and the reservoir of all blemishes, the sinners have no other course than the nectar of Kṛṣṇa's story. This alone is the merit in this terrible Kali age that men are freed from the bondage of their acts by means of narrating the glory of Kṛṣṇa only. Sacrifices, gifts, penance, rites, knowledge, meditation gave success in (ages) like Kṛta. In the same way, O brāhmaṇa, the narration of (Viṣṇu's) name (leads to success) in Kali. Therefore, for the emancipation of men born in the Kali age, you should relate Śrīmad Bhāgavata, by composing which, O dear one, your mind will be pleased and people will be blessed.

The lord said:

111-121. Having thus ordered Vyāsa of unlimited lustre, he, O dear one, constantly singing the virtues of Viṣṇu, went as he desired. After Nārada had gone, Vyāsa who saw everything, composed this great text, viz. Śrīmad Bhāgavata. Having taught the four Vedas to Paila and others according to the rule, he gave all the Purāṇa-texts to Sūta. That text of the Bhāgavata was heard by the son of Lomaharṣana, when it was being told to the king Parīkṣit by Śuka. O daughter of the (Himālaya) Mountain, he properly told it to sages like Śaunaka. It is above all Purāṇas and best among them. Men whose heart is attached to it find interest in nothing else. In their minds, Kṛṣṇa, son of Nanda, shines. O you mother of the chief of (my) attendants, I have told you the entire greatness of Śrī Bhāgavata, which you had asked me to narrate for crossing over the (mundane) world. A man who devoutly listens to or he too who reads with approval the greatness (of Śrī Bhāgavata) along with many historical accounts leading to devotion and salvation, obtains the highest position. Having studied it, a brāhmaṇa would obtain (the knowledge of) the Vedas, a kṣatriya would get victory, a vaiśya (would obtain) wealth, and a śūdra gets the best position by just listening to it.

CHAPTER ONE HUNDRED NINETYNINE

The Glory of Yamunā

The sages said:

1. O Sūta tell us the glory of Yamunā in detail—to whom it was spoken, and by whom it was spoken—along with a story.

Sūta said:

2. Once Pāṇḍu's son, desiring to hear auspicious knowledge from Saubhari, went to his place, and having saluted him, asked him like this:

Yudhiṣṭhira said:

3. O brāhmaṇa, tell me about that holy place which is (the best) among the holy places on the bank of Yamunā, and which is (even) superior to the land of the birth of Viṣṇu.

Saubhari said:

4-8. Once the two pre-eminent sages, Nārada and Parvata, moving in the sky, (while) looking (here and there), saw the very beautiful Khāṇḍava forest. From the sky they descended there and sat on the auspicious bank of Kālindī, and having rested awhile, entered her water to bathe. King Śibi, son of Uśīnara, hunting in the forest, saw the two, and waiting for them to come out, sat on the bank of the river. The two who after having duly bathed had put on garments, who were saluted by the king with his head (bent down), sat on the bank. Seeing thousands of golden sacrificial posts there, Śibi, free from pride, spoke to Nārada and Parvata:

Śibi said:

9-10. O pre-eminent sages, tell me, whose sacrificial posts these are. Who performed a sacrifice here—(was it) a god or a man? Leaving holy places like Kāśī, which man performed a sacrifice here? What peculiarity, O treasures of knowledge, does it have (in a greater extent) than other holy places?

Nārada said:

11-14. Formerly Hiraṇyakaśipu, having conquered deities like Indra, secured the kingdom of the three worlds, and entertained great pride. His son was Prahlāda, highly devoted to Nārāyaṇa. The wicked (Hiraṇyakaśipu), whose auspiciousness had perished, bore a great malice against him. Due to that malice, Viṣṇu, taking up the body of Nṛsiṁha, instantly killed the lord of demons, and gave the kingdom of heaven to (Indra) the lord of heaven. Having obtained his own position, the lord of gods, remembering the virtues of Viṣṇu, and saluting Bṛhaspati's feet with his head (bent down) said to him:

Indra said:

15-16. O preceptor, Viṣṇu, the supporter of the world, taking up the form of Nṛsiṁha, gave me the kindom of deities. I desire to worship him with sacrifices. O Guru, tell me (about) a pure place and also (about) the brāhmaṇas. You, doing good to us, should not delay in this matter.

Bṛhaspati said:

17-19. For you there is the charming and extremely holy Khāṇḍava forest which contains (the trees like) ketakī, aśoka, bakula and (also) bees intoxicated by honey. There is Yamunā, auspicious, holy and purifying the three worlds. On remembering her she gives heaven, and on death Brahmā's position. O lord of gods, if you desire the continuous well-being of your relatives, worship Viṣṇu with many sacrifices on her bank.

Nārada said:

20-27. Having heard Bṛhaspati's words, and quickly getting into a vehicle, Indra came to this forest of him which caused happiness, along with Bṛhaspati and the materials of sacrifice. Having come here, and having seen this forest, he obtained great joy. Prompted by Guru, Indra, choosing the seven sages, the sons of Brahmā, the brāhmaṇas, worshipped the lord of the world with sacrifices. The lord, pleased with him, came, along with Brahmā and Śiva, to Indra's sacrifice, where there was a great festivity. That Indra, of a crooked mind, seeing the triad of gods, quickly got up from his seat, and along with the sages, saluted them. Quickly getting down from their vehicles, they sat near him on seats of excellent gold, and shone like fires on altars. With Śiva and Brahmā who had white and red bodies, Viṣṇu, of a dark complexion, wearing yellow garments, shone like a cloud on two peaks. Indra washed their feet and took that water on his head. Being full of joy, he spoke sweet words:

Indra said:

28-37. O gods, this sacrifice performed by me has become instantly fruitful, since you, difficult to see even by meditating saints are seen (by me). O Viṣṇu, you alone have taken up the three forms. Yet as in a crystal, the appearance of multiplicity in you in respect of qualities is false. As fire concealed in pieces of wood does not manifest itself without friction, in the same way you remaining in the hearts of your devotees (do not manifest yourself) without deep devotion. Devotion to you alone, would be helpful to all beings. By that (devotion) entertained by Prahlāda, gods became happy. O god, we, given to sensual pleasures, have our hearts screened by your Māyā. We, the servants of your feet, do not know your nature correctly. O Brahman, O Mahādeva, since you two also are the preceptors of the world due to his greatness, you are not different from him. Whatever is said with words, thought of by the mind is his Māyā only. So all are away from that pair(?). He who sees this entire visible world to be unreal, would not think of (sensuous pleasures). O Śiva, those who resort to Viṣṇu's feet, cross the water held by you on your head. O Brahman, may I have, in existence after existence, a great liking for his feet, resembling lotuses. Due to it being agitated by her (Māyā's) glance, the entire world, Mahat etc. springs up. There is none else given to kindness like you who give happiness (even) to your enemies. That which is described as your kindness, that removes the misery of your people is (just) (due to) ignorance, O Nṛhari.

Nārada said:

38-46. Having thus praised Viṣṇu, the lord of gods remained bent before him. He who had applied (i.e. concentrated) his mind with a desire to hear his words, looked great.

The sages, having thus heard the praise of Ramā's lord, done by Indra in the assembly, said: "Well (done), well done." (They said:) "O Indra, (even) the devotion of those who practise severe penance for a hundred years is not like your devotion to Viṣṇu. The Yoga with eight parts, by means of which glory is obtained, is not easy. The refuge of men is renunciation with equanimity of mind and devotion to him. When the dedication of that act which is performed with the wealth earned in pursuance of the duties of one's own caste is made to Viṣṇu, that is devotion, giving happiness. He should not censure other deity, (and) him who salutes (the deity) with Viṣṇu in his mind. He should not ignore Vedic words. Such a devotee is dear to those who everyday listen to the virtues of Viṣṇu, who sing his glory, who remember him, resort to him, worship him, who salute him with servitude, who form friendship with him, who offer him their possessions, who do not desire salvation etc. O Indra, you also devoutly propitiate the lord of the world. Do not desire anything from him. Then you will be blessed."

Nārada said:

47. When Indra was thus advised by the sages, Viṣṇu, the lord, having heard about the devotion that was done to him, that could be resorted to by all, and that would cause the crossing of the three worlds, spoke sweet words to Indra in the assembly.

CHAPTER TWO HUNDRED

The Episode of a Bhilla and a Lion

The lord said:

1-15a. O lord of gods, it is no wonder that these very wise sages respect and honour my devotion, (leading to) my position, since these who teach knowledge to those living in the three worlds, always propagate the Vedic path that has perished. You, though attached to the enjoyments in heaven, have devoutly approached me. What wonder is there, since Bṛhaspati is your preceptor. O best of gods, free from desires, worship me with sacrifices with many gifts. You will quickly reach my position which is near. At every sacrifice present many prasthas (particular measures) of jewels. This place will be called Indraprastha. O Brahmā, having brought Sarasvatī and Gaṅgā purifying the world, fashion here the best holy place (called) Prayāga. O Śiva, you establish here Kāśī and Śivakāñcī and Gokarṇa. Always live here along with Gaurī. O sons of Brahmā, proficient in metaphysical and worldly knowledge, fashion here seven holy places by means of the power of your abstract meditation. O Guru, you set up the holy place Nigamodbodhaka. Here the knowledge of Vedas would be had even without studying (them). The two highest souls would have the recollection of their former existence. I shall found here very beautiful Dvārakā, where Gomatī has joined the sea. O Indra, I shall also fashion here Kośalā and Madhvaraṇya, where I shall descend through the bodies of Rāma (i.e. Balarāma) and Kṛṣṇa. I shall also fashion here Badaryāśrama, the abode of Nara and Nārāyaṇa, where, O chief of gods, I shall always live. With a desire for your good only, I shall found the two excellent holy places, Haridvāra and Puṣkara. I shall found here all the holy places that are in Naimiṣa, on the Kālañjara mountain and the bank of Sarasvatī.

Nārada said:

15b-26. O Śibi, having heard those auspicious words of Viṣṇu, and having done and seen that, Brahmā, Śiva and others did as was said (by him). That lord of the gods again worshipped

Lakṣmī's lord with many sacrifices in this place full of all holy places. In front of Kṛṣṇa, he gave prasthas of jewels to brāhmaṇas. 'May this Nārāyaṇa, the soul of all, be pleased with me.' Since then this holy place is called Indraprastha. One who dies at this holy place full of all holy places, is not reborn. The brāhmaṇas, having received those prasthas of jewels given by Indra, gave him there, in the assembly, a blessing that would not be fruitless: "O Indra, may Govinda be pleased with this gift of you. May you also have steady devotion for him. O lord, in this land of (sacred) rites formerly you, having a desire, performed a hundred sacrifices. Due to that religious position you obtained a place among the gods. Now you, without any desire, have worshipped Viṣṇu with sacrifices. Falling from your position, you will be (born) as the best brāhmaṇa. There (i.e. in that existence) also, you, worshipping Viṣṇu in accordance with your (caste-)duty, will remember the act like the sacrifice that you did. On remembering that, you, abandoning your house and going to holy places with your father, will come to this Śakra-tīrtha. Resorting to the fourth stage of life you will caste your body here. Then you, having a divine body, will get into an aeroplane brought by the attendants and bright like the sun, and will reach the position of Śrī Hari (i.e. Viṣṇu)."

Nārada said:

27-32. Having heard this blessing of the brāhmaṇas and their words indicative of the future, the lord of gods was extremely delighted, O Śibi. Having honoured with (gifts of) wealth etc. Brahmā's sons, the priests at the sacrifice, Indra, honouring Bṛhaspati, went to heaven. O Śībi, Indra, full of devotion for Viṣṇu, having ruled there, with his religious merit exhausted, came down to Hastināpura. There was a brāhmaṇa, Śivaśarman (by name), who had mastered the Vedas and Vedāṅgas. His wife was Guṇavatī, of a very significant name. To her was born Indra, who served Viṣṇu, at an auspicious time. Astrologers were called. Seeing the auspicious time they said:

The astrologers said:

33-36 O Śivaśaraman, this your boy will be dear to Viṣṇu. He wlll emancipate your family. We are telling the truth and not a lie. When he will have the body of thirteen years (i.e. when he will be thirteen years old), he, rich with knowledge learnt (i.e. got) by him, will marry. Then having produced a good son he will be an anchorite. The wise one, wandering to holy places, will renounce the world. There is the excellent river in Indra's Khāṇḍavavana. On her bank is Hariprastha. He will die there.

Nārada said:

37-44. Having heard the auspicious words uttered by the astrologers, he then named his son Viṣṇuśarman. Having dismissed them by (giving them) wealth, the intelligent one thought: 'I whose son will be Viṣṇu's devotee, am blessed. This son will accomplish for me the four stages of human life. He will die at the holy place. Who else is lucky like me?' Thinking like this in his mind, Śivaśarman got performed the ceremony to be performed at the birth of a child through the brāhmaṇas on an auspicious day. And when the son completed seven years, the best brāhmaṇa performed, in his eighth year, his thread ceremony in the month of Caitra. O king, after having imparted him education till the twelfth year he united the son with a wife, O Śibi. The intelligent Viṣṇuśarman having produced a son on his wife made up his mind, free from carnal desire, for visiting holy places. Having approached his father, and having saluted both his feet, the very wise Viṣṇuśarman, remembering the sages' words, said:

Viṣṇuśarman said:

45-49. O father, allow me. Having resorted to the third stage of life, causing good company, I (shall) worship Viṣṇu. Wife, house, wealth, children, friends are perishable. A wise man is not attached to them like bubbles on water. By means of Vedic study and progeny I have paid off the two debts (of the sages and forefathers). I, free from desires, (now) desire to offer a sacrifice to Viṣṇu. Having given up attachment for the constituents of nature I desire to stay at an excellent holy place, as long as my destiny allows.

Thus address by the son, the very intelligent father, remembering the words of the astrologers, and being desireless for (i.e. disgusted with) the mundane existence, said:

Śivaśarman said:

50-54. This is the time for resorting to the fourth stage of life for me also who am free from egoism. Having abandoned objects of senses like poison, I shall resort to the nectar in the form of Viṣṇu. O son, in this old age, my mind does not find delight in the house like an elephant brought from a forest and tied. Your younger brother Suśarman will support the family left by us two, like knowledge supporting a man forsaken by wealth and family. Your mother, a loyal wife, will (like to) follow me, renouncing the world, as brilliance follows the sun at the end of the day. Therefore, we too, not known by (i.e. without the knowledge of) your mother and thinking of Viṣṇu's lotus-like feet, (shall) go, O dear one.

Nārada said:

55-78a. Thus thinking, the two, desiring salvation, leaving (the members of) the family (that were) asleep, moved out of the house, and went. O Śibi, the two, free from egoism, wandered, and came to the excellent place, Śakraprastha, causing auspiciousness. Viṣṇuśarman who had come here, having seen the sacrificial posts laid by him in his former birth, remembered his contact with Viṣṇu. And the intelligent one said to his father: "Formerly (i.e. in my former birth) I was Indra. With a desire to please Viṣṇu, I performed sacrifices here. Here only, Viṣṇu, loving his devotees, was pleased with me. The brāhmaṇas, the seven sages, were pleased by me with prasthas of jewels. They only gave me devotion to Viṣṇu, salvation and birth. All, Viṣṇu and others, have put up holy places elsewhere. This holy place, Indraprastha, is full of all holy places. The best sages had told that I would die here only. After that I would obtain Viṣṇu's feet. I remember all this. These two, Gaṅgā and Sarasvatī, were brought from his own world by Brahmā; due to their contact this is called Prayāga. This is Kāśī, Śiva's city, in the eastern region of Prayāga. At the distance of four hastas there is an island. A man dead on it is not reborn. At the western region of Kāśī, at a distance of eightyfour hastas, there is Śivakāñcī founded by Śiva and giving salvation to the dead. This holy place called Gokarṇa, is very dear to Śiva. It is established on a portion of land measuring eight hastas. To the west of the chief holy place is this auspicious Dvārāvatī. A man dead within a distance of two hundred and eighty hastas from here gets four arms. Then to the eastern region of this is Kośala, dear to people. It measures seventytwo hastas and its sight is meritorious. This is Madhuvana, O dear one, founded by Viṣṇu himself, which is to the west and which measures forty hastas. O dear one, to the north of this is the abode of Nara and Nārāyaṇa. It stands on a piece of ground measuring fortyfour hastas. This holy place is Haridvāra, situated in the south of it. It is seen on a piece of land measuring one hundred and twenty hastas. This is the holy place Puṣkara, the crest-jewel of holy places. O dear one, it is situated on a piece of ground measuring forty-eight hastas. At a distance of one krośa from Prayāga, in the eastern direction, are seven holy places of the seven sages. This is the group of seven holy places. Near the seven holy places there are many other holy places, in which at every step a dead man becomes one with four arms. At a distance of one krośa from Prayāga, in the western region, is the holy place named Nigamodbodhaka, formerly founded by Guru. The distance between the seven holy places and Nigamodbodhaka is great. O dear one, this is the holy place Indraprastha, formerly founded by deities. It is extended up to a yojana in the east and the west. The great sages have said that four yojanas to the south of Yamunā is the limit of Indraprastha. He who casts his body here in (the confluence of) the three deities, is unborn."

Nārada said:

78b-79a. O Śibi, hearing these words of his son, the brāhmaṇa Śivaśarman having a doubt, said to his son, truthful of words.

Śivaśarman said:

79b-82. How should I know that formerly you were the lord of gods; you performed sacrifices here; you pleased the brāhmaṇas with (presents of) jewels? O son, do that by which I would have the truth of what is told by you. Wherefrom did you hear about this limit of Indraprastha, since from the time you had understanding you did not leave the house? From me only you have studied the four Vedas with the Aṅgas. How did you have the knowledge of the acts done in the former birth?

Viṣṇuśarman said:

83-85. Formerly the sages had given me a boon causing the recollection of the former existence. This recollection of this holy place is had by me from them only. O father, bathe here in this holy place, viz. Nigamodbodhaka. You will obtain knowledge difficult to obtain, giving you the ability to recollect your former birth. You will recollect even my behaviour in my former existence by touching the water of this holy place. I tell you the truth, O father.

Nārada said:

86-101. When the best brāhmaṇa Śivaśarman, after having heard this was ready to bathe in the holy place Nigamodbodhaka for the recollection of his former birth, there came running a bhilla followed by a lion. His limbs were full of great fear; he was panting; he was overcome by fatigue. He was of a harmful nature; he killed (people) on the way; he always robbed merchants. His body was dark. His hair was tawny. He was short. His eyes were like those of a cat. He had a lance in his hand; his figure was fearful. The man existed as it were by sin. Then seeing at a distance after him a lion the father and son quickly climbed a nearby tree, and remained (on it), saying, 'O Kṛṣṇa, free us from this untimely death.' O best king, the bhilla, seeing the lion (pursuing him) faster to seize him, was afraid, and proceeded to climb up the tree. The impetuous lion seized him, climbing (up the tree) at his feet, knocked him down with his back on the ground, and mounted on him. The bhilla too, who was pained and was under (the lion), tore the lion's belly with his lance in such a way that the mass of his entrails, smeared with a stream of blood came out. The lion, with a piteous roar, pounded the bhilla's head, and he died instantly. When the two died, there came down, O king, attendants with a group of two aeroplanes, that were fashioned with crystal stones, that were decorated with multitudes of jewels, that had charming pictures (painted on them), that were adorned with snow-walls, that had windows (decked) with rubies, the bells of which were tinkling, that had charming raised seats, that had cushions, that shone with lofty flags, that had high arches, that looked beautiful due to a hundred doors, that were clear like mirrors due to their floors resembling new corals, along with (i.e. in which were seated) two attendants whose complexion was like fresh clouds, on whose ears were charming rings, who had in their hands conches, discs, maces and lotuses, who had put on yellow garments, whose eyes resembled fully bloomed lotuses, the anklets round whose feet were making a deep (tinkling) sound, who had rows of bracelets round their forearms, whose chests looked charming due to pearl necklaces, whose faces had curly hair over them, whose couples of eyebrows had cast down the bow of Cupid.

102-111a. The bhilla and the lion, even before life left them, gave up their bodies and remained in a natural state due to the power of this holy place. The attendants of Viṣṇu, bringing the aeroplanes near them, who were having no dress or form, said to them: "O bhilla, best of men, O lion, the lord of beasts, know us to be Viṣṇu's attendants who have come from Vaikuṇṭha (or from Viṣṇu). We shall take you to his place. It is true. There are no distresses there. Getting into your respective aeroplane, go quickly. Do not tarry." The bhilla and the lion, got into their respective aeroplanes, and full of amazement, spoke to the attendants of (Viṣṇu), the lord of Lakṣmī: "O best deities, listen to our words. Due to your sight knowledge of the highest truth is produced (in us). In this existence we have not done the slightest good act. By your favour we are having the recollection of our former deeds. We ate flesh; we were engaged in killing animals; our mind and senses were cruel; we were born in sinners' families; we cause fear when looked at. In such a world, we were sinners. Due to what religious merit, we have seen (you)? Due to what religious merit shall we have absorption into Śrī Hari?"

The two attendants said:

111b-117. Indeed due to your dying at this holy place, formerly fashioned by (Bṛhaspati,) the preceptor of gods, you saw us, and (would get) the wonderful absorption (into Viṣṇu). You will soon obtain (i.e. reach) the position of the lord of Lakṣmī. Sins like the murder of a brāhmaṇa roar till the time this holy place of Bṛhaspati is not seen. As darkness perishes on sunrise, in the same way sins perish on seeing Nigamodbodhaka.

This holy place, called Indraprastha, purified Indra. Here he worshipped Viṣṇu with sacrifices with many presents. Viṣṇu pleased (by them), gave him a boon. Hear (it): "O Indra, those men, even killers, who cast their bodies at your holy place, full of all holy places, are equal to me."

Nārada said:

118. Speaking like this, the two best attendants took the two and went to Viṣṇu's place, having gone to which a man does not get drowned in the ocean of the world (i.e. the worldly existence).

CHAPTER TWO HUNDRED ONE

Śarabha's Story

Nārada said:

1-2. The two, the father and the son, got down from the tree, and seeing that even sinners got the position of Viṣṇu, were very much amazed. The best brāhmaṇa Śivaśarman, having heard the praise, expressed by the (two) attendants, of the holy place, spoke to Viṣṇuśarman, his son:

Śivaśarman said:

3-6. The bhilla and the lion have easily reached that position which is not easy to be reached by the brāhmaṇas even with penance practised. Observe the greatness of the holy place. It is not possible to praise in appropriate terms this best holy place, due to the power of which those who had committed sins from birth to death have obtained identity of form with Viṣṇu, O son? What a great disparity there is between the divine birth of Brahmā, which is from pure Sattva and difficult to be had even by gods on the one hand, and the Tamas-born lion and bhilla on the other! But this holy place is having a wonderful efficacy. O dear one, a being after having reached the end (of the fruits) of his actions. falls from the position of Brahman. (But) a being meeting death here (in this holy place), fashioned by (Bṛhaspati) the preceptor of the gods, has no fall from Viṣṇu's position.

Nārada said:

7-16. O king, the best brāhmaṇa, having actually seen the greatness of this holy place of Bṛhaspati, proceeded to bathe there. Having washed his face, teeth, feet and purified his mind, and having put on a garment with five hems, and having tied his tuft of hair, he remembered Viṣṇu, with the recitation of the verse *Aśvakrāntā* . . . He touched the clay on the bank, made a mark (on his forehead) with it, and again got into the water. There, plunging into the water and facing the current, he again got up. Remembering Viṣṇu and Gaṅgā, purifying the people, he again plunged. Again getting up he remembered the seven cities[1] like Ayodhyā; again dedicating his mind to Govinda, he plunged into the water. Having bathed duly he put on garments that were washed; and having come out the best brāhmaṇa put a mark (on his forehead). The restrained one put darbhas into his hands, on his feet and tufted hair. He duly performed the sandhyā (prayer) and offered oblations of three kinds. The honoured one made a respectful offering to the Sun with flowers, and the best brāhmaṇa, putting his folded palms on his head, saluted (the Sun). The best brāhmaṇa offered worship to Viṣṇu whose feet are revered by the world, beginning with an invocation and ending with an offering of eatables. Having performed the rites and seated comfortably, he, remembering fully the acts of his former birth, said to his son like that:

Śivaśarman said:

17-26. O Viṣṇuśarman, O dear one, your words are not false, since due to a bath here I had the recollection of my deeds in the former birth. O glorious one, listen to what I tell you. Formerly I was born in the family of wealthy and religious merchants. My father named Śarabha lived in the city of Kānyakubja. Resorting to the wealth of piety he obtained much

1. Saptapurī—The seven cities that are said to be so sacred that death at any one of them is the giver of eternal happiness. They are: Ayodhyā, Mathurā, Māyā, Kāśī, Kāñcī, Avantikā, and Dvārāvatī.

wealth by trade. He, with his body seized by old age and his mind afflicted by anxiety, passed a long time, (but) a son was not born to him. The best merchant day and night thought like this: 'My wealth, though collected to a large extent, is in vain without a son. Even a rich person having no son is indebted to his dead ancestors, as a cloud full of water but not showing (it), is to the cātakas. A man conquers the three worlds by means of progeny having piety as the foremost (virtue), as a king conquers an enemy difficult to conquer by means of power[1] of three kinds. Pure progeny pleases parents of good minds as sweet and true words that are spoken please friends and foes. The glory of the father enhances by means of the son's prosperity, as the pure water of the ocean by means of the moon. Therefore, a man should strive with his body or wealth to beget a son. Without him the two (i.e. the body and wealth) of men, having (momentary) life like that (of a flash) of lightning, are useless.'

27-34. When he was thinking like this, the excellent sage, Devala, having suprasensual knowledge, came there to give (him) a boon. Seeing him coming (my) father got up from (his) seat, and giving him a respectful offering and water to wash his feet with, saluted the sage with his head (bent down). Having made him sit on the seat offered with his own hand, my father asked the best sage Devala, of divine appearance: "O best sage, welcome to you. (I hope) there is happiness in your family, and the religious observances like penance and study of the Vedas are free from obstacles. I hope, guests come to your hermitage at the (proper) time. I hope, the trees in your hermitage bear fruits as desired by you. I hope, tigers etc. coming to your hermitage do not entertain hostility towards deer etc. as brothers towards their brothers. Your moving about on the earth gives joy to the householders. How (can it be) otherwise? How can they, engaged in (the affairs in) their houses, have your sight? O sage, granted that you, having your mind fixed on the dust particles on Viṣṇu's feet have absolutely no desire for anything; but quickly tell me about the purpose of your arrival."

1. Śakti: regal power. It has three parts or constituents: Prabhu-śakti or Prabhāva-śakti (the majesty or pre-eminent position of the king himself); Mantra-śakti (the power of good counsel); Utsāha-śakti (the power of energy).

Śivaśarman said:

35. Thus addressed that sage Devala, honoured by gods, desiring to know the thought in his mind, said to the great trader:

Devala said:

36-41. O best merchant, you have righteously collected much wealth, with which, O you knowing piety, perform obligatory and optional rites. A man gets respect in the king's assembly due to wealth, as a good (i.e. brave) warrior gets success in a battle due to valour. A householder, getting wealth, makes a great advance, as a bull, getting grains ripe in autumn, gets nourishment, O chief merchant. Relatives and other people do not leave the wealthy persons as bees do not abandon a tree with flowers containing honey. Due to want of wealth, the householders are fully reduced to feebleness, as the lakes without water in summer. O chief merchant, that ample wealth is there in your house. Why then, are your limbs feeble? (Please) tell me, if it is not a secret.

The merchant said:

42-45. You are like the fathers specially engaged in instructing (people) in their welfare. What is there to be concealed by men like me, who are (just) like your sons? O best sage, due to your favour I am fully happy. I am unhappy only due to want of a son in my old age. Know that the feebleness of my limbs is due to that, O best sage. I am afraid (of the repayment) of the debt to my dead ancestors, and of falling down (due to the non-repayment). O sage, suggest an expedient by which I shall have a son. For people like you there is nothing that cannot be done on the earth.

Śivaśarman said:

46-47. Having heard these words of the best merchant, Devala, having made his mind steady for a moment, and with his eyes closed, thought. Devala, having suprasensual knowledge, saw the obstacle in my father's having a child, and recollecting (it) said:

Devala said:

48-62. O vaiśya, I shall tell you what beautiful idea this your religious wife formerly had in her mind. 'O Gaurī, O you dear to Śambhu, when I shall be pregnant, I shall please you with foods having the six flavours;[1] (so also) with incense, rows of lights, tāmbūlas, dances, songs coming out of lutes, and smearings of various kinds.' Your wife having promised like this in front of her friends remained devoutly waiting for the time (of pregnancy). This your wife conceived in that month only. Then all her friends of affectionate hearts spoke to her: "O fortunate one, the pregnancy longed for by you, has been bestowed on you. Therefore, do what is promised to the goddess. Otherwise, there would be an obstacle due to the change wrought by her. Goddesses give boons or curses when they are (either) propitiated or angered." Thus addressed by her friends your highly virtuous, loyal wife, full of joy, modestly said to you: "O lord, I desire to worship Gaurī fulfilling all desires, due to whose grace I have had my desired object." O best merchant, hearing these auspicious words of your wife, you took her to be pregnant. Being delighted with great gaiety you instantly ordered your servants to bring the requisites of worship. You then gave her all the things brought by them, so also honey, food, grapes, perfumes, etc. Then she, calling all her friends, said to them: "O friends, taking the collection of materials brought for the worship of Ambikā, you, taking the requisites of worship, go to the temple of Ambikā, and please the goddess with worship laid down by the rules. In our family a pregnant woman does not move out of the house. Therefore, I shall not come. You (please) go to worship her."

63-81. Thus ordered, the friends, taking the materials (of worship), went to the temple of Ambikā, which was the abode of intoxicated bees moving (here and there). It was crowded with groups of mango trees on which flocks of cuckoos were sporting. It was adorned with swans, cranes and geese. There were spotless lotuses. It was surrounded by parrots and (other) birds talking about the virtues of Mahādeva. There were the friends of Umā engaged in sprinkling garlands and creepers. There the ground was purified by light plantings of the steps

1. Ṣaḍ-rasa: The six flavours: pungent, sour, sweet, saltish, bitter, and astringent.

of the lord of Umā. There were celestial trees on the boundary of the water bound by crystal stones. It was resounding with (the sound of) the gandharvas that were singing, accompanying the dance of Pārvatī's lord. There the mango tree, campaka trees, koraka trees were slightly tossed by gentle breezes. The bowers of creepers had the echoes of the notes of the dancing peacocks. It was brightened by her sports, and had flashing brightness like that of jewels. Those (friends) whose husbands were alive went there and saluted the daughter of the (Himālaya) Mountain; and going round her (image) keeping (it) to their right, they said with devotion: "O Jagadambā, salutation to you. Give us happiness, O you who are dear to Śiva. Accept this offering brought for your worship. There is a merchant Śarabha by name. He has a charming wife. She longed for pregnancy. This worship of you is for having had it. Due to your grace, O you dear to Śambhu, she had that foetus (i.e. she became pregnant). We have laid before you this offering to worship you. In her family a pregnant woman does not move out of the house. Therefore, O goddess, she has not come; be pleased and accept this (offering)." O vaiśya, having said like that to her, the friends of your wife offered the offering duly and worshipped her with sandal etc. Not receiving any reply from Gaurī, they returned home. They told their friend that Śiva's beloved was dejected. Hearing these words of them, the vaiśya woman, being uneasy, thought: 'Why was Gaurī not pleased? She knows my devotion for her. She knows the worship I offered to her. How can the internal (thoughts) and external (behaviour) of men be not known to (deities) like her? She also knows the reason for which I did not go there. Why was she not pleased by the offering made by me? I do not see any other reason for her dissatisfaction, except my not having gone to that charming temple. What has gone by cannot be changed. After I am delivered of the foetus, I shall go to her temple for worshipping her. Salutation to that wife of Mahādeva. May she cause happiness.' O vaiśya, speaking like this, your wife remained carrying the foetus.

Śivaśarman said:

82. O Viṣṇuśarman, the father, knowing this former account, asked the very wise, best sage, Devala:

The merchant said:

83-84. O sage, that your daughter-in-law offered the worship as promised. Tell me the cause of Pārvatī's dejection; since she herself knows the reason why she did not go there, and it was also told to her friends. Then why did she become dejected?

Devala said:

85-86. O best merchant, listen, I am telling you the reason for which Pārvatī's disappointment, destroying the foetus, took place. When her friends had returned after worshipping Skanda's mother, Vijayā full of curiosity, said to Pārvatī:

Vijayā said:

87-88. O Girijā, these ladies devoutly made an offering to you. Then, O you of an excellent face, why were you not pleased? To please you they worshipped you with incense, lights and offerings of food. (Instead of being pleased) why are you, on the contrary, disappointed?

Devala said:

89. O merchant, hearing these words of her friend, the goddess, honoured by excellent gods, told her friend Vijayā, the cause of her dejection.

Pārvatī said:

90-96. I know, O friend Vijayā, that the merchant's wife was unable to move out of the house through lack of discrimination for pregnancy (*corrupt reading*). Her friends, prompted by her, came to worship me. (Deities) like me do not accept the worship offered through others' hands. Had her husband come that would have been well. Her foetus neglected by me will fall out (immaturely). O friend, if a lady causes that vow which she herself cannot practise, to be practised by her husband, then the vow of the two does not fail. Or, after having asked (the permission of) her husband, she of a concentrated mind, (could get it practised) by a pre-eminent brāhmaṇa. Since she did not come herself and did not worship me, therefore, I have made her pregnancy void and fruitless. If again, the couple will come and devoutly worship me then they will have a son.

Devala said:

97-101a. O merchant, that curse was not heard by you, or your wife or the friends, so also the favour granted by her. Due to this ignorance of you two, not knowing the counter-rite giving happiness in this world and the next, a son was not born to you. O merchant, I have told you this reason for your not having a child as formerly Vasiṣṭha had told king Dilīpa. As having heard that the king propitiated Nandinī, in the same way, along with your wife propitiate Gaurī, fulfilling desires. As she, being propitiated by king Dilīpa gave him a son, similarly propitiate Gaurī; she will give you a son.

The merchant said:

101b-103. O sage, who is that king Dilīpa, and who is that Nandinī, having propitiated whom that best king obtained a son? Why did the king, leaving the gods like Śiva, giving the fruits to the three castes, propitiate her only for (obtaining) a son? O sage, tell me all this that I ask you. Hearing it, I, with my wife, shall serve that daughter of the (Himālaya) Mountain.

Śivaśarman said:

104. O Viṣṇuśarman, the sage, having heard these words spoken by the polite merchant, my father, commenced telling him Dilīpa's account, very holy in the world.

CHAPTER TWO HUNDRED TWO

The Story of King Dilīpa

Devala said:

1-16a. O very wise one, listen to the divine, wonderful account of king Dilīpa, which removes the sin of those who hear it. In Vaivasvata Manu's family was (born) the best king Dilīpa like Prācīnabarhis in Svāyambhuva Manu's (family). That king, best among the religious, protecting the earth justly, pleased the people with his rich virtues. The queen, the wife of that king, the daughter of the lord of Magadha, named Sudakṣiṇā, was like Śacī to the lord of heaven. Even after a long time had passed, a son was not born to the queen. The sovereign, the lord of Kośala, thus thought in his mind: 'I have held (under my control) the earth adorned with the gems like the ocean, the great Meru mountain etc. There is nothing wanting that should lead to my disgrace. At the proper time I have practised the three objects of human life. I have not opposed it. Yet in the mind of me who am childless, there is no happiness. With sacrifices I have worshipped Viṣṇu; so also the best gods like Indra. Everywhere on the earth I have got fashioned tanks, groves and wells. I have, with devotion, satisfied brāhmaṇas and guests with (presents of) cows, land, gold, garments, and with meals having the six (kinds of) tastes. Having justly uprooted the kings in battles for the maintenance (of piety), I have increased my treasury with great wealth. Those who went astray, who were arrogant, who violated their duties, who were averse to their dead ancestors and deities, and who (therefore) deserved punishment, were punished by me. On the five parvan days, the day sacred to Viṣṇu, to the Sun, on a day on which a rite in honour of the dead ancestors is performed, on the tenth and eleventh days I have not waited upon my wife. I never ignored my wife who had bathed at (the end of her) menstrual period; so also (I approached her) even at other times when requested by her. At that time I had sexual intercourse with her who had a passion for it. Thus I have resorted to religious practices, worldly pursuits and carnal pleasures at the proper time. Due to what defect in my queen am I not having a child? Vasiṣṭha, my preceptor, who knows the past and the future will alone tell me the defect due to which a son is not born to me.'

Devala said:

16b-26a. Thinking like this, the king, deciding to go to his preceptor's hermitage, entrusted Kośala with rich treasures to his ministers. Then having worshipped God, the creator of beings, the couple, desiring a son, proceeded to the preceptor's hermitage on an auspicious day. The couple, seated in a chariot, having gone over the path, reached after some days the holy hermitage of the preceptor. There the sage received the guests that had come there after the offering made to all deities. It purified the sages in it and the guests also with the rising mass of smoke of the material offered into the fire. It was dull due to the (slow-moving) deer whose bellies were full due to the mass of shoots of dūrvās. In the hall of the hermitage the flock of female deer was entering from all sides. It was full of noise of groups of birds gathering on the trees which they had turned into their abodes. There were tigers and (other) beasts, that had given up their mutual hostility. The sound of the recitation of the Vedas made by great sages engaged there in muttering (hymns) and meditation, had ceased for a while. There the boys were engaged in sports during intermission of study. In it the couple saw Vasiṣṭha performing the rites. He was seated on a holy seat and was steady, and was waited upon by Arundhatī. He (i.e. Dilīpa) saluted the preceptor's feet, and his wife saluted the ladies of (the family of) him. The preceptor gave him a blessing, and Arundhatī gave her one. Preceptor Vasiṣṭha, the greatest among the adorable, honoured the guest with respectful offerings, and asked him like this:

Vasiṣṭha said:

26b-30. O greatest among kings, I hope everything is all right in your kingdom, in your family and with the people following their respective practices. O hero, I hope you have protected the earth righteously. (I hope) your treasury is growing like a righteous thought for good practices. O king, I hope your excellent villagers and citizens are not transgressing their limit like the oceans. I hope due to love, due to moving together and association, the couples in your cities act like Lakṣmī and Viṣṇu. O best king, I hope, the voluntary vows of your subjects are fruitful like the Haricandana[1] tree in heaven.

Devala said:

31-33. Having asked like this, that greatest sage, Vasiṣṭha, pre-eminent among sages, fed the king with eatables procured

1. Haricandana: One of the five trees of Paradise. The five trees are: Mandāra, Pārijātaka, Santāna, Kalpa, and Haricandana.

through the power of his abstract meditation. That old Arundhatī, of a generous mind, and full of respect, fed the queen with various dishes of cooked food. The steady sage, having held the hand of the king who was fed and had saluted him and who was seated comfortably, again asked him.

Vasiṣṭha said:

34-46a. O king, what is the use of the kingdom of heaven to that king whose kingdom has the seven constituents,[1] in which the subjects are engaged in their duties, in which kinsmen and relatives are pleased, where the soldiers know the science of weapons and missiles, in which friends are obedient, where the enemies are subdued, where the minds (of men) are devoted to Kṛṣṇa's worship? O lord, the religious kings of the Ikṣvāku family, having produced sons, and having entrusted the kingdom to them, proceed to practise penance. You are young. You have not (as yet) seen the face of your son. Why have you, abandoning your kingdom like that, come here?

The king said:

O brāhmaṇa, with a desire for (going to) heaven, I, having abandoned my kingdom like that, have come to your hermitage to practise penance. O brāhmaṇa, you have told the truth that (kings) born in Ikṣvāku's family, entrusted their kingdom to their sons, and went to the penance-grove. As childhood has passed, so this youth that has come will also pass; and certainly old age will come. There is no doubt that a man meets death after old age. O brāhmaṇa, when I die, to whom will this kingdom, without a son's birth, go? Tell me that, O preceptor. Therefore, I who remain in the kingdom without a child, have no feeling of mineness for it, without it. O you my preceptor, you know the three objects of human life. O you treasure of penance, quickly tell me the defect after seeing it through meditation, due to which a son is not born to me. Having heard it, I shall adopt a remedy against it to obtain a child.

---

1. Saptāṅga: the seven constituents of a kingdom: king, ministers, friend, treasury, people, forts, and army.

Devala said:

46b-47a. Having heard these words of the king, Vasiṣṭha, seeing through concentration the cause of the obstruction in (the birth of) a child, spoke:

Vasiṣṭha said:

47b-53a. Formerly, O king, you, having waited upon the chief of gods, and remembering this your young wife who had bathed (after her menstrual period) started for your home. O king, on the way of you who, being eager to have a child, were hurriedly going, stood under a divine tree the desire-yielding cow. You produced great anger in her by not saluting and not doing pious acts like saluting the dust of her venerable feet. With great anger she cursed you: "A son will not be born to you till you do not serve my progeny." You desiring a son, and therefore going quickly to give her (your semen after) menstruation, and thinking of that only, did not hear the curse nor did your charioteer hear it due to the noise caused by the axles. With this your young wife propitiate her young granddaughter, the cow Nandinī, along with her calf. She will give you a son.

Devala said:

53b-54. While Vasiṣṭha, the sage, was speaking like this that Nandinī, with her udders having (milk) flowing from them through affection, came there. Seeing her, the best sage Vasiṣṭha, with his heart delighted, saw her, and showing her to the king, again said to him:

Vasiṣṭha said:

55-57. O king, this (cow) of an auspicious name has come just when remembered. Therefore, know that the accomplishment of your object is near. There is no doubt that when you propitiate her by going after her in the forest and your young wife propitiates her in the hermitage, she will, through her favour, give you a son. O best king, O archer, graze her in such a way that no wild ferocious animal would attack her.

Devala said:

58. Then the ascetic (Vasiṣṭha) gave the king who talked

little and to the daughter-in-law a good hut to pass their night in. There the king with his mind controlled along with his wife passed the night, sleeping on the ground covered with grass.

CHAPTER TWO HUNDRED THREE

Dilīpa Obtains a Son by Propitiating Nandinī

Devala said:

1-19. Then in the morning, the king taking (with him) the cow Nandinī worshipped by the queen with flowers went to the forest. Like her shadow the king followed the divine (cow). He too ate roots etc. after she had eaten young grass etc. After she had sat in the shade of a tree, he sat there. He drank water after she had drunk. The king thus served the preceptor's desire-yielding cow by (offering her) soft grass, driving away flies and scratching her (body). Purifying the king's body with dust-particles raised by her hoofs, she returned to the hermitage in the evening. Nandinī, as it were, loaded with the great burden of the mission of the king, appeared to be going slowly bent by the great burden. The queen taking to her sandal, sacred rice grains, articles of food, incense etc. went forth to (greet) her near the harmitage in the evening. The queen after duly worshipping and repeatedly saluting her and having gone round her keeping her to her right, stood before her with the palms of her hands joined. She (i.e. the cow) remaining steady accepted that worship devoutly offered by the queen and went to the hermitage with the two. O vaiśya, when Dilīpa of a firm vow was thus propitiating her, twentyone days passed. Then, with a desire to know that king's devotion, she, of a fearless heart, entered Himālaya's cave containing young grass. A lion whose arrival was not noticed by the king observing the beauty of the Himālayan peaks, forcibly seized Nandinī. The cow, as it were, afflicted, wailed much with a piteous sound, (thus) producing pity in the heart of the king. Then hearing her wailing, the lord of the world withdrew his eyes from the peaks of Himālaya. The king seeing a lion of sharp claws (seated) upon the cow with tears flowing on her face, was afflicted. Seeing her seized by the lion, the archer put his right hand (on his back) to take out an arrow from the quiver. The lord of the earth, taking out an arrow from the quiver, fixing the arrow on the string, fully drew the string to kill the lion. When the lion looked towards him, his entire body was paralysed. The king could not discharge the arrow. He, therefore, was amazed. Seeing the king like that, the lion, making him still more amazed, spoke in a human voice.

The lion said:

20-28. O king, I know you to be Dilīpa, born in the solar family. You too know me to be Śiva's attendant called Kumbhodara. O hero, this devadāru (tree) which is within the range of your sight is protected by Pārvatī of an affectionate heart like her (own) son. Once, O great king, the soft bark of this (tree) was very much torn by a wild elephant scratching his temples (against it). Noticing it like that, Pārvatī, full of pity, kept me, turning me into a lion, here, to protect it. And she said to me: "O Kumbhodara, listen. Living here you eat whichever animal would come here." Since then, O best king, I, obeying her order, obeyed by all gods, have been staying in this cave. You should not be amazed at your body being paralysed. On this Himālaya Mountain Śambhu's great Māyā prevails. You cannot strike me like another (ordinary) lion, as the lord (Śiva) mounts on Nandin after getting on my back. O hero, go back; protect this (your) body, the means of (accomplishing) all objects. This cow has come as my prey through destiny.

Devala said:

29. Hearing these words of him, along with the address as 'O hero', the king with his body paralysed replied to him:

The king said:

30-37. O lord of beasts, I salute Śiva, the cause of the creation, maintenance and destruction of the world, and Pārvatī, the mother of the world. O lord of beasts, as their servant you are respectable to me. Having heard the words which I (shall) speak, direct me as to what I (should) do. You know, Vasiṣṭha, Brahmā's son, is our preceptor. This is his cow, Nandinī by name, accomplishing all objects. He has given (i.e entrusted) her to me to propitiate her for the birth of a child (to me). For a few days she has been properly propitiated by me. This mother of a young calf is seized by you in the mountain-cave. It is not possible for me to release her forcibly from (you), a servant of Śiva. How can I go to that sage without her? She is the granddaughter of the desire-yielding cow, fit to be served by the world. There is no other cow like this with which I shall please him. Therefore, release this best cow, and have me for your meal. I give you my body tarnished by infamy. (Having done) like this, there will not be the loss of the sage's religious rite, and you will also have your meal. I, giving up my life for the cow, shall reach an excellent position (i.e. salvation).

Devala said:

38-41a. O best merchant, when the lion, on hearing this, remained silent, the king, conversant with religious practices, lay, looking up, before him. On him who was expecting the very unbearable jump of the lion fell the shower of flowers dropped by best gods. Hearing the words, 'O son, get up', the king got up. He saw (there) the cow like (his) mother and not the lion. To him, who was amazed, Nandinī said:

Nandinī said:

41b-43. By means of the illusion in the form of the lion, I tested you. O king, due to the sage's power (even) Yama cannot think of seizing me; then what other animals can to do so? By offering your own body you were ready to protect me. Therefore, I am pleased with you. Ask for your desired boon.

The king said:

44-47. For (deities) like you there is nothing that is concealed in the (hearts of) beings. Therefore, O mother, you know it. Give it to me. Give me a son, continuing my family, born to the daughter of the king of Magadha. For pure ones like you, nothing is impossible.

Saying so the king with his eyes fixed stood before her in silence with his palms joined and expecting a reply from her.

Devala said:

Hearing these words of the king, Nandinī, accomplishing the objects of the manes, gods, sages, men and (other) beings said these words:

Nandinī said:

48-49a. From a cup made of leaves drink to your satisfaction my milk, O son. Ordered by the preceptor you will again drink the remaining in the hermitage. You will have a son, continuing your family and knowing (the use of) weapons and missiles.

Devala said:

49b. Thus addressed by that granddaughter of Surabhi, he politely said to her:

Dilīpa said:

50-53. O mother, I shall drink the remnant of your (milk) only after the completion of the rite. Having drunk the nectar of your favourable words I am satiated. I do not desire anything else like a cātaka desiring water from the row of clouds (only). Having served you I have had the source of everything as a dullard has due to learning honoured by all men. Even the curse given by your grandmother has become a boon for me. Wherefrom, except you, can I get a son? How could I have had your sight? It has led to a boon only. O mother, (deities) like you are to be propitiated. Nobody would desire poison from Mahādeva, giving the three goals of human life.

Devala said:

54-58. Hearing these words, the cow, being pleased, said: "Well (said), well (said)", and being very proud, went with him to the hermitage. As on the previous day, the king's wife worshipped her on that day also. The cow, as it were, the accomplishment of (the king's) object embodied, became pleased. The lotus-eyed (wife) of the king, seeing the pleased face of the king, knew that the object for which an effort was made, has been accomplished. Then the couple, along with the cow to whom worship was duly offered, went to the blessed preceptor. The best sage, the treasure of suprasensual knowledge, seeing them with their lotus-like faces pleased, delighting them, said:

Vasiṣṭha said:

59-64. O king, I know the cow is pleased (with you), for the lustre on your face today appears to be unprecedented. Surabhi (the divine, desire-yielding cow) and the divine tree are known to fulfil desires (of beings). Having propitiated her (grand-)child, if the object is accomplished, what wonder is there? The tree gives every desired (object). She (i.e. Surabhi), the innocent one, even though remembered from a distance (gives the desired object). Then, what will she not give like the divine river, when devoutly served (by remaining) in her vicinity only? Through my (supernatural) knowledge, I knew the test given to you by her. O king, you too preserve your righteousness as I am favourably inclined to you, as devotion is to the supreme soul, Lakṣmī is pleased with Viṣṇu, or Pārvatī is attached to Śiva. Highly devoted to the worship of the cow, you with your wife, pass the night here. O great king, you who have completed the rite will go to your city tomorrow.

Devala said:

65-68. O merchant, he, having, along with his wife, thus propitiated the cow, having obtained his desired object, having furnished his chariot, secured his preceptor's order, and went home. After a few days Raghu was born to that Dilīpa. The race of Raghu is well-known on the earth by his (i.e. Raghu's) name. O merchant, that man who will read this account of Dilīpa, will obtain wealth, grains, sons on the earth. O excellent Śarabha, you too, along with this (your wife), worship according to your own way and quickly propitiate Gaurī. She will also give you a son, the chief of your family, endowed with virtues, and sinless.

Śivaśarman said:

69. The sage, having narrated this very charming and aus-

picious account of Dilīpa to Śarabha, and having instructed him as to the manner of worshipping Ambikā, took to his desired path.

CHAPTER TWO HUNDRED FOUR

The Story of a Merchant Śarabha and a Demon Vikaṭa

Śivaśarman said:

1-3. O Viṣṇuśarman, then Śarabha, taking the materials of worship went with his wife to the temple of Śrī Caṇḍikā. Having duly bathed there, they, full of devotion, worshipped Caṇḍikā with flowers, incense and lights with a desire for (getting) a son. Ambikā, devoutly propitiated by them for seven days, spoke with a clear mind (these) words directly addressed to them:

Pārvatī said:

4-7. O merchant, by means of your very firm devotion I am pleased with you. O good one, I shall give you a son for whom you are striving. Go to the Khāṇḍava (forest) of Indra. Do not delay. There is the excellent, very auspicious holy place called Indraprastha. There is the holy place, fulfilling all desires and fashioned by Bṛhaspati. With a desire to have a son, bath there. By means of a bath there, O dear one, you will have a son. O dear one, by bathing there, I obtained Skanda, the killer of foes.

Śivaśarman said:

8-14. Hearing these words of the goddess, my father, with his wife, came here and with a desire for (having) a son bathed (here). The intelligent one gave a hundred cows with household materials to brāhmaṇas after having gratified gods and the dead ancestors properly. After having stayed there with their minds controlled for seven nights, the couple with their lotus-like faces blooming due to having secured the desired object, went home. In the same month my mother conceived; and when, day by day, nine months passed, I was born in the tenth auspicious month. O Viṣṇuśarman, the old account which I told you, was heard by me from my father when I was twenty years old. Once my father, seeing me capable of managing the household affairs and being detached from everything, handed over to me (the management of) the house. He, having his mind attached to Govinda and a religious nature, condemning addiction to objects of senses and repeatedly praising devotion for Viṣṇu, said to me:

The father said:

15-25. O you intelligent one, old age has come to me. My hair has grown grey. I shall resort to the lotus-like feet of Viṣṇu, that are resorted to by the good. That man whose mind becomes clear and quite steady due to service to him, is self-contented, and does not long for anything. Having no desire for pleasure and aversion to pain, and experiencing the natural (results of) good or bad deeds, he, at the end of them, casts his body and becomes unborn (i.e. is not reborn). Wealth gives excessive pleasure till the bliss of self-realization is not obtained. When it is obtained, it (i.e. the former) is small like buttermilk as contrasted with nectar. This Māyā of Viṣṇu is strong. It deludes a man. He like one intoxicated by liquor, does not know what is beneficial and what is not. The lord causes, as he wills, active worldly life or its absence, through knowledge or ignorance; for his sport is like that of a child. O dear one, when an act as told in the Veda is done by one desiring its fruit, it is great active worldly life. They (i.e. the acts) should be dedicated to the lord. As burnt seeds do not grow in spite of effort, similarly acts dedicated through desirelessness to the lord of the universe do not (fructify). Salvation is the destruction of (the fruits of) acts that give pleasure or pain. Bondage is their origin. This is the verdict of the holy texts. Therefore, I doing acts as told in the Vedas and not desiring their fruits and having devotion for Viṣṇu in my heart, am moving in (i.e. visiting) the holy places. Thus experiencing the (fruits of) acts that were commenced, and not censuring others, I shall destroy the disease due to (the life in) the world by drinking the medicine in the form of the company of the good.

Śivaśarman said:

26. O Viṣṇuśarman, listen accurately to what I said to my father after I had heard these words of him:

The merchant's son said:

27-33. The people are difficult to please; they will not give you any credit. (They will say:) He has gone leaving the bad family being dejected with it. These feet of Viṣṇu purify the three worlds. (Even) when remembered from a distance they remove sins. Why do you leave them? O father, even a sinful person who dies in Magadha, has his sins washed in Gaṅgā. He goes to heaven. Do not give up the auspicious (Gaṅgā), (since) sixty thousand sons of the noble Sagara, who were burnt by Kapila's anger, went to heaven due to her touch. O father, do not go elsewhere after abandoning her; that is a series (of steps) leading to heaven, that even brings about salvation, and is resorted to by those who desire salvation. Do not disregard Gaṅgā honoured by gods, (which is) in your vicinity. O glorious one, she, when resorted to, will give you what you desire. Even if lower animals, through ignorance, would die in her water, they would become Brahman. How do you abandon her?

Śivaśarman said:

34-47a. Hearing these words my father to whom sacred law was dear, being averse to all objects of senses, lived in the house. Everyday he thrice bathed in Gaṅgā, and always went to the house where a Purāṇa would be (read). O son, once listening to the greatness of Yamunā-tīrtha, the wise one heard about the greatness of this holy place. The religious merit of this holy place full of all holy places is a hundred times better than holy places like Avimukta, Haridvāra, Prayāga, Puṣkara, Ayodhyā, Dvārikā, Kāñcī, Mathurā and others. My father, having heard what the learned son had told him, went, unnoticed by all, to this holy place, after abandoning the house. My illustrious father, serving the feet of Viṣṇu like us came here with a desire for salvation. Bathing thrice (a day) at the Nigamodbodhaka Tīrtha he, the wise one, doing his rites and being desireless, lived at this best holy place—the abode of the unborn—for a few months. Once he had very severe fever. Due to the great pain (caused) by the fever he, losing his consciousness, fainted. For a while the father remained in the condition of unconsciousness. When later he regained his consciousness he thought like this: 'Oh! misery has befallen me. My very intelligent, religious son, who would console me, with my body hot due to fever, is away. I have not atoned for the very fearful sin of illicit intercourse. What would be my fate? (If) my son will come I shall give him the wealth which I have hidden in my house and which even I have not seen.'

Śivaśarman said:

47b-51a. While he was thinking like this, a traveller, troubled by rain, afflicted by cold, and with his body trembling, entered the hut. Seeing him asleep, the traveller again went near him, and knowing him to be an ascetic saluted him with (i.e. by bending) his head, and said to him: "O sage, why are you sleeping? The evening has come. This sun is setting. This is not the time for sleeping for you." When the traveller had just uttered these words, Śarabha, my father, with his body hot with fever, somehow spoke to him:

Śarabha said:

51b-58a. O traveller, listen to the words which I am speaking to you. Listening to the course of my fate you do (what is proper), O good one. I am a merchant named Śarabha. My house is in Kānyakubja. Though prevented by my wife, friends and son I came here on hearing the greatness of this holy place told by my son. O good one, some months have passed after I came here. Now for the last three days I have been suffering from fever. My life had departed. Today it has come (back) again. O good one, some portion of my life still remains (to be passed). I have come (back) after having seen Yama's place, and due to my good fortune you have come here. O friend, take me to my house; I shall give you much wealth after reaching home. O you treasure of kindness, favour me. Dig a portion of the land here and take my wealth.

Śivaśarman said:

58b-60a. Having heard this, the wicked-minded rustic, addicted to sensuous pleasures and greedy of wealth, said to him: "I shall do as told by you." Speaking like this, and digging the wealth from that piece of land, the traveller placed it before Śarabha and said:

The traveller said:

60b-61. O chief of merchants, I have taken out this your wealth from the piece of land. Quickly give (some money) to me to bring a palanquin; having placed you, suffering from fever, in it, I shall take you to your place.

Śivaśarman said:

62-76. Thus addressed by him, he gave him three golden palas. He too took that money and went to the city of Lavaṇa. O son, having stayed there for a night, he, having paid a couple of palas, brought a palanquin with attendants and carriers. The wicked one took the two palas for himself only. Having put the excellent merchant, Śarabha, in the palanquin, the traveller, hastening the carriers, started for Kānyakubja. The traveller, repeatedly making him (i.e. giving him) who was oppressed with thirst, drink a small quantity of water collected from that holy place in a water-pot, proceeded. Then, on the way, they got to the bank of a lake to eat (food). Having bathed and eaten food, they hastily moved from that place. Having crossed some portion of the land, they were oppressed by thirst. (The traveller) drank the water from the water-pot and made Śarabha also drink it. Then a very fierce demon, Vikaṭa by name, moving in the solitary forest, saw them going. Seeing them, he, with his mouth open, and overcome by hunger, and causing the earth to tremble with the strokes (i.e. the plantings) of his feet, speedily ran (to them), and coming near them speedily, he seized the traveller and the carriers at their testicles and he, moving in the sky, whirled them. He dropped them who were dead due to being whirled only, on the ground. He ate their flesh and drank blood from their testicles. Thinking, 'Where will this man suffering from a disease go from my presence? I shall (first) eat him up, and then drink the water', that chief among the demons then threw water from the water-pot on his face. As soon as the water was thrown he had the recollection of his former birth. He turned away from killing that Śarabha. He also got the recollection of the sin committed by him in his former existence, due to which he obtained demonhood though he was born as a brāhmaṇa. The demon, having recollected his sin, and having got knowledge, quickly approached Śarabha (my father) and said to my father:

The demon said:

77-78. "O best man, who are you? And who are these men whom, I, a mean demon, of a fierce form. devoured? Of which excellent holy place is this water, due to whose power even a sinner like me had the recollection of my former existence?"

The merchant said:

79-86. O best demon, I am a merchant. My home is in Kānyakubja. Travelling to (various) holy places I came to Indraprastha. There I suffered from fever due to fate. O you having bad ways, then an idea to go home arose in me. Some traveller troubled by rain came there. I requested him to bring a palanquin and take me home. And this is that wise traveller who quickly brought a palanquin and having put me in it, had proceeded to my house. Now that traveller and the carriers of the palanquin have been eaten by you. Hear of which holy place this water is. In the Khāṇḍava Vana of Indra there is the excellent river Yamunā. On her bank is the best holy place called Hariprastha. The preceptor of gods lives there. The holy place accomplishes everything (and is called) Nigamodbodhaka, drinking the water of which you got the recollection. I have told you all this that you had asked me. O demon, I shall ask you something. Tell (i.e. answer) me quickly about it. Now (and) here you will recollect the deeds in your former existence. Tell me what sin you committed, due to which you became a demon.

The demon said:

87-100. Listen. I shall tell you everything. Formerly I was a brāhmaṇa (born) in the family of those proficient in the Vedas. I was wicked and sinful. While playing with dice everyday with those conversant with it, I lost much wealth, mine as well as of my father. My father having reported my act to the king, formerly got me having no wealth, out of the house. I went to a village nearby. There was a friend, the best brāhmaṇa named Devaka. He, respecting me, allowed me to live comfortably in his house for a long time. When my friend had gone somewhere, I, afflicted by sexual urge, forcibly enjoyed his beautiful wife. At that moment only that very chaste lady, drinking strong poison, died. Seeing her (dead) I ran away at the dark night. I who was running (away) was arrested by the officers of the king. Saying, 'This is a thief', they cut off my head. Causing me to take up a body full of torment the servants of Yama threw me into the terrible Raurava hell by Yama's order. Having experienced severe torture there for sixty thousand years, I obtained demon-hood due to that sin only. O chief of merchants, I have passed a hundred years as a demon. I (shall) tell (you) that remedy due to which I (shall) get salvation. O good one, you gave me religious merit. I shall speak (i.e. tell) it. Listen carefully to that by which this water of the excellent holy place got into my mouth. O merchant, in that same existence I observed the vow of Viṣṇu's day (i.e. Ekādaśī) due to company and not (my) desire, and kept awake at night. Having bathed on the Dvādaśī-day I got ready to eat also. (At that time) some devotee of Viṣṇu, having Viṣṇu's form, came to my house. Seeing him I got angry and uttered abusive words: "O hypocrite, O wicked one, why are you going amidst the ladies?"

101-109. When, addressed by me, the wise one, who looked equally upon respect or disrespect, silently went out of my house, my loyal wife, coming towards him, fell at his feet and brought the good man to the house. Though insulted by me, the noble one did not get angry. He was delighted when honoured by her, since he was one to whom enemies and friends were alike. She, having seated him on a seat (said to me): "O lord of my life, make him enjoy (i.e. offer him) food. Conquer the three worlds." Thus addressed by the chaste one, I, with a gloomy face, spoke to the noble-hearted one, of a pleasing face, "(Please) get up, pacify your hunger." Speaking like this, I, prompted by my slender-waisted (wife), again seated him on a seat and washed his feet. To the judicious one I offered a plate full of food. My good wife gave (i.e. poured) water on his hand. I was repeatedly prompted by her. The virtuous one, free from perturbation, went at will, muttering. 'Hare Rāma, Hare Kṛṣṇa.' O merchant, due to this religious merit which I, prompted by my wife, did in the previous existence, this water of the holy place was brought to me.

Śivaśarman said:

110. O Viṣṇuśarman, when the demon got up after saying these words, the traveller and the carriers, having divine bodies, spoke in the sky:

The traveller and the carriers said:

111-115. O chief merchant, O good one, though we met with death immaturely, we obtained godhead after drinking this water due to your favour. O chief of merchants, since we went with you through greed of wealth, our desire for wealth had not left (us) even at the time of death. By the power of the water of this best holy place in our belly, we secured at death the friendship of the lord of wealth. O lord, we salute you; we are going to the city of the lord of wealth in aeroplanes which are brought by his attendants, which are decorated with various jewels. Go to the holy place Nigamodbodhaka. Do not delay. O good one, along with you quickly emancipate him also.

Śivaśarman said:

116-117a. O dear one, speaking like this, they went, all around, to the northern direction, producing sound in the sky and on the earth with small bells of the aeroplanes. Then my father, the merchant, spoke to the demon:

Śarabha said:

117b-118. Get up. Quickly take me to the holy place Nigamodbodhaka. I, suffering from fever, cannot go there on foot. There is none else except you, who (would) take me to that holy place.

Śivaśarman said:

119-122. The demon, comforting the merchant with the words 'All right' put him on his shoulder, and speedily went to that purifying holy place. Both, the chief merchant and the demon, just bathing at the best of all holy places, stayed there. I having heard about the great agony of my father, and urged by my mother (to go to him) moved from my house. Having come here, I saw him, suffering from severe fever. I saluted him with (i.e. by bending my) head. He blessed me and said:

Śarabha said:

123-125. O dear one, why have you come here along a distant (i.e. long) path? My friend, a demon by name Vikaṭa, has come here, and (is) staying here doing his own rites. Get up, and fall at his feet (i.e. prostrate before him) like a staff. You should not be afraid of him who has given up harmful acts. Now, having reached this holy place, he stays near me.

Śivaśarman said:

126-127. Thus told by my father, that noble Śarabha, I got up and fell at his feet (prostrating myself) like a staff. He raised me (seizing me) with my arms, and closely embracing me and giving me a blessing said, "Welcome to you, O my friend's son."

The demon said:

128-129. O dear one, you are fortunate that you have come here on hearing your father's very severe suffering due to fever. Performing the rite with water mixed with sesamum-seeds, you will be free from the debt of your dead ancestors. Having bathed perform your rites; (thereby) you will remember your former existence.

Śivaśarman said:

130-143. O dear one, thus told by him, I, remembering the auspicious and inauspicious acts of the former existence, entered the holy place having excellent water. Having duly bathed here, I came near my father. I asked him the account of the demon: "Why has he become religious-minded?" Having heard the account of the demon, the carriers and the traveller, I praised this best holy place. Thinking, 'I shall go home when my father will be free from the disease', I stayed there for ten days. Within (those) ten days, while I watched (i.e. before me) the death of my father occurred in the (half) quantity of the water of this best holy place. Then, Viṣṇu, having a body like a fresh cloud, and holding Lakṣmī close to his bosom, came after having mounted

Garuḍa. He had put on yellow garments; had four arms; his lotus-like eyes were tawny. He was served by the divine Brahmā and others along with Andhakārin, and by the kinnaras singing the hosts of his virtues. He was being praised on all sides by Hāhā, Hūhū and others. Giving my father identity with his own form, and putting him on Garuḍa, and surrounded by Brahmā and others, Viṣṇu went up to heaven. Seeing my father's sameness of form with Viṣṇu, I thought, when, at that time, there sprang the truth in my heart: 'It is the greatness of this crest-jewel of holy places that in half of its water a being that is dead becomes four-armed. I shall rightly not at all leave this best holy place having a strong efficacy urged by thirst for the disease in the form of wealth. I shall stay in this hut of my father till (I get) freedom from the (fruits of) acts that have been commenced on the earth.' Having thought like this and performed proper rites (in honour) of my father, I stayed (there) with a desire for salvation along with the demon.

CHAPTER TWO HUNDRED FIVE

The Efficacy of Nigamabodha

Śivaśarman said:

1-10. Once that best demon, having seen a milch cow plunged into mud, entered it to take her up. 'There is a great religious merit in (i.e. due to) protecting a cow. The protector would go to heaven.' He who was thinking like this was seized by a crocodile (literally, a water-elephant). He was taken down into the water. With his belly full of water, and with his body pressed by him, he died instantly. He resorted to a divine form; an aeroplane with an attendant was brought near him sent by gods led by Indra. I asked the chief of the demons, going (to heaven) after having died here in this great holy place, very difficult to be reached, and giving salvation, "O intelligent and divine one, how did you reach heaven?" Thus addressed, he said, "O innocent one, I longed for it." When that meritorious one had gone to heaven, the place of the meritorious ones, I, remaining alone, was taken to Viṣṇu, the good resort. With a concentrated mind, I, while going, standing, sleeping, keeping awake, bathing, constantly meditated upon that lotus-eyed one only. "O Viṣṇu, I have sought lhe shelter of your lotus-like feet. I have no longing for the position of Brahmā, Śiva or Indra." O dear one, making my mind free from the (longing for) objects of senses, and soliciting that Puruṣottama (i.e. Viṣṇu) only, I lived at this great holy place.

Viṣṇuśarman said:

11-14. When, while staying at this great holy place, you died, then how did you get a birth again? This is my doubt. The traveller and the carriers, on their having ignored the restriction (laid down) at this holy place due to greed for money, met with death from the demon (and) went to heaven on drinking the water of this great holy place. So also the demon meeting with, at his will, death from the crocodile, went to heaven while you were looking on (i.e. in your presence). There is no (re)birth (for a man whose) death takes place there.

Nārada said:

15. O Śibi, having heard the auspicious words of his son, Śivaśarman told him the former account, the cause of his birth.

Śivaśarman said:

16-19. O Viṣṇuśarman, listen to this cause of my birth. I am telling it to you. Having heard it, be free from doubts. Once when I had resorted to meditation while worshipping Viṣṇu, Durvāsas, irascible by nature, came to my hermitage. Not aware of his having arrived (there), I, intent upon meditation on Viṣṇu, remained in that condition recollecting (Viṣṇu's) name for a long time. The sage, standing for a while, full of anger and with his eyes red, spoke loudly to himself these (words):

Durvāsas said:

20-25. Oh! I, Atri's son, born from the womb of Anasūyā, a portion of Śiva, am thus excessively neglected by this human being: This wicked man even ignores me who caused Indra to fall from the kingdom of the three worlds! Who are you that are not afraid of me who am like the destructive fire at the end of the world, since I have the greatest worth barring (that of) the three gods? How is it that that deity whom he is meditating upon, does not advise him that Yama has come in an embodied form? Indeed he is meditating upon Viṣṇu, the lord of the world, being satisfied with the nectar of meditation upon whom he does not have the knowledge of his surroundings. Let him meditate upon Viṣṇu, Brahmā, Śiva, or any other (deity). He should be punished by me by all means. He has disregarded me.

Śivaśarman said:

26-45. Thinking like this, he roused me, and with his eyes red due to anger, cursed me who had become conscious. "How will that desire, which you, ignoring me, had in your mind at the time of meditation, come true at all?" O dear one, when, after having spoken like this, the sage born of Atri, moved (to go), I dreaded with fear, seized his feet, and said like this: "O best sage, forgive me; give up your anger. (People) like me do not properly know the deeds of (sages) like you. Now you have given a fearful curse to me who am innocent. Favour me who am polite. Show favour for the end of (i.e. ending) your curse." Thus addressed, Durvāsas, giving up his anger, became cool. O darling, is it not proper, since he is Śiva (himself)? The wise one said to me: "You, being the best brāhmaṇa, will meet with death here only, and will not be reborn." Having thus favoured me that Śiva (i.e. Durvāsas) left, after staying there that day and being honoured by me with a hospitable reception. I, having thought that the sage's words would not be untrue, and repenting in my mind, went home: 'Oh! to me, having my hermitage in a holy place, and constantly meditating upon (Viṣṇu) the sight of Lakṣmī's lord has become difficult to have in this existence, like that of a cloud to a cātaka in Caitra and Vaiśākha, causing heat? Wherefrom has this one, causing obstacle in my course to Vaikuṇṭha come like a cloud (coming in the way) of a man who has set out (on a journey)? It is not the fault of the sage. It is indeed the desire of that Viṣṇu only. Having well appeared before me, he has given me another (i.e. a new) existence. I, scared of the worldly existence, should seize the lotus-like feet of Viṣṇu, as a traveller heated by the heat of summer (takes to) the shade of a tree. What is the use of the transient wealth, children, wife and other relatives to me who am muttering 'Govinda, Paramānanda (the highest joy), Rāma.' Not censuring other acts, and resorting to Viṣṇu, and remaining like a neutral person among the members of my family, I shall enjoy what is destined.' O dear one, thnking like this, I, after having bathed in the water sacred to Viṣṇu, came home after a few days. I told my mother and relatives about the death of my father. Hearing (the news) they lamented; they did not know that this (worldly existence) is transitory. Having no longing for the worlds like Satya, I remained in the house and died on the bank of Gaṅgā, resorted to by the sages. Due to the curse of the sage Durvāsas, I was born in the family of Viṣṇu's devotees. Having died at this holy place, I shall reach Viṣṇu's feet.

Nārada said:

46-51. O noble one, thus the two best brāhmaṇas talking to each other about the sins committed by them in their former existence, and thinking about Viṣṇu's foliage-like feet, remained at the holy place fashioned by the preceptor of gods. Thinking about and remembering Viṣṇu, of lotus-like eyes, of four arms, having a body dark blue like a cloud, and shining with his weapons and ornaments, they got absorption into Viṣṇu. The story of this excellent holy place which is the one called Indraprastha has been told. O Śibi, listen to its fruit. A man obtains the same fruit by devoutly listening to it as is obtained by him on bathing in Gaṅgā or by giving away his daughter (in marriage). There is no doubt that that fruit which is produced on the earth at the birth of a son, or by a bath in the water of Godāvarī when Jupiter is in the Zodiacal sign of Leo, is obtained by listening to it. There is no other holy place giving all objects than this best holy place, by dying at which even lower animals become four-armed (ones).

CHAPTER TWO HUNDRED SIX

A Woman Should Never Desert Her Husband

Saubhari said:

1. That religious king, the wealthy Śibi, having heard those words of the sage Nārada, was pleased in his mind, and (thus) spoke to the best one:

Śibi said:

2-3. O sage, you have properly described the greatness of this excellent holy place Nigamodbodhaka. I have heard it; that removes sins. O sage, there are hundreds of holy places in this Indraprastha. Tell me the greatness of some other holy place, if there is any.

Nārada said:

4-17. O king, I shall tell you what formerly took place in this Dvārakā which is situated within Indraprastha. Listen to it from me. In Kāmpilya there was a certain brāhmaṇa, Cupid embodied as it were. He attracted the hearts of all women with his excellent amorous actions. He was skilled in the science of music. His voice was sweet like that of a cuckoo. Once, that very intelligent one, holding a lute in his hand, repeatedly playing upon it, singing, without an equal, with voice sweet like that of a cukoo, moved in the city. Having heard the sound of his song, full of melody and protracted tones, the wives of citizens abandoned their domestic work and went (to him). Fascinated by his handsome form, they could not bear the force of lust. Hearing the song actually they were disturbed. What other self-controlled and wise person than the two (viz. Brahmā and Śiva) is able to conquer Cupid who created a longing for Sarasvatī in the mind of Brahmā, or who made half of Śiva's body to be given to Pārvatī? And women are fickle by nature. Even the chaste ones were unable to put up with the excitement caused by Cupid. What could be said, O king? Cupid is difficult to be conquered in the world. They went everywhere he, singing with his throat and lute and fascinating with his tone, went. Their husbands, sons, brothers and fathers came there, and threatening them, took them (back) to their own homes, O king. When they again looking for him, approached him, the citizens told the account to their king. The king too called the best brāhmaṇa and asked him in private: "O best brāhmaṇa, tell me by means of which charm you fascinated the women in the city. I shall give you much wealth. Othewise I shall drive you out of my kingdom. There is no doubt about it."

Nārada said:

18. Hearing these words of the king, the best brāhmaṇa, the ocean of handsomeness and virtues, spoke to him true words.

The Brāhmaṇa said:

19-21. O king, I, a beggar, have neither a charm nor a herb; but all the women in your city have no control over their senses. O king, the women in your city cannot put up with the force of lust on seeing my handsome form and hearing the sound of my songs. O great king, what can I do? O lord, what is my fault? The order of the king, like (the fruits of) former acts, can never be resisted.

Nārada said:

22. O king Uśīnara-Śibi, when the brāhmaṇa was telling like this all citizents, coming together, spoke thus to the king:

The citizens said:

23-27. O king, this brāhmaṇa has fascinated the wives of the citizens. They do not remain in their houses. They cannot be stopped by us. O lord, if this one who infatuates the women lives in the city, then today (only) we shall go to other countries. Our bull-god of the nature of havya and kavya (oblations to gods and dead ancestors) has gone(?). They have started going after him like a cow from the field of sinners. O lord of men, we, abandoned by glory, have no other shelter to seek. They will follow him as the female elephants follow their lord. How can Lakṣmī (wealth) remain in a vacant house? Since these three, viz. piety, worldly riches and house, depend upon the wife, one that depends upon the wife's piety and wealth cannot remain, when the two are lost.

Nārada said:

28. When the citizens were speaking like this, their wives came to the king, sat there, and thus spoke to one another:

The wives of the citizens said:

29-31a. Our minds open excessively on seeing this brāhmaṇa of a charming form as lotuses in the water do on seeing the lord of the day and they close in his absence as the white lotuses close without the moon: come, together we shall seize (and take) him before the king. He is not fit to be killed, nor are we. What will the king do?

Nārada said:

31b-33. Saying so, they hurriedly seized the best brāhmaṇa, when their own husbands were watching and in front of the king himself; and they said to him: "O lord of our minds, come to our house, and quickly pacify (the agony) tormenting our hearts. Today we cannot remain (i.e. live) without you." Hearing these words of them, the brāhmaṇa replied:

The brāhmaṇa said:

34-40. I am your son; you are my mothers. Leaving your houses, why are you wandering? Propitiate your own lords, since, when the husbands are propitiated, wives certainly (enjoy) the two worlds, and Viṣṇu, the lord of gods, is pleased. (And) when he is pleased, what is difficult to be obtained? That woman who, forsaking her own husband, resorts to another (man) with a desire for enjoyment, invites censure and goes to a fearful hell. She, the deceiver of her husband, lives there till the end of the kalpa. Again having moved out of it, she reaches the state of an inanimate object. Even from there, she obtains beasthood for many existences. Then freed from that (stock) she is born as a crippled one. Knowing the sinful course to be like this, turn away from Cupid. Otherwise at the end (i.e. fall) of your body, you will go to a very fearful hell. You will not have the pleasure that you desire to get from me. It is your sin, since it is a fall of a human being.

Nārada said:

41-43. Having heard his words like these, and seeing the faces of their husbands, they hung down their faces through shame like creepers struck by a (stormy) wind. The very terrible fire of lust of the women in the city went out due to the cold water in the form of the words of the chap. O king, all of them, condemning Cupid as one that fascinates even gods like Brahmā, Indra, got up, and walked (away).

The women said:

44-52. Fie upon this, committing sinful acts, an axe to the wood in the form of good character! He who has struck Cupid for the happiness of passionate beautiful women, is blessed. What should we say to Rukmiṇī, venerable to the world, who carried in her womb this Rāhu, named Pradyumna, eating the Moon of the good character of women? If that mean god comes within the range of our sight again, we shall throw him into the fire of the eye of the lord (Śiva) by meditating upon him. He, the sinful one, whom Viṣṇu, delighted in self, created, made Viṣṇu dear to (or the lover of) sixteen thousand women. Then what can be said about us?

Having thus censured that Cupid, the women praised that best brāhmaṇa who preserved his own character and that of them also, O king. 'Blessed is that mother of this (best brāhmaṇa) who gave, birth to this excellent brāhmaṇa who vanquished Cupid and preserved the virtue of others! Fie upon us who were laughed at by the king's men, who were vanquished by Cupid, and by whom great sin was committed through speech and mind!' All the women who were thus thinking, who were of the same view, being admonished by the brāhmaṇa's words, went to their respective houses. Then king Kāmpilya also, having honoured that brāhmaṇa with garments and ornaments, sent him to the house of that good man.

53-63. As time went on, the powerful lord of Kārūṣa besieged lord of Kāmpilya and his city with armies (i.e. a large army). A great war took place between the two. He (i.e. Kārūṣa king) got him killed. He plundered the entire city and the brave ones were killed everywhere. Those women eating (i.e. drinking) Kālakūṭa (poison) died. They had not made any atonement for that sin. Due to that sin all those were born as demonesses with huge bodies and causing fear in the city of the demon called Bhīṣaṇa. All the women in the city were killed by Hanūmat, occupying the banner of the chariot of Viṣṇu relishing sacrifices. The same were again born as demonesses on the path to Maru. They were oppressed by hunger and thirst, and caused fear at their sight. Thus due to the sin committed by means of speech and mind, they obtained two existences, mixed with (i.e. along with) the existence as demonesses. Due to their sin the two cities along with their kings were destroyed. Therefore, O lord, women, fearing sin, should never resort to another lover even through speech or mind. Women desiring salvation should not desert their husband even though he is diseased, dull, poor or blind. O Śibi, I have told you in great detail about the sin produced through devotion to another lover by means of speech or mind, so also the fruit of it obtained by these (women). By the drops (of water) of the pious Dvārakā, seen by those going to Indraprastha, falling on their bodies, the women in the city reached heaven after abandoning the severe condition of corpse-eaters, which they had reached due to their having resorted to another lover, and obtained the form of divine ladies delighting gods.

CHAPTER TWO HUNDRED SEVEN

The Story of Vimala

Saubhari said:

1. O son of Dharma, having heard these words of that noble Nārada, king Śibi politely spoke these (words):

Śibi said:

2. O best sage, how did those demonesses, moving on the path to Maru, get the water from this Dvārakā?

Nārada said:

3-9. O king, listen to the story, pure and destroying sin, of a brāhmaṇa named Vimala, living in the valley of the Himālaya (mountain). In the Himālayan valley lived a brāhmaṇa by name Vimala. He honoured gods, sages, his dead ancestors, and guests. He was engrossed in worshipping Viṣṇu's feet. He knew the Vedas, the Vedāṅgas and religious practices. His mind was (devoted to) listening to the Purāṇa containing the hosts of Viṣṇu's virtues. In his old age a son was born to him due to Viṣṇu's grace. The father then named him Haridatta (literally, given by Viṣṇu). He duly performed his (sacraments like) shaving etc. Haridatta received (the knowledge of) the Vedas from his teacher. Having duly studied the Vedas, having paid the fee of the teacher, he, being detached, took to renunciation, (having) completely (dropped) the two stages (viz. the second and the third) of human life. On coming to know that act of him, his mother who loved her son, bathing (i.e. making wet) her pair of breasts with tears due to separation from her son, wept.

The mother said:

10-16. O dear one, like a bee abandoning coarse grass, where are you going, leaving me who am helpless, and your father stricken with old age? Due to service of the feet of Viṣṇu, I got you in my old age. You have resorted to his feet for salvation after having abandoned me. O dear one, I was certainly a fool, since having propitiated that eternal Viṣṇu I longed for you, the unsteady one, for getting happiness. O child, you are intelligent since you are resorting to Viṣṇu, the all-in-all. You too are looking upon this transient world as permanent. What should I do? Where should I go? Māyā cuts off my understanding, as a strong person having a weapon cuts off a plantain tree producing good fruits (right) from its roots. Blessed was king Daśaratha who died due to agony (caused by separation) from Rāma. Fie upon me who am (still) sustaining my life (even) after separation from my son! Come, appear before me, emancipate me. O dear one, O ocean of virtues, speak to your father words consisting of (the words from) the Vedas.

Nārada said:

17-20a. Weeping like this, O king, the mother fell on the ground like a digit of the moon due to its being cut off (from other digits) given to Rāhu. O best king, the brāhmaṇa sage came there. Seeing her fallen on the ground, he said: "What is this? Why has she, with her hair dishevelled and garments and ornaments disordered, fallen on the ground? Is Haridatta well?" All those her friends said to that Vimala, O king:

The friends said:

20b-21. Your son, Haridatta, having studied the Vedas, having paid the teacher's fee, and being highly devoted to Viṣṇu, has renounced the world. Due to the grief caused by separation from him she has fallen on the ground.

Nārada said:

22. Having heard these words of them, the very wise Vimala roused his wife with this nectar of his words.

Vimala said:

23-26. O (my) wife, get up. Listen to the words spoken by me. Why have you fallen down and are dejected? Your son who, knowing this (world to be) transient, has resorted to Viṣṇu's foliage-like feet, is blessed. You too, his mother, whose son has served the feet of Viṣṇu, are blessed. He will also undoubtedly emancipate me, (our) family, and men born in our family, O auspicious one. What a lot of difference is there between this unsteady world, and the service of Viṣṇu's feet, giving an eternal world! Thinking like this kings like Bharata resorted to Viṣṇu. So (has) your son (done), O chaste one. Unless a wise man, free from lust, resorts to the foliage-like feet of Viṣṇu, in every existence (of him) his wife, wealth, house, body, relatives cause grief to him.

Nārada said:

27. Thus admonished by him, the wise one, she got up from the ground, and with a piteous voice spoke to her husband:

The wife said:

28-31. O darling, I understand all that you have said well. I am very much tormented since I do not see a leader for our family. What is the use of service to Viṣṇu, when there is the great holy place in the form of a son? Even if we meet with death in our house only, we shall have (the fruit of) both the worlds then (i.e. when we have a son). Men indeed should try to beget a good son; since sons emancipate their ancestors from the ocean of the mundane existence. O you very intelligent one, if you desire a son, the foremost in the family, then, with a desire to have a son, resort to the creator and supporter of all beings.

Nārada said:

32-36. Hearing these words of her Vimala, the brāhmaṇa, said: "With a desire to have a son, I shall go to Brahmakṣetra Prayāga." Saying so, the brāhmaṇa set out and went to Haridvāra. Having duly bathed there, he then went to Indraprastha after a few days. O brave one, having bathed there (at the holy place) giving (whatever is desired) to everyone that solicits, in the evening, and having eaten (food) he slept at night on the bank of Yamunā. Near that Vimala sleeping at night, the lord of gods along with all holy places quickly came after having mounted on a swan. Having come he raised Vimala, desiring a son; and the best got spoke sweet words.

Brahmā said:

37-43. I know the desire hidden in your mind. Since there is no way to fulfil it, listen to the reason. Once all gods, led by me and Śiva, gathered on the peak of Meru, and praised Viṣṇu for success. Being praised by gods like me lord Viṣṇu was pleased then, and said: "Choose (a boon)." Thus addressed by Viṣṇu, all gods, having received (from him) a boon as desired, went to their respective houses. I said: "O lord of gods, give me an excellent boon. May my holy place, Prayāga, give all the desired objects. May another holy place of me at Indraprastha be a hundredfold (meritorious). O sinless one, I have properly chosen it from you." Having heard these words of me, the lord then said to me: "Let it be so," and again spoke (certain) words. Listen to (those) words.

The lord said:

44-56a. In Indra's Khāṇḍava forest there is an auspicious holy place on the bank of Yamunā, called Indraprastha. Those who die there are equal to me. O Brahman, my own city of Dvārakā is a hundredfold more meritorious than when formerly it was at the shore of the ocean. A man who, having ignored it, resorts to another holy place, does not obtain the fruit of (a visit to) the holy place. This statement is not false. A man would obtain the merit said to be accruing from all holy places. The city of Dvārakā preserves another illusory holy place. He who, having bathed at other holy places, and having performed various rites, will come here, will certainly get the fruit of those holy places.

O best brāhmaṇa, having spoken these words, Viṣṇu disappeared. I too went to my world situated below Vaikuṇṭha. Kāśī is said to be a hundredfold more meritorious than Prayāga, my holy place. Similarly the hilly place Nigamodbodhaka is a hundredfold more meritorious than Kāśī. This group of seven holy places is said to have the fruit equal to the three. O brāhmaṇa, to him who goes to Prayāga without ignoring these three, I give his desired objects. Not otherwise. Some sages say that the seven, Ayodhyā etc., are equal in merit. Indraprastha is said to be hundredfold superior to those. O brāhmaṇa, having come to that holy place Śrī Dvārakā, which gives all the desired fruits, bathe there with the desire for a son. When the hundred names are uttered, unlimited religious merit accrues from them. This holy place will give you a son, the foremost in your family; and due to your bathing here, Viṣṇu will be pleased.

Nārada said:

56b-58. Speaking like this, Brahmā, the lord of the chief of gods, vanished. Vimala also then bathed, and offered oblations to gods etc. Thus said the pious one: "O Dvārakā, dear to Kṛṣṇa, give me a son, your devotee. Salutation to you." When the brāhmaṇa spoke like this, there was (heard) a divine voice.

The divine voice said:

59-60a. Due to the favour of this holy place, the crest-jewel of all holy places, you will have a son, knowing the truth of religious practices and continuing your family. Go home; do not delay. The bath is well done.

Nārada said:

60b-69. Having heard that (divine) voice, he, trusting in the birth of a son (i.e. trusting he will have a son), took water of Dvārakā in a water-pot, and left (the place). On the way he met his friend living on the Malaya mountain. He was going (back) home after having visited all holy places. He told him all the account consisting of his dialogue with Brahmā. He too was amazed on hearing what had taken place at the holy place of Dvārakā. The pious one said: "O friend, listen to my words. I desire to visit all those holy places that are fashioned in Bhārata. O friend, take me to that holy place, granting all desired objects and show it to me. On the earth those friends who oblige their friends are excellent. In the world none is like them—(even) the father, the mother, or the son. All relatives desert a poor man. But friends, afflicted by his grief, do not leave the friend. A friend emancipates his friends plunged into the ocean of mundane existence. Having taught me the devotion to Viṣṇu, capable of destroying existences, you have become my best friend. O oblige me. O brāhmaṇa, show me the best holy place called Dvārakā."

CHAPTER TWO HUNDRED EIGHT

The Greatness of Dvārakā

Nārada said:

1. Taking the brāhmaṇa (with him) Vimala came here to Dvārakā. And the two wise ones with a desire for devotion for Viṣṇu bathed there. In the sky there was again heard the divine voice, deep like that of clouds.

The divine voice said:

2. Listen, O best brāhmaṇas, this is Viṣṇu's holy place. You

will have, due to the grace of this holy place, devotion for Viṣṇu, due to which people abandon the strong infatuation due to Māyā.

Nārada said:

3-4. The two best brāhmaṇas having heard the incorporeal speech, said to each other: "This is Viṣṇu's favour." The two, having duly bathed there and obtained great devotion for Viṣṇu, saluting him and talking to each other walked.

The brāhmaṇas said:

5-7a. As we two, walking on the path came in contact with each other, as on the earth contact with a house and wife etc. takes place, so the future separation of us, being on the way, is (but) proper. So is (the contact and separation from) the wife, son etc. being in the mouth of tiger in the form of Death. That man who realising the contact with wife and sons to be transient, would ever resort to and worship Viṣṇu, is blessed.

Nārada said:

7b-11a. "(Please) remember me. I am your servant, resorting to your feet. You may send me a message." Saying like this, they went home. O king, listen, how that friend of Vimala, going along the path, brought about the liberation of the demonesses. The brāhmaṇa, while going, reached that place void of water, where the demonesses scorched by sins stood oppressed by hunger and thirst. Then they, seeing from a distance that brāhmaṇa with a pot containing water in his hand, said to one another:

The demonesses said:

11b-13a. Some traveller, holding a pot of water in his hand is coming. Our hunger and thiist will be at least partially satisfied. We shall eat him up and drink the water in the pot in his hand. We are oppressed by hunger and thirst for a hundred years.

Nārada said:

13b-21. One said: "Having first eaten his hot liver, then having drunk his blood, I shall gain life." The other said: "How much material does he have, O Gajānanā? Even for me, Vyāghrānanā, it is not seen to be enough for drinking." Another one called Rathacakrā, (said): "Hear my words. From one I shall fashion an ear-ring, and a girdle from (other) intestine." Another one said: "I, skilled in gambling, will play dice in the gambling hall with his sixteen teeth, made black from one side." All of them, thus speaking among themselves, ran to the brāhmaṇa, with their mouths opened, tongues lolling and bright great arms. Seeing them coming, the brāhmaṇa was overcome by fear. O king, he protected himself all round, as told in the Vedas. The demonesses of fierce valour having come (to him), stood away from him. O king, they were repelled by his lustre and hymns. And they said: "Tell us, who are you? Wherefrom have you come? Seeing you our mind is delighted. O brāhmaṇa, what will be the fruit of touching your feet? Therefore, place your lotus-like feet on our heads."

Nārada said:

22a. Hearing their words Haridattaja (Haridatta's son?) said:

The brāhmaṇa said:

22b-23. I am a brāhmaṇa who has come after visiting holy places. Now I am going to Puṣkara. What do you desire? Since, if I am able to give it, I shall do so.

The demonesses said:

24. O brāhmaṇa, tell us in which holy places you bathed. All those are meritorious. Liberate us from this bad existence, giving terrible agony due to great hunger and thirst.

The brāhmaṇa said:

25-38. From my hermitage I went first to Haripura, Avantī. From there I went to Dvārakā. Having bathed in the water of Somodbhavā, I went to the holy place Prabhāsa situated on the shore of the sea. Then I bathed at the highly purifying Setunibandha. From there I came to the very holy Kiṣkindhā where Rāma had killed Vālin, the lord of the host of monkeys. From there I came to the Sarasvatī temple situated on the bank of Narmadā where Sarasvatī, served by all, dwells. Then I reached

Veṇī, saluted her and saw the two cities Śivakāñcī and Viṣṇukāñcī in the southern part of India, due to having died where a man becomes Śiva and Viṣṇu. From there I reached Utkala where lord Viṣṇu, actually giving the four ends of human life and the desired objects to his devotees dwells. Having duly worshipped him, and eaten the eatables offered to him, I went to Gaṅgāsāgara which was his favour only. Then having duly gratified gods, sages and (my) dead ancestors, I came to that place where Gaṅgā had a hundred faces (i.e. flew in a hundred courses). Then having gone to Gayā and having duly offered piṇḍa, endowed with Tulasī blossoms, sandal and water to the dead ancestors, I came to Kośala, to Śarayū which by means of her touch cloudy due to the water, had purified all people. There is a holy place called Gopratāra difficult to be reached (even) by gods. O demonesses, there I did the acts like bathing etc. From there I reached Kāśī, the capital of the lord of Umā. Having saluted god Viśveśvara, so also Bindumādhava, I devoutly bathed in the Jñānavāpī at Maṇikarṇikā. Having stayed there for three nights, I again came to Prayāga where actually Brahmā (lives) on the fourteenth day of the bright half of Pauṣa.

39-49. At a dawn of Māgha, having bathed there, again from there I came to Naimiṣa on the bank of Gomatī, where all holy places, with their enchantment dwell. From there I reached Mathurā where there is the holy place called Viśrānti. Near it is a holy, excellent pool called Asikuṇḍa. There very holy Yamunā giving everything and having the holy places of Kṛṣṇagaṅgā, Dhruvā, Krūrakeśī, Kālī exists. On both her banks are forests shining with splendour and producing all holy places. Having bathed in them and drunk (their water) a man is not born again. From there I came to the holy, excellent city of Hastināpura. There is the best river Gaṅgā that rose from lotus-like feet of Viṣṇu. Then coming to the place of Nārāyaṇa situated in the Himālayan region and seeing Mādhava (there), I came to Kedāra. Having worshipped Viśveśa (there) and having drunk the water of Haṁsā (lake), I came to the very holy Haridvāra, on the bank of Gaṅgā. Having bathed there and having gratified gods, sages and (my) dead ancestors, I came to Kurukṣetra where there is Prācī Sarasvatī. There too, I with my senses controlled, performed all rites, and having worshipped Viṣṇu's lotus-like feet I went to Puṣkara. On the way my friend named Vimala, going from the holy place Indraprastha, met me.

50-60. O demonesses, the brāhmaṇa, causing me to return, took me to the holy place Śakra-(i.e. Indra-)prastha, giving all (desired) objects. There is holy Dvārakā fashioned by Viṣṇu himself. There I actually saw Viṣṇu, not in form but through words. There he and I bathed to obtain devotion for Viṣṇu. Viṣṇu, of the form of Kṛṣṇa, gave it to him and me. We heard Viṣṇu's words, but did not see his form. We secured devotion for him. From that place I came to Puṣkara. O demonesses, I tell you that this water in the water-pot is from that holy place called Dvārakā, the chief among holy places. I have told you what you had asked me. Seeing this bad plight of you, compassion is produced in my heart. Tell me what I should do. I am at your disposal. Let knowledge come to you.

Saying so, he sprinkled them with (that) water. Due to the touch of that water they remembered all the acts in their (various) existences, and gave up their powerful demonish bodies. Obtaining divine bodies, and turning into celestial nymphs, they got into an aeroplane that had come from heaven, and saluted the brāhmaṇa. And they said: "O best brāhmaṇa, due to contact with the water from Dvārakā we are freed from demonhood, and are (now) going to heaven. O brāhmaṇa, there is no other better holy place giving all desired objects than this Dvārakā situated in Indraprastha."

Nārada said:

61-68. Speaking like this, O king, they got into the aeroplanes. And ordered by the brāhmaṇa, they went by that (aeroplane) to the eastern direction. A man, hearing the greatness of this Dvārakā situated on the bank of Yamunā, is freed from sins, O king. The same fruit as is had by giving meals to a hundred brāhmaṇas as desired by them, is produced by listening to this greatness. O king, as happiness is experienced on worshipping Viṣṇu, similarly (it is had) by listening to the greatness of this Dvārakā. That fruit which is got by giving twenty palas of gold (to a brāhmaṇa) at the time of the solar eclipse and the lunar eclipse, is obtained by one hearing the greatness of this (Dvārakā). Having heard (the account of) the acquisition of a son by Vimala, (a man) obtains a son; and hearing (the account of) the acquisition of his friend's devotion (a man) secures the best devotion. He who, endowed with devotion, listens to (the account of) the liberation of the demonesses, goes like them in an aeroplane to heaven. O best king, I have described to you the greatness of Dvārakā that should be resorted by men in the three worlds and that is situated at Śakratīrtha. Tell me, what other (account) more meritorious than this, I should relate to you. No delay should be done in (securing) one's bliss.

CHAPTER TWO HUNDRED NINE

The Story of Brāhmaṇa Mukunda

Yudhiṣṭhira said:

1-2. O Saubhari, of which holy place, situated at Śakratīrtha, did the sage Nārada describe the greatness to Śibi? Therefore, a desire to hear it is produced in me. Tell me who have bowed (to you) the meritorious dialogue between Śibi and Nārada.

Saubhari said:

3. O Dharmarāja, king Śibi, having heard the description (made) by Nārada, and also the greatness of Dvārakā, respectfully asked him only.

Śibi said:

4-5. O son of Brahmā, O greatest god, I have heard the excellent, wonderful greatness of Dvārakā situated on the slope of Indraprastha. O sage, if there is any sacred story (about someone) in Ayodhyā, then tell it to me who am thirsty of drinking the nectar of your words.

Nārada said:

6-24. As to this there is a holy account, destroying great sins, of a barber and Mukunda, a diligent brāhmaṇa. Both the barber, the killer of a brāhmaṇa, and the king who died prematurely, went to heaven due to the favour of Kośalā. The city is situated on the bank of Candrabhāgā. There was a sinful, censurable barber, Caṇḍaka by name. The sinful one snatched the wealth of others through stealing. He killed the travellers with weapons and nooses etc. and robbed them (of their possessions). He was always engaged in gambling and (drinking) liquor, and hankered after others' wives. He broke the walls of temples, and sold the bricks and stones. Near his locality lived a brāhmaṇa, endowed with wealth, knowing the Vedic rites, and named Mukunda, O king. Once at night he with his limbs loosened after fatigue due to coitus had fearlessly slept, having embraced his young wife. That Caṇḍaka entered at night the house of that Mukunda to snatch away ornaments etc. (found) in the mansion. Taking whatever was (found) outside the mansion, he went home, and again entered the brāhmaṇa's house. He made a great effort to break the door; (but) he was blocked by iron bolts and was unable to open it. He then climbed (over the wall) and entered the brāhmaṇa's house. The cruel one, holding a sword in his hand, entered the mansion. There he saw the couple, asleep and alarmed. To snatch away the golden ornaments, he approached them. The barber, after having taken many ornaments lying on one side of the bed, extended his hand to snatch away ornaments (put) on his body. The brāhmaṇa was awakened by the thief's touch and was overcome by fear. He did not say anything; (but) closing his eyes remained there only. When the sinful thief took the ornaments from his body and moved, the brāhmaṇa unable to bear the loss of his wealth, came from behind him, and seized him with his hands. O king, the thief also struck the brāhmaṇa with his sword. With his pierced belly, he cried. 'O father, O mother.' People shouting "What (happened)?" came near him. They saw him with his entrails coming out and his body smeared with blood. And they asked Mukunda: "Who has done such an act?" With great difficulty he too spoke like this to his relatives:

Mukunda said:

25-26a. This is the result of my deeds done in the previous birth. None (else) gives pleasure or pain to a human being. These are just (the results of) piety and impiety. Their root lies in one's former act(s).

Nārada said:

26b-28a. Speaking like this, he was troubled by great agony. O king, at that time, when his friends were looking on (i.e. in the presence of his friends) he cast his life. O kind, then his mother, a chaste brāhmaṇa-lady wept after putting his head, adorned with ear-rings on her lap.

The mother said:

28b-35a. O son, you, reaching the final stage (i.e. dying) have destroyed me, as the day's grace is destroyed by the sun going to the western mountain. O very intelligent one, this body (of you) which is fit for being smeared with sandal, has, having plunged me into the ocean of affliction and grief, been greyish due to dust. Your habit of chewing tāmbūla is certainly being perpetuated by its being mixed with emission of blood. Those very eyes of you which formerly surpassed the beauty of lotuses have now become, as it were, covered with a mass of darkness. O child, get up, get up. Teach your students. At the end of the Vaiśvadeva (sacrifice), honour the guest that has arrived. Your friends, standing at the door, have called you. Go to them. Give them whatever is to be given to them, and take from them whatever is to be received. Oh, Oh! Give reply to me. I fall at your feet. Otherwise, I shall cast my life near you.

Nārada said:

35b-36a. Saying so, the mother of Mukunda, then fainted. His wife, taking his head on her lap, wailed:

The wife said:

36b-41. O lord, O ocean of virtues, listen to my words. If for some reason you are angry with your mother, speak out to me. O good one, formerly you never resorted to silence like this. Some younger brother has insulted you. This parrot in the cage does not eat food without you. Give him well-cooked food, so also to the sārikā uttering indistinct but sweet words. Teach the parrot and the sārikā the series of names of Viṣṇu (like) 'Rāma, Rāma; Hare Kṛṣṇa'. Get up. The two are very clever. What offence have I done to you, that you are not talking to me? I have well preserved the wealth which you have given to me. O lord, I will not wait till the delivery of your lustre (i.e. semen) that you have put into me. I shall follow you.

Nārada said:

42-44. Having thus lamented, that dear wife of Mukunda, desiring to follow him, stopped weeping. O king, then the ascetic, the preceptor of Mukunda, called Vedāyana, wandering over the earth went to his house. "Where has Mukunda gone? The mother and the wife of the intelligent one are not seen." Thus he then asked the female servant.

The female servant said:

45-47a. O preceptor, some thief killed my master at night. He took (away) all the ornaments and silken garments of the daughter-in-law. Falling dead, he (i.e. his body) is at the top of the mansion. His mother, the daughter-in-law, his brothers, fallen into the ocean of great grief, are weeping near him.

Nārada said:

47b-49a. Having heard these words uttered by the female servant, the ascetic, going up to (the top of) the mansion saw his dead disciple. Seeing his relatives weeping excessively near him, the wise one desiring to take them up from the ocean of grief, said to them:

Vedāyana said:

49b-59. O mother, tell me whether you are thus lamenting for his body or his soul. Tell me the truth. (Your) lamenting is not proper for both (the body and the soul). This body, an aggregate of the elements, is earned due to (i.e. as a result of) deeds commenced (by one in one's existences). When they are exhausted, the elements get separated from them. The coming together of them with the deeds is the birth of men. When they perish, the getting separated of them (i.e. the elements) is the death (of men). Since the coming together or getting separated of the beings is due to their deeds, the wise should not lament for the dull body, dependent on (the deeds). Birth and death are seen in the soul due to the beginningless illusion. (A man) thinks them (to be there) due to his looking upon the body as the soul. (In reality) they are not there. When that (notion of identifying the body with the soul) is removed, he (becomes) that pure, formless Brahman which is self-illumined, the cause of the world, itself beyond a cause (i.e. having no cause), distinguished with virtues, which is eternal, which is knowledge, joy and which always illumines the world with its lustre. The tongue never licks it. The eyes never see it. The ears never hear it. The nose never smells it. The skin never touches it. It is beyond the senses. It is self-illumined; it is self-sighted. It is never the object. It is beyond the mind. It cannot be grasped even by the intelligence. Deities of pure sattva that are the forms of its incarnation serve it, but do not understand its form which is beyond the existent and the non-existent. Such is the nature of the (highest) soul. What man would be so foolish as to be angry with it, since it is neither produced, nor does it perish?

CHAPTER TWO HUNDRED TEN

Mukunda Goes to Heaven

Nārada said:

1-15. Having thus enlightened them with words expressing the highest truth, the ascetic got done his (obsequial) rites. The learned one stopped the young, pregnant wife of Mukunda, who insisted on following her husband. O king, having taken his bones, his brother, along with the anchorite, went to drop them into the water of Gaṅgā. O king, the brāhmaṇa (Mukunda's brother) and the ascetic reached along with the members of a caravan this holy place Indraprastha after a few days. O king, in this Kośalā which is in Indraprastha on the bank of Gaṅgā on earth, they slept at night. Keeping the bundle of the bones between themselves, the two, fatigued due to the journey, went to sleep. When, at night the members of the caravan had slept, a dog came there to take away cooked food etc. The dog, repeatedly smelling the kitchen, licking the vessels, at times tolerating the stroke of a staff, moved in the entire camp. Then being struck by someone on the head, he ran from there like a hen-pecked husband struck by his wife but unable to retaliate. The dog again entered the same place with a desire to lick the vessels containing food, as he was struck with staffs and bricks, like a poor person loving a prostitute (enters her house) with a desire for enjoyment. Thus wandering, the dog (came) where the two were asleep, and took away the bundle of bones. Having carried it for a distance, he tore the bundle with his teeth and seeing the fleshless bones in it, threw them into the water of this Kośalā. The moment the bones were thrown into this water, O king, Mukunda, seated in a divine aeroplane, came there. Seeing his preceptor and younger brother asleep, he gently awakened them. O king, he, of a divine form, having saluted his teacher, said:

Mukunda said:

16-19. O my preceptor Vedāyana, I salute you. O my younger brother, my blessing to you. Due to your favour my bones have fallen into this holy place. This I, having died, having gone to hell and got its fruit, have secured a divine course due to the grace of this holy place. I have come here to salute you, my preceptor, who are a holy place. I, going to heaven in this divine aeroplane, saluted you, this holy place, and saw (i.e. met) my brother. (Please) allow me. I (shall) go to heaven causing happiness.

Nārada said:

20. Hearing these words of Mukunda, his preceptor Vedāyana with his amazement removed, said to him seated in the aeroplane.

Vedāyana said:

21-22. O Mukunda, tell me the truth. After your death, to which world did you go, from where you are now going to heaven, O dear one? O dear one, what happened there? Who is the ruler of that world? What kind of subjects are there? What are the religious practices? Tell all that.

Mukunda said:

23-28a. O preceptor, I shall tell you what took place after (my) death. Now my recollection is revived due to the favour of this holy place. When that wicked barber Caṇḍaka killed me, Yama's very fearful servants came (there). They were tawny-eyed; their hair was red; their bodies, nails and lower lips were dark. They were short; had long feet, short noses and projected teeth. They said to one another: "Take him, take him, by the order of Yama, to (Yama's) city (called) Saṁyamanī only." Speaking like this, very angrily they put me into a body being tormented; fastening me by fierce nooses they struck me with iron mallets. I who was being taken by them, being overcome by grief, wept very much on the path having heated sand on it; and I was again beaten by them. And being firm, they, very much deriding me, said:

Yama's messengers said:

28b-33. Since you offended against your preceptor explaining (to you) the eternal Brahman, what will you do before Yama? You will have to see his fierce face. You will have to experience the fruit of that fearful sin. O sinner, due to that sin only you died prematurely.

Saying so, in a short time they took me to Saṁyamanī, Yama's city, situated in (an area of) many yojanas, where king Yama himself dwelt. Having saluted king Yama, and having placed me before him, they reported to him about me: "This sinful brāhmaṇa is brought." Seeing me, king Yama said to the members of his assembly:

Yama said:

34-35a. O members of the assembly, being well attentive, listen to my words. When Brahmā assigned me this charge, he, the grandsire of the worlds, spoke to me like this:

Brahmā said:

35b-37. You, the lord of Saṁyamanī, will punish impious

people. O son of the Sun, punish them in accordance with their offence. You should throw into hells these two, committing major sins, viz. one who does not support his parents and one who offends against his preceptor. The punishment would be staying in each hell for a myriad years. O you lord of the (Southern) quarter, you have not to show compassion to these two.

Yama said:

38-41. Therefore, O members of the assembly, by Brahmā's words I do not take pity on a man offending against his preceptor or not supporting his parents. This brāhmaṇa has offended against his preceptor. Due to that offence he met with an untimely death; and he, unfit to be seen, is brought (here) by my servants at my order. O servants, first throw him into the fearful Raurava (hell) for a myriad years; and taking him who has offended against his preceptor out of that (hell), throw him again into another (hell) for that much period. Then quickly let him stay for the proper period in all the hells.

Mukunda said:

42-51. O preceptor Vedāyana, O master, the servants, by Yama's order, took me to the fearful Raurava (hell), and fastening me with chains, threw me into it. There, O dear one, I experienced very severe, poignant agony, so that even a moment was passed as a yuga by me. Staying there I passed thirty days painfully. Today on this thirty-first day I have come out (of it), when (my) bones fell into this most excellent holy place. Due to the grace of this holy place my sin due to offending against my preceptor, perished instantly; and I went to heaven. I shall happily live in heaven as long as fourteen Indras (rule the heaven). The subjects that live in Yama's city cause fear to sinners, but are pleasing to the pious. The young women there have faces like those of lions, elephants, boars; have large fangs, plump bellies; have faces like those of cats; have tawny hair; and have long feet and long hands. When I became free from the sin due to the favour of this holy place, I saw in Yama's abode the subjects of divine forms. All of them were truthful in their speech, were full of modest behaviour, had worn divine ornaments, and were adorned with divine garments. O dear one, I have told this (in reply to) what you had asked me. (Please) allow me to go to the city of the lord of gods.

Nārada said:

52. That ascetic, having heard these words spoken by his disciple at that time, again asked that brāhmaṇa, Mukunda, O king:

Vedāyana said:

53-55. From your childhood and with affection for your preceptor, you learnt everything from me—Veda with the Pada (-pāṭha) and Krama-pāṭha (the two ways of reciting the Veda), along with the science of words (i.e. grammar). You excellently served me with devotion. O good one, in you reside the virtues of the good like tranquillity, control etc. O dear one, tell me, so that I shall understand it properly, how you committed the sin of offending against your preceptor.

Mukunda said:

56-62. I have never disobeyed them who gave me birth, performed my thread-ceremony, those who supported their daughters and the Vedas, so also him who made me wear the sacred thread. I served my mother-in-law and my father-in-law like a servant. I did not also disobey you who taught me the holy texts. (But) I offended against him who was the family priest, the preceptor of my family, and who had mastered the Vedas and the Vedāṅgas. (Please) listen to it. The settled rule of our family is: 'If a righteous son is born in our family, then his umblical cord is cut off after a cow, or a gift (equal to) her (value) is given to the family priest.' O dear one, when a son was just born to me only on an auspicious day, I, the foolish one, did not perform the rite of (i.e. befitting) my family. Due to my not performing it, I offended against my preceptor. I have told (you) all this as to how I committed a sin by offending against the preceptor. Now permit me. It (shall) go to heaven.

Vedāyana said:

63-64. Due to the favour of this auspicious Kośalā, situated within Indraprastha, the recollection of the previous existence appears. O Mukunda, due to which religious merit were your bones dropped in this holy place? O sinless one, tell it (if) you have its recollection.

Mukunda said:

65-69. (One) evening a brāhmaṇa came to my house. I duly gave him a seat and food. He too, having eaten as he desired, slept on a good bed. At night his entire body suffered from a very severe fever. Troubled by it, the brāhmaṇa did not get sleep. In the morning only he died. When his death took place, O preceptor, I performed all the rites like cremation and dropped his bones, according to the sacred rule, in Gaṅgā. Due to that religious merit my bones fell into this auspicious holy place, named Kośalā, fashioned by Brahmā.

Nārada said:

70. O king, the brāhmaṇa, having thus told his account, and having a charming body like that of a god, quickly went to heaven in an aeroplane. It is told how he met his death at the hands of the thief and obtained heaven through the grace of this best holy place.

CHAPTER TWO HUNDRED ELEVEN

Caṇḍaka's Fate

Nārada said:

1-3a. O Śibi, I have told you the entire excellent account of Mukunda. Listen also to the account of the barber Caṇḍaka from me. O king, on the day when Caṇḍaka killed the brāhmaṇa Mukunda, the citizens heard that news. Hearing that they clearly reported like this to the king:

The citizens said:

3b-4. O king, Caṇḍaka has killed Mukunda, the best brāhmaṇa, and has taken (away) his ample wealth. Do what is proper. You are the protector of us (your) subjects, and the chastiser of the bad.

Nārada said:

5-7. Hearing this, the king with his eyes red with anger, said to the minister who was by his side: "Listen to what these (citizens) say. Quickly bring that sinner. Otherwise I shall kill you. O most sinful one, get up, get up, (and) do (what leads to) the happiness of the good. A king in whose country his subjects are harassed by thieves and who does not protect them from them (i.e. the thieves), goes to hell."

Nārada said:

8-10a. O Śibi, having heard these words of the king, the minister quickly mounted his horse, and with a hundred foot-soldiers went to Mukunda's house, and asked his relatives: "Who killed Mukunda? Tell me the truth. By the order of the king I shall kill the sinner."

Nārada said:

10b. Hearing these words of the minister, the relatives of the brāhmaṇa said:

The relatives of the brāhmaṇa said:

11-12. O minister, Mukunda was killed by Caṇḍaka, the barber. This is his turban that had fallen when he was running away. The young wife of Mukunda herself has seen the sinner. What shall we do? We have plunged in the ocean of grief.

Nārada said:

13-19. Hearing these words of the relatives of the brāhmaṇa, the minister went to the house of that sinful barber. Quickly he got down from the horse and with some foot-soldiers went into his house and saw him asleep. Ordered by him the foot-soldiers seized him by his hair that moment (only) and they raised that sinful, mean barber from (his) bed. When the sinful barber saying, "What is this? what is this?" opened his eyes, he saw him (i.e. the minister). Recollecting his act—the sin that he had committed at night—he, for a moment, remained with his face hung down and realising (that) Yama had stood over his head. Getting him arrested by his foot-soldiers, the minister took him to the king, and thus spoke to the king: "O king, this barber Caṇḍaka, the killer of the brāhmaṇa, has been brought. I shall quickly do what you order."

The king said:

20-22. O best minister, O you who know religious practices, O long-lived one, listen to my words. Here there is this clean, best river, Candrabhāgā. Those who cast their lives here go to the place of gods. Therefore, this wicked barber should not be killed here. If (he would be killed) outside the boundary of five krośas of this (place), he would go to fearful hells. Make no delay.

Nārada said:

23-30. Thus addressed by the king, the best minister prompted cāṇḍālas to kill him at the king's order, O king. The cāṇḍālas taking him up on the other bank of Candrabhāgā to a place at a distance of two yojanas, cut off his head. The sinner became a serpent having a deadly body, living in the hollow of a dhava tree, and with his mouth producing flames of poison. The dhava tree dried due to the fire from his hissing as a pool full of water dries due to the heat of the sun. Due to the sinner's going there the dhava tree and the land around it, with the grass etc. cut off, became a barren land. O Śibi, once there came a caravan from the southern region. It especially was going to Nārāyaṇa's hermitage, called Badara. On the way a brāhmaṇa had joined the caravan. O king, carrying on his shoulder a holeless wooden box containing the bones of his father and mother, he was going to drop them into the water of Gaṅgā giving the desired objects even to sinners.

31-41a. He too came there to the forest where the serpent was and kept the box made of red rods at a secluded place. Coming there the serpent raised a rod with his hood. When the box was partially opened, he entered the box. The rod returned to its original position. The serpent, dreadful due to poison, remained motionless there in the box only. Then in the morning all of them moved from that place, O king. The brāhmaṇa also taking the box covered with a blanket on his head, proceeded to Gaṅgā.

O king, the caravan of the pilgrims reached this pure Kośalā after some days. Then the brāhmaṇa, sick due to cold opened the blanket which covered the box there on the auspicious slope of Ayodhyā. The serpent too who had no food (for a long time) got his food, i.e. air, and throwing up a strong rod, moved out of it. Seeing the serpent to have moved out, all men, saying 'A serpent, a serpent', and with clods in their hands, went there. While the serpent was running (away) he was hit by one of them. While the pilgrims were watching he cast his life. Giving up his serpent-body, he obtained godhead, difficult to be obtained. Getting into a divine aeroplane, he spoke these (words) to the people:

The serpent said:

41b-44. O brāhmaṇas from the south, hear my words. Formerly I was a mean barber named Caṇḍaka who killed a brāhmaṇa. Due to the great sin of the murder of a brāhmaṇa, I became a serpent in (this) desert. Having experienced the miseries in the hell for five lakhs of years, I have passed two myriads of years in this existence as a serpent. Due to the favour of this holy place, I have obtained excellent godhead. Therefore, this sacred place giving all (desired) objects should not be abandoned; from it, I, a sinner, have reached heaven.

Nārada said:

45-50. Thus that sinful barber, having reached a censurable existence, went seated in an aeroplane to heaven. The southerners, becoming ascetics, lived at that sacred place—whose grandeur they had seen—only, with their minds (fixed) on the lotus-like feet of Viṣṇu. That best brāhmaṇa, noticing the greatness of this holy place and having developed faith in it, dropped his parents' bones there. When the pieces of the bones fell there, his parents, seated in a divine aeroplane, came there at that moment only. And, while (other) people were listening, they said to their son: "O son, live long; be happy in the world with wealth and grains. Due to your having caused the liberation of both of us, you will obtain salvation. This is not false." Due to the dropping of the bones, both—the fruit that the son would have by offering piṇḍas into Gaṅgā and the parents' going to heaven—took place.

CHAPTER TWO HUNDRED TWELVE

The Efficacy of Kośalā

Nārada said:

1-6a. Speaking like that, the brāhmaṇa's parents, of divine forms, got into the excellent aeroplane, and went to Viṣṇu's city. Their son, having lived there in Kośalā only for three days, went home, thinking about the grandeur of the holy place. This, O king, is called Kośalā by the wise. I shall tell (about) it to you whose mind has a curiosity to listen to it. Having gone to that Kośalā, the brāhmaṇa chaps from the south, desiring to die (there), lived in it giving proper objects. One of them going to Nārāyaṇa's place after ignoring it, was stopped by Viṣṇu in the guise of an old brāhmaṇa. He thus spoke to the brāhmaṇa:

The old brāhmaṇa said:

6b-15. O best brāhmaṇa, ignoring this auspicious Kośalā, where are you going? O brāhmaṇa, this holy place Indraprastha is the best of all holy places. O son, here is this Kośalā, dear to Viṣṇu, and giving salvation. Success will not come to you there, where you are going after ignoring this giving a position free from all desires; and Viṣṇu will be averse to you. O brāhmaṇa, if you desire salvation, then this holy place will give you that object, with the desire of which, you, after taking a pledge, will bathe at this holy place. O brāhmaṇa, even within the range of your sight (i.e. when you were seeing), a serpent became a god. Due to the favour of this the brāhmaṇa couple resides in heaven. How then do you, even after having reached it due to the dawn of good fortune, and even after being convinced on seeing its greatness, ignore it? O fool, you appear to be like one who, after being oppressed by thirst, leaves the ocean of nectar, and goes to muddy water. Your fate appears to be like that of him who, being deluded, throws into a well the desire-yielding gem that was in his hand. Your fate is that of a foolish man who, after having propitiated Viṣṇu, desires the worthless pleasure of senses. No man goes (to another place) after having ignored this Kośalā, giving all desired objects. One who bathes here, goes to heaven. One who dies here lives among the immortal.

Nārada said:

16. O king, having heard (these) words of Viṣṇu, upholding the welfare of brāhmaṇas, he spoke to the brāhmaṇa, "Badarikāśrama is the best."

The brāhmaṇa said:

17-21. O best brāhmaṇa, in me who have heard about the grandeur of the small village, faith is produced by means of these words of you. I have never heard about this holy place, Indraprastha. O old one, how is Kośalā (situated) in it, where actually Viṣṇu (lives), and where the meditating saints are liberated. How should I ignore that meritorious hermitage and stay here as Viṣṇu, having himself come (here), and telling me like this, would stop me? O brāhmaṇa, this holy place is superior to Badarī. So, though driven to that hermitage, I shall not proceed (to it). Desiring salvation (I have come here). Otherwise I would not have stayed here.

Nārada said:

22-23a. When the brāhmaṇa spoke like this, Viṣṇu, the four-armed one, giving up the ordinary form (of a man), and having a divine form, said to the noble brāhmaṇa, desiring salvation:

Viṣṇu said:

23b-28. This Indraprastha is best of all holy places. As Śiva is among all those who know Brahman, as Gaṅgā is among rivers, as Himālaya is among mountains, as Garuḍa is among birds, as Śakra is among gods, as Nārada is among Viṣṇu's devotees, as the Sun is among luminaries, as the Milky Ocean is among oceans, as brāhmaṇa is among castes, as the grandsire is among the created, as the son of Kausalyā is among the incarnations of Viṣṇu, so is this holy place Indraprastha the best of all holy places. A man, without or with a desire, sometimes goes to a holy place. At every place I myself am the giver of the fruit. A devotee who goes (to another holy place) by ignoring Kośalā situated in Indraprastha, does not obtain the fruit from the protector of the host of the givers of fruits.

Nārada said:

29-35. Having thus heard those words, and having seen that excellent form, and having saluted Viṣṇu, the brāhmaṇa left. The lord, the soul of the universe, instantly disappeared. He devoutly worshipped that brāhmaṇa as the supreme principle. Having come there to Kośalā the brāhmaṇa told the entire account to all his companions, O king. Those noble brāhmaṇas from the south, did not eat there and abandoned their ordinary bodies. Just then, Śrī Viṣṇu mounted upon Garuḍa came there with his attendants in those many aeroplanes shining with lustre. They, with divine forms, seeing him and the aeroplanes with attendants, fell prostrate like staffs on the earth. All the brāhmaṇas, having divine knowledge and bodies praised that god of divine form whose lotus-like feet are adored by gods.

The brāhmaṇas said:

36-44. Salutation to you who have a body shining like an atasī-flower, who have covered yourself with a yellow garment, who have various lotuses put on the bright ear-rings, who have put blue small lotuses on your ears. Devotion to you is indeed the desire-yielding creeper (tree) which, when resorted to, gives what is desired by the mind. Similar is this your Kośalā with objects of enjoyment. The two are secured through your grace. We salute your lotus-like feet saluted by respectable hosts of gods etc., thought of by delighted groups of meditating saints, and the root of salvation, the source of the highest joy. O lord of Lakṣmī, we have reached your form, distinguished with charming marks like Śrīvatsa etc.; yet we long for your service, secured and honoured by Nārada and others. (Even) Lakṣmī, residing within your chest (i.e. in your heart) does not have that happiness which is obtained by those who have become your servants. O lord of Lakṣmī, Śrī Maheśa knows it. He and none else has experienced it in the world. Among us, even having no attachment, he is to be honoured. The best sages like Nārada, your devotees, worship the lord of the worlds, due to him. Śambhu, though his heart is full of the joy due to Brahman, is satisfied only by serving you. Full of devotion to you he repeatedly dances excessively to receive your virtues. For this reason human beings who have secured your service, have no desires.

His two doorkeepers, with your marks on their bodies reach their own abode through delusion(?). Your desire is with reference to this world. Quick fall of your worlds never takes place. Who would know your Māyā which is difficult to be known by gods like Brahmā, Śiva etc.?

Nārada said:

45. That lord, eager to reach his place, being thus praised by them, said with a voice deep like that of clouds, to the southerners.

The lord said:

46-52. O brāhmaṇas, due to the grace of this Kośalā you have obtained absorption into me. You will also obtain my service. O brāhmaṇas, from today this excellent holy place of me will be known by the great name 'Dakṣiṇakośalā', where, Rāma, born as Daśaratha's son, will kill Rāvaṇa. That where a poor wise man goes up to Vaikuṇṭha is called Uttarakośalā by all excellent sages. Even he who would live here without that (i.e. knowledge) goes to heaven. They say that this Dakṣiṇakośalā is ten times superior to it. Some best sages describe it to be eleven times superior. I think the difference between that and this is: My attendants carry to Vaikuṇṭha one who dies there; while I myself take him who dies here; putting him on Garuḍa I absorb him into myself.

Nārada said:

53-55. O king, having thus spoken to those brāhmaṇas, and taking them (with himself) and himself praising the greatness of this holy place, Viṣṇu went to Vaikuṇṭha. O lord of the world, I have told you the reason for which the wise call her Dakṣiṇakośalā. O best king, I have described to you the greatness of Kośalā which destroys the sins of Kali, which is desired for reaching the feet of the Lotus-eyed (Viṣṇu); (now) I shall tell you the account that took place in Madhuvana.

CHAPTER TWO HUNDRED THIRTEEN

A Śrāddha at Madhuvana Is More Meritorious

Nārada said:

1-7. O dear one, O Śibi, Viṣṇu, who was pleased, established (this) city, this Madhuvana for Indra. Here is this holy place called Viśrānti, best in the three worlds, giving salvation to the very wise men, holy and resorted to by the good. O king, Viṣṇu, the universal soul, lives in the form of Śrī Kola (i.e. a bear) at this best, meritorious holy place called Viśrānti. O king, it is said that he who has always propitiated Viṣṇu during many existences, dies here. On the very bank of Kālindī (i.e. Yamunā) another holy place called Viśrānti, is fashioned by Viṣṇu himself, where Kaṁsa was hurled down. O king, the two are equal in merits giving Vaikuṇṭha. Due to the dawn of good fortune, it, giving all (desired) objects, is obtained. To you I shall tell the importance of this holy place, having heard which you will obtain the fruit of bathing in all holy places.

8-16. O king, there lived a poor brāhmaṇa named Kuśala in the auspicious city of Kirāta in the land at the foot of the Himālaya mountain. His wife of a bad conduct was fondly attached to a man of a bad character. The unchaste woman deluded her husband with her (bad) acts. Her husband deluded by her was unable to ward her off. He, the poor one, was intent on obeying her orders, and was (i.e. lived), as it were, bought (by her). People ridiculed the brāhmaṇa, the husband of the unchaste woman. He too, scared of the ridicule, did not stir out of the house. She put on very costly silken garments and ornaments given by her paramours. The wicked one, though ridiculed, was not ashamed. Due to his servile nature she, the wicked one, contemptuously gave her husband old garments taken off from the bodies (of others). That her own husband who was thus slighted by the unchaste woman, being very much afflicted by grief, ate (i.e. drank) poison at night and died. The wanton woman was then scared of the king due to her bad conduct. She spoke (these) false words: "I shall follow my husband." O king, her friends, tutored by her only, went near her, and speaking like this, stopped her.

The friends said:

17-22. O deer-eyed woman, why do you do this worthless act, that you are ready to destroy your body resembling gold? O friend, what happiness did you get from this poor, incapable (husband), not industrious, and filling his own belly? Nourish this young son? Except you, who is his guardian? O beautiful lady, all of us will die, if you die. O you beautiful lady, look after this your house; rise. Let this your son, who will give happiness later, be victorious. All the relatives desire your life (i.e. that you should live). Get up. Do what is desired in their minds by your relatives. O good one, all your friends due to affection for you, are weeping. Stop them who are much grieved (from weeping) by giving (i.e. speaking to) them your words.

Nārada said:

23. That wicked one, having thus heard their words flowing from righteousness, raised her face, and making her own relatives listen, said:

The friend said:

24-28. I know that the proper words that you spoke are indeed true. Yet women must respect their husbands, giving (the merit of) both the worlds. O friends, listen to words uttered by me and following the code of laws. If it is proper, permit me (to follow my husband). That woman, even though she is a sinner, who, devoted to her husband, follows her dead husband, lives with him for a long time in heaven. Women should never desert their husbands even though he is poor or diseased. He, alive or dead, should be followed (by them). This is (i.e. thus says) the ancient holy text. Thinking thus in mind, O friends, I am following my husband. He (i.e. son) will live by his fate. What shall I do to him?

Nārada said:

29. Thus addressed, her wicked friends, giving a wicked counsel, said to her, deluding all people by means of her righteous words:

The friends said:

30-33. O you lady of beautiful eyebrows, first desert us and then follow your husband, O dear one. All of us are unable to put up with separation from you. You, destroying us, and following your own husband, will have little religious merit and great sin. How can you obtain heaven? You well looked after this husband of yours, when he was alive. O friend, you have done what is laid down for a husband and his wife. As long as this your son is unable to have his livelihood, he will live by your fortune.

Nārada said:

34-45. Thus addressed, she turned away from following her husband. She got performed his obsequial rites by her son. Then after some time she thought of getting his thread ceremony performed, got it performed by brāhmaṇas after having given them the wealth given to her by her paramours. The boy born in adultery[1], whose thread-ceremony was performed, who knew the real nature of human soul, quickly went out of the house, and was highly devoted to Viṣṇu. Having secured the company of the good, and given up his trifling body, he went up to the perpetual world, not accessible to the meditating saints. When the son went out she was unhappy in her mind. O king, on the same day she again dallied with her paramours. When she was thus dallying with her paramours, in course of time old age, destroying the arrogance of beauty, came over to her. Seeing her body stricken with old age, she was abandoned by the paramours. She spoiling the character of the group of other (women), became a go-between. Then she snatched the cow, along with her calf, of one brāhmaṇa; and, O king, she sold it for some money. O king, thus she passed some time (working) as a messenger. Then her dry body became worthless. When leprosy overcame her body, her five limbs—hands, feet, and the nose as the fifth, dropped. When, she who was reduced to such a condition, did not get food, she was taken to the market by a maid servant. There she, appealing to people with piteous words, and being despised, filled her belly.

1. **Kuṇḍa: A son born in adultery. A son born of a woman from someone who is not her husband, and when the husband is alive.**

46-51. O king, a brāhmaṇa, knowing all the Vedas, a great orator, who lived near, seeing her, spoke these words: "Sin gives pain to people in this world and the next. Therefore, men, afraid of pain, should not commit a sin. A man who, having committed a sin, performs an expiation, has not committed the sin; so he would not get its fruit. He who, having repeatedly committed sins, does not perform an expiation, meets the same fate as this woman, in this world and in the next. In this world she committed a host of sins. She will suffer its fruit here only, and also in a hell. In the holy texts an expiation is seen for all sinners, but not for women averse to (good) deeds."

Nārada said:

52-63a. Speaking like this, the best brāhmaṇa, afraid of seeing her, again and again remembering Viṣṇu, and saluting the Sun, left. O king, she, thus suffering the fruit of her acts, obtained by herself, became miserable and died after a few days. No burning on funeral pyre of her, the sinful one, was done. Cāṇḍālas dragged her by (seizing) her hair, and took her out of the city. At the time of her death, Yama's servants came (there), and making her take up a body that caused torment, they took her to Yama's city. That god, gentle to the pious and actually hated by the sinners, seeing her again, turned away his face. Yama, thus turning away his face, ordered his servants: "As pronounced by me, throw her into the Raurava hell." Thus addressed, the servants remembering the acts which she had done, took her and threw her, with her face (turned) down, into that fierce Raurava. In that Raurava (hell) she remained for one period of Manu. Later she was born as an alligator eating the flesh of the dead in a cremation ground. There also, she, eating excessively the flesh of the dead, got the fruit, viz. misery. of her acts. Once that brāhmaṇa who was born from her womb in the stock of brāhmaṇas, and who was roaming came there to the cremation ground. The sage's son, seeing her eating the flesh of the dead, thought for a moment in his mind, and recognised her to be his mother. Recognising her to be his mother, he said to himeslf:

The sage's son said:

63b-66a. Today I shall emancipate her from the ocean of

misery. Oh, a being is not freed, except at (the end of) the period of suffering (the fruit of his sins), from the sinful deed done by himself. She passed in the hell the period called (i.e. that was equal to) the period of a Manu, and with men she has passed here a hundred years. How much has she to experience (the fruit of) her great sin hereafter?

Nārada said:

66b-67. Thinking like this, he, closing his eyes, again thought by means of his sacred knowledge. Having noticed the fearful condition, with his divine sight, of that sinner, the best brāhmaṇa again said to himself, O king:

The sages' son said:

68-71. Oh! her liberation is not seen (to be possible) even after a hundred kalpas, except her dying at a holy place, or submitting herself to (Viṣṇu) the lord of Lakṣmī. Or she will not obtain heaven except by my offering piṇḍas at Gayā, even for hundreds of kalpas. In this birth of her she will never have these two—death in the region of a holy place, or liking for serving Viṣṇu. The (only) cause of the emancipation of her, the sinful one plunged in the ocean of sins, will be a śrāddha performed by me at Gayā.

Nārada said:

72-73. Thinking like this, the pious one went to his father's hermitage. He told his father the entire cause of his mother's misery. Having heard the son's words telling (about) his mother's misery, the best sage spoke to his son who had bowed his neck (i.e. head):

The sage said:

74-82. As a king, knowing polity, takes the sovereignty of his enemy in a war, O dear one, quickly raise your mother from this miserable condition. If a son, capable of emancipating his mother or father from misery, does not emancipate them, he goes to hell. Having received water and piṇḍas from their sons at an excellent holy place, the dead ancestors go to heaven from hell, and from heaven to Viṣṇu's place. Therefore, get up quickly. Go to Khāṇḍava-vana. There is the holy Yamunā, resorted to by the best sages. On her bank is Hariprastha, full of all holy places. Then there is the holy Madhuvana set up by Viṣṇu himself. Having duly bathed there, and having done your (usual) rites, offer a śrāddha to her, your mother, and (also) perform (other) rites. When a śrāddha is offered there by you desiring heaven for her, she abandoning the strong body of an alligator, will reach Viṣṇu's world. O dear one, the good have declared that the religious merit (due to offering a śrāddha) at Madhuvana, is a hundred times more than the one due to offering piṇḍas at Gayā. O dear one, now the Sun has entered the Zodiacal sign Libra. O son, go and offer a śrāddha to your ancestors.

CHAPTER TWO HUNDRED FOURTEEN

The Greatness of Madhuvana

Nārada said:

1-9. O king, having heard these words of his father, he quickly went to the holy Madhuvana, a hundred times holier than Gayā. Then the learned brāhmaṇa spoke to the brāhmaṇas living at that holy place, and again having invited them after some time, spoke to them words of welcome. Then having washed their feet and worshipped them with sandal etc. he made respectful offering at their feet, and similarly himself sipped (water). Then taking the brāhmaṇas he seated them at the place of the śrāddha. And filling the pot (used) for the rite with darbhas, water, tulasī (leaves), flowers, sandal, sacred rice grains and sesamum-seeds, he remembered Viṣṇu. The brāhmaṇas thrice recited the verse: *Devatābhyaḥ*.... Then he tied it containing sesamum-seeds with darbhas that were purified, in the directions beginning with the east, in the proper order with (the recital of) the hymn *Agniṣvātta* ....With the hymn *Rakṣobhūta*...he tied the ends of the garment worn round the waist into a knot. Then taking the pledge, he gave darbha seat to the brāhmaṇas. Then the best brāhmaṇa invoked his dead ancestors. Then giving respectful offering into their hands, he turned down the vessel and made it lie on its face. Having offered sandal etc. he, with his sacred thread hanging down over the left shoulder, sipped water. Then the brāhmaṇa gave the pots after having his sacred thread (once) hanging down over the left and (once) over the right shoulder.

10-24. Permitted by the brāhmaṇas, he offered oblations like ghee into the fire. Then he filled those vessels (with water), O king. With his hand turned up and down he took the vessels and taught by the brāhmaṇas he recited (the hymn) *Pṛthvī tvā*... With (the reciting of) the hymn *Asaṁskṛtapraṇītānām*... the brāhmaṇas offered seats with the darbhas strewn (there) with their points in the southern direction. O king, with (the reciting of) the hymn *Agnidagdha*... he put food mixed with ghee and along with water on the seats made by darbhas. Again, with his sacred thread hanging down over the left shoulder, he sipped a mouthful of water. He asked them, "Are you satisfied?" They replied, "We are satisfied." He took the permission of those brāhmaṇas to eat the remaining food. The brāhmaṇa made an altar of the measure of the length of twelve aṅgulas, and drew a line facing the south with a darbha. He laid the firebrand with (the reciting of) the hymn *Ye rūpāṇi*... in the direction of fire. O king, he duly offered darbha-seats and six piṇḍas only to them who were, in the former existence, his mother, father, so also to their parents, i.e. his grandfathers, so also, O best king, who were his maternal great-grandfather and paternal grandfather, along with their wives. Having worshipped them with sandal etc. and having cast off the middle piṇḍa and after having smelt the pot containing the piṇḍas, he put it on his left shoulder. Then taking the vessel containing water, and reciting (the hymn) *Vāje vāje*...again offering respectful oblation to their feet, he pleased them with presents etc. Having followed them up to the door, and having secured their permission, the brāhmaṇa dined along with his relatives, O king. O best king, when the best brāhmaṇa, after thus finishing the śrāddha of his ancestors in the pious Madhuvana, and with his mind tranquil, started for his father's hermitage, he met on his way those who had eaten at the śrāddha. They, seated in six aeroplanes, adorned with divine ornaments, wearing celestial garments thus spoke to the best brāhmaṇa:

The ancestors said:

25-26. O child, O best brāhmaṇa, ask for an excellent boon. You, performing a śrāddha at this holy place, have emancipated us. Due to your favour we have become Viṣṇu's attendants. O you very intelligent one, ask for what is desired in (i.e. by) your mind.

The sage's son said:

27. Who are you? Wherefrom have you come? How did you become (Viṣṇu's) attendants? Why do you grant me a boon without my having obliged you?

Nārada said:

28. Hearing these words of the son in his former existence, the father, who had died after taking poison due to grief, said:

The father said:

29-35. O brāhmaṇa, I am your father, a brāhmaṇa, in your former existence. I was very much troubled by your unchaste mother. Being extremely afflicted, I took poison at night, died prematurely, and, therefore, became a demon: O dear one, after being turned into a demon, I passed a period of Manu and one hundred and fifteen years (in that condition). Now in the (hundred and) sixteenth year, when you performed a śrāddha in this meritorious holy place Madhuvana, I attained godhead. This aeroplane sent by Indra along with attendants and a host of the celestial nymphs has arrived from heaven for me to get in. I, along with the attendants and the host of celestial nymphs, have, while going to the heaven after getting into the excellent aeroplane, come here to give you a boon. Ask for a boon. God bless you. We can't brook any delay. Indra, mounted upon the elephant Airāvata, is waiting for me.

Nārada said:

36-37a. O king, thus telling his son his own account, and giving him the devotion for Viṣṇu (as) asked by him, he went to heaven. Then his mother spoke to him, her son in the previous existence:

The mother said:

37b-41. Due to your favour I have become a goddess and am freed from sins. O best brāhmaṇa, I, though a sinner, have become the friend of Śacī, when you performed the śrāddha at this holy place called Viśrānti. O glorious one, ask for what is desired by your mind. I shall give it to you, since the words of us, the deities, are never falsified. O best brāhmaṇa, you know the sin due to which I, after staying in the hell for a long time, became an alligator in the cremation ground. O son, allow me (to go). Śacī, surrounded by hosts of celestial ladies is waiting for me in the sky.

Nārada said:

42-43. O king, his mother too, having thus spoken to him, her desireless son, went after being saluted by him with his head (bent down) to heaven. Then his grandfather, having similarity of form with Viṣṇu, again spoke (these) words to his grandson, the best brāhmaṇa.

The grandfather said:

44-46. O child, O child, live long. Obtain what is desired by you. Due to your favour we have crossed over this ocean of mundane existence, difficult to cross. O child, I am your grandfather, and this is your grandmother. The chaste lady followed me who had died, and soon obtained residence in the same heaven (as of Viṣṇu). When today you performed the śrāddha-rite at Viśrānti, we have obtained similarity of form with Viṣṇu in his heaven.

Nārada said:

47-48. O best king, the brāhmaṇa, after having spoken like this, went along with her, his wife, to Vaikuṇṭha after having crossed Brahmā's world. O best king, listen attentively to the words, the brāhmaṇa, his great-grandfather spoke to him, which I am telling you.

The great-grandfather said:

49-54. O child, O glorious one, I am your great-grandfather. As a result of my causing an abortion, I obtained the stock of (i.e. was born as) a pig. Then I went out of it, and being oppressed by my sin, became a dog. Then I became an inanimate object on the best mountain, Vindhya. Then I who for a long time remained in that condition of an inanimate object, was forcibly uprooted by an elephant. Then at that time only you performed the śrāddha at this excellent holy place. And therefore I was freed from that inanimate condition and got an excellent residence in the city of the lord of yakṣas. O best brāhmaṇa, permit me. Due to your favour I (shall) go. With the desire to see you I have come here, and have seen you of a pious appearance (and) the Madhuvana, the best of all holy places.

Nārada said:

55. Thus addressed by him, the sage's son, knowing religious merit, asked, after saluting his great-grandfather with (having bent) his head to him, his great-grandfather:

The sage said:

56-57. O dear one, you were born in a great brāhmaṇa family. How did you, O great one, commit the sin of causing abortion, due to which you obtained (i.e. were born in) a series of censurable stocks? O illustrious one, tell me that if you recollect (it).

The great-grandfather said:

58-66. O best brāhmaṇa, formerly, in the existence of a brāhmaṇa, I maintained myself by the employment of spells and amulets. Due to greed of wealth, I, with my understanding destroyed due to (ill) luck, gave them (clients) medicine for conception and abortion; for greed would take away the understanding of those having no wealth, as the sun takes away the water of the canals in the hot season. O dear one, when a man's understanding perishes, he certainly commits a sin. Due to the sin he gets (into) a hell, and from there goes to (i.e. is born in) a bad stock. In that existence, one pregnant woman asked me: "O brāhmaṇa, shall I give birth to a son or a girl?" Then I said to her: "A daughter will be born to you. (Therefore) I shall give you a medicine for the birth of a son." Thus addressed, the woman, the crest-jewel of the foolish, seized my feet and gave me a pala of gold. She said to me: "I have given birth to six daughters. You have now told (i.e. predicted) the seventh. After her birth I shall not live. O brāhmaṇa do that by which I shall not give birth to another daughter destroying my life."

67-79. Hearing these words of her, I again said to her: "At the time of your delivery I shall give you a medicine (capable of) generating a son." Saying, "All right" and having heard me she went home and believing in my words, remained waiting for that time. When she had gone, I became anxious like this. Listen as to how I became so. I (shall) tell it. 'She convinced of the birth of a son, gave me a pala of gold. I did not know what (i.e. a boy or a girl) would be born to her. What should be done in this case? How would that (gold of) a measure of a pala remain in the house of me who am poor?' Thinking like this, I handed over to her maid that medicine causing abortion and made her give it to her. Due to that medicine she aborted in the third month (of pregnancy). The sign of either a boy or a girl was not noticed. She, dejected due to the abortion, came to my house, and having no hope for the birth of a son, demanded (back) the gold. Then I showed her powder of bricks (mixed) with ash, and mixed with turmeric powder and with water. "O mother, for the birth of a son to you I have prepared this powder. For preparing that I required double the money that you had given me." Thus addressed by me, she ignored the powder, and went home, saying to me, "O brāhmaṇa, I shall take it from you at the proper time." O dear one, I have thus caused a very fearful (sin of) abortion, due to which I roamed in three very censurable stocks. Now due to your favour I am freed from the state of an inanimate object. O best sage, permit me. I (shall) go to the auspicious Alakā.

Nārada said:

80-82. O king, his great-grandfather, speaking like this, and saluted by him with his head (bent down), went to the northern direction in a beautiful aeroplane having rows of small bells with gandharvas dancing (in it) and charming with jewelled ramparts. Then the great-grandmother of the brāhmaṇa seated in an excellent aeroplane, spoke to her great-grandson, O great king:

The great-grandmother said:

83-85. O you of a good vow, due to this religious merit you have not to go anywhere else except the temple marked with Viṣṇu's lotus-like feet. O sage, this my sinful husband is your great-grandfather. He, of a very wicked mind, though warded off by me, committed a sin. He too, of a very sinful mind, is liberated by you from the ocean of misery. Who is able to describe your virtues?

Nārada said:

86-96. Speaking like this, she too went to her husband's world, O best king. With that same husband she rejoiced in Alakā for a long time. Then all those—grandfather etc.—got into the aeroplanes along with their wives and went to heaven. The best brāhmaṇa went from that holy place to his father's hermitage. And he described to his father the full account. He also went along with his family to Madhuvana and prepared a hut of leaves near Viśrānti. The best sage, bathing three times (a day) at the holy place called Viśrānti, did not even long for Viṣṇu's world. O king, once, while bathing in the water he wondered: 'When shall I see Viṣṇu?' O king, when the excellent sage was wondering like this, Viṣṇu, seated on the king of birds, hastily came (there). He came along with Lakṣmī (close) to his chest; he had four arms. The complexion of his body was like a fresh cloud. He was covered with a garment with the colour of lightning. His large chest was shining with the Kaustubha (jewel). He held a conch, a disc and a lotus. His neck shone with a garland of wood-flowers. His earrings had the shape of crocodiles. His eyes resembled the blooming lotus-flowers. His hands were tawny, and feet had good soles. Covering the directions with the mass (of lustre) like that of the moon, he spoke to the best brāhmaṇa, illumining him with his lustre:

The lord said:

97-99. O best brāhmaṇa, this is the meritorious place known as Viśrānta, and sacred to me. It gives all desired objects on one's bathing in it. Today at the time of your bath you longed for my sight. I have presented it, difficult to be obtained by gods, to you. O brāhmaṇa, give up this human body. Take up a divine one. Mounting on the lord of birds, come to my place along with me.

Nārada said:

100. O king, having heard these words of the lord of Lakṣmī, the chief of sages, bowing down, praised him (by remaining) in the water only.

The sage said:

101-107. O lord of Lakṣmī, your beautiful lotus-like feet have lovely lotuses offered to them. They destroy the torment of the mundane existence and are saluted by gods. O lord, those beings that are deluded by your Māyā here, can never be liberated without your grace. O lord, due to their resorting to holy places, and their company with the good, devotion (for you) in (these) men is produced due to your grace. O Viṣṇu, he who, having heard the narration of your merits uttered (i.e. made) by many good people and destroying all sins, repeats it, would not fall into the cavity of a mother's womb. O lord of Lakṣmī, the mind of your man (i.e. devotee), (though) fallen into the great going (of the mundane existence) and covered with dust (i.e. passion), does not, like an excellent gem, give up its purity. The man who having horripilation on his body falls (prostrate) like a staff at your lotus-like feet, takes his family to your place, longed for by all meditating saints. O lord, this very soul, deluded by your Māyā roams along all paths, (but) by means of the glances of your charming eyes, crosses the ocean in the form of the world.

Nārada said:

108-111. Praising Viṣṇu like this, the best sage, saying, 'Victory to you', fell at his feet (prostrating himself) like a staff. Lakṣmī's lord, raised the best sage fallen at his feet like a staff, and the universal Soul put him and (the members of) his family on Garuḍa and went to Vaikuṇṭha. O Śibi, I have told you the greatness, destroying all sins, of Madhuvana, O king. What else do you desire to hear? A man who listens to this (account) is freed from all sins.

CHAPTER TWO HUNDRED FIFTEEN

Budha Infuriated and Appeased

Saubhari said:

1. O Yudhiṣṭhira, having heard these auspicious words of Nārada, modest Śibi Auśīnara said to him:

Śibi said:

2-4. O sage, from your mouth (i.e. from you) I have heard about the greatness of Madhuvana; but there is some doubt in my mind. How was he, of a pious mind, who liberated all his kinsmen, the son of a wanton woman, in two existences? O revered one, tell this. You virtually know everything—the past, the present, and the future also, O Nārada.

Nārada said:

5-9. Once all sages gathered at Haridvāra on the tenth of the bright half of Jyeṣṭha connected with all festivals. There they having duly bathed and performed their (respective) auspicious rites, rested on the surface of Himālaya with their hearts at ease. Into the company of the sages, there came Budha, Tārā's son, full of excessive handsomeness and, as it were, another Cupid embodied. Seeing him coming all the sages got up. Saluted by him with his head (bent down), they again sat down. Seeing the regard shown to Budha by the pre-eminent sages, the sage's son thus asked his father, O lord:

The sage's son said:

10. O father, who is this that has come (here), who is another Cupid in handsomeness and very much respected by sages like Vyāsa?

Nārada said:

11. The pious, best sage, having heard these words of his son, said to him who had insisted (on knowing who Budha was):

The father said:

12. This is the intelligent, great son of Bṛhaspati, the pre-

ceptor of gods, and born of Tārā, and the perpetuator of the family of the Moon.

The son said:

13-15. O father, how have you spoken irrelevant words? How is he the son of Bṛhaspati as well as the perpetuator of the family of the Moon? O father, the Moon was born of Anasūyā from the chief of the sages, viz. Atri. How can this son of Bṛhaspati perpetuate his family? O father, this is a great doubt lurking in my mind. O best brāhmaṇa, remove that doubt of your child who is confused.

The father said:

16-24. O dear one, formerly Bṛhaspati's glorious wife named Tārā was forcibly kidnapped by the powerful Candra (i.e. the Moon). Kidnapping Bṛhaspati's wife the Moon took her to his house and dallied with her for a long time. O dear one, after some time she conceived. Then Bṛhaspati appealed (to Candra to return) his wife. Candra too, overcome by pride and puffed up by his power, did not give her (back). Then, O dear one, Bṛhaspati, getting ready along with gods like Indra, started fighting with the powerful Candra. To help Candra Śukra then came there to the battle that was commenced with the demons. Then a great war for Tārā took place. All people will look upon (that battle called) Tārakāmaya as important. In that very terrible war (both) gods and demons were killed. O dear one, no one was victorious or defeated. Then Brahmā came there, and stopping that fierce battle, gave, after admonishing the Moon, Tārā to Bṛhaspati. Bṛhaspati, seeing Tārā to be pregnant, was angry, and in the presence of Brahmā (said to) Tārā in the gathering of the gods and demons:

Bṛhaspati said:

25. O Tārā of unsteady eyes, listen to my words. Whose child do you bear—of Candra or of me?

The father said:

26-27. O dear one, when that beautiful (Tārā) who was abashed and was thus repeatedly asked, did not say anything to him, then he (i.e. Budha), who was born (of her) and was angry, said to his mother when the gods and demons were looking on (i.e. in the presence of the gods and the demons).

Budha said:

28. Why do you not, giving up your sense of shame, declare my father? See the power of my curse.

The father said:

29-32. When, speaking like this, he was on the point of cursing her after taking water, she gently said: "Candra is your father." When the chaste lady spoke like this, Candra gladly took this Budha, his own son, and went home. Bṛhaspati also took that Tārā and went home. Brahmā, (other) gods, and demons also went home. I have told you all this that you had asked me as to how he, born of Bṛhaspati's wife, perpetuates Candra's line.

Nārada said:

33-34. Hearing these words of his father, the sage's son laughed loudly and said to his father: "This is the son of a wanton lady, born in adultery."

The father said to the son:

O son, don't speak (like) this. He, knowing (what is going on in) the heart of every being will, understanding your words, curse you.

Nārada said:

35. O king, when the sage had spoken like this, the son of Candra understood what he had said, and while all the sages were listening, he said:

Budha said:

36-46. O best sages, may you listen to my words; and think whether they are good or bad. Do not delay. To see you who know the truth, I have come here. I have not in the least offended anyone. (Then) why do the infatuated ones insult me through jealousy? I long to see you to make my life fruitful. It is the very nature of the wicked that they, like the cuckoos with sweet notes, sometimes upset the good though innocent. The wicked do not abandon their wicked nature even in the company of the good, as the ocean becomes saline even in the company of the water of Gaṅgā. Oh! (see) the wickedness of the hunter that he kills the deer leading life like sages, moving in the forest, and knowing their own songs(?). What offence have the fish done to the wicked fishermen that they kill them moving in the water at a sacred place? It is their very nature. The good also do not give up their nature in the company of the wicked, as the sandal trees, though surrounded by serpents, do not abandon their coolness. The good dance (with joy) even at the prosperity of their enemy. Then what to say of (the prosperity of) one belonging to their own party? The best sages are eager as the peacocks are (at the sight) of a cloud. The good sustain even their bodies for the good of others, as my father bears the digits for the sake of manes, gods and men. To the good the continual rise (of others) causes joy, as the cool rays of my father (the Moon) cause joy to the white water lilies.

Nārada said:

47-51. Angrily speaking these words, Budha cursed that sage's son: "You too quickly become, like me, a son born in adultery on the earth." Having heard the curse given by Budha, the father made his son fall at his (i.e. Budha's) feet, saying, "(Please) forgive (him)". And he said, "This boy does not know your grandeur. It is not proper for (persons) like you to be angry with this boy. Forgiveness is the nature of a good man who is angry for some reason, as coolness in the nature of water heated by fire. Therefore, having forgiven him quickly favour this child having no discrimination, for forgiveness is the essence of the good."

Nārada said:

52. (Budha,) the son of Candra, thus addressed by him, gave up his anger, and with a cool mind favoured him.

Budha said:

53-58. O sage, this your son after being born in adultery on the earth, will obtain the perpetual place after a sacred thread is given to him (i.e. after his thread-ceremony).

O best king, due to the curse of Budha the sage's son obtained birth as a son born in adultery, and liberated his dead ancestors. Having heard this purifying greatness of Madhuvana, a man gets the entire fruit of a horse-sacrifice. The mind of those men who keep in it the excellent significance of this greatness, is not overpowered by objects of senses. There is no doubt that those highly intelligent ones who will recite and listen to this (description of the) greatness will go, after casting their body, to Viṣṇu's world. I have described to you this ceaselessly pure account of Madhuvana, which delights the lord of Lakṣmī, which promptly cuts off the mass of blemishes due to Kali, which is the cause of warding off the senses going astray (and of leading to) the pious form (of Viṣṇu).

CHAPTER TWO HUNDRED SIXTEEN

The Greatness of Badarikāśrama

Nārada said:

1-12. O king, this Badarikāśrama is situated in the region of just eleven dhanus (i.e. forty-four hastas) from this Madhuvana. To you I shall describe the wonderful greatness of this excellent holy place. One listening to it is free from fear. O king, there was in Magadha a truthful, restrained brāhmaṇa named Devadāsa, who was, as it were, another Dharma. Proficient in all lores he was, as it were, another Bṛhaspati. Like Prahlāda, the king of demons, he pleased Viṣṇu. Though he had a wife, he had conquered, like Śiva, Cupid. Like the sage Viśvāmitra he was always engaged in good acts. He was honoured in the house of Magadha's lord, as Droṇa in Kuru's house. Like Bali, lord of demons, he was disposed to giving gifts to worthy recipients. His wife by name Uttamā was excellent with virtues like Lakṣmī. She was engaged in serving her husband like Janaka's daughter (Sītā). He had one intelligent son named Aṅgada; and he had one daughter Valayā by name, having excellent marks. Of them the son was elder, the daughter was younger, O king. The best brāhmaṇa got them married in due course. O king, that daughter, endowed with auspicious marks, who was married, went to her father-in-law's house after some time. The very intelligent Aṅgada who knew all holy texts and who was adorned with the splendour of youth, bore the burden (i.e. the responsibility) of the household. Once that best brāhmaṇa, seeing his son to be capable of managing the duties, said to his wife, O best king:

Devadāsa said:

13-21. O good lady, listen to my words proper for this time; (and) then quickly do what is fit, O good one. This old age has come. Causing the limbs to tremble as a storm causes to tremble a ripe fruit, it will cause the body to fall. O you of a good vow, it will also make dull the brightness of the eyes, as the morning time makes dull the brightness of the stars along with the moon. Like an iron fetter this old age will lessen the speed of the stumbling feet at every step. Therefore, O auspicious one, as long as this old age does not become advanced, we should quickly do what is good to us. O fortunate one, a house, sons, friends, brothers, parents are perishable. So also is wealth etc. A wise man is not attached to them. Therefore, I, with my senses controlled, will wander, in the manner of an anchorite, about all holy places and will see Viṣṇu. Then, O auspicious one, taking to renunciation at an excellent holy place, I shall cast my body at the end of the fructification of my karmas. If thus I would be free from life, salvation would be (possible) for me who have properly placed my mind at the lotus-like feet of Lakṣmī's lord.

Uttamā said:

22-25. What man or woman (except one) having no sense would take delight in the perishable mundane existence, leaving Viṣṇu (i.e. and leave Viṣṇu), the perpetual abode? Therefore, O lord of my life, take me, serving your lotus-like feet with you, and quickly lift me up from the ocean of the worldly existence. This (our) glorious son Aṅgada has become capable of sustaining the burden of the household. This auspicious daughter-in-law will help him. That foolish man or woman, who, when his or her son is capable (of looking after the household), would not be detached, is deprived of bliss.

Nārada said:

26. Having thus talked to each other, that couple called their son Aṅgada on the same day and told him:

The couple said:

27-33. O Aṅgada, know us to have our limbs drooping due to the appearance of old age. At some holy place we shall strive for our spiritual good. Devoutly worshipping Viṣṇu is said to be the highest good. For that only the desireless good people strive on the earth. They who have no attachment for objects of senses, who look equally upon all beings, who are neither delighted nor dejected due to pleasure or pain, are alone the good men, serving the feet of Viṣṇu. By merely seeing them a man is blessed. A wise man, eager to see him (i.e. Viṣṇu), and wandering about the holy places, would see him by good luck. Therefore, O Aṅgada, having placed on your two long arms the burden of (maintaining) the family, allow us to go on a pilgrimage. O son, if, in course of our pilgrimage, we may see a good man, then we would be blessed.

Nārada said:

34-36. Thus addressed by the parents, the son spoke good words: "You have told this to be the emancipation of the entire family. Quickly order me what beneficial thing to you I should do. I always obey the orders of you whose feet are respectable (to me). Take with you the excellent wealth stored by you for giving gifts at holy places. So also take me with you as a servant to serve you."

Nārada said:

37-41a. Speaking like this, and taking money (with him) he went with them for a couple of krośas; and somehow sent back by them, he came home. They took some money with them, and thinking, 'May Viṣṇu come to us' lived there for three days, eating bulbs, roots and fruits. O king, when the couple set off from that place, they met a siddha on their way.

Saluted by both of them with their heads (bent down) he sat down. When the chief of siddhas was seated, they asked him thus: "Tell (us) who you are, wherefrom you have come, what you desire to do".

The siddha said:

41b-46. O best ascetic, I am a siddha. My house is at Kalpagrāma. I have come from Indraprastha. There I saw a great wonder. There is the siddha Kapila resembling Viṣṇu in merits. Learning Sāṁkhya from him I lived in his hermitage. Once my celebrated teacher, Kapila, went from his hermitage to the very holy (place) called Badarī, to bathe in the water of Yamunā. There one wild buffalo, oppressed by thirst, entered the water of Yamunā, and having drunk it, recollected his former existence. The wild buffalo, having recollected his past deeds, quickly came out of the water and saluted (my) teacher, Kapila; and when I was listening, the buffalo spoke with a human voice, which I (shall) tell you today. Listen to it, (which is) very wonderful.

The buffalo said:

47-48. O you Kapila, O you who are a portion of Viṣṇu, O you lord of the siddhas, tell me who have bowed to you, what the name of this great holy place is. Due to the touch of the water of this excellent holy place, I got (the recollection) of my deeds in the past existence, O illustrious one.

The siddha said:

49. Having heard these words of the buffalo, the great sage, though he knew his account, laughed and said these words:

Kapila said:

50. O best of buffaloes, who were you in your former existence? What deed did you do then, due to which you obtained (i.e. were born in) the stock of the buffalo?

The buffalo said:

51-61. O best sage, listen to the account of my former existence. Formerly I was a king, the mighty chief of Kaliṅga.

Deluded by passion I did not know (i.e. discriminate between) my wife and that of another. I took away the wealth of sinless merchants of good conduct. O king(?), I, being fearless, wandered at night in the city to dally with beautiful wives of others. I, deluded by Cupid, at night lived in that house in which I saw a beautiful woman, as an elephant lives in a field. Sporting there fearlessly, and snatching wealth from that house, I returned to my house after a few days. By day I seated in my assembly made two city-lads fight a base duel in front of me. Regarding the boy who put down (the other boy) as rich, I forcibly took the wealth, little or much, of his father. Saying, "This one due to his cowardice is not fit to live in my city", I killed him who was defeated, O sage. The citizens seeing the king to have begun behaving like this, abandoned the city, and went to another country. Durvāsas, the great sage born of Rudra, while roaming over the earth once came to my city. Then all citizens, gathering together approached him. Saluting him, they spoke to him these words acquainting him with their misery:

The citizens said:

62-71. O son of Atri, O best sage, O treasure of pity, favour us. Turn to piety this king, engrossed in doing unrighteous deeds. Due to the dawn of our good fortune you have come (here). Rescue us like a raft from this ocean of misery due to the king who is transgressing its limits. O best sage, the greedy one took away our wealth. The passionate one spoilt chaste and innocent ladies. Many children aged about ten years were killed by him. O great sage, this king is the store of innumerable faults.

The buffalo said:

Having heard these words of the citizens, that sage, the son of Atri, thinking, 'He must be punished', came to my assembly. Seeing the naked sage coming, I stopped him through my servants, saying, "He is not fit to be seen." I many times ordered my servants: "Stop him whose figure is like that of a buffalo, with his entire body smeared with dust." Then the servants quickly went to stop him. Just by means of a 'hum' sound the sage reduced all of them to ash, as you did Sagara's sons, protecting the sacrificial horse of their father. Seeing the servants to be completely reduced to ash, I quickly got up and was about to enter my house. The best sage, addressing me as "O sinner", cursed me:

72-77. "Now become a buffalo in a great forest." Thus cursed by him, I gave up the royal body; I became a buffalo in a great forest in the Maru country, O sage. O best sage, I lived there for a long time. Hear due to which religious merit I have come here. I had got constructed many reservoirs of water, wells, and tanks. I had (also) planted many mango trees on (the sides of) the path. O god, due to that religious merit, I did not fall into a hell. And I got the contact of the water of this holy place. I have thus told you about the righteous and unrighteous deeds in my former birth, due to which I reached this holy place, and due to which I had reached the buffalo's stock. Due to the touch of the water of this excellent place, I remembered my former existence. O sage, tell me how I shall be free from this miserable stock.

Kapila said:

78. This holy place of Lakṣmī's lord called Badarī is very meritorious. Bathe here, you will quickly obtain what is in your mind.

The siddha said:

79-80. O great sage, having heard these words of the king, he, desiring heaven, entered (the water of) the holy place to bathe. When, having bathed there with a desire (to go) to heaven, he came to the bank from the water, Indra came there just at that moment from heaven.

Indra said:

81. O lord of Kaliṅga, give up your body of the buffalo. Receiving a divine body come to my heaven. You bathed (here) with a desire to (reach) heaven; you have secured that abode of gods.

The siddha said:

82-83. Thus addressed by him, he then abandoned his body of buffalo, and securing a divine body, he mounted upon the lord of elephants. Having mounted upon the lord of elephants, and remaining in the air for a moment, and saluting the god with his head bent down, he praised the sage Kapila.

The Kaliṅga-king said:

84-92. O highest lord, salutation to you, the cause of absolute knowledge, the bridge to all Vedic sciences, and an enemy of those who oppose them. The flow of the Sāṁkhya (principles) causing the knowledge of the absolute truth among the human beings whose minds are overpowered by illusion, is due to you, O lord. O sage, you punish and throw into stocks of lower animals those who give up what is laid down in the Vedas and behave as they like. All regents of quarters like Indra are under your control. Afraid of you, the chastiser, they do what you desire. You, the soul of all, caused the gods to incarnate in each former yuga to destroy those opposing the practices laid down in the three Vedas. O lord, those enemies of gods who were killed by you, gave up their sorrowful bodies and reached Viṣṇu's heaven. O lord of the world, order me to go to heaven. Also favour Indra, with your nectar-like glances, who is bowing to you. O lord of gods, by the favour of you and (the holy place) called Badarī, I have given up my miserable body, and have got a virtuous body. O you treasure of grace, by your favour, I am, after mounting upon the lord of elephants, going to heaven willingly.

The siddha said:

93-96. Thus praising Kapila, the lord of gods, and saluting his feet, the Kaliṅga-king went to heaven. O brāhmaṇa, I, attending upon my preceptor, saw this wonder and also liberation from sin at Badarikāśrama. In the three worlds there is no better holy place giving all (desired) objects. If you desire the highest good, go there with your wife. O brāhmaṇa, to take my old father desiring salvation (and) having no other yearning to Badarī, I am going home.

Nārada said:

97-101. O king, after having narrated the greatness of this excellent holy place called Badarī, the siddha went home. Then after some time that brāhmaṇa (Devadāsa) along with his wife, visiting (various) holy places, reached Indraprastha where the two were taken to his own abode by him (i.e. Vāsudeva) (appearing) in his own body (*corrupt reading*). The siddha also, having quickly brought his father from his house, bathed him, desiring salvation, there only at that excellent holy place. The old father of that siddha, saluted by gods, was also taken to his own abode by Śrī Viṣṇu. This (holy place) called Badarī, is in Indraprastha. The lord would give all the objects desired by the minds of those bathing here. O king of a modest mind, I have described to you its holy greatness. Having heard it, a man will never fall into a mother's womb (i.e. he will bever be reborn).

CHAPTER TWO HUNDRED SEVENTEEN

The Greatness of Haridvāra

The king said:

1-5. O good one, you have described to me the greatness of Badarī, having heard which my mind has become pure, O sage. O best sage, this excellent, wonderful greatness of Śakraprastha gives all the four goals of human life. O Nārada, there is no other holy place than this, which is the best, which gives salvation even to lower animals, which destroys sins just when it is seen. O Nārada, from you, giving delight, I really desire to hear about the greatness of Haridvāra which is in it. O sage, by the description of this holy place situated in Śakraprastha, emancipate me who am a poor person due to wanton deeds indulged in because of ignorance.

Nārada said:

6-19. O illustrious one, listen. I shall describe to you the greatness of Haridvāra, giving the fruit of a horse-sacrifice. I shall tell you today how a sinful cāṇḍāla went to heaven. O lord, listen to it attentively. In Dharmakṣetra Kurukṣetra there lived, outside the city, a sinful cāṇḍāla known as Kāliṅga. He cheated the citizens' boys, five or six years old, forcibly took them to a forest, and killed them there, O king. Having killed them, the mean one took away silver, golden ornaments, and jewels etc. from their bodies. At night he entered the houses of the good to snatch away wealth. Aiming at the wealth of travellers, he killed them in a lonely forest. Once, on the day of a solar eclipse, people desiring to make various presents came to Kurukṣetra from many quarters, O king. O king, having, on that solar eclipse day, duly bathed there, and having duly given presents, the people went home. One, best among merchants, having much wealth, proceeded towards his house after all men. He, seated on a horse, had twenty foot-soldiers in front of him. That great sinner Kāliṅga proceeded after him for (snatching) his wealth. After having traversed (the distance of) a few camps, the mean man, the cāṇḍāla could not wait (as) he did not get an opportunity to rob his wealth. Even with force he was unable to seize his wealth. The merchant was accompanied by twenty men, while he was alone. O king, the sinful (cāṇḍāla) came for (snatching) the merchant's wealth. At night he entered his camp to take away his wealth. But one of the merchant's men keeping a watch, noticed the sinner while entering.

20-25. Seeing him about to give a blow, the man keeping the watch, even while lying, seized him by both his feet, O king. The man, keeping the watch, seizing his feet, and awakening other people, was struck by the thief just with his hand. Other people, hearing (the sound) seized him who was running away. Again striking him who had seized him, he ran away. O king, one of the (merchant's) servants having a bow, struck the mean one who was quickly running, from a distance only. As soon as he was struck by the arrow, he quickly gave up his life. The thief killed two followers of the merchant, O king. The three, getting into excellent vehicles brought by the attendants, remained in the sky, and spoke these words to the merchant.

Kāliṅga and the merchant's servants said:

26-27. O chief merchant, O good one, this Haridvāra is an excellent holy place in Indraprastha which is propitious even to sinners. O merchant, we three who died at this excellent holy place, will now go to heaven. Good luck to you.

Śrī Nārada said:

28-30. O Śibi, speaking like this the three went to heaven, the place of those who do good deeds and where many things of enjoyment are obtained according to (one's) desire. O king, when the night had passed, the merchant burnt the dead bodies of his two servants and dropped their bones here. O king, when the bones were being dropped at this holy place, the two servants came back here from heaven, and said these words to the merchant:

The two servants said:

31-36. O chief of the merchants, O good one, due to death at this holy place on the earth, even sinful beings undoubtedly go to heaven. O merchant, if the bones of a being who dies on a dry land, fall into the water of his holy place, he would stay in Satyaloka. Due to the bones of us who died on a dry land being dropped in the water (of this holy place) we have reached Brahmā's world, and will stay here as long as Brahmā lives (here). Since the bones of the thief who died on a dry ground did not fall in the water of this holy place, he went to heaven, O king. Finding out his body also quickly drop it into (the water of) this place, so that, O best god, he too will obtain our state. Good men should always oblige others. They should never mind even a very bad turn done by the bad.

Nārada said:

37-49. Speaking like this the two illustrious ones went to Viṣṇu's city(?) due to their bones being dropped into the water of the holy place of Haridvāra. O illustrious one, the merchant looked for the thief's body to burn it; but, O king, he did not find it. Again returning to that crest-jewel of all holy places, viz. Haridvāra, O great king, he bathed there only with the desire: 'Having produced good sons, having pleased brāhmaṇas and my kinsmen by (giving them) wealth earned righteously, and having propitiated Viṣṇu by serving him, and having died at you (i.e. at this holy place) only, I shall go to Viṣṇu's abode. O lord of the holy places, salutation to you. You must do this.' With this desire, O king, the merchant bathed with all his servants at that holy place giving all desired objects, and then went home. Having gone there the intelligent one produced sons on his wife and pleased his kinsmen by (giving them) wealth earned righteously. O king, having propitiated Lakṣmī's lord with great devotion, he died at this holy place, due to which he would reach

Vaikuṇṭha. O king, I have thus described to you the greatness of this holy place Haridvāra. Listen to the fruit (obtained) by listening to it. A man would obtain that fruit which he would obtain by giving a droṇa (approximately 30 kilograms) of sesamum seeds (to a brāhmaṇa) in Māgha. The fruit due to listening to (the account of) the greatness of this (holy place) is the same as by giving gopīcandana, and eating from brahma-leaves(?). The same fruit as is obtained on keeping awake in the last watch of the Prabodhinī Ekādaśī would be obtained by listening to (the account of) the greatness of this holy place. There is no other holy place on the earth, giving the fruit of the four goals of human life, like this Haridvāra in Indraprastha.

CHAPTER TWO HUNDRED EIGHTEEN

The Greatness of Puṣkara: Puṇḍarīka's Story

Nārada said:

1-2. O illustrious one, listen to the very wonderful greatness, causing propitiousness, of the holy place Puṣkara, situated here. Viṣṇu, the lord of all gods, being pleased due to the grace of that holy place would live in Puṇḍarīka's house for a month. His younger brother, though engaged in committing sins, obtained salvation here only.

Śibi said:

3-5. Who is that righteous Puṇḍarīka? What act did he do, due to which the lord, being pleased, lived in his house? O sage, tell me all that how his sinful younger brother reached Śrī Hari's place due to the grace of this holy place. Listening to its greatness I am not being satisfied.

Nārada said:

6-9. In the Vidarbha-city, there lived a brāhmaṇa called Mālava, who was very famous, who knew the Vedas, who was tranquil, learned and highly devoted to Viṣṇu, who worshipped deities, sages, dead ancestors, and fed beings and men. He was not addicted to the objects of senses, and was free from greed and folly. Once that illustrious one went to bathe to the very holy Godāvarī, when Jupiter had entered the Zodiacal sign Leo. To offer (to brāhmaṇas) there he took ten thousand palas of gold from his house. The righteous one going along the way thought in his mind:

Mālava said (to himself):

10-16. From my house I have taken ten thousand palas of gold to be given (to brāhmaṇas). They are not to be given to anyone. They are to be given to a respectable good man. That which is given at the proper place and time to a worthy brāhmaṇa who has not rendered any service (to the giver), would be inexhaustible. The righteous sage, himself living by gleaning corn, having given what was obtained by gleaning corn to Durvāsas, gave up his own position, and went to the highest one. King Bali, the lord of the demons, knowing Vāmana to be a worthy recipient, gave him, even his enemy, the three worlds earned with his own arms (i.e. power). Therefore, to please Viṣṇu, I should give my wealth, earned righteously, to a worthy recipient. I should not long for its fruit. My sister's son, the pious Puṇḍarīka, who is the crest-jewel of all worthy recipients, will come when called from (the city) called Gaja. Half of the wealth brought by me I shall give to that worthy recipient, my sister's son. The remaining I shall duly give to learned brāhmaṇas.

Nārada said:

17-21. O king, then that best, pious brāhmaṇa Mālava, reached after a few days the holy Godāvarī. His sister's son, Puṇḍarīka, the pious one, joined him. O king, he had come there before that Mālava. Having duly bathed there, on the day when (the Sun) entered Leo, he gave half of his wealth to Puṇḍarīka, saying, "May Viṣṇu be pleased with me." That pious Puṇḍarīka also, having bathed in the water of Godāvarī, gladly gave the fourth part of his wealth to learned brāhmaṇas. He (i.e. Mālava), having bathed there and given gifts according to his capacity, spoke to his sister's son who was going home, O king:

Mālava said:

22-27. Tell (i.e. convey) my salutation to the elders and blessings to the younger, since, our union here has become (i.e. proved) to be momentary. Similarly our union with our sons, wife is momentary. Therefore, that wise man who gets detached from the mundane existence, where the union is momentary, would certainly be fit for Viṣṇu's favour. Due to viṣṇu's grace, a being would be interested in good company. Then in him is produced a desire to hear about Viṣṇu's playful acts. Having heard Viṣṇu's playful acts narrated by the good, he with a strong desire narrates them and then merely remembers Viṣṇu. Then he has love for serving Viṣṇu's feet. Then a man quickly crosses (the mundane existence) as a great ocean with a raft. For this reason, the good, the wise exert in deeds. O pious one, therefore, you also exert.

Nārada said:

28-34. Thus speaking, he, with his face bedewed with tears, dismissed his sister's son, with his eyes full of tears and went (home). The pious Puṇḍarīka also proceeded to his house. O king, after a few days, he came to this auspicious place. He saw his younger brother called Bharata, fallen on the ground, breathing, and smeared with blood flowing out of his wounds. Weeping loudly, he asked his brother: "Due to what are you reduced to this condition? For what purpose have you come here from (your) house?" O lord of kings, when Puṇḍarīka was asking like this Bharata afflicted by great pain, instantly died. O king, while men and his preceptor were watching, a wonderful vehicle with attendants descended from the sky. Having got into it, that Bharata, though he had committed sins, became one of a divine body, saluted his elder brother, and said these words to him:

Bharata said:

35-44a. O very intelligent Puṇḍarīka, due to the grace of this holy place, Puṣkara, I, though a sinner, secured a position in heaven. O brother, though you know my fierce deed, yet I shall today tell it (again), (because) some (part of it) is unknown to you. I dallied with the prostitute Prabhāvatī, and spent much money on liquor in her house. I lost in gambling whatever wealth I had earned by stealing. I ate the remnants of the offering to Śiva on Śivarātri, for which you blamed a brāhmaṇa named Jebuka. O Puṇḍarīka, you know this deed which I did. O brother, you do not know the deed which I did when you went to Godāvarī. I shall tell you that also. When you had left, and a fortnight had passed, I learnt from people words difficult to be borne by a man, viz. that the maternal uncle had called Puṇḍarīka to give him wealth. 'Having killed Puṇḍarīka, my uterine brother, I shall snatch away the wealth taken by him which (our) maternal uncle has given him; and with that great wealth I shall please Prabhāvatī. I shall play with a gamester and those who know it (i.e. gambling).'

44b-47. Thinking like this I remained blocking your way, to kill you and to take much wealth from you, O you very intelligent one. When the wealth was (to be) taken possession of (by me), O brother, from somewhere a caravan of merchants came, where I had slept at night, O very intelligent one. Then at night a thief entered the place full of the men of the caravan to snatch the wealth of the merchants. When the thief, after having taken some wealth, ran away the servants, crying, suddenly ran after him.

The servants said:

48. Catch him, catch him. He is a thief going away hurriedly after having snatched much wealth in the midst of us (though) many.

Bharata said:

49-54. O brother, having heard these words of them, I suddenly ran after him in front of them with a desire to seize whatever he had snatched. Then the merchants' servants with swords in their hands, taking me to be his protector, and having a sword in my hand, struck me quickly. I, a sinner, killed an excellent brāhmaṇa among them (though he was) saying, 'I am a brāhmaṇa', with a sharp-edged sword. The merchants' servants killed me with edges of swords (i.e. sharp-edged swords). In the morning the merchants went to the kingdom where they wanted to go. Then you came here and saw me breathing and with my body smeared with blood flowing (from the wounds), and dead due to unconsciousness caused by the injury. O brother, I have thus told you what for I had come here, and I have also told you how I met with a premature death.

CHAPTER TWO HUNDRED NINETEEN

The Greatness of Puṣkara; Puṇḍarīka Attains Absorption into Viṣṇu

Nārada said:

1. Hearing these words of him, the noble-minded Puṇḍarīka spoke to his brother, when his companions were listening:

Puṇḍarīka said:

2. O Bharata, tell me if you know due to which religious merit you died at this holy place. Your sin is quite well-known.

Bharata said:

3-7. O Puṇḍarīka, listen. I am telling you which religious merit I did in this existence, which gave (i.e. brought) me (to) this holy place. Once, after having snatched wealth, I, while coming back to my house, saw a dead, helpless child of someone in the market. Putting it on my head, taking it to the auspicious bank of Gaṅgā and adorning it with a garment etc. I performed his funeral rites like burning his body. I spent all the wealth I had obtained through gambling. Due to that religious merit I secured (i.e. I reached) this holy place, bringing auspiciousness. Perform funeral rites of my body after burning it.

Śrī Nārada said:

8-16. O king, when the funeral rites were performed, even the sinful Bharata went to heaven by the favour of this holy place. Now listen as to how Viṣṇu, Hari, lived for a month in Puṇḍarīka's house by the favour of this holy place. The pious one seeing that Bharata got felicity at this holy place, thought in his mind that this holy place gives desired objects. That wise Puṇḍarīka bathed at this holy place with this desire: 'May Viṣṇu in his original form live in my house during the month of Māgha'. Having bathed with this desire he went home. O best king, Puṇḍarīka told his brothers about the death of Bharata at this holy place giving all (desired) objects. They too, with their minds covered by Māyā, having heard it, lamented. Then Puṇḍarīka, doing his (usual) rites at home, and being highly delighted, lived in his house thinking that Viṣṇu would come due to his penance. On the full-moon day of Pauṣa he celebrated a great festival, thinking that Hari would certainly come to his house the next day. He adorned his house by sprinkling it with sandal mixed with water, smearing it with cow-dung, and by arranging the quadrangle with pearls. He fed two hundred brāhmaṇas with various kinds of food. He gratified them with profuse presents.

17-21. Singing at night with those skilled in playing on various musical instruments and singing sweet songs, he kept awake with his kinsmen. In the morning having dismissed all those singers etc., he with his mind longing for Viṣṇu's arrival sat in his house. Then sending back his vehicle from the vicinity of his (i.e. Puṇḍarīka's) house, he (i.e. Viṣṇu) entered his house to do what was desired by his man. That Puṇḍarīka, having seen that Viṣṇu to have arrived, quickly got up from his seat, and saluted him by (bending down) his head, O king. That pious one, delighted to see Viṣṇu, having worshipped him by offering him materials of worship etc. said to him, seated on a seat:

Puṇḍarīka said:

22-29. You have very clearly done what removes the torment of the mundane existence. O Viṣṇu, you, causing preservation, stay here, till this pure penance would come to an end. Your Vaikuṇṭha, free from all blemishes, exists there only where all your servants, serving (you) live. We have heard from the mouths of the good that, O lord, Viṣṇu lives in that house where your deeds are described. They indeed are the good, in whose speech remains your name, in whose hearts remains your handsome form, and in whose ears remain your virtues. They indeed are the good whose heart (longs) for your service, and on whose heads are the remains of an offering to you. O lord of Lakṣmī, they alone are the good whose mind (views equally) their enemy and their friend, so also their gain and loss. O lord of Lakṣmī, they alone are the good whose mind is not affected by emotions. The good live where you live; you live where the good live. So knowing (me) to be good live in my house during (the month of) Māgha.

Nārada said:

30. Viṣṇu, having heard these words of that Puṇḍarīka, and brightening the quarters with the lustre of his teeth, said (these) words:

The lord said:

31-33. O you very intelligent one, you are the best among the virtuous men on the earth, since with a desire for my company you bathed at the holy place. O brāhmaṇa, get up. Bathe in the water of Gaṅgā in Māgha. At the end of Māgha, on the full-moon day, I shall bathe you at Puṣkara. All that entire fruit due to bathing in the month of Māgha at Prayāga, would be (obtained) due to bathing (just) on one day at the holy place, Puṣkara.

Nārada said:

34-42a. That best brāhmaṇa, Puṇḍarīka, thus addressed by Viṣṇu, bathed in the water of Gaṅgā, when the sun had slightly risen. Puṇḍarīka actually worshipped the lotus-eyed (Viṣṇu) with tulasī(-leaves), blooming flowers, barley, saffron, sandal, and he waved five lights of camphor before the lord of Lakṣmī, whose body was made fragrant with incenses of agaru. Having fed the lord of the world with four kinds of food, he fanned him lying on a jewelled bed with chowries. He shampooed the feet of the lord of Lakṣmī. He gave him a tāmbūla with camphor. Taking a mirror in his hand the best brāhmaṇa stood in front of Lakṣmī's lord when he was tying the turban. Thus the brāhmaṇa passed the entire month of Māgha in worshipping (Viṣṇu) destroying the mundane existence and living in his house. Then on the full-moon day at the end of Māgha, he saw Garuḍa waiting in front of him, who had come there on merely being remembered by the lord of Lakṣmī. Seeing him, the lotus-eyed (Viṣṇu) said to Puṇḍarīka:

The lord said:

42b-46. O best brāhmaṇa, listen to the words which I am speaking to you. I have given you—viz. that I lived (in your house) for a month—(what was desired by you), when you had by chance gone to the holy place Puṣkara situated in Indraprastha for a bath. O you very intelligent one, today having mounted upon the lord of birds with me go to that Puṣkara (again) which is the crest-jewel of all holy places. O brāhmaṇa, since I am at your disposal, I shall give you, bathing at the place giving the four goals of human life, whatever you desire. Your brother Bharata, though a sinner, desiring heaven got it when he died there. What else can be spoken about him?

Nārada said:

47-52. O lord of kings, having thus spoken to the best brāhmaṇa and putting him on the lord of birds, he came to that best holy place. From Puṇḍarīka's body a flash went out along with his vital breath and reached Viṣṇu's position. O king, Puṇḍarīka, by means of a bath at the holy place Puṣkara, situated in Indraprastha, obtained absorption into the lord. Thus by the solicitation of the holy place, even Viṣṇu happily lived in his house like his relative. Who can describe the greatness of Puṣkara situated in Indraprastha? I have described only a part equal to one fraction of a crore. O king, by devoutly listening to or by reciting the greatness, a man obtains the fruit of a horse-sacrifice.

CHAPTER TWO HUNDRED TWENTY

The Greatness of Prayāga: Mohinī's Story

Nārada said:

1-4. To you I am describing devoutly the very meritorious greatness of the auspicious Prayāga, the principal among holy places. O king, there was a gandharva (named) Viśvāvasu, well-known in the world. Once he went to Brahmā's assembly on Sumeru to sing. Viśvāvasu saw there the lord of gods resorted to by all hosts of gods, seated on an excellent seat, O king. O king, near the seat of Brahmā he saw Indraprastha, as if it was another lord of the world, seated on an excellent seat.

5-8. He saw the lord of gods and the chief of holy places waving chowries on the heads of Brahmaprastha and Indraprastha, O king. O king, he also saw there other divine holy places, standing with the palms of their hands joined in obeisance, at a distance from the two. In front of the two he sang an excellent Gāndharva-rāga. Leaving the gods he went to Satyaloka with the holy places. Then, O lord of kings, the intelligent Viśvāvasu, seeing the grandeur of the holy place Indraprastha, spoke these words to Hāhā.

Viśvāvasu said:

9-13. O best of gandharvas, in the world this holy place called Indraprastha is very wonderful among the heaps of (i.e. many) holy places, since he was seated on a seat near that of Brahmā who is the lord of the movable and the immovable, and whose lotus-like feet are saluted by the gods. Even the chief of the holy places standing behind, waved chowries on his head, (thus) becoming his servant. Then what can be said about other holy places? (All) the holy places that are there grant as a fruit (of a visit to them) the three goals of human life; but this holy place Indraprastha grants (all) the four goals. The holy places stationed here are Dhruva in merits. Their great merits cannot be described even by Śeṣa.

Nārada said:

14. O king, the intelligent Viśvāvasu, seeing the grandeur of Indraprastha like this, which was purifying and giving all desired objects, went home.

15-20. As Śakra, lord of Śacī, is the greatest among gods, and Brahmā is superior to him, so is this Prayāga the best of all holy places. Indraprastha is superior even to that, O great king. O king, I shall tell you the account of the prostitute Mohinī, which took place at Prayāga which is seen within it. O king, on the bank of river Narmadā there is the city Māhiṣmatī. In it was a prostitute named Mohinī, who had ample wealth, was endowed with beauty and youth, and skilled in dancing and singing.

She, greedy of wealth, committed many sins. She killed seven brāhmaṇas and many maid servants. She, the sinful one, also many times caused their abortions. In this way she passed her good (i.e. valuable) youth in sinful acts.

21-28. Then after some time old age came to her body. She with her body afflicted by old age and with her desire for sensual objects gone, did not have a longing for young men, nor did they have (any longing) for her, O king. About her wealth, earned sinfully, she did not confide in anyone. She did not give it (to anyone); she did not enjoy it herself; she did not deposit it somewhere. Once, at night, she being awakened, thought like this: 'Whose will this wealth earned sinfully be when I am dead? It will take me to a dreadful hell. The maid servants and their husbands will enjoy that wealth of me. Then now, why should I not make a good use of it?' Thinking like this, she resolved upon doing righteous acts and constructed gardens, tanks, wells, reservoirs of water and temples. Near the city she fixed a place where water is distributed to travellers in summer; and she gave them food (also), O great king. Near her house she put up a guest house for foreigners to stay in. And she also gave them excellent food.

29-37. O king, when that Mohinī was thus engaged in righteous acts, in course of time old age came to her, and sometime she thought: 'Though I have spent much money on righteous acts, yet I still have much more wealth in (the form of) gold, silver etc. I shall voluntarily give it to learned brāhmaṇas.' Thus she thought. Thinking like this Mohinī invited the brāhmaṇas of the city. O king, when they, realising that the acceptance of the wealth from her was fearful, she divided her wealth into two parts. O king, she gave one part to her maid servants and the other to foreigners. She herself became destitute. Knowing that her death was imminent, her maid servants left her, took the wealth, and went (away) as they liked thinking that wealth which would be given by her when she would be free from fever (was already with them). She, after having observed eighteen fasts, was then free from fever, as (a part of the span of) her life was still left, O king. O king, she had one maid named Jaradgavā. Being careful, she actively waited upon her with (i.e. by giving her) salutary diet etc.

38-43. After a few days she was fit to take full diet. With (a sense of) shame she ate in the house of that Jaradgavā. 'Here (i.e. in the world) I have lived happily. Now misery has come to me. I shall not live in poverty.' Thinking like this, she went elsewhere. While she was going to a forest, the thieves of the city, thinking 'This is Mohinī, going after taking wealth', struck her. O king, not finding wealth with her, they left her breathing in that very forest. Then, O king, some anchorite, carrying water from Prayāga in a water-pot came to the forest. Then seeing her fallen with her body wounded by weapons and asking for the water by means of signs made by her hand,

The anchorite said:

44-50. Who are you? Who has wounded your body with sharp weapons? Why have you, all alone, come to this lonely forest? O auspicious one, with a desire to do good this water of Prayāga, situated in Indraprastha, is brought by me due to good luck.

Thus addressed by him, she, unable to speak, opened her mouth to drink water, with the desire, 'May I be a queen'. O king, when this water of Prayāga was dropped into her mouth, that prostitute Mohinī gave up her life. At the time of her departure she longed for the status of a queen. Therefore, she, being born in the house of the lord of Kerala, became due to drinking the water of the holy place, the wife of king Vīravarman endowed with (good) family, (good) character, wealth, prosperity, in the Draviḍa country. The lotus-eyed one had a body yellowish like gold. Therefore, her father named her 'Hemāṅgī'.

51-53. Once that Hemāṅgī, adorned with golden ornaments, went to the house of Kalā, her friend and the minister's daughter. There she was bathed (after being smeared) with barley oil, was fed with various foods, and was seated on an excellent seat. With her braid tied with flowers, and adorned with thin silken garments, and having a tāmbūla in her mouth, she said to Kalā:

Hemāṅgī said:

54. O Kalā, speaking sweetly but indistinctly like a cuckoo, understand my words. Show me the thing which is wonderful in your house.

CHAPTER TWO HUNDRED TWENTYONE

The Greatness of Prayāga: Hemāṅgī and Vīravarman Go to Vaikuṇṭha

Nārada said:

1-3. O king, that Kalā, thus addressed by the king's wife, got brought a golden box from her treasure, and put it before (her). She said, "O queen, O wife of the great king, this is a very wonderful book. There are pictures in it. Having opened the book a little, see what it contains. By seeing the pictures in it your mind will be delighted."

4-12. Thus addressed by her, the queen got the box opened by her maid and took with her hand the book that was in it. In it she first saw succinctly (the pictures of) the incarnations. Then she saw the globe having an expanse of fifty crores of yojanas. In it she saw a region full of darkness. Between the two stood the Lokāloka mountain, O king. Then she saw the seven islands surrounded by seven seas. So also in them, she saw rivers, mountains and continents, O very wise one. The wife of the king saw this Bhāratakhaṇḍa. She saw the chief rivers like Yamunā, Gaṅgā. O king, the illustrious one saw this auspicious Indraprastha along with Vraja on the bank of Yamunā. O king, the high-minded one seeing in it the holy place fashioned by Brahmā, recollected the act(s) done by her in her former birth. Then silently getting up she, determining, 'I shall not eat (food) till I leave for the holy place', hurriedly went home. Then only, that Hemāṅgī, loving the chief holy place, said to king Vīravarman, dear to her like her own life:

Hemāṅgī said:

13-19. O lord of my life, listen to my righteous words, and carry them out quickly, O illustrious one. (My desire) will be fulfilled. Formerly I was a prostitute. I committed many sins in my youth and in my old age I had a mind to do pious acts. I spent righteously the wealth I had earned sinfully. O king, when I who was penniless, went out of my city and was going in a forest, thieves who were sinful, who were tormented by improper poverty, struck me, with a desire to grab (my) wealth. The thieves, with their desires frustrated, leaving me, with my body wounded with sharp weapons, and breathing (but) unconscious, there, went (away). Then an anchorite carrying the water of Prayāga situated in Indraprastha, came into that forest. The ascetic seeing me lying in that condition there asked me: "Who are you? Wherefrom (have you come)? Why and by whom were you hit?"

20-24. I then did not say anything, but asked for that holy water. He put it into my mouth, and I abandoned (my) body. Hearing that that water fulfils all desires, I desired, O lord, at the time of the departure of my life: 'May I be (born as) a queen.' Due to the grace of that holy place I became your wife practising acts of a good family and of a very good character. O king, now I desire to see, along with you, that chief holy place Prayāga situated in Indraprastha and giving all desired objects. O king, I have taken this pledge that I shall eat food only when I proceed to that chief holy place, O lord.

The king said:

25. O you of unsteady eyes, how would I know (to be true) what you said? Convince me, O good one; I would do what you said.

Nārada said:

26a. When the king said like this, there was a voice in the sky.

The divine voice said:

26b-27. O king, your wife has spoken the truth. Having gone to the auspicious Prayāga, the best of all holy places situated in Indraprastha, bathe there; you will get whatever you desire.

Nārada said:

28-33. Having heard the words coming from the sky the king prostrated himself on the ground like a staff, and said, "I salute him who spoke those words." Then having called his minister, and having entrusted the kingdom to him, he, getting into an excellent chariot, went with her to the excellent holy place. After a few days the king came here with Hemāṅgī. The king with his wife drank the water at the chief holy place. The couple bathed there at that auspicious holy place, giving all desired objects, desiring 'May I reach Vaikuṇṭha with this body.' When the couple had just bathed there, the best gods (Brahmā and Viṣṇu) having the swan and the eagle respectively as their vehicles arrived there. Seeing them who had come there, that king Vīravarman, with a concentrated mind, saluted by (bowing) his head, and praised them.

The king said:

34-41. Salutation to you, O best gods, having dark and tawny bodies and wearing garments like gold and red lead. I salute you, having mainly (qualities of) sattva and rajas, the wonderful lords of Vaikuṇṭha and Satyaloka, having four and two hands, and carried by best birds. I salute by (bowing) my head bent through good thoughts, you, giving good liberation and pleasures to men having detachment and attachment, and with your lotus-like feet saluted by gods. O you whose lotus-like feet are saluted by gods, nobody knows your original form, since you are beyond Prakṛti and transcend the mind and speech of man. O you highest soul, that man is blessed who, thinking this world to be transitory, resorts to your lotus-like feet saluted by hosts of sages. This holy place, where your feet are resorted to, is indeed difficult to be reached by men worshipping you, and it gives all desired objects. Yet these two are to be resorted to for salvation, not secured through any other (means). He who resorts to it with any other desire (than salvation) is (indeed) duped. Desiring to conquer all worlds the good, resorting to you and to this place giving salvation, do not long for anything except it.

Nārada said:

42. When having thus praised the lord of gods and the lord of the worlds, the king remained (silent), then that Hemāṅgī spoke, O king:

Hemāṅgī said:

43-46. O lord of Lakṣmī, O you having eyes like lotus petals, O Brahman having a high seat, and venerable to Sarasvatī, I salute you; if you favour me of a mean heart, then (help me to) cross this ocean of the mundane existence. O lord, due to the grace of this holy place I became a queen. I had your view difficult to be had even by gods. You two know the hearts of all; you have given us the best, which we two had longed for at the time of bathing.

The best gods, thus praised by both, had their faces pleased, and they said to the couple:

Viṣṇu and Brahmā said:

47-48. O Hemāṅgī, you are blessed since you, due to the contact with this holy place, have emancipated your husband whose mind was attached to the pleasures of the kingdom. Such a salvation is difficult to get for kings attached to objects of senses. Your husband has a wife like you due to the grace of this holy place.

Nārada said:

49-53. Speaking like this, and looking at Garuḍa, the best of birds, the two best gods (and the couple) went to Satyaloka, O lord of men. There they (the couple) were all duly honoured by Brahmā, O king. Then they stayed there for some time at the request of him. O king, then with the couple Viṣṇu, mounting on Garuḍa, went to Śrī Vaikuṇṭha. O king, I have thus told you the greatness of the chief holy place, which is meritorious, destroys all sins, leads to success and gives sons. A man who would listen to or read this account daily would go to his desired place. I have told the truth.

CHAPTER TWO HUNDRED TWENTYTWO

Kāśī, Gokarṇa, Śivakāñcī, Tīrthasaptaka and Bhīmakuṇḍa

Nārada said:

1-8. O king Śibi, listen. I am describing to you the excellent, meritorious greatness of Kāśī giving success and long life. O king, formerly in the auspicious Kṛtayuga there was a tree called śiṁśapā in Kāśī situated on the slope of Indraprastha. There was a crow that had made its nest on the tree; and below it in the hollow (of the tree) lived a great serpent. Once his wife laid a couple of eggs in the nest and went somewhere. She did not come back to her nest. O king, that crow took care of the couple of eggs; lived high up on that śiṁśapā tree only. Once at night a great storm came and it broke the śiṁśapā tree from its root though strong. Then at the root of the śiṁśapā tree shattered by the storm, the crow and the serpent were crushed and died. The tree, śiṁśapā tree, (the serpent and) the crow etc. had divine bodies, and getting into three aeroplanes, went to Viṣṇu's abode.

Śibi said:

9. O divine sage, due to what religious merit did they reach the city giving salvation? Who were they before that? Tell (me) all that, O Nārada.

Nārada said:

10-14. There was a brāhmaṇa named Śravaṇa in the Kurujāṅgala country. His wife was Kuṇḍā by name, and his brother was Kuranṭaka. That Śravaṇa ate, without having bathed (first), sweetmeats. Due to that sin he became (i.e. was born as) a village crow. His brother Kuranṭaka was a strong atheist. He stopped (following) the path laid down by Śrutis and Smṛtis, and censured deities. Due to that fault he became a deadly serpent after his death. Śravaṇa's wife Kuṇḍā shared the sins of both (of them). Therefore, she got the condition of an immobile object (viz. the tree) which was resorted to by both (Śravaṇa and Kuranṭaka). O king, I have told you this that happened in their former existence.

15-20. Hereafter I shall tell you about their religious merit due to which they reached the charming city of the lord of the world, viz. Kāśī, O king. Once they were returning home from another village. Seeing the cow of a traveller fallen into a well and being urged by him they took her out. Hearing what they told, Kuṇḍā said: 'Well (done).' Due to that religious merit they met with death at Kāśī, on the slope of Indraprastha, which is difficult to have, and went up to Vaikuṇṭha. O king, I have told you this excellent greatness of Kāśī. Tell me what else you desire to hear.

Śibi said:

21-22. O sage, you mentioned three holy places of Śiva: Kāśī and Śivakāñcī, and the other (i.e. the third) one, viz. Gokarṇa. O great sage, you have told me the greatness of one viz. Kāśī, Tell me, if there is any, the greatness of Gokarṇa and Śivakāñcī.

Nārada said:

23-30. O king, Gokarṇa is a very purifying holy place of Śiva only. A man dying there would be Śiva; there is no doubt about it. If a being would die there on land, in water or in the air, he after becoming Śiva, shines on the peak of Kailāsa. One dying here at the holy place of Gokarṇa is not born again. Shining like Śiva, one obtains salvation at any time. O king, O lord, O very intelligent one, I shall describe to you the greatness of this Gokarṇa also, which I had heard from Brahmā's mouth. This frontier mountain of a meritorious appearance is seen near Gurutīrtha at a distance of two miles from Prayāga. On it was a very cruel bhilla named Karkaṭa. His wife was Jarā by name. She had killed (her) five husbands. That Jarā prepared a sweetmeat (mixed) with poison to kill Karkaṭa, (her) sixth husband. The noble bhilla heard about it from the mouth of his sister. That very cruel Karkaṭa set about killing that young woman.

31-39a. When the king of the bhillas, with a sword in his hand, came to kill her, she, realising that he was ready to kill her, went (away). Being frightened and desiring (to save) her life she ran to a forest. That Karkaṭa, with a sword in his hand, seized her here at the holy place of Gokarṇa. Having cut off her head with the sword, and having dropped her body into the water of the holy place Gokarṇa, he went to his place. That sinful Jarā also met with death there at Gokarṇa. She became the friend of Pārvatī on the peak of Kailāsa. I have told you this glory of Gokarṇa. I shall describe to you the holy greatness of Śivakāñcī. O lord, the same bliss which I told (is obtained) in Gokarṇa is also obtained in Śivakāñcī situated on the slope of Indraprastha. Here god Śiva, on propitiating Viṣṇu, the lord of all gods, obtained the status of the chief devotee and metaphysical knowledge.

Therefore, we all, the sons of Brahman, always propitiate him, with a desire to get good devotion and knowledge.

39b-48. O king, here the demon Bāṇa, observing a fast, propitiated Maheśvara for a hundred years with a desire to have qualities like him. The god was pleased with him and gave him the status of his attendant. And he himself became forever the protector of his city. O king, this city formerly belonged to the magnanimous Viṣṇu. Viṣṇu, pleased with the penance of Śiva, gave it to him. Here formerly a very wonderful event took place. A brāhmaṇa, a devotee of Śiva, reached Vaikuṇṭha here. O king, there was a religious brāhmaṇa by name Heramba. With his body, mind and words he was always engaged in worshipping Śiva. O king Śibi, once the noble one, Śiva's devotee, while visiting places holy to Śiva, came here to Śivakāñcī. The intelligent one did not leave this charming (holy place). Later he died in its water. There only the attendants of Mahādeva (i.e. Śiva) took the best brāhmaṇa and proceeded to the Kailāsa mountain by his (i.e. Śiva's) order. In the middle came the attendants of Viṣṇu from Vaikuṇṭha. They forcibly set out to take that best brāhmaṇa from them. There was a great battle between the attendants of Viṣṇu and Śiva.

49-56. In that battle none got victory or defeat. Viṣṇu, seated on Garuḍa, came there from Vaikuṇṭha. Śiva, the supporter of the three worlds, seated on his bull, also (came) there from Kailāsa. Then the two looking at each other's face, laughed (i.e. smiled) and only watched the great battle waged by their attendants in the sky. Then Viṣṇu warded his own attendants and those of Śiva off the battle in the sky, and putting the brāhmaṇa on Garuḍa, Viṣṇu went to Śiva's abode, surrounded by Śiva, Śiva's attendants and his own attendants. The glorious one while going along the way was saluted by gods. Led by Śiva he entered his abode, showing the brāhmaṇa the beauty of it. Then from that Kailāsa, Viṣṇu, saluted by Śiva with great devotion went to Vaikuṇṭha. The glorious brāhmaṇa also obtained the sight of Viṣṇu due to the grace of this holy place and enjoyed in the vicinity of Viṣṇu. O king, I have told you this grandeur of Śivakāñcī.

57-64. Listen very attentively to (the holy place) named Tīrthasaptaka. O great king, this holy place gives the fruit of the four goals of human life (to one who) visits it, comes in its contact, thinks about it or even (merely) remembers it. O king, great sages like Vasiṣṭha stayed there and practised severe penance for the creation. The religious Marīci also bathed here for (getting) a son; and the glorious one obtained an excellent son, viz. Kaśyapa. Atri also pleased here the best gods by his penance, and obtained three sons from them—Soma, Durvāsas and Datta. The pious Aṅgiras also obtained, due to the favour of this holy place, sons. They, the brāhmaṇas, viz. the Āṅgirasas, were born in his family. Pulaha also got a son, Dambholi, of excellent virtues, who was, O king, Agastya in olden times. By bathing in this holy place Pulastya, practising penance, got a son, the glorious Kubera, Śiva's friend. Kratu too had thousands of sons (called) Vālakhilyas.

65-67. Due to the favour of this holy place they were perpetual celibates. Vasiṣṭha too, practising severe penance, got seven sons, Raja and others. O best king, I have described its greatness. O king, there are many other holy places also, like Kapilāśrama, Kedāra, Prabhāsa. O king, their greatness cannot be described even by Ananta even during a million years; then how (can it be described) by (persons) like me?

Saubhari said:

68-71. Having spoken like this, Nārada, the best sage, extolling Viṣṇu's virtues went to Śiva from the sky. O king, Auśīnara Śibi, having heard about the grandeur of Indraprastha from the sage's mouth, regarded himself blessed. The king, having duly bathed there at Indraprastha, and having performed all auspicious rites, went to his city. O lord, I have described to you the greatness of Indraprastha, the holy place purifying people and situated on the bank of Yamunā.

72-77. O best king, in Kali (age), people, void of faith, will not have regard for this Indraprastha, the crest-jewel of all holy places. That fruit which is obtained by listening to the eighteen Purāṇas and Bhārata is produced by (listening to) the greatness of Indraprastha. That fruit which is obtained by means of a lakh of baths at dawn in the month of Māgha would be had by devoutly listening to (the description of) the greatness of this (holy place). O king, he who devoutly listens to (the description of) its greatness, would gratify his dead ancestors, gods and sages. That fruit which is had by means of the vows like Kṛcchra, Atikṛcchra, Parāka, and Cāndrāyaṇa, would be had by devoutly listening to (the description of) its greatness. O king, that fruit which is due to all sacrifices like the horse-sacrifice would be had by devoutly listening to (the description of) its greatness.

Sūta said:

78-80. King Yudhiṣṭhira having thus heard the greatness of Indraprastha from Śaunaka Saubhari, went to Hastināpura. Then having instructed his brothers led by Duryodhana, he went to the auspicious Indraprastha with a desire to perform a Rājasūya sacrifice. Having brought from Dvārakā, Kṛṣṇa, his family-deity, the king performed the Rājasūya sacrifice.

81-85. Thinking that this holy place could give salvation even to the abusive (Śiśupāla), Kṛṣṇa killed Śiśupāla there. Śiśupāla too, due to dying at that holy place only, got absorbed into Kṛṣṇa, giving all (desired) objects. Bhīma fashioned a very extensive pool at the place where Śiśupāla was killed, and the (Rājasūya) sacrifice was performed. Bhīma fashioned there a very extensive pool with his mace. It is known as Bhīmakuṇḍa, and has become purifying on the earth. There is no doubt that that fruit which is had by bathing in Yamunā at Indraprastha is had (by bathing) in that pool.

Sūta said:

86-90. That holy place will forgive the faults of a living being who stays there by practices like going round it for a year. The man who goes round it every year, would not be tinged with the evils (committed) at the holy place and sins. He who does not go round (it) does not get sanctification at the holy place. Therefore, those who desire a fruit should go round it. He who reciting Viṣṇu's names goes round it, obtains at every step the fruit of presenting a brown cow. The man who goes round Indraprastha on the fourteenth day of the dark half of Caitra, is blessed, and is freed from all sins.

CHAPTER TWO HUNDRED TWENTYTHREE

Gem of a Formula

Śaunaka said:

1-2. O glorious Sūta, you are blessed that you make us, plunged very much in the ocean of the mundane existence, drink a large quantity of nectar. O good one, tell us, desiring to cross the worldly existence, the gem of a formula, pure due to devotion, of which the mobile and the immobile are full.

Sūta said:

3-4. O Śaunaka, listen. I shall tell you the very wonderful gem of a formula, which the noble Vasiṣṭha spoke to Dilīpa. Once Dilīpa having saluted Vasiṣṭha, the best brāhmaṇa, his preceptor, asked him as you did (now).

Dilīpa said:

5-9. O revered one, you have particularly told me all the practices, so also practices with those of castes and the stages of life and the daily and occasional obligatory rites. O best sage, I have also heard the kingly duties, sacrifices, gifts (to be made) at holy places and vows etc., which give inexhaustible pleasures in heaven. Now I desire to hear about the ancient path leading to salvation. Tell me about it along which I can luckily go. What is the best of all sacred formulas, the only medicine for all the diseases in the worldly existence? What is the best formula giving salvation to all human beings? Tell all that truthfully and for the love and regard (that you have) for me.

Vasiṣṭha said:

10-11. O king, you desiring the good of all the world, have asked well. I shall, in private, tell you a great secret, emancipating (you) from the worldly existence. Formerly all holy sages intent on (performing) sacrifices and (giving) gifts, asked Nārada, Brahmā's son, the best sage:

The great sages said:

12. O revered one, by what formula shall we go to the

highest position? O glorious one, tell that to us. Please favour us.

Nārada said:

13. Formerly all meditating saints—Sanaka and others—asked in private Brahmā about the path to salvation, very difficult to be obtained.

Brahmā said:

14-20a. O meditating saints, listen to this wonderful secret. All gods and sages having penance as their wealth do not know it. The immutable god Nārāyaṇa told it to me at the beginning of the creation. He, along with the great goddess was worshipped by me. Then the immutable Nārāyaṇa was pleased with me. He gave me the status of the creator and all the literature having its origin in the Veda, so also illuminating formulas, pervasive and non-pervasive. Then I spoke to the god, the ancient Puruṣottama (i.e. Viṣṇu): "O revered one, by what formula (can) men cross the mundane existence? Tell me about it truly for the good of all people. Which of all formulas, is the one without (i.e. not requiring) initiatory rite, which gives men the highest place (even) by being uttered once (only)?"

The lord said:

20b-27. O glorious one, you, desiring the good of all the people, have asked well. Therefore, I shall tell you the secret by means of which men would reach me. Of all the formulas the gem of a formula is auspicious. It gives the highest position even when it is remembered just once. The two gems of (i.e. in) the formula (are:) Lakṣmī, Nārāyaṇa). *Nyāsa* (assignment?), *Prayati* (purification?) and *Śaraṇāgati* (approaching for shelter?) are necessary. The formula 'Lakṣmī-Nārāyaṇa' gives all fruits. Understand in succession the names of the gem of a formula(?). Merely by its utterance I am always pleased. A man born in a (noble) family, an ascetic, one who has mastered the Vedas and Vedāṅgas, one who is given to (performing) sacrifices and (giving) gifts, one resorting to all holy places, so also one who has taken a vow, one who speaks the truth, or even an ascetic having knowledge—is not entitled to the formula. He should carefully avoid it.

Brāhmaṇas, kṣatriyas, vaiśyas, women, and others—all are entitled to it if they are my devotees.

28-33. The excellent formula should be given to those who do not seek the shelter of any other (deity than Viṣṇu), who do not serve any other (deity than Viṣṇu), who do not (try to) reach any other (deity than Viṣṇu). Even if recited once it gives a quick fruit to the afflicted. It keeps away another (i.e. re-)birth even of haughty beings. (If) an afflicted person, or an inquisitive person, or one longing for wealth, or a wise person or a king seeks my shelter (but) once, he would obtain all his desired objects. It should not be told to him who is not initiated, to him who is not a devotee, to a proud person, to an atheist, to a greedy person, to one who is averse to (i.e. who has no) faith. It should not be told to him who has no desire to listen (to it); to him who does not abide by Śiva, to him who is free from lust, anger, hypocrisy, greed, so also to him who resorts to me with steady devotion, this excellent gem of a formula should be duly told.

34-37. (The devotee should observe) rules with regard to place and time, (should have) exact determination of foes and friends, (should know) the nyāsa,[1] mudrā[2] etc., along with the initiatory rite; he should have his body marked with (the impression of) my disc, so also do my worship, should dedicate his actions to me, should seek my shelter only. With great confidence in me he should assign all fruits to me. He should not possess anything. He should avoid talking to non-devotees of Viṣṇu or saluting them. He should also avoid saluting or worshipping other deities than (me).

38-44. Rules like this are declared for him who submits himself (to me). To a man endowed with such qualities, the excellent gem of a formula should be told. I, Nārāyaṇa, ancient Viṣṇu, am its seer; so also I, the ocean of affection, am its deity, along with Lakṣmī. I, Nārāyaṇa, the lord of the entire world, the glorious one, of a good character, fortunate, omniscient, omnipotent, with my desires always fulfilled, omnipresent, having every-

1. Nyāsa: Assignment of the various parts of the body to different deities which is usually accompanied by prayer and corresponding gesticulations.

2. Mudrā: Certain positions of the fingers practised in devotion or religious worship.

one as my relative, ocean of the nectar of pity am with Lakṣmī said to be its deity. Its metre is said to be the goddess Gāyatrī, having twentyfive syllables. He should twice assign seven, six, three, five, two or six limbs(?) He should meditate upon me, along with Lakṣmī not separated from me, of the form of the universe, having in my hands a disc, a conch, a mace, and a lotus, and of a divine form. He, being restrainted and pure, should worship me along with Lakṣmī seated on my left lap, with this gem of a formula, and with sandal, flowers and offerings. O lord of the beings, even if I am worshipped once I am pleased.

Brahmā said:

45-48. O lord, you have properly told this excellent secret, so also the power of the gem of a formula, which gives every success to men. You are the father of all the worlds, so also their mother and preceptor. You are the master, friend, brother, recourse, refuge and friend. O lord of gods, I am your servant, disciple and friend. Therefore, O you ocean of pity, you told this excellent (formula) to me. Now with the desire for the good of all people, tell fully accurately the initiation of this gem of a formula for its proper practice.

The lord said:

49-54. O child, listen, I shall tell you the great rite of the initiation of this gem of a formula. To secure my resort, a man should first resort to a preceptor. The preceptor (should be) endowed with (the knowledge of) the Veda, (should be) Viṣṇu's devotee, free from jealousy, (should) know the formula, (should be) devoted to the formula, (should) always resort to the formula and (be) pure. He should belong to a good school; he should be proficient in the science of Brahman. He should not follow any other (deity than me); should not have any other aim (than me). He should be a brāhmaṇa, free from anger, attachment, and greed. He should teach good behaviour, should long for salvation, and should know the highest soul. A preceptor, a friendly one, having these qualities, who would teach (good) practices is called a preceptor. He who depends upon his preceptor when taught good behaviour, is steady in (obeying the preceptor's) order, is said to be a disciple by the good.

55-64. A preceptor should teach the excellent gem of a formula to a disciple having these characteristics, and endowed with all virtues. On a Dvādaśī day, or when the Sun is in the Śravaṇa constellation or on some day holy to Viṣṇu, a good preceptor should initiate the pleased (disciple). He should get fashioned the Sudarśana disc or the Pāñcajanya conch out of gold, silver, copper or bell-metal. Having bathed it with pure pañcāmṛta,[1] he should worship it before me. He should duly worship it with sandal and flowers, with (the utterance of) the formula. There he should establish fire in accordance with statements from his own Gṛhya (sūtras). The preceptor, the best brāhmaṇa, should offer ghee (into the fire) to the accompaniment of the formula. He should make oblations one thousand and eight times, or one hundred and eight times with the repetition of this gem of a formula or other auspicious formulas sacred to Viṣṇu. With (the recitation of) the hymns like the Puruṣasūkta he should offer ghee and milk into fire. The best brāhmaṇa should drop the disc and the conch into that fire. The preceptor, to the accompaniment (of the formula) of six letters should offer ghee into the fire twenty times. The preceptor, taking a heated disc, should make a mark (with it) and with the conch, to the accompaniment of the formula, on the left and the right arms. Having finished the remaining rite, he should again perform the worship. Then having brought a pitcher full of pure water, having consecrated it with (that) formula only, he should sprinkle (the water) on his head.

65-67. The preceptor should teach the formula to the disciple who has put on a white garment, has sipped water, is polite, has put on the sectarian mark. He should explain the meaning of the formula, and especially its operation. The disciple who has received the formula, should honour the preceptor with ornaments etc. O best god, he who, in this manner, learns the formula from a preceptor, Viṣṇu's devotee, goes to (the place) of Viṣṇu, not otherwise.

---

1. Pañcāmṛta: The collection of five sweet things used in worshipping deities. They are: milk, sugar, ghee, curd and honey.

Nārada said:

68-70. The father, Viṣṇu, having thus spoken to the Creator, marked him with his own disc, and he himself gave (i.e. taught) him the formula. O best sages, the god, that lord Brahmā, my father, the lord of all worlds, duly gave (i.e. taught) the formula to me also. Therefore, O best sages, O brāhmaṇas, you too, putting on (the mark) of the Sudarśana (disc), seek the shelter of Viṣṇu's couple of feet.

Vasiṣṭha said:

71-80. All the sages, thus addressed by Nārada, the divine sage, and entitled to the two (feet of Viṣṇu) went to the highest position of Viṣṇu. Therefore, O royal sage, you too desire absorption into Viṣṇu after putting on (the mark of) Sudarśana according to the proper rule of initiation. Seek the shelter of the two feet of Viṣṇu alone. Brahmā, the lord of all the people and the three worlds, himself told me and Nārada also this excellent formula. Nārada taught the formula, exclusive devotion (to) and seeking refuge (of Viṣṇu) to the great sages like Śaunaka living in Naimiṣāraṇya. O king, the great sages, deities, siddhas, sādhyas and demons do not know this most secret formula. I too gave to Parāśara, Śakti's son, this formula. O king, I shall tell you also this great secret—the couple of Lakṣmī and Viṣṇu, exclusive devotion (to) and seeking the refuge (of the two). There is no greater formula than the couple. I tell you the truth. In the worlds there is no practice superior to this. Formerly Brahmā told the truth, repeatedly (told) the truth that there is no other god than Viṣṇu who gives salvation to men. Service to him alone would be salvation, which would cut off (the fruits of) all acts.

CHAPTER TWO HUNDRED TWENTYFOUR

Bearing the Marks of a Disc etc. Essential for a Brāhmaṇa

Dilīpa said:

1-3. O revered one, tell me all about (it) full of the nectar of devotion to Viṣṇu. Listening to (the account of) devotion to Viṣṇu, that brings happiness, I am not at all satisfied. O best sage, except the ocean of the nectar of devotion to Viṣṇu, what else is the refuge in the fearful forest of the mundane existence to men who are always tormented by the fires with huge flames in the form of the three torments? O great sage, tell (me) in detail the varieties of devotion to the highest soul that are constantly practised by the sages.

Vasiṣṭha said:

4-5. O lord of kings, you ask well about the means of emancipation of men from the worldly existence, viz. devotion to Viṣṇu, the highest lord, which always brings happiness. Formerly goddess Pārvatī asked the same great question to Śiva, worshipped by the world, on the peak of Kailāsa.

Pārvatī said:

6-10. O god of gods, Mahādeva, O killer of Tripura, O lord of gods, tell me about devotion to Viṣṇu, which gives salvation to all human beings. So also the different deities that are worshipped, the hymns, and the various ways of the worship, and the nature of that Viṣṇu, and his qualities like splendour, the nature of his heaven, reaching which (a devotee) does not return (to his world), and due to which the lord Viṣṇu brings about creation, maintenance and destruction. That is the great abode of Viṣṇu reaching which (men) do not return (to this world). With this or that act or means, sinful men, with their minds addicted to objects of senses, reach the highest place. Due to your love for me tell all that to me in detail.

Vasiṣṭha said:

11. Mahādeva, the killer of Tripura, thus asked by the great goddess, saluted Viṣṇu, and with great affection said (to her):

Rudra said:

12-17. Well, O great goddess, O you desiring the good of all people, you ask me well (to tell you) the excellent greatness of (Viṣṇu) the lord of Śrī. O Pārvatī, you are blessed; you have earned religious merit; you are Viṣṇu's devotee. O good one, I am always pleased with your (good) character, beauty and virtues. I shall, O Girijā, tell you about the best devotion (to Viṣṇu), the manner of (reciting) his hymns, and about his form. Viṣṇu, the ancient Vāsudeva is the truth. He is the highest soul, the highest Brahman, the highest light, and greater than the great. He is Acyuta, Puruṣa, Kṛṣṇa, the eternal one, the benevolent lord, the eternal and omnipresent one, the stable one, Rudra, the witness of everything, and the lord of created beings. He is the sacrifice, the lord of sacrifice, and actually the lord of the Veda. He is Hiraṇyagarbha, the sun, the lord creating and sustaining the worlds.

18-28. He is to be described by the letter *A*, is the lord, and the lord of Śrī, the Earth and Nīlā. He is the lord of immortality, and of that which grows with food. He has a thousand heads; he is the soul of all; he has a thousand eyes and a thousand feet. Having touched the earth on all sides, he has stood above it by ten fingers. He is Ananta, the lord of Lakṣmī, Ramā; he possesses qualities and is without them, and is great. He is the lord of all worlds, he has splendour, is omniscient, and is unlimited. O Pārvatī, I shall tell you as I can, the greatness of that Vāsudeva, the chief in the worlds, and the lord of the worlds. With Brahmā and the deities it is impossible for me to describe it, the meaning of all Upaniṣads determined in the Vedānta. I shall also tell you the kinds of his worship. Listen, I shall tell them separately. The marking with Viṣṇu's conch and disc is said to be the first (worship) of Viṣṇu. (Other varieties are:) putting on rectangular marks, accepting hymns of (i.e. holy to) him, worshipping (him), muttering, meditating (on him), recollecting his names; so also narration (of), listening to his (accounts), saluting (him), serving his feet; so also taking the water (flowing) from his feet, and taking food after offering it to him. (So also) serving those who belong to him, faith in the vow of Dvādaśī, planting the Tulasī (plant). (Thus) the devotion to Viṣṇu, the holder of the Śārṅga bow and the god of gods is said to be of sixteen kinds for freedom from the bondage of the mundane existence. Viṣṇu is always venerable to all gods, so also to me, and especially to brāhmaṇas. Therefore, a brāhmaṇa should everyday duly worship Viṣṇu.

29-37. Having marks of his signs he doubtlessly reaches the feet (or the position) of the lord of Lakṣmī. A brāhmaṇa should have the marks of a conch and a disc at the roots of his arms, (and) for removing all sins the marks should be made after these are heated in fire. Having duly put on the mark of a disc or a conch and a disc or of the five weapons (of Viṣṇu), he should begin his religious duties. Having worn the mark of the disc heated in fire at the roots of his arms, he avoids the fearful city of Yama, and goes to the highest position of Viṣṇu. All that worship, hymns, muttering (of hymns) of him who worships Viṣṇu without (having on his body) the mark of a disc perishes. The brāhmaṇa who having marked (his body) at the roots of arms with a disc heated in fire, (then) mutters the hymn, would obtain salvation. The best brāhmaṇa having put on the mark of Sudarśana disc heated in fire and having duly made offerings should appoint (a brāhmaṇa) for the rites. All the śrāddha (offered) by him who feeds (a brāhmaṇa) without the mark of Viṣṇu on his body, becomes fruitless, and his dead ancestors leave disappointed. One should honour at a śrāddha a brāhmaṇa having (on his body) the mark of Viṣṇu's disc, and should carefully avoid one without the mark of Viṣṇu's disc (on his body). One should present a cow, land, gold to him having a mark of the disc (of Viṣṇu on his body).

38-46. Whatever is given to (a brāhmaṇa) not having the mark of a disc (on his body) is given to a demon. Those who have marks made with a disc heated in fire at the roots of their arms, get freed from all sins, and go to the highest position of Viṣṇu. To him whose body is marked with a disc heated in fire, all holy places and sacrifices have come. There is no doubt about it. A brāhmaṇa, not having (the mark of) the disc (made) duly, would be unrefined. Nothing would come to him even if he performs a thousand sacrifices. A brāhmaṇa, having knowledge not easily obtained, but not (having the mark of) the disc made duly, is condemned among all people, and would fall from the status of a brāhmaṇa. As Viṣṇu, holding the conch and disc is worshipped by the souls (i.e. men), similarly a brāhmaṇa, having (on his body) the marks of the disc etc. deserves to be honoured by all. A brāhmaṇa, even though he knows all the Vedas, or is proficient in all holy texts, would fall without having (i.e. if he does not have) (the mark of) the disc duly made (on his body); if he is without the mark or the marks of a conch or a disc, he should be put on a donkey and be driven out of the city. Vāsudeva Janārdana is untouched by the primordial matter (Prakṛti). O goddess, a brāhmaṇa having the mark of Viṣṇu's disc is just like that. Therefore, a man should have, at the roots of his arms, the (marks of) heated disc and conch of Viṣṇu, which burn the stream of sins (produced) due to the contact of matter.

47-50. He should have, at the roots of his arms, the marks made with heated disc and conch. Women and śūdras should always have those made with scented sandal (-paste). At the root of the arm of a brāhmaṇa the mark of the disc should be made with a heated (sign). Marks with heated (signs) must be duly made (on the body) of a brāhmaṇa. For the success in (rites prescribed by) the holy and the Smṛti texts, so also for being entitled to worshipping Viṣṇu, (the mark of) the disc should be duly had. For accomplishing the status of Viṣṇu, and for getting knowledge, a man should burn his body with (i.e. have marks of) heated conch and disc, after duly having offered oblations into fire.

51-53. A brāhmaṇa should not mark his body with any other symbol than that of Viṣṇu—with other symbols than the conch, disc, mace, sword and the Śārṅga (bow) of Viṣṇu. He should burn his body with marks (made with Viṣṇu's symbols). He, whose body is burnt with (i.e. has) other marks, is not entitled to (performing) rites. One should avoid a brāhmaṇa not having the disc (-mark) from a distance. In the world one should not look at a brāhmaṇa who is not a devotee of Viṣṇu as (one does not look at) a cāṇḍāla. Viṣṇu's devotee, even if he is outside the castes, purifies the three worlds.

54-59. Therefore, O you of a charming face, brāhmaṇas should duly have marks (on their bodies). Brāhmaṇas (with their bodies marked) with Viṣṇu's disc are refined and noble for acquiring mastery of hymns, knowledge and for salvation. Brāhmaṇas without (marks of) Viṣṇu's disc are not refined. As it is urged by the holy texts, especially brāhmaṇas, living in all stages of life, should duly have (the mark of) Viṣṇu's disc. Those who know the Vedas consider that a brāhmaṇa should have (the mark of) Sudarśana on his right arm, and (that of) the conch on the left. The wearing of (the mark of) the disc etc. is told in the Mahopaniṣad (the great Upaniṣad texts); so also in the Sāman (Veda), Yajur (Veda) and the Ṛg (Veda), O you of a beautiful face. O Viṣṇu, the other ancients have the marks of your pure lotus, disc for crossing the ocean of existence, at the roots of their arms. Others have other marks of you.

60-64. The extensive disc is known as Caraṇa. Pavitra is an old and auspicious word. Burnt by the disc they would cross the ocean of sins. Viṣṇu's disc is the lord of the hymns (brāhmaṇa-spatyam?) and has always pervaded the world. Those whose bodies are not burnt (with it) do not go to the highest position. Those whose bodies are burnt with (it) go to the highest position. Know from me the names of Viṣṇu's disc in succession: Pavitra, Caraṇa, Nemi, Sudarśana, Haricakra, Sahasrāra (having a thousand spokes), Prākṛtaghna (killer of the mean), Lokadvāra (a gate to the good world), Mahaujasa (very bright). Purify us with the Brahmanhood, pure and burnt in fire. Purify us with that Pavitra, having flames of you, O Agni.

65-69. May the Pāvamānya (hymns) purify me with the thousand-edged disc with which they always protect themselves. The disc of the Creator is bright with metal plates and golden. We knowing the hymn purify it (already) purified by it. The unaging disc with the felly is the eye of the noble one. Having put it on gods reached a high position. Therefore, (the marks of) the weapons should be duly put on particularly by brāhmaṇas, especially by Viṣṇu's devotees. The noble one of a pure heart, who having the Ūrdhvapuṇḍra (perpendicular marks of sandal on the forehead) and the mark of the disc, meditates on Viṣṇu's position, by means of singing the hymn always reaches (god Viṣṇu) higher than the highest always remaining in his heart.

70-74. Those devotees of Viṣṇu, having stuck to (i.e. round) their necks the garland of Tulasī or lotuses or a rosary, having the marks of conch or disc at the roots of their arms, or those having the Ūrdhvapuṇḍra (the vertical lines) on their foreheads, quickly purify the world. Beings are not sorry for those who preserve (but) do not properly carry (the mark of) the extensive disc of the lord of heaven. Those who carry the disc very firm(-ly marked) with (the proper) rite on their arm(s), quickly occupy, by means of their lustre, a high place in the sky. He who has at the root(s) of his arms the disc mark of Viṣṇu, the highest soul (made) by heating (the disc) in the sacrificial fire, crosses the great ocean of the mundane existence, and goes to the pure world of the highest lord. A man should make at the roots of his arms the marks with the heated discs etc. He should also get such marks put on (the bodies of) his wife, children, servants and beasts etc.

75-80. O you of an excellent face, all holy texts tell this. In the history (books) and the Purāṇas the same thing is told. The mark of devotion to Viṣṇu is said to be of two kinds: external and internal. The external (mark) is (produced) by means of a conch, a disc etc. The internal (one) is freedom from attachment. One having similarity between the external and the internal is said to belong to Viṣṇu. Therefore, the disc etc. are said to be the first (external) mark pertaining to Viṣṇu. The internal (mark) is realising the soul after being free from the faults due to Cupid (i.e. passion of love). So also showing compassion to all beings, tranquility and absence of greed for the objects of senses. So also having no attachment for sons, wife etc.; and delight in the study of Yoga; serving the highest lord by means of undistracted application to devotion. Therefore, marking with (Viṣṇu's) weapons like the disc is said to pertain to Viṣṇu. Vaiṣṇavatva (the status of belonging to Viṣṇu) cannot be had without the marks of the disc etc.

CHAPTER TWO HUNDRED TWENTYFIVE

The Efficacy of Ūrdhvapuṇḍra

Śaṅkara said:

1-4. O you of an auspicious appearance, I shall tell you the greatness of the Ūrdhvapuṇḍra (vertical Vaiṣṇava mark on the forehead). The best brāhmaṇa would be free from the bond of the worldly existence just on having it. Within the large and very charming space in the Ūrdhvapuṇḍra, Viṣṇu, god of gods, is seated with Lakṣmī. Therefore, the body of him, on which there would be the mark, is the clean, auspicious temple of the lord. That devotee of Viṣṇu, who has the mark made with white clay, has bathed at all holy places, is prepared for all sacrifices.

5-8. The brāhmaṇa having the mark is honoured among all people, (and) getting into an excellent aeroplane, goes to the highest place of Viṣṇu. The best brāhmaṇa should put on the mark thrice (a day), for purification of all sins, and for obtaining the fruit of performing sacrifices and digging wells and doing other acts of charity. (A man) seeing one having the mark, is freed from all sins. By saluting him devoutly he would obtain the fruit of all (kinds of) charity. The dead ancestors of him who will feed a brāhmaṇa having the mark are undoubtedly pleased for crores of kalpas.

9-14. O you of an auspicious face, he who, having the mark, performs a śrāddha, would obtain, for crores of kalpas, the fruit of the śrāddha (performed) at Gayā. The religious merit of the sacrifices, gifts, penance, muttering (of hymns), sacrificial rites etc. of one having the mark is endless. All the sacrifices performed, wells dug, and other charitable acts done by him who does any act without having the mark, are useless. That human body which is without the mark should not be seen at all. It would be like a cremation ground. All the rites etc. which a man without the mark would do, are taken (away) by demons; and he goes down to hell. A brāhmaṇa well-versed in the Vedas, should have the mark with white clay. The wise one should never have it in an oblique manner even in a misery.

15-18. Brāhmaṇas should have the mark. The mark of kṣatriyas should be round; that of vaiśyas should be strip-like; that of śūdras should have three lines. The mark should be made with clay; the round one with musk; the strip-like one with sandal; and the three-lined one with sacred ash. The vertical mark is recommended for all. It is not prohibited. A kṣatriya etc. also, if he is Viṣṇu's devotee should have it. Brāhmaṇas are not to have the oblique or the strip-like mark. And they are not to worship any other (deity) than Viṣṇu, the highest lord.

19-23. O goddess, if a brāhmaṇa, learned and born in a noble family has put on (the mark of) sacred ash, one should avoid such a brāhmaṇa, as a pot in which liquor is left as the remnant. The mark of three lines is the practice for those who are śūdras and like śūdras. There is no doubt that a brāhmaṇa having the mark of three lines, falls. The very noble ones, interested in the good of all living beings, should have a puṇḍra with a gap like the shape of Viṣṇu's foot. A man should have the mark in accordance with the precept, resembling the foot of Viṣṇu and having a gap in its centre; for that is Viṣṇu's temple. He should have the mark which is good, pleasing, has the shape of a staff, good sides, which is very charming, very beautiful, and which has a gap at the centre.

24-27. Therefore, O you of an auspicious appearance, brāhmaṇas and women should always have the mark which has a gap, has the shape of a staff, and is very beautiful. In the large and very beautiful gap at the centre of the vertical mark, Viṣṇu is seated with Lakṣmī. That mean brāhmaṇa who would have a gapless vertical mark, expels Viṣṇu along with Lakṣmī seated there. There is no doubt that there always is a dog's foot on the foreheads of those mean brāhmaṇas who have a gapless vertical mark.

28-40. Therefore, in order to attain the same world as of Viṣṇu, a brāhmaṇa should always have a mark with a gap, with turmeric, and having auspiciousness. For securing absorption into Viṣṇu one should, with great devotion, bring the clay from the pool on the Veṅkaṭa mountain, and make the vertical mark (with it). A devoted person should bring the clay from the root of Tulasī of (i.e. dear to) Śrī Kṛṣṇa, and should make the vertical mark (with it). Viṣṇu is pleased with him. Or the best brāhmaṇa, having brought the pleasing clay from the auspicious, charming pool (i.e. sacred to) Viṣṇu at Dvārāvatī, should make the mark (with it) in order to secure all desired objects. He who, having brought with great devotion, clay from the banks of Gaṅgā, makes the mark with it, would obtain the fruit of all sacrifices. Due to having the mark (with) sandal, turmeric, so also (with) ash from the sacred fire one is said to control everything. He should bring the clay from that place which is sacred to Viṣṇu. One should get the clay from the top of a mountain, the bank of a river, the root of a bilva (tree), a reservoir of water, the coast of a sea, an anthill, especially from a place sacred to Viṣṇu, and from the place where the water used for Viṣṇu's bath always flows, for having the mark. A man, taking clay with water flowing from Viṣṇu's feet, and having puṇḍra marks on the limbs of his body at Śrīraṅga, Veṅkaṭagiri, Śrīkūrma, the auspicious Dvārakā, Prayāga, Narasiṁha mountain, Varāha, a Tulasī-grove would get absorption into Viṣṇu. For having the mark clay should be taken from that place wherefrom the noble devotees of Viṣṇu take it. A dark mark is said to cause peace. So also a red one is said to bring about control. They say that a yellow one leads to riches. The white one leads to salvation and is auspicious.

41-50. They say that a round, oblique, gapless, short, long, protracted, thin, crooked, ugly mark, one with its top closed or with its root cut off, with a line missing, inauspicious, rough, fixed, one that is not drawn with the finger, not having fragrance, or inadequate is unfortunate. One should draw it with clay beginning with the root of the nose. Starting it from the middle of the eye-brows, he should have a gap in it. The gap should be of the measure of two fingers, and the sides of the size of a finger. With white clay he should draw a better and auspicious mark. He should meditate upon Keśava (as staying) on his forehead. (He should meditate) upon Nārāyaṇa (as staying) in his belly, Mādhava (as staying) in his chest, and Govinda (as staying) in his throat. (He should meditate) upon Viṣṇu (as staying) in the right side of his belly and Madhusūdana (as staying) in his right arm. (He should meditate) upon Trivikrama (as staying) in (the right side of) his neck, and Vāmana (as staying) in his left side. (He should meditate) upon Śrīdhara (as staying) in his left arm, and Hṛṣīkeśa in (the left side of) his neck. (He should meditate) upon Padmanābha (as staying) in his back, and place Dāmodara in the lower part of his spine. And with the water for washing it (he should meditate) upon Vāsudeva (as present) in his head. He should draw the mark of the measure of four fingers on his forehead, both the arms, on both (the sides) of the back, and on the neck. On the belly and near its sides a long one of the measure of ten fingers is recommended. On the arms and chest a mark of the measure of eight fingers is recommended. Thus a brāhmaṇa should always have twelve marks.

51-59. He should, after meditating upon those images with

their respective hymns, have the marks (on those respective limbs of his body). In the gap he should have (i.e. put) auspicious turmeric. They say, kṣatriyas should have four marks and vaiśyas should have two. One mark is laid down for women and śūdras. He should have four marks on the forehead, on his chest, and on the arms. Two are laid down for the forehead and the chest and one for the place where the hair is separated. Of all the marks, the vertical one is said to be the first (that should be put) on the forehead. As laid down, it should be had in the order of the forehead first. One should have the images of Vāsudeva etc. in the four vertical marks. In two he should have the two (images of) Govinda and Kṛṣṇa and one of Nārāyaṇa. O Girijā, I have thus told (you) the manner in which the puṇḍra is had. The triad of one resembling the aśvattha-leaf, the reed-leaf, or the lotus-leaf, is said to be 'Mohana'. A pure, great devotee of Viṣṇu, should, in case of a controversy, have a vertical mark of the shape of a staff. Those, the roots of whose arms are marked with Sudarśana, so also all of whose limbs are marked with the vertical puṇḍra, who have lotus garlands and rosaries, protect the people from contact with heaps of sins.

CHAPTER TWO HUNDRED TWENTYSIX

The Meaning of the Mantra (Formula)

Śaṅkara said:

1-5. At (the time of) a nyāsa or worship, one should resort to Viṣṇu's formula (mantra). The highest position is not had by means of a formula not sacred to Viṣṇu. If the former couple of sacred names (i.e. the one mentioned above) is imparted by one who is a non-Vaiṣṇava, then one should again receive it from a follower of Viṣṇu. Even if a man has studied a thousand branches (of the holy texts), even if he was initiated into all (kinds of) sacrifices, even if he is born in a good family, he should not be a preceptor if he is not a follower of Viṣṇu. That follower of Viṣṇu who properly imparts the two sacred names, should be known as the preceptor, tearing off the bond of the mundane existence. A brāhmaṇa should, after resorting to a preceptor, live (with him) for a year. The preceptor, knowing his behaviour, should impart him the formula.

6-9. Having first done the sacraments as burning his body (i.e. putting sectarian marks on it), he should then utter the formula, after burning, putting the sectarian mark and giving a name (to him). Then he should teach his disciple of a pure heart. The rite of burning with (i.e. putting marks like) the (heated) disc (etc.) is called tāpa (or burning). The sectarian mark is said to be vertical and the name (accepted by) the Vaiṣṇava sect is pronounced. Then in accordance with the rule (about the mantra) the teacher should teach the formula to the disciple. (He should teach him) nyāsa, the eight-syllabled or any other formula sacred to Viṣṇu. O you of an auspicious face, here nyāsa is of a high value to the followers of Viṣṇu.

10-12. Therefore, for them nyāsa is said to be superior. A brāhmaṇa highly devoted to nyāsa is said to be the best. There is no greater mantra than a nyāsa. I am telling you the truth. Nyāsa and the couple of mantras are synonyms for devotion. Learn it from me. After having instruction in the two, he should practise all rites. He who is not entitled to both does not deserve to perform all rites.

13-16. Therefore, the best brāhmaṇa, having studied the two, should study the eight-syllabled formula properly. The formula is said to be eight-syllabled due to the inclusion of (the syllable) Om. The wise say that that is a sacred formula which naturally has Om at its beginning. Except at the beginning of all formulas Om is not naturally there. One should use it before (i.e. at the beginning of) all formulas. O you of an auspicious face, the sacred syllable Om is Brahman. It is the chief of all formulas. One should use it at the commencement of all formulas.

17-21. At the root-formula Om is naturally settled. The first (syllable) is *Om*, having one letter. Then is (the word) *namaḥ* having two letters. Then in proper order are the five letters *Nārāyaṇāya.* Thus the formula, accomplishing all objects, should be known to be eight-syllabled. It removes all sorrows; it is glorious; it contains all formulas; it is auspicious. Its seer is Nārāyaṇa, and (he) himself, the lord of Śrī, is its deity. Its metre is the divine Gāyatrī and origin is Om. The power of the formula is goddess Śrī who is never-failing. The first foot is said to be the letter *Om*; the second to be *Namaḥ*, and the third to be *Nārāyaṇāya*. Thus the three feet are told.

22-26. The letters *a*, *u*, and *m* form the syllable *Om*, which is Brahman's word, and is of the nature of the three Vedas. Viṣṇu is expressed by the letter *a*, Śrī by the letter *u*; the letter *m* is the servant of these two, and is said to be the twentyfifth (letter). It is said by the wise that *a* expresses Viṣṇu's form. The sages say that *u* expresses the form of the goddess Śrī. The letter *m* expresses the soul, the puruṣa, the twentyfifth (principle of the Sāṁkhyas). The elements are expressed by the class of letters beginning with *ka*; and the senses are denoted by the class of letters beginning with *ca*. The class of letters beginning with *ṭa* and that beginning with *ta* denote knowledge, so also the letters like *dha* (indicate the same). The mind is expressed by the letter *pa* only; and ego by the letter *pha*.

27-30. Mahat (i.e. Intellect) and Prakṛti (Primordial Matter) (the principles enunciated in the Sāṁkhya System) are (respectively) expressed by the letters *ba* and *bha*. The soul is said to be the letter *ma* and is said to be the twentyfifth (principle). It is different from the body, the senses, the mind, the vital breath; and has no other means. He is the remnant of the lord, is denoted by *ma* and is sentient. Some say that *ma* indicates just the emphasis. According to them the principle of Śrī is expressed by the letter *va* (*ma*?) only. As the sun's lustre does not go away from him, so Lakṣmī does not go away from him. Viṣṇu, the ocean of auspicious qualities, is expressed by the letter *ā*.

31-36. The lord of Śrī is the remnant of all souls, is the seed (i.e. source) of the world, and the highest person. He is the author and the sustainer of the world, the lord, and people's kin. (Lakṣmī) always controls the worlds, does not go away from Viṣṇu. She is mother of the entire world and Viṣṇu's charming wife. Here (i.e. in the mantra) the letter *u* expresses Śrī, who is the support of the world. The wise say that the letter *ma* expresses the soul, the servant of the two (i.e. Viṣṇu and Lakṣmī). He is the support of knowledge, has knowledge as his quality, is sentient, and is beyond Prakṛti. He is not insentient; he is without any modification; is uniform in nature and has (no other form than) his own form. He is subtle, eternal, pervading, of the nature of intellect and joy, is of the nature of ego, immutable, the soul, of different forms, and eternal. He cannot be burnt, cannot be cut off, cannot be made wet, cannot be dried, and is indestructible; he is (thus) endowed with such qualities and is an effect of the highest (soul).

37-42. The letter *ma* expresses the individual soul, always dependent. He is the servant of Viṣṇu only and of none else. Thus is determined his servitude to be mediocre. O sinless one, the meaning of *Om* should be known like this. I have explained it (to you). O auspicious one, the exposition of *Om* (is done) by means of the remnant of the meaning, the formula(?). In this world, he who is the servant of another, does not get freedom. Therefore, with (the help of) the mind one should turn away Mahat and Ahaṁkāra (i.e. Intellect and Ego). That act which is done by the knowledge of one's means, is also prohibited. The letter *ma* is (i.e. stands for) ego, and the letter *na* prohibits it. Therefore, with his mind only he gets freedom from the ego. Every accomplishment is due to the mind. Otherwise he would perish. Whatever is with the mind is said to be the ego.

43-46. One having egotism has absolutely no happiness. He whose mind is deluded by egotism sinks in the blinding darkness. Therefore, his freedom through mind is not prohibited. He is dependent upon the lord and lives under his influence. Therefore, the sentient is not the author of the means. The mobile and the immobile exist due to the will of the highest lord. Therefore, he would completely give up the application of his own power. Due to the lord's power there is nothing that is not obtained by him.

47-53. Having placed the burden (i.e. the responsibility) on that lord of Lakṣmī, he should do acts of (i.e. sacred to) him only. The highest soul, Viṣṇu, is the master. I always belong to him. His mind should be employed according to the desire of that lord only. Thus it is noble when egotism and sense of mineness are abandoned by the mind. In the mundane existence the sense of mineness is the root of the bondage due to the deeds. Therefore, a wise man should avoid Mahat (Intellect) and Ahaṁkāra (ego) with (the help of) the mind. (Now) O you auspicious Girijā, I shall explain (to you) the word *Nārāyaṇa*. *Nārā* is the assemblage of the souls. This Puruṣa (Nārāyaṇa) is their refuge. And they are his abode; therefore he is said to be *Nārāyaṇa.* The entire world—the sentient and insentient objects—is heard, is seen. He, who always remains after pervading it, is said to be *Nārāyaṇa.* The groups of all men are said to be *Nārā.* He is their refuge and support. Therefore, he is said to be *Nārāyaṇa.* The wise know the principles produced from *Nara* (i.e. the Supreme Spirit) as *nārā.*

54-59. They alone are his abode. Therefore, he is called *Nārāyaṇa,* by whom the world, after devouring it even at the end of the kalpa, is supported, and by whom it is again created. Therefore he is said to be *Nārāyaṇa.* The entire world consisting of the mobile and the immobile is called *Nāra.* To it he is connected; therefore he is said to be *Nārāyaṇa.* The *Nāra*—the host of men —is his abode or refuge. Therefore, he is always called *Nārāyaṇa* by the sages; from him spring the worlds, as the massive foam in the ocean. Since they again merge into him, therefore, he is said to be *Nārāyaṇa.* He is (residing) at the eternal position, is eternal, and is always free and alone enjoys; he is the lord of the entire world. Therefore, he is called *Nārāyaṇa. Nārāyaṇa* is the highest Brahman. *Nārāyaṇa* is the highest principle.

60-64. *Nārāyaṇa* has remained after pervading whatever is seen or heard within and without this world. Hari, Nārāyaṇa, Acyuta is the Supreme soul with the sins destroyed. He resides within all beings. He is divine, always (all) alone, and is eternal. He is the seer and is what is to be seen. He is the listener and is what is listened to also. He is the one that touches and is also what is touched. He meditates and is what is meditated upon. He is the speaker and what is spoken. He is the knower and what is known. He is the sentient and insentient world. All that is said to be Hari, the lord of Śrī, Nārāyaṇa. He, the Supreme Being, has a thousand heads, a thousand eyes, a thousand feet. Having pervaded all the worlds he stands above them by (the measure of) ten fingers.

65-69. All that was and will be is Nārāyaṇa Hari. And he is the lord of immortality and the Virāṭ; the Supreme Being (grows beyond) by the means of food. He alone is the Supreme Being, Viṣṇu, Vāsudeva, Acyuta, Hari, Hiraṇmaya, and the lord; he is immortal, eternal, auspicious (Śiva). He is the master of the entire world, is the lord of all people, and the master. He is Hiraṇyagarbha, the Sun, is Ananta (the endless) and the great god. The word *Bhagavat*, so also the word *Puruṣa* and the word *Nirupādhi* stand for Vāsudeva, the soul of all. The god, the lord Viṣṇu, the highest soul, the friend of the world, the only ruler of the movable and the immovable is the greatest refuge of the ascetics.

70-73. That one who is naturally merged into the sound uttered at the beginning of the Veda and who is settled in the Vedānta (i.e. the Upaniṣads), who is the greatest, is the great god. That one, viz. Viṣṇu, who is (indicated by) the letter *a*, the one who is Nārāyaṇa Hari, is the eternal Supreme Being, the highest soul, the great lord. Sages use the word *Īśvara* (i.e. the lord) also for him in whom wonderful glory exists. Unconditional lordship exists in Viṣṇu. The ancient words of Veda have described him as the soul, the lord. Therefore, in Vāsudeva the great lordship exists.

74-88. Due to his splendour he is *Tripād* (literally, having three feet). He is the lord of sport. He, the soul of all, has two kinds of grandeurs and glory. He who is the lord of Śrī, Bhū and Nīlā is called the lord. Therefore, mastery over all exists in Vāsudeva. He is the lord of sacrifice, is the sacrifice, the enjoyer of sacrifice, the performer of sacrifice, the lord, the enjoyer of sacrifice, the Puruṣa (i.e. the deity) of sacrifice. He alone is the highest lord. He is the lord of sacrifice. He is the enjoyer of the oblations made to gods and all offerings to the dead ancestors. He is immutable. He, Hari, is the lord here. All goblins and demons go away from his vicinity. He, Viṣṇu, who became Virāṭ and Hari, is himself the highest lord, who pleases the three worlds. With him as the complete oblation gods performed a sacrifice. Those who have a double row of teeth are born from that sacrifice. From that sacrifice with all the oblations sprang *ṛks*, *sāmans*. From it sprang horses, cows, men etc. The entire world consisting of the mobile and the immobile sprang from the body of the Supreme Being consisting of everything. The castes were his face, arms, thighs and feet in due order. From his feet the earth came up and the heaven from his head. From his mind the moon was produced, and the sun from his eye. Fire with a thousand eyes (sprang) from his mouth, and the ever-moving wind from his breath. From his navel came up Brahmā, the sky, the movable and immovable world. Since the entire world came up from the eternal Viṣṇu, therefore, Viṣṇu full of all, is called Nārāyaṇa. Hari, having thus created the world again devours it, as a spider does the web produced from its saliva. Since, having curbed Brahmā, Indra, Rudra, Yama and Varuṇa, he subdues them, therefore, he is called Hari. This ancient Supreme Being having put the world in his belly, sleeps in the coating of (his) Māyā, which has become an ocean. (In the beginning) here this Viṣṇu, Nārāyaṇa, Acyuta was alone.

89-93. Brahmā, Rudra, gods, great sages, this heaven, this earth, the moon, the sun, the stars, the world, the (cosmic) egg covered by Mahat (were) not there. O auspicious one, since the entire world was held by that Hari (in his belly) and was again created at the time of creation, therefore he is said to be Nārāyaṇa. O Pārvatī, service to him is described in the formula by the dative case. This entire world, beginning with Brahmā, is his slave. Knowing the meaning to be like this one should then use the formula. O you of an excellent face, without knowing the meaning of the formula, one would not get success, so also enjoyment, devotion and salvation.

CHAPTER TWO HUNDRED TWENTYSEVEN

The Description of the Vibhūti of Tripād

Pārvatī said:

1-2. Tell me in detail, the importance of the meaning and the words of the sacred formula, so also the lord's *vibhūti* (divine properties) and his qualities. O lord of all gods, properly tell me all about that highest abode of Viṣṇu, and about the kinds of his *vyūhas* (divine manifestations).

The lord said:

3-7. O goddess, listen. I shall explain to you the nature of the highest soul; so also the *vibhūti* and group of qualities of that Viṣṇu. That great, Supreme Being who is mentioned as Viṣṇu, Nārāyaṇa, is the lord of the worlds, and the eternal highest soul. The lord has hands and feet on all sides, has eyes on all sides. Having all worlds and great abodes in it (i.e. his body) he stands above the minds of men. The lord of Lakṣmī, Puruṣottama, has thus a multiple nature. For enjoyment with the goddess he takes up divine and auspicious forms. His is a large body. His form is like that of fire. Viṣṇu took to the form of a youth and a boy. He enjoyed with Lakṣmī, the mother of the worlds, as the Moon with rays (producing) nectar (enjoys with) his moonlight.

8-13. This (lord) of the goddess of the world is a young boy, ever young. Having handsomeness like that of a crore of Cupids he remains at the highest place. For his enjoyment there is the highest sky; for his sport the entire world. The two kinds of Viṣṇu's vibhūti are due to his enjoyment and sport. He always remains enjoying. Sometime he withdraws his sport. Due to his having a (special) power, he has both enjoyment and sport. The pervading with his third step is done in the highest abode. One step of him was here also. His vibhūti with the third step is perpetual, (while) the step (on the earth) is non-perpetual. That eternal auspicious form of the lord has stayed in the highest abode. It is infallible, eternal, divine, and has always resorted to youth. It is always enjoying the goddess Lakṣmī and is surrounded by Lakṣmī and the earth. This Lakṣmī of Viṣṇu, the mother of the world, is eternal and imperishable.

14-21. O you of an auspicious face, as Viṣṇu is omnipresent so is Lakṣmī. This ever auspicious wife of Viṣṇu rules over the world. She has hands and feet on all sides. She has eyes and heads on all sides. This Nārāyaṇī, the mother of the world, is the resort of the entire world. The entire immobile and mobile world has resorted to (i.e. depends upon) her glance. The existence and the dissolution of the world is due to her opening and closing (her) eyes. This great Lakṣmī is the first of all. She has three constituents (viz. sattva, rajas and tamas). She is the greatest goddess. She of a visible and invisible form, remains after having pervaded everything. The great goddess having seen the entire universe void, filled that entire (universe) with her own lustre. That Lakṣmī is the Earth only, well-known as goddess Nilā. Being the support of the world, she has resorted to the form of the earth. She herself would be of the form of Nīlā due to her liquid form of the nature of water etc. She has obtained the form of Lakṣmī. She is of the nature of wealth and speech. Thus, she, the goddess of the world, has resorted to Viṣṇu. O you of an auspicious face, all the varieties of knowledge would be (i.e. are) her forms.

22-23. Everything that has a beautiful form is said to be her body only. It remains in women as beauty, good character and behaviour, and good fortune (in the form of having their husbands alive). O Girijā, her beauty is at the head (i.e. top of the beauty) of all women. By means of the glance of her, of a strong vision, Brahmā, Śiva, Indra the lord of heaven, the Moon, the Sun, Kubera, Yama, Agni obtain ample affluence.

24-28. He who, after getting up in the morning would recite these auspicious names of her, viz. Lakṣmī, Śrī, Kamalā, Vidyā, Mātā, Viṣṇupriyā (dear to Viṣṇu), Satī, Padmālayā (having a lotus as her abode), Padmahastā (having a lotus in her hand), Padmākṣī (lotus-eyed), Lokasundarī, Bhutānām Īśvarī (She who controls the beings), Nityā, Sahyā (literally, bearable), Sarvagatā (omnipresent), Śubhā (auspicious), Viṣṇupatnī, Mahādevī, Kṣīrodatanayā (daughter of the Milky Ocean), Ramā, Anantā (endless), Lokamātā (the mother of the world), Bhū, Nīlā, Sarvasukhapradā (giving all pleasures), Rukmiṇī, so also Sītā, Śubhā (auspicious), Sarvavedavatī (possessing all Vedas), Satī, Sarasvatī, Gaurī, Śānti, Svāhā (the oblations offered to gods), Svadhā (the oblations offered to dead ancestors), Rati, Nārāyaṇī, Viṣṇu's eternal beautiful wife never leaving him, obtains wealth and faultless riches and grains.

29-37. I here invoke Śrī who has golden complexion, who is attractive, who has a golden and silver chaplet, who is moonlike, full of gold, Lakṣmī, who does not go away from Viṣṇu, who is perceptible through her fragrance, who is haughty, always nourished, who is the goddess of wealth, who controls all beings. The great goddess thus praised in Ṛgveda gave all the pleasure of affluence to gods like Śiva. This ancient wife of Viṣṇu controls this world. The entire mobile and immobile world resorts to (i.e. depends upon) her glances. He, the indestructible, immutable Supreme Being, on whose chest the goddess like Agni's lustre, rests, is actually the lord of all. He is the affluent Nārāyaṇa, the ocean of the quality of love. He is the lord, is good-tempered, amiable, omniscient and all-powerful.

His desires are always fully gratified; he is a natural friend and companion. He is the ocean of the nectar of compassion. He is the shelter of men. He is the giver of heaven, salvation and happiness to his devotees. He is the mine of pity. I shall fully do service to that Viṣṇu. In all conditions like time and place the form of the lord of Kamalā is well-established. A man would easily obtain service to Viṣṇu.

38-42. Having thus known the meaning of the sacred formula, a man should properly practise devotion to him. All this immobile and mobile world is under his control. Lord Śrīmat Nārāyaṇa is the lord, the master of the worlds. He is the mother, the father, the son, the kinsman, the abode, the refuge and the shelter. The lord of Śrī has auspicious qualities; he gives the fruits of all desires. He is the lord of the world, who is described as qualityless in the holy texts. He is said to be so in the sense that he is devoid of Prakṛti-born qualities associated with what should be abandoned. The falseness of the display of which is (indicated) by passages found in Vedānta, i.e. all that is seen, consists in its being transient. In this case also, the Prakṛti-born form of the (cosmic) egg itself is perishable.

43-48. In the same way the transitoriness of the Prakṛti-born forms is explained. The meaning is: O great goddess, the Prakṛti has come up for the play of Viṣṇu, the god of gods, entitled to sport. This egg (i.e. cosmos) having Prakṛti as its source is charming as it is complete with the four and ten worlds, oceans with islands, four kinds of beings and mountains with very lofty peaks. It is endowed with qualities more than ten; it is covered with seven covers. By means of that time only which moves in the form of (the measures of time like) kalā,[1] kāṣṭhā,[2] the creation, maintenance and destruction of the world would be (i.e. take place). A day of Brahmā is of the duration of four thousand yugas. As many years' (duration) is a night of Brahmā, whose birth is not known. When the end of Brahmā comes, he would be destroying everything.

49-51. The worlds existing in the (cosmic) egg are burnt by the destructive fire at the end of the world. Then all the souls are

1. Kalā: A division of time variously computed as one minute, 48 seconds, or 8 seconds.

2. Kāṣṭhā: A measure of time, 1/30 kalā.

put into the Prakṛti (i.e. the personified will) of Viṣṇu. The cover of the egg, the beings, are merged into the primordial matter. That primordial matter is the support of the entire world, and has resorted to Viṣṇu. By means of her the lord always brings about the creation and destruction of the world. The lord has created the illusion in the form of the world for his sport.

52-54. She (called) Avidyā (ignorance), Prakṛti (primordial matter), Māyā (illusion), Guṇatrayamayī (consisting of the three constituents, viz. sattva, rajas and tamas), Sanātanī (the ancient one) is ever the cause of creation, maintenance and destruction. This Yoganidrā (Viṣṇu's sleep at the end of a yuga), the great illusion, the Prakṛti having the three constituents, unmanifest, Pradhāna is the sport of Viṣṇu that does not change. Due to Prakṛti only the creation and destruction of the world would always take place. The place of Prakṛti beyond calculation is imperishable, dense darkness.

55-59. On the boundary on the side above is Virajā; on the lower side the ancient one is limitless. She in her gross and subtle condition has subdued the entire world. Creation and destruction are said to be the two states of expansion and contraction of her. Thus all beings are within Prakṛti. Then all this great world within Prakṛti is void. Thus the excellent form of (his) vibhūti is of the form of Prakṛti. O daughter of the (Himālaya) Mountain, listen to the vibhūti of the Tripād (liberally, having three feet or steps). The river Virajā is between Pradhāna and the highest heaven. She, the auspicious one, is caused to flow with the water produced by the sweat of the Vedāṅgas. At the other side of her, in the highest heaven is the ancient vibhūti, viz. Tripād (i.e. Viṣṇu).

60-63. (The nature of the highest place of Viṣṇu is:) immortal, eternal, continual, endless, the highest position, pure, full of sattva (i.e. goodness), divine, immutable and Brahman's place. It is unchanging and has the lustre equal to that of many crores of suns. It is full of the Vedas, is pure, and free from creation and destruction. It is beyond calculation, unaging, continual, free from wakefulness and sleep etc. It is golden; it gives salvation; it gives bliss and happiness. It is without similarity or excess (i.e. nothing is equal or superior to it). It is without a beginning or an end. It is auspicious. It is wonderful due to lustre; is charming; is always the ocean of joy.

64-67. Viṣṇu's highest place is endowed with these and other qualities. The sun, or the moon, or the fire does not illumine it. That is the highest place of Viṣṇu, after going to which (beings) do not return (to the earth). That is Viṣṇu's highest abode, which is eternal, continual and fixed. Even for hundreds of crores of kalpas Viṣṇu's place cannot be described by me, or by Brahmā, or by hosts of best sages. O dear one, the unfallen lord stays at that place; one may or may not know him. It is immutable; it is a mystery (even) to the Vedas (or it is a secret of the Vedas); in it all gods were seated. There is none who can describe it. What can one do with a ṛc? Those who know it are these, seated here.

68-75. O goddess, the wise ones always see that highest abode of Viṣṇu, which is indestructible, eternal, divine, and is like an expanded eye. It is not impossible for deities like Brahmā, Rudra to enter it. The best meditating sages see it through knowledge, the path of the holy texts. I, Brahmā, gods and great sages do not understand the significance of all the Upaniṣads. On understanding it I shall tell it, O you of a good vow. At that highest place of Viṣṇu, called good and auspicious, cows with many horns and very happy created beings live. They say here is the abode of Viṣṇu, dressed as a cowherd. With the cows and cowherds of pleasant appellations the great abode shines. It has the complexion of the sun. The unfalling lustre, viz. Viṣṇu's place is beyond darkness. It is Brahmā's prop. That is a pure, good ancient world. At this highest position, the eternal place, in which the vulgar do not find a place, the two, young Śrī and the ancient (Viṣṇu), being watchful, stayed.

76-80. Bhū and Nīlā, dear to Viṣṇu, are the two sisters from there. Here the old Sādhyas, and all the ancient gods dwell. Those of an auspicious appearance, and great ones sought out heaven. There the learned watchful brāhmaṇas kindle (the fire). The wise brāhmaṇas, desiring its contact, go to that place. That highest place of Viṣṇu is called Mokṣa (liberation). Those free from bondage obtain (i.e. reach) that happy place. Reaching it they do not come back (i.e. are not reborn). Therefore, it is called

Mokṣa (liberation). Mokṣa is the highest place (state); it is divine, immortal, the abode of Viṣṇu; it is indestructible; it is the highest abode; it is Vaikuṇṭha, the eternal place. It is nitya (eternal), the highest heaven, the best and the sanātana (ancient). These are the synonymns of the highest abode of Viṣṇu. I shall (now) explain in detail the form of the vibhūti of that Tripād.

CHAPTER TWO HUNDRED TWENTYEIGHT

Description of the Highest Heaven etc.

Śrī Mahādeva said:

1-6. The worlds of the vibhūti of Tripād are said to be innumerable. All they are made of pure sattva, and are called bliss and happiness. All they are eternal, free from change, and void of attachment etc. that are worthy of being abandoned. All are golden, pure, and have the lustre of crores of suns. They are full of all Vedas, are divine, and free from lust and anger. They are resorted to by those who take joy only in devotion to the lotus-like feet of Viṣṇu. They are completely happy due to continuous chanting of the Sāmans. All are of the nature of the five Upaniṣads and have the lustre of the Vedas. All of them are covered with divine men and women full of the Vedas. They are adorned with lakes having water in the form of only the flavour of the Vedas. They have the immobile objects in the form of the holy texts, the codes of law and the Purāṇas. It is not possible for me to describe the full expanse of (these) worlds.

7-13. Only the distance between Virajā and the highest heaven is said (to be covered by them). That place should be enjoyed by those who resort to the unmanifest Brahman. That absolute position which gives joy and happiness due to the experience of one's own self is called *Niśśreyas*, *Nirvāṇa*, *Kaivalya* and *Mokṣa*. Those who are nourished by the happiness due to their interest in devoutly serving the lotus-like feet of the lord of Śrī, and whose intellect is small, desire mokṣa, void of happiness. (But) the high-souled, noble ones who serve the feet of the lord go to that highest abode of Viṣṇu which gives pleasure (derived) from Brahman. That place of Viṣṇu (called) Vaikuṇṭha is crowded with diverse communities. It is covered with ramparts, splendid rooms and great mansions. In it is a divine city called Ayodhyā. It is covered with ramparts rich in gems, gold and pictures, and with portals. It has four gates and is covered with jewelled principal gates. It is protected by door-keepers like Caṇḍa and Kumuda. At the eastern gate there are Caṇḍa and Pracaṇḍa, and at the western there are Bhadra and Subhadraka.

14-18. Jaya and Vijaya are in the west, and Dhātṛ and Vidhātṛ are at the northern (gate). The other doorkeepers are: Kumuda, Kumudākṣa. Puṇḍarīka and Vāmana. (So also) Śaṅkukarṇa, Sarvanetra, Sumukha, Supratiṣṭhita. These are said to be the regents of the quarters in this city, O you of an auspicious face. It is covered with crores of rows of houses resembling fire (brightness). It is endowed with eternal divine women and men, who have mounted (i.e. stepped into) youth. In the centre of the city there is the charming harem of the god. It is possessed of jewelled ramparts, and adorned with jewelled arched doorways. It has many splendid rooms, principal mansions, and palaces. On all sides it is adorned with bevies of divine celestial nymphs and ladies.

19-24. In the centre is an open hall with a high royal place. It is furnished with a thousand pillars (decked) with rubies, is full of gems and is beautiful. It is full of divine pearls and is adorned with chanting of Sāmans. At its centre is a charming, beautiful throne full of all Vedas. It is always surrounded by deities like Dharma (i.e. Righteousness), full of the Vedas, and by Piety, Knowledge, Great Affluence and Detachment having shining bodies. It is also surrounded by Ṛg, Yajus, Sāman and Atharvan (Vedas) in (due) order, and in a bodily form. Śakti (i.e. power), Ādhāraśakti (i.e. supporting power), Cicchakti (i.e. power of mind) always auspicious, so also the powers of the deities like Dharma are called Śakti. In the centre of it live the rays of Fire, the Sun, and the Moon. So also (there live) Kūrma, the king of serpents, Vainateya (i.e. Garuḍa) and the lord of the triad (of the Vedas). All the Vedas and the hymns have resorted to the condition of a seat?

25. The divine seat, full of all syllables is known as the seat

of practice in abstract meditation. At its centre is an eight-petalled lotus, bright like the rising sun.

26-39a. In it in a bright pericarp the Supreme Being, the lord of gods, is seated with the goddess, O you of a beautiful appearance. He is dark like the petal of a blue lotus. He has the light like that of a crore of suns. He is a young boy, is glossy (or affectionate) and is covered with (i.e. has) delicate limbs. He resembles a full-blown red lotus. He has delicate, lotus-like feet. His eyes are like the full-blown lotuses; is marked with a couple of fine, creeper-like (arched) eye-brows. His nose is good; he is endowed with good cheeks; he has good ears and a lotus-like face. He has teeth resembling pearls. His coral-like lips have a smile on them. He resembles the full moon; his lotus-like face has a charming smile on it. He shines with ear-rings resembling the colour of the young sun. He is adorned with very glossy, dark and curly hair. His hair is tied into a braid having (the flowers of) mandāra and pārijātaka. He is adorned with the Kaustubha (jewel) resembling the rising, morning sun. He shines with a conch-like neck to which garlands and golden wreaths are attached. He shines with very high, large shoulders resembling those of a lion. He is adorned with four plump, round and long arms. He is adorned with rings, bracelets and armlets. His large chest is adorned with good ornaments like the Kaustubha, resembling crores of young suns. He is adorned with a garland of wood-flowers. He has a lovely navel which is the place of origin of the Creator. He is endowed with (i.e. has put on) a soft yellow garment resembling the morning sunshine. His feet are beautiful due to various gems. He shines with two bracelets. He has a row of nails resembling the moon with the moonlight. Acyuta is the treasure of the handsomeness and beauty of a crore of Cupids. He (i.e. his body) is smeared with divine sandal. He is adorned with a divine garland. He shines with his raised arms that have held the conch and the disc. So also (he shines) with the other two hands granting boons.

39b-46. On his left thigh is seated goddess Mahālakṣmī, the great deity. She has a golden complexion and is deer-eyed. She has (put on) a wreath of gold and silver. She is endowed with all (auspicious) marks; and her body has (just) the commencement of youth (i.e. the body is youthful). She has (put on) jewelled ear-rings. Her hair is dark and curly. Her body is smeared with divine sandal, and she shines with divine flowers. Her fine hair is decked with flowers of mandāra, ketakī and jasmine; her eye-brows are good; her nose is fine; her buttocks are good (i.e. plump); her breasts are plump and raised. She resembles the full moon. Her lotus-like face has a charming smile on it. She is adorned with ear-rings resembling the colour of the young sun. Her complexion resembles gold purified with fire. Her ornaments are made of gold purified by fire. She is endowed with four hands. She is adorned with a golden lotus. She is abounding in various beautiful gems. She is also adorned with necklaces, armlets, bracelets and rings. She shines with a couple of big lotuses held in both her hands. Her hands are graced with golden ornaments called citrons.

47-50. In this way the lord, the great god, always shines in the highest heaven with Mahālakṣmī never leaving him. On his two sides are seated the auspicious Dharaṇī and Nīlā on an auspicious seat. And on the tips of the petals in the eight directions are seated the Śaktis (i.e. the powers embodied) like Vimalā. Vimalā, Utkarṣiṇī, Jñānā, Kriyā, Yogā, so also Prahvī, Satyā and Īśānā, are the (eight) powers of the highest soul. Endowed with all (auspicious) marks, they, holding divine chowries, having moon-like lustre, delight their lord, Acyuta.

51-54. (There are also) bevies of celestial nymphs, and five hundred women. They live in the harem and are adorned with all ornaments. All they have lotuses in their hands, and have lustre like that of crores of fires. They are endowed with all (auspicious) marks, and have faces resembling the moon. The king, the Highest Being, surrounded by them shines. He is also surrounded by Ananta, Garuḍa, and other principal gods like Kārtikeya. He is also surrounded by other servants, eternally liberated. The highest Being, fond of enjoyments and affluence, delights with Ramā.

55-57. O auspicious Girijā, in this way the lord of Vaikuṇṭha shines in the highest place. I shall explain to you his vyūhas (manifestations) and worlds. In the east of the Vaikuṇṭhaloka is the abode of Viṣṇu. In the southeast is Lakṣmī's abode. In the south is Saṁkarṣaṇa's abode. In the southwest is (the abode) of Sarasvatī. In the west is the abode of Pradyumna. In the northwest is the place of Rati. The land of Aniruddha is in the north.

58. In the northeast is the Śānti-loka. This is the first covering. Then there are twentyfour worlds in a sequence beginning with Keśava.

59-65. The second covering of Vaikuṇṭha is called Śubha. The third auspicious covering consists of the worlds of Matsya, Kūrma, etc. The fourth auspicious covering has the worlds Satya, Acyuta, Ananta, Durgā, Viṣvaksena, Gajānana, Śaṁkha, Padma, Nidhi. In the great directions are the worlds of Ṛg, Yajus, Sāman and Atharvan. So also of Sāvitrī, Garuḍa, Dharma and Sacrifice. The fifth covering is said to be inexhaustible and full of all Speech. So also (there are) the conch, the disc, the mace, the lotus, the sword, the bow, the plough also, and the pestle. The worlds are (thus) equipped with all weapons and missiles. The sixth indestructible covering is said to be consisting of hymns and missiles. Then (there are those) of Indra, Agni, Yama, Nirṛti, Varuṇa, Vāyu, Soma, Īśāna. The seventh is said to be (occupied) by the sages. The Sādhyas, the hosts of Maruts, the Viśvedevas, all are eternal (residents) in the highest abode. So also are other gods.

66-71a. In the material world they are the transient gods. The holy text says: 'The great ones sought out the heaven.' Thus the highest place shines with those liberated, eternal ones fond of enjoyment. The powerful lord shines with the divine queens. The sun does not illumine it; nor does the moon, nor does the fire. Having reached it, the ascetics of acute vows do not return (to the earth). Those who are devoted to the formula consisting of two (divine names) only go to that immutable (place). (It is) not (reached) by means of Vedas, sacrifices, study, gifts, auspicious vows, austerities accompanied by fasts, and other expedients. That eternal, ancient place is to be reached by means of the formula of a couple of names only, so also by means of concentrated devotion or submission.

Pārvatī said:

71b-73. O lord, you have well explained the nature of heaven. How did he dwell in the highest heaven, in the whole territory? For what purpose did he dwell (there)? What is the purpose of (his) sport? How did the lord, the highest god, living in the world consisting of pure sattva live with his vibhūti mixed with rajas and tamas?

Rudra said:

74-75. In his Tripād-vibhūti the glorious highest lord, living with the goddess, and always having his sole enjoyment, is delighted. That great illusion, Prakṛti, the resort of the world, having joined the palms of her hands, extolled the highest god.

Mahāmāyā (*the Great Illusion*) *said*:

76-90. Salutation to you, the dwelling-place of the three worlds. Salutation to you of the form of the universe. Salutation to you, the ancient one. Salutation to you, the cause of the origin of the world. Salutation to (you) the lord of Śrī, Bhū, Līlā; to Nārāyaṇa. Salutation to you the glorious one; to Viṣṇu, having the Śārṅga (bow). Salutation to you of the form of all gods, to Viṣṇu, to the triumphant one; to you of a thousand forms, and to you Ananta. Repeated salutations to Acyuta, the one having no modification, and of a pure, good form, and having a form that has no beginning, middle or end. Salutation to you, Hiraṇyagarbha, Yajña (i.e. Sacrifice), to the highest soul, to the soul of all beings, and to the refuge of all beings. Salutation to Brahman, to Light, to you of the form of the universe, to you of pure feet, to the supreme soul, the highest (being). Salutation to you, Saṁkarṣaṇa, Rudra, the prop of all beings, to Hayagrīva, to the blazing Kāla (i.e. Death), to Viṣṇu. Salutation to you, O man (i.e. the chief deity) of sacrifice, of the nature of the oblations made to deities and dead ancestors. Salutation to the lord of beings, to the Sun of auspicious lustre, to Agni, enjoying oblations offered to gods, and to him, the soul (or of the nature) of sacrifice. Salutation to the procreator, to the cause of creation, maintenance and destruction. Salutation to him who is to be known by the Upaniṣads, and of the nature of four souls. Salutation to you, Brahmā, Viṣṇu. Salutation to Śaṅkara (literally, doing good) also. Salutation to you having the three qualities and the cause of creation, maintenance and destruction. Salutation to you the qualityless one, living in the hearts of all. Salutation to that Viṣṇu, the unmanifest, watching the worlds. Salutation to Nārāyaṇa, the lord of Śrī, of the form of six qualities, to him full of unending qualities, and the giver of all objects. Salutation to Vāsudeva having the form of five states. Salutation to you having the five and nine different vyūhas (manifestations). Salutation to Yajña-varāha; repeated salutations to Govinda, to the unchanging one, to the pure one, and to the adversary of what is fit to be abandoned. Salutation to you, Rāma, Kṛṣṇa, Narasiṁha. Salutation to you, Keśava, remover of the affliction of the worlds.

91-96. You, Viṣṇu, are the refuge of all the worlds. O lord of the god of gods, be pleased for the good of all worlds. All the sentient beings, having no support and shelter, stay in me. They are bodiless, formless and without all senses. They are without the practices of religious austerities, and always experience misery. O Keśava, please give them worlds and bodies. O omniscient one, create as before the vibhūti (glory) of your sport. O great lord, see, the entire sentient and insentient, mobile and immobile (world) is deluded by me for (your) sport. O Viṣṇu, create with me the material egg. Having put into the mundane existence, piety and impiety, pleasure, pain, and resorting to me, please indulge in sport. Do not tarry.

Śrī Mahādeva said:

97-101. The highest lord, thus addressed by the deity Māyā, entered her, and started creating the world. He who is called Prakṛti-Puruṣa (Matter and Lord), here is Acyuta. He alone is lord Viṣṇu. He entered the Prakṛti. In the Prakṛti he created Brahmā and (other) beings, resorting to Mahat (i.e. intellect). From this Mahat, Ahaṁkāra (Ego) sprang up. From that Ahaṁkāra, the triad of the constituents (guṇas) came up. From the three constituents the creator of the universe produced the subtle elements. At that moment only the gross elements sprang up from the subtle elements. From Brahman, of the nature of the three constituents, Oṁkāra (i.e. the syllable Om) first came up.

102-107. Vāyu (i.e. air) sprang from Ākāśa (i.e. ether); from Vāyu, Agni (i.e. fire) came up. From Agni, water sprang up; and from water the earth is said to have sprung up. The elements—ether and others—were created one after another. Their qualities—sound, touch, colour, taste and odour (were produced). The great lord, having created and taken the guṇas one after another, and having mixed them up, created the very great egg of the world and those that merged there, which are fourteen in number. In it Viṣṇu created gods like Brahmā, divinities, lower animals, human beings and four kinds of immobile (objects). Then in him having lotus-like eyes he created the great creation. There, the former (souls) remaining in Prakṛti, are born from him in the stocks of gods etc. in accordance with their former deeds.

CHAPTER TWO HUNDRED TWENTYNINE

A Description of Viṣṇu's Vyūhas

Pārvatī said:

1. Tell me in detail about the excellent creation of gods. How were the ancient ones like Brahmā, the best in heaven, were born? Tell me also in detail about the incarnations of the lord.

Rudra said:

2-7. Ether, Air, Fire, Water and Earth were created in due succession. Brahmā created the unfathomable ocean of water among them. In this which had become an ocean, Viṣṇu, taking all the beings, slept the sleep at the end of a yuga, on a leaf of a fig-tree in the water that was his Māyā. Desiring to create the world he had the sleep at the end of a yuga. Madhusūdana (i.e. Viṣṇu) enjoyed for a long time with that Māyā. On her he generated the excellent Time. So also the divisions of Time like Kalā, Kāṣṭhā, and of the form of a fortnight, a month etc. At that time the lotus in the form of Viṣṇu's navel, which was of the shape of a bud, began to expand. The very bright one was the origin of the world. There the very intelligent Brahmā sprang up. He, desiring to create the world, and impelled by the quality of rajas, praised the highest god having his sleep at the end of the yuga.

Brahmā said:

8-15. Salutation to you, Viṣṇu, the cause of creation, maintenance, and destruction, to you adorned with the ornament of the world, to you the affluent one and of the form of the universe. Salutation to god Brahmaṇya (i.e. the creator), beneficial to cows and brāhmaṇas and beneficial to the world; repeated salutations to Kṛṣṇa, to Govinda. Salutation to (you) of the form of Pradhāna (i.e. Prakṛti) and Time, to the Highest Being, the god. Salutation to (you) of the form of the visible world and not having the form of it. Repeated salutations to Nārāyaṇa, Viśva, the lord of the universe, to the lord of Śrī, Bhū, Nīlā, to Brahman, the highest soul. Salutation to Vāsudeva, of the form of the universe and having the Śārṅga bow, to the lord of the triad (of the Vedas), to Hari, of the form of the lord of the universe. Salutation to you, perfect with endless auspicious qualities. When you, full of the world, sleep, the entire world sleeps. O lord of the world, in the visible world, everything mobile and immobile is covered (by you). You alone are the cause, the agent, and the effect due to the three constituents (viz. sattva, rajas, tamas). You alone are the creator, the one who meditates, and the maker. You remaining in the pure sattva (quality) keep awake. Whence can you have sleep? O god, worlds, the ancient ones, have abided in you.

Śiva said:

16-19. Thus addressed by Brahmā, the highest god Viṣṇu, freed from his sleep at the end of the yuga, got up from that bed. The inconceivable Acyuta, the lord of the worlds, having controlled his sleep at the end of the yuga, commenced creating the world at that moment. Having thought, the Highest Being then created the entire world. Then the lord created in the lotus of his navel all the worlds, the golden egg lying in the water, the seven islands limited by oceans and having land and mountains, with the frying pan (like) egg.

20-24. The lord, Viṣṇu, took his place in the egg. Then with his mind devoted to the supreme spirit, Brahmā meditated upon Viṣṇu. At the end of the meditation a drop of perspiration was produced from his forehead. That drop, of the shape of a bubble, in a moment fell on the earth. O you of an excellent face, I, having three eyes, a trident, and adorned with the crown of the matted hair, was born from that bubble. With modesty I asked the lord of gods: "What shall I do?" Then god Viṣṇu, with delight, thus spoke to me: "O Rudra, you will bring about a fierce-looking destruction of the world, (after) actually being (my) portion, viz. Saṁkarṣaṇa, O you of an excellent face."

25-29. O goddess, from that Nārāyaṇa, I, the fearful one, was born. Having entrusted me with the destruction (of the world), Viṣṇu just again produced from his eyes the moon and the sun, that remove darkness. From his ears he produced Vāyu and directions, and Indra and Agni from his mouth. The lotus-eyed one produced Varuṇa (and) Mitra from his nostrils, and all gods with the Sādhyas and hosts of Maruts from his arms. (He produced) gems and herbs from all the pores of his skin. On (i.e. from) his skin (he produced) mountains, oceans and beasts like cows. Brāhmaṇa was created from his face, and kṣatriya from his arms. Vaiśya sprang up from his thighs and śūdra from his feet.

30-39. Having thus created the entire world, remaining insentient, the lord of the universe remained in it in a universal form. As without the power of that Viṣṇu it did not have winking, therefore, the ancient Viṣṇu alone is the life of the entire world. He alone, the highest soul, being of an unmanifest nature settled down. Brahmā himself proceeds with creation, maintenance and destruction. That ancient Vāsudeva is full of six qualities. From himself having the qualities (of sattva, rajas and tamas) he made his form, the world, into four. The lord of the form of Pradyumna is endowed with all grandeur. He having obtained the position of the inner controller of the lords of creation, time, and people, properly brings about the creation. Then to the high-souled one he gave the Vedas along with the Itihāsas. Brahmā, the grandsire of the world, the portion of Pradyumna, (thus) born of the portion, brings about the creation and maintenance of the world. Lord Aniruddha, endowed with power and lustre, and having got the position of the inner controller of Manus, kings, time and people looks after the maintenance. Lord Saṁkarṣaṇa, Mahā Viṣṇu, endowed with knowledge and power, after assuming the position of the inner controller of time, all beings, Rudra and Yama destroys the world.

40-44. Thus the state of the inner-controllership of self consists in his being the innermost soul. Matsya, Kūrma, Varāha, Narasiṁha, Vāmana, Rāma, Paraśurāma, Kṛṣṇa, Buddha and Kalki are the ten Vibhavas (incarnations) of Brahman, the highest soul. The group of six qualities is said to exist in Nṛsiṁha, Rāma and Kṛṣṇa. The highest state of the god is like one lamp being produced (i.e. lighted) from another lamp. O auspicious Girijā, that is the state of this Viṣṇu. Listen. The highest heaven Vaikuṇṭha, the excellent Viṣṇuloka, his own form Śvetadvīpa, the excellent Milky Ocean are said to be the four-fold Vyūha (manifestation of god) by the great sages.

45-50. The auspicious origin of Vaikuṇṭha is in the covering of water. It is (bright) like a crore of fires. All that is imperishable like Dharma. It is resorted to by fragrant trees like mandāra and fires. It is full of many gems, is divine, and contains crores of aeroplanes. That which is said to be the highest abode has characteristics like those. In that excellent city of Vaikuṇṭha, bright with various jewels there is a charming, excellent abode called Devajayārāma, which has four doors and has golden ramparts and arched doorways. It is guarded by doorkeepers like Caṇḍa and Kumuda and others. It is filled with divine residences full of various jewels. On all sides it is extended up to five thousand billion yojanas. It is filled with crores of mansions as lofty as thousand yojanas.

51-58. It is adorned with divine men and women who have entered youth. The women and men here look splendid with all good marks. They resemble Śrī Viṣṇu in form, and are adorned with all ornaments. They are covered with divine garlands and garments, and are adorned with divine sandal (paste). They, accomplished with eight syllables of the formula (mantra), through devotion for the lord of gods, of sixteen kinds, rejoice (there), O you naturally charming one. Entering his place, they rejoice as liked by their mind. Having gone into it, and remaining with Viṣṇu, they never return. With their souls intact, the auspicious ones in the company of Viṣṇu, the wise ones, always obtain happiness like that of him. (Those) ones of auspicious hearts having here and there entered Viṣṇu's worlds, again obtain heaven, like the beings living in heaven. Like Lakṣmaṇa, Bharata and Saṁkarṣaṇa and others they are also born in Satyaloka according to their desire. Then by that (path) only they go to that eternal, highest place. The devotees of Viṣṇu do not have the bondage due to acts and birth.

59-66. The wise say that being Viṣṇu's servant is liberation. Being bound by the lord of gods is not described as a bondage. Viṣṇu's servants are free from all bonds and from blemishes. All worlds up to that of Brahmā are characterized by returning (i.e. one has to come back to the earth after esiding there for some time). They are marked by karmabandha (bondage due to acts), have friends like (i.e. are accompanied by) misery, cause, fear, result in great exertion, and cause the destruction of birth, O goddess. The enjoyment of pleasures by men is (just) like food mixed with poison. The deities, getting angry on seeing men with (the effects of) their (good) deeds exhausted, drop them into the mundane existence, having the bondage due to deeds. Therefore, O goddess, the pleasures in heaven cause trouble in many ways. A meditating sage should avoid it which is transient, fraudulent and mixed with misery. He should always remember Viṣṇu, the medicine destroying the mass of all miseries. Merely by the utterance of (Viṣṇu's) name they obtain the highest position. Therefore, O Gaurī, a wise man should desire (to go to) the heaven of Viṣṇu. With undistracted devotion he should worship the lord, the ocean of pity. There is no doubt that he having all knowledge and virtues does protect him.

67-80. Therefore, having muttered the very pious, auspicious formula of eight syllables, he obtains Viṣṇu's world, giving all desired objects. The glorious Viṣṇu, seated on the jewelled couch (bright) like the rays of a thousand suns, (placed) in a divine hall, shone. The glorious Viṣṇu is seated on a divine lotus-seat, (placed on) a divine golden seat, which is held by Śaktis supporting it, which is full of many jewels, which has many colours; the seat is on the eight-petalled lotus, auspicious like the eight letters of the formula, having the auspicious mystical letter of Lakṣmī, and having the lustre like that of crores of young suns. To his right side is the world's mother, Hiraṇmayī (full of gold). She is holding the divine chowries. She is adorned with divine garlands. With her hands she has held a pot of jewels, a citron, and a golden lotus. To his right is goddess Pṛthivī (the Earth), bright like the petals of a blue lotus. She is having various ornaments and is adorned with beautiful garments. In her upper hands she has held a couple of beautiful red lotuses. With the other two hands the goddess has held a couple of vessels of corn. Holding divine chowries, the Śaktis like Vimalā who are graced with all (good) marks, are seated on the tips of the petals. Among them is seated glorious Acyuta, Hari. He is adorned with hands having divine ornaments like the conch, the disc, the mace and the lotus, and ornaments like armlets and necklaces. He shines with ear-rings like the sun rising in the morning. The lord, enjoying (himself), served by the eternal gods mentioned before, lives in the eternal city of Vaikuṇṭha in the Satya (world). The rich, eight-syllabled formula takes the wise siddhas and never others to that Viṣṇu's world. O you of an excellent face, I have thus described to you the first Vyūha.

81-86. O you of a good vow, I shall explain to you the second world of Viṣṇu. This world of Viṣṇu is known as eternal and is said to be the best among the worlds. That large, meritorious, pure, auspicious world, full of goodness shines like a thousand mid-day suns (shining) simultaneously. Even at the end of the kalpa that very great world would not merge (into Brahman). It is not possible for me or the gods like Brahmā to see it. On all sides the whole of it is full of the groves of the desire-yielding trees. It is endowed with oblong lakes full of nectar-like water. It is graced with divine lotuses full of gold and jewels. It is covered with crores of divine ornaments resembling lightning. It is graced continually with Sāmans, cooings of cuckoos etc. and with trees and flowers carrying fragrance.

87-90. It is covered by divine women and men aged less than sixteen, rich with the grace of all (good) marks, and almost divine ornaments. Women, with their delighted husbands worship Lakṣmī's lord in charming regions in that land. They always obtain the happiness fit to be obtained through his grace. They sing the great deeds of Kṛṣṇa, giving great joy. Very beautiful, auspicious women, having lotus-like eyes, lotus-like feet, resembling Lakṣmī, having divine garlands and garments sport (there).

91-96. Men, holding conches, discs, maces and lotuses,

adorned with ornaments, having garlands, wearing yellow garments, are there. Due to mutual touch the pleasure of devotion for Viṣṇu and delight of the men and women sporting there, grow day by day. In it is the charming and graced harem of Viṣṇu. It is endowed with sandal, agaru-sandal, camphor, saffron and water. It is all around decorated with many flowers and halls. In it, on a divine, beautiful and soft bed which is covered with a bright cover, which is on the lotus-seat, and which is under the shade of the desire-yielding tree, and which has the covers of flowers, rich in the beauty of divine fragrance, the ancient Viṣṇu, the lord of gods, is seated with goddess Lakṣmī.

97-107. He is like crores of moons. He is adorned with divine ornaments. His face is adorned with a pair of soft nostrils of a fine complexion. He shines with glossy, large and beautiful cheeks. He has dark and curly hair. His eyes resemble petals of a red lotus. He has put flowers of mandāra, ketakī, jasmine and white lotuses on his head. His lips are like glossy bimba-fruits. His lotus-like face has a beautiful smile on it. He shines with rows of teeth that shine like priceless pearls. His body is smeared with haricandana. He is having a mark made with musk. He has lovely elevated shoulders and four long arms. He has beautiful sprout-like hands resembling the japā-flower. He has his broad chest adorned with Śrīvatsa and Kaustubha. He is adorned with very beautiful divine wreaths full of pearls. He is covered with a yellow garment like (the light of) the early morning sun and the moonlight. He is adorned with lotus leaves along with anklets decked with rubies. He is adorned with rows of nails like the moon without a spot. His feet and lotus-like hands are soft like red lotuses and fair. He is adorned with a couple of arms having a conch and a disc. With the other two he has clung Lakṣmī's body to his chest. With her he shines like a cloud to which lightning has clung. His couple of auspicious and soft feet is like gold purified by fire. Here the ancient Viṣṇu, the lord of gods, sports.

108-117a. (Lakṣmī is) like gold purified by fire. She is adorned with all ornaments. She is adorned with very glistening and curved sapphires like the row of the digits of the moon. She is adorned with the divine flowers of mandāra and pārijāta. The ends of her hair are beautified by ear-ornaments, and resemble bees. With her stout and raised breasts she presses Viṣṇu's chest. She is adorned with ornaments like armlets and necklaces. She, the beautiful wife of the lord of all worlds, is always full of youth (i.e. she is ever young). There she eternally sports with the lord of the worlds. That Vāsudeva only, attracting the minds of all beings, and giving the desired objects to men, plays in this entire world. Around him are the eight powers—the eight bodies of Lakṣmī. (They are) Ramā, Rukmiṇī, Sītā, Padmā, Padmālayā, Śivā, Sulakṣaṇā and Suśīlā; they protect that place (lit. world) with weapons like conches, discs, maces, lotuses and śārṅgas (bows), and with lotus-like arrays formed around. Thus, O you of an auspicious appearance, I have properly and in brief described to you the form of the second (Vyūha). It is not possible to describe it in detail. Those who mutter the twelve-syllabled formula giving pleasure always obtain (this) eternal, auspicious, indestructible (world).

117b-123. The world of Viṣṇu can never be obtained by means of Vedic studies, sacrifices, vows and fasting, except by serving (Viṣṇu). Therefore, a devotee should worship Viṣṇu with an undistracted mind. He obtains the highest divine power, freeing him (self) from the bondage of (i.e. due to) his deeds. O goddess, the second, indestructible Vyūha is said to be like this. O Pārvatī, listen. I shall describe to you the third great Vyūha. O you very intelligent one, on the northern shore of the ocean is the Śvetadvīpa. There Viṣṇu stays to allow his view to the meditating sages like the noble Sanaka. Sanaka, Sananda, the third, viz. Sanātana, so also Sanatkumāra, Jātas, Voḍhu, Pañcaśikha—these very bright meditating sages are the sons of Brahmā. They are detached from all enjoyments, are pure, and are always of pure qualities. They enjoy only the flavour of the pleasure due to seeing the lord.

124-133. Viṣṇu dwells there in the vicinity so that Nara, Nārāyaṇa, etc. who reside in the Śvetadvīpa, should (be able to) see him. In the Śvetadvīpa, resembling crores of suns, bright due to being full of various jewels, resorted to by great meditating sages, and free from fear, there are charming parks (having trees) like pārijāta. (The place is) crowded with santāna-creepers, adorned with sandal-trees containing blooming white and blue lotuses, and reservoirs of water. In it is an auspicious, charming city called Airāvatī. It shines with many divine halls full of various jewels. It is occupied by divine women and men, and full of many mansions. In it is a harem crowded with jewelled trees. It is covered with many lofty mansions, resembling the young sun. In it is a pavilion which is divine, which is graced with gems and gold, and made fragrant with the fragrance of sandal, agaru-sandal, camphor and saffron. It is adorned with canopies rich in beauty with various flowers. It is crowded with celestial damsels, and graced with the chanting of Sāmans. At the centre there is a throne bright like the sun or fire. In it there is an eight-petalled lotus like another orb of the moon. In it, in the pericarp, is seated Viṣṇu. He is like pure gold, and is adorned with a necklace of pearl.

134-138. He has four powerful hands holding a conch, a disc, a mace and a lotus. He is graced with a necklace, armlets, bracelets and rings. He has lovely feet resembling golden lotuses. He is graced with rows of white nails like santānaka (flowers). He is adorned with youth proper for the age and form of (a lad of) sixteen years. He is graced with an upright, fragrant mark (Ūrdhvapuṇḍra) made with saffron, and the parting line of hair. He is well covered with a white garment resembling the foam of nectar that was churned (out of the ocean). He is graced with white ear-rings made of pearls. He, whose body fascinates the world, is seated on the lotus-seat.

139-145. On his left lap is seated the goddess of a divine form. She, Lakṣmī, is worthy of him in character, good qualities etc. She resembles lotus-filaments, is graced with the advent of youth, is endowed with all (good) marks, and has ornaments of gold purified in fire. She has put on a divine garland and garment; her hair is dark and curly. She, shining with four arms, is adorned with armlets. She shines with pearl-necklaces; her hair is graced with mandāra (flowers). Her nostrils are soft; she is graced with rows of bright teeth. She has put on the mark of musk on her forehead. The tip of her nose is graced with pearls. She has stout and raised breasts like golden pitchers. Her body is smeared with divine saffron. She is graced with a divine garland. The goddess holds in her lotus-like hands a vessel containing garments, a citron, a mirror, a golden lotus. Around Viṣṇu there are these Śaktis (powers) of her, resembling her:

146-150. Īśā, Vāsyā, Mahādevī, Jāhnavī, Kamalālayā, Sāvitrī, Sarvagā, Padmā are said to be (her) Śaktis. Sraddhā, Medhā, Dhṛti, Prajñā, Dhāraṇā, and Śānti, (so also) Śruti, Smṛti, Dhṛti, Medhā, Vṛddhi, Buddhi, Manīṣiṇī, are said to be Lakṣmī's maids, doing all (pieces of) work. The deities like Ananta and Garuḍa are the usual servants. The eternal deities like the Sādhyas, the hosts of Maruts, pleased with enjoyments obtained through his (her?) favour, serve him (her?) in the palaces, mansions, groves and cities. The eternal ones avoiding what should be abandoned and what is fruitless, always and continually play there.

151-153. Those who, full of faith, constantly mutter Viṣṇu's formula, those who are engaged in the Dvādaśī-vow, go to his immutable position. O Girijā, the ancient world of Viṣṇu cannot be reached by means of Vedas, gifts, sacrifices or even by vows. The place of Viṣṇu can be reached by men with undistracted devotion. Therefore, one should always worship Viṣṇu with undistracted devotion.

154-155. One should narrate (his account), (should utter) just his name, should meditate upon him, should always mutter his formula, should devoutly offer oblations to, and propitiate the omnipresent one giving all desired objects. O you of beautiful buttocks (i.e. beautiful one), I have told you about the third Vyūha and nature of the highest soul as described by the ancient ones.

156-168. Hereafter I shall explain (to you) the excellent fourth Vyūha. To protect the gods, he, resembling crores of moons, lies on the extensive, auspicious bed of Ananta, in the Milky Ocean adorned by Indra, and covered by youths like Indra. Padmanābha, Acyuta, Hari is seated on a divine seat. He resembles a dark cloud. His eyes are large like lotus-leaves. He is graced with a crown resembling a crore of suns. He shines with two divine ear-rings, bright with various jewels. He is covered with a yellow garment resembling the early morning sun or the moonlight. He is graced with the palms of his hands and soles of his feet resembling bright red lotuses. He is graced with necklaces, armlets, bracelets and rings. He is adorned with hands having the conch, disc, mace, Śārṅga (bow) and sword. He is graced with the desire-yielding trees rich in good flowers, fruits and branches. He is graced with the navel-lotus (the place) of the birth and death (i.e. the origin and destruction) of the universe. His body is smeared with yellow sandal. He is adorned with all ornaments. He has tied his very glossy, dark, curly hair into a braid with divine, charming flowers of mandāra, pārijāta etc. He is graced with a soft, high nose and a pair of high shoulders and knees. He is graced with feet having anklets and having gems and corals. He is graced with rows of nails like the spotless moon. His lotus-like face has lips resembling the aśoka-flowers. He is beautified with rows of teeth bright like priceless pearls. He is graced with a smiling face resembling the full moon. He has entered youth. He is glorious. He is bright with tender limbs. He is the refuge of all the people and gives the fruits to all the people.

169-175. The goddess is worthy of him in qualities like beauty, character etc. She resembles gold purified by fire, and has ornaments of gold purified by fire. She is young; has a beautiful form; she is endowed with charm, (good) character and qualities. She has covered herself with a white garment resembling the form of the Milky Ocean. Her hair is decked with the flowers of mandāra, ketakī and jasmine. She has the mark of musk on her forehead. The parting of her hair is graced with a gem. She has the beauty of many complexions. She is adorned with ear-ornaments. She smiles beautifully with her red lips having the light like the coral. She is well graced with glossy hair resembling intoxicated bees. Her waist is slender. Her eyes are large. Her breasts are stout and raised. She has four charming hands. She is adorned with all ornaments. The goddess has held a couple of auspicious golden lotuses in her raised hands. She has remained closely embracing her lord with the other two (hands). With her glances she is constantly looking at the gods.

176-180. O Pārvatī, the gods constantly looked at by the goddess are fortunate. There gods, siddhas, cāraṇas, kinnars, remaining in the hall, and with their eyes full of the tears of joy constantly sing to the goddess. The lord of gods, being praised by the gods like Brahmā, Rudra harassed by the demons, granted fearlessness to the gods. Hari, the lord of all gods, having granted fearlessness to gods, started killing the demons for the protection of the world. O you sinless one, I have thus explained to you Viṣṇu's fourth Vyūha. O you of an excellent face, what else do you desire to hear? I shall tell it. You are fortunate; you are blessed. You are a devotee of Viṣṇu.

CHAPTER TWO HUNDRED THIRTY

The Fish Incarnation of Viṣṇu

Pārvatī said:

1-2. O venerable one, please tell me duly taking what form the lord of gods, Viṣṇu, killed the demons. O Śiva, tell me in detail the grandeur of the forms (i.e. incarnations) of the Fish, the Tortoise of (i.e. taken by) the Greatest (lord).

Mahādeva said:

3-11. O goddess, listen with an alert mind. I shall tell (you) the grandeur of Viṣṇu and the nature of his incarnations of the Fish, the Tortoise etc. As from one lamp another is produced (i.e. lighted), so would be the forms of the highest lord. The grand incarnations of the god are said to be auspicious and of various forms. There are also images of the highest lord that are worshipped. Brahmā, due to his being the Creator, is the universal lord and a great joy. Bhṛgu, Marīci, Atri, Dakṣa, and Kardama, so also Pulastya, Pulaha, Giriśa and Kratu are said to be the nine lords, in succession, of the created beings. Venerable Marīci generated Kaśyapa. O you of an auspicious appearance, Kaśyapa had four wives: (They were:) Aditi, Diti, Kadru and Vinatā also. Aditi gave birth to gods of shining appearance. Diti (gave birth) to demonic sons who were Tāmasa by nature. Some very great demons were: Śambūka, Hayagrīva, and the very mighty Hiraṇyākṣa; so also Hiraṇyakaśipu, Jambha, Maya and others. Makara, of a very severe penance, and very powerful, went to Brahmā's world.

12-14. The powerful one, having duped Brahmā, seized the Vedas. Having seized the holy texts he entered the great ocean. Then the whole world became a void, and religious practices got mixed. There were no studies. There was no offering made to deities. The practices of the castes and the stages of human life were ignored. Then god Brahmā, surrounded by hosts of all gods, went to the Milky Ocean, and seeking refuge of god (Viṣṇu), praised him.

Brahmā said:

15-23a. Favour me, O god, O lord, O you seated on the serpent-couch, O lord of all gods, O soul of all gods, O you full of Vedas, O Acyuta. You are the first seed of the world-tree. In the middle (i.e. in its maintenance) you are superior to all. In the end (i.e. at the time of its destruction) you are Śiva. You move according to your will. You alone sustain the ancient world of the form of sentience. You are the unmanifest, the origin of the elements, the Pradhāna (i.e. the Primordial Matter) and the immutable Puruṣa. You, the Highest Lord, are the original, middle and the final form of the world. You, the Highest Being, are the refuge of all worlds. You are the origin of the beings. You are a great being. You are the cause of the group of the elements. You, possessing a soul and resorting to Ahaṁkāra, are divided into three. You are the origin and the end. You are the great Vāyu (air) that moves everywhere. You are, and you are not, the origin. You are fire, the treasure of lustres. You, the great lord, are the water, the life of all worlds. O you highly intelligent one, you are the earth, the support of the moving. You are the supporter of the earth. You are the rivers, the ocean, and you alone are the origin of everything. You are the divine sage; you are all the beings, O Highest Being. People urged by you only indulge in good or bad (acts).

23b-25. The Vedas, assaulted by the demon, have entered the great ocean. This entire world—immovable and movable—has the Vedas as its support. The Vedas alone are the limits on all sides of all (religious) practices. The gods are eternally satisfied with the Vedas. Therefore, O Keśava, please bring (back) the Vedas.

Śrī Mahādeva said:

26-31. Viṣṇu, the highest lord, thus addressed by Brahmā, resorted to the Fish-form and entered the great ocean. Resorting to the form of a crocodile, he, honoured by the gods, killed that very fearful demon, after tearing him with the tip of his mouth. Having killed him, and taken all the Vedas, the Vedāṅgas, the Upāṅgas, he, of a great lustre, gave them to that Brahmā. The Vedas seized by the demon, were mixed up with one another. The intelligent lord, of the form of Vyāsa, made them distinct. By Vyāsa, the noble one, the Vedas were separated. Thus, he, with his Fish incarnation, protected all deities. Oh! at that time Lakṣmī's lord made the world free from affliction by giving (back) the Vedas. He, the venerable Vāsudeva, Hari, full of all gods, being extolled by groups of gods and siddhas, and with his feet worshipped by the meditating sages, vanished.

CHAPTER TWO HUNDRED THIRTYONE

Durvāsas Curses Indra

Śrī Rudra said:

1-5. O dear one, I shall duly explain to you that grandeur of the Fish (incarnation) of Viṣṇu, that is saluted by all people. Listen with a concentrated mind. The very lustrous son of Atri, well known as Durvāsas, is wrathful, agitates all the world, and has (practised) severe penance. He, my portion, the brāhmaṇa sage, always causing fear to all, and the treasure of penance went to the Himālayan surface (i.e. region). He, worshipped by kinnara women, lived there for a year. (Then) the sage, desiring to see Indra, went to heaven. At that time he, of a great lustre, saw Śacī's lord, the great god, mounted on an elephant and being honoured by all gods.

6-9. Seeing that, that Durvāsas, having a severe penance (to his credit), with his mind delighted and full of modesty, gave him the garland of pārijāta (flowers). The lord of the deities, received that garland, and placing it on the head of (his) elephant, went to Nandana (garden). The intoxicated elephant, took the garland with his trunk, pressed it and threw it on the ground. Then that

Durvāsas of a great lustre got angry, and with the fire of his anger ablaze, cursed Indra.

Durvāsas said:

10. Since endowed with the entire prosperity of the three worlds, you are slighting me, therefore, the prosperity of the three worlds will surely he destroyed.

Rudra said:

11-18. Indra thus cursed went back to his city. Then Śrī, the mother of the worlds, vanished in a moment. When Lakṣmī vanished, the three worlds vanished. When she, to whose glance the entire world of the immovable and movable resorts, vanished, everything perished. All gods like Brahmā, gandharvas, yakṣas, kinnaras, fiends, demons, serpents, men and goblins, beasts, birds, insects, all immovable and movable objects, all of them were not looked at by Lakṣmī, that mother of the world. All of them were reduced to poverty and experienced misery. Gods, oppressed by hunger and thirst, and being dispirited, cried. Clouds did not shower. All reservoirs of water were dry. All the trees became dry, and were without flowers and fruits. Then gods, along with fiends, demons and goblins, being oppressed by hunger and thirst, went to Brahmā of unlimited vigour, and said to him, the grandsire, the lord of the god of gods and born in a lotus:

The gods said:

19-21a. O venerable one, the three worlds are oppressed by hunger and thirst. No oblations are offered into fire to a deity. The (three worlds) are without all religious practices. All gods, demons and human beings, oppressed by hunger and thirst, have sought the shelter of you, the protector, the lord of all worlds. O lord of gods, please protect the creatures oppressed by hunger and thirst.

Rudra said:

21b-22a. Hearing these words of (i.e. uttered by) them he who respected others and who was the grandsire of all worlds, being very much pleased, spoke to them all:

Brahmā said:

22b-27. Listen, O all gods, demons, gandharvas and men. All this has come to (us) due to Indra's misdeed. This great, fearful fire of universal destruction has come up. O gods, since that very high-minded Durvāsas became angry, all the three worlds perished due to his anger. The silly one, with his mind full of anger, and excited by anger, has said: "Let the three worlds and Lakṣmī, disappear." Due to his curse goddess Lakṣmī, dear to Viṣṇu, the mother and the supporter of the worlds, the great goddess, disappeared. The mother of the worlds, due to being looked at by whose glance the worlds become happy, did not look at (i.e. cared for) the worlds experiencing misery.

28-32. Therefore, all of us will go to Viṣṇu, the excellent one, staying in the Milky Ocean, and will worship the eternal god. When the lord of gods is pleased, this world will be happy.

Deciding like this in his mind, Brahmā, accompanied by hosts of gods, went to the Milky Ocean with sages like Bhṛgu. On the northern coast of the Milky Ocean, the deities like Brahmā, Rudra etc. worshipped Viṣṇu according to rules laid down for worshipping the god. Muttering the eight-syllabled formula, and the Puruṣa-sūkta, and meditating on him with undistracted minds, they offered oblations to the highest god. They praised him with divine hymns and saluted him in various ways.

33-36. Then the venerable one, being pleased and being praised by great sages, stood within the sight of all gods (i.e. appeared before them). Seeing the mighty lord of all worlds, who was full of all gods, who had mounted upon Garuḍa, who had held a conch, a disc and a mace, who had worn a yellow garment, who had four arms, whose eyes resembled lotuses, who had Śrīvatsa and Kaustubha (marks) on his chest, who was adorned with a garland of wood-flowers, who was graced with a crown, a necklace, armlets and anklets, they praised him with shouts of victory and continually saluted him.

37-38. The revered one kindly said to all the deities: "I am a giver of boons. O gods, choose a boon." Thus he spoke (to them). Hearing these words, all gods led by Brahmā and with the palms of their hands joined, said these words to the god:

The gods said:

39-40. O venerable one, now all these three worlds, along with gods, demons and human beings, are afflicted by hunger and thirst. Therefore, O Viṣṇu, we have sought your shelter. Protect all this world. None else would ever be able (to protect it).

Rudra said:

41. Acyuta, the highest lord, thus addressed by all deities, thought and spoke to these gods led by Brahmā, these words:

The lord said:

42-46. Due to the curse of the son of the sage Atri Lakṣmī disappeared. The world will be endowed with grandeur due to her looking at it with (i.e. casting) her glance. Therefore, O gods, all of you led by Śiva and Brahmā, extract the Mandara mountain, and put it into the Milky Ocean. O gods, making the Mandara mountain encircled by the king of serpents, the churning rod, churn with the (help of) the fiends, gandharvas and demons, the Ocean. Then Lakṣmī will appear for the protection of the world. There is no doubt that you, looked at by her, will be very lucky. Concealed (in the Ocean) in the form of a tortoise I myself shall hold the (Mandara) mountain, and entering with my strength into all gods (I shall make them) stronger.

Rudra saia:

47-48. O you of lotus-like eyes, when all the deities were thus addressed by Viṣṇu, they, led by Brahmā, spoke to the lord of gods: "Well, well." Being praised by best gods, and saluted by all the worlds, venerable, glorious Acyuta, the prop and the god of all, looking equally everywhere, vanished.

CHAPTER TWO HUNDRED THIRTYTWO

The Rise of Goddess Lakṣmī

Śaṅkara said:

1-6. Then all the hosts of gods and the very powerful demons extracted the Mandara mountain and put it into the Milky Ocean. Then the powerful lord Viṣṇu, the creator of the beings, and of unlimited valour, supported, in the form of a tortoise, the mountain. The eternal, immutable, omniscient one, whose body has no beginning, middle or end, who is of a universal form, who is the lord of the worlds fit to be worshipped, supported the excellent mountain with one arm only. Then all gods and demons churned the Ocean, after encircling the Mandara mountain with the lord of serpents. Then when the Milky Ocean was being churned by the very powerful deities for generating (i.e. taking out) Lakṣmī, all the great sages fasted, observed restrictions and also muttered Śrīsūkta.

7-10. The divine excellent brāhmaṇas recited (the hymn Viṣṇu-) Sahasranāma. All the sages who desired to mutter (the formula of) Lakṣmī-Nārāyaṇa-Viṣṇu, fasted on the Ekādaśī day of the bright fortnight when the great ocean was being churned and muttered the excellent Śrī-hymn. The topmost brāhmaṇas, the best sages meditated upon and worshipped (the deity). Then at that time when the great ocean was being churned, at first there came up the very strong Kālakūṭa poison which was very painful, very fierce, and which was like the fire of universal destruction.

11-15. Seeing (it), all gods and demons, being frightened, fled away. O you of beautiful eyes, then seeing the best gods frightened and fleeing away, I said to them: "O you all hosts of gods, do not be afraid of the poison. I shall drink this strong poison, Kālakūṭa." Thus addressed by me, all the gods, led by Indra and bowing, very much praised me with the words 'Well, Well'. On seeing the strong poison, like a cloud, having come up I meditated in my heart upon the eagle-bannered god Viṣṇu, resembling the rising sun and holding a conch, a disc, and a mace.

16-21. Having meditated (i.e. when I meditated) with a concentrated mind upon that lord along with Śrī and Bhūmi, having earrings of gold purified by fire, remover of all miseries, and on my having muttered the great hymn of the name and form (of Viṣṇu) along with Mahālakṣmī, all that poison, which was very fierce, which was the first one, which was fearful to all, which was (capable of) destroying all the worlds, was digested (by me) due to the three names of Viṣṇu, the omnipresent one. He who, being restrained, would devoutly mutter the three names of Viṣṇu, viz. Acyuta, Ananta, Govinda, beginning with Praṇava (i.e. Om) and (also) ending with Om, has no fear of death, so also the great fear due to poison, disease and fire. The wise, restrained one, who would mutter the great hymn—the three names—does not have fear of Death; then from where else (can he have it)? Thus with (the muttering of) the three names I drank that poison.

22-24a. Then the gods, pleased and very much amazed, praised me. Having saluted me the gods again churned the Milky Ocean. O beautiful lady, when the ocean was being churned by me and the gods, Jyeṣṭhā Devī, covered with gems, wreaths and garments came up. When the goddess came up, she said: "What should I do?" Then all the hosts of gods repeatedly said to the goddess:

Gods said:

24b-32. We give you the place in the charming interior of the house of those where quarrel takes place. Having inauspicious (qualities), live there. Giving misery and poverty to them who, being liars, always speak harsh words, and who of impure hearts, sleep in the evening, stay in their house. There is no doubt that you will always stay at that place where there will be potsherds, hair, ash, bones, fire of the chaff or charcoal. O you inauspicious one, always live, along with Kali, in that house which is marked by potsherds, bones, ash, hair etc. O great goddess, resort to him who, the stupid one, very much covered with sin, sips water without cleaning his feet. People cleaning their teeth with chaff, charcoal, potsherd, stone, sand, (a piece of) garment, (or of) hide, will be (i.e. are) mean. O goddess, causing poverty, always live in the house of those who eat sesamum, flesh of animals struck with a poisoned weapon, kaliṅga, pot-herb, garlic, mushrooms, viḍvarāha, bilva, kośātaki-fruit, bottle-gourd, and onions.

Rudra said:

33-45. Having thus ordered Jyeṣṭhā, dear to Kali, all the gods, well-composed, again churned the Milky Ocean. O you of an auspicious face, then goddess Vāruṇī came up. Ananta, the lord of serpents, took her of beautiful eyes. Then Surā (spirituous liquor), adorned with all ornaments, came up. She graced with all (auspicious) marks became the wife of Garuḍa. Then bevies of celestial nymphs and divine and very strong gandharvas endowed with handsomeness and engaged in sweet singing, came up. Then Airāvata came up. Then the horse Uccaiḥśravas came up. Then came up Dhanvantari, Pārijāta and Surabhi giving all desired objects. Indra with a pleased mind accepted all these. Then in the morning when the sun rose on the Dvādaśī day, and when the Ocean was again churned by gods led by Indra, Śrī, Mahālakṣmī, the auspicious goddess of all the worlds, being praised by great sages with pleasing faces, came up. She resembled a crore of young suns, and was adorned with golden armlets. She was seated on a golden lotus and was graced with all (auspicious) marks. Her eyes were large like lotus-petals. Her hair was dark and curly. Her body was smeared with divine sandal. She was adorned with divine flowers. She had (put on) all divine ornaments decked with various jewels. Her waist was slender. She was the mother of the world. Her breasts were stout and raised. She had four hands. Her eyes were large. Her face was like the full moon. She held with her lotus-like hands adorned with all ornaments, a pot of jewels, citron, and an auspicious couple of golden lotuses. On her bosom she wore a garland of unfaded lotuses. They saw that great goddess, desiring the good of all worlds.

46-54. Seeing her, the controller of all beings, the mother having a lotus-garland, Nārāyaṇī, world's mother, having a place in the heart of Viṣṇu, all the deities were pleased. In heaven groups of gods beat drums strongly. The sylvan deities continuously showered flowers. The chief gandharvas sang and bevies of celestial damsels danced. So also auspicious breezes blew. The sun was very bright. The fires burnt noiselessly; the ten directions were bright. Then from the Milky Ocean the Moon came up. He, Soma (i.e. the Moon), the brother of the mother (Lakṣmī), was pleasant. The Moon, the lord of the stars, became the maternal uncle of the world. Then Tulasī, Viṣṇu's wife, purifying the world, and the mother of the world came up for the worship of Viṣṇu. Then all the gods, with their minds pleased and all desires fulfilled, put (back) the (Mandara) mountain as before (in its own place), and led by Śiva and Brahmā, approached the mother (i.e. Lakṣmī). Having praised her with the (hymn Viṣṇu-) sahasranāma, they recited the text of the Śrīsūkta. Then, O goddess, she, being pleased, said to all gods:

Śrī said:

55a. O best gods, ask for a boon. Well-being to you. I am a giver of boons.

Rudra said:

55b. With their figures bent and palms of their hands joined, the gods said to Lakṣmī:

The gods said:

56-59a. O Kamalā, O goddess, O you dear to all gods, be pleased. Always rest on Viṣṇu's chest. Never go away (from there). O goddess, always look after the three worlds. O highest goddess, you, to whose glances the entire immovable and movable world resorts, are eternal. Gods, looked at (with favour) by you, are powerful. You are the mother of gods like Rudra. (Their) splendour is due to your glance. We desire this, O goddess. Salutation to you, O mother of the world.

Rudra said:

59b-62a. Thus addressed by all deities, the great goddess, the mother of the world, the one dear to Viṣṇu, said to the gods: "Let it be so." Then Viṣṇu, lord of Śrī, holding a conch, a disc and a mace, manifested himself as before in the Milky Ocean. Then the gods, having saluted Viṣṇu, praised him. All the auspicious (gods) with their faces delighted and with the palms of their hands joined said:

The gods said:

62b-63a. O lord of all, accept the goddess Lakṣmī, never leaving you, as your dear queen for the protection of the world.

Rudra said:

63b-70. Having said like this, all gods led by Brahmā and along with the sages, and with their eyes full of tears of joy, placed the goddess and the god, adorned with divine garments, divine wreath and various jewels, on a divine seat, full of various jewels and resembling the young sun, and worshipped Viṣṇu seated with Lakṣmī. They also worshipped the goddess with sandal, incense, lights, and offerings of eatables full of nectar, and with extraordinary fruits. Goddess Tulasī, delicate and auspicious, came up from the nectar. With that they properly worshipped Lakṣmī's couple of feet. Gods overcome with tears full of joy, having gone round him, keeping him to their right, three times, and having saluted him, praised him with eulogies. Then venerable Viṣṇu was pleased. With Lakṣmī, the lord gave them boons desired (by them). Then gods, men and others were very much delighted. They were purified by Lakṣmī's glances. They had profuse grains and wealth. Being extremely healthy, they obtained great happiness.

CHAPTER TWO HUNDRED THIRTYTHREE

Ekādaśī as a Day of Fast

Śiva said:

1. Then for the good of all the world the lord along with the goddess, delighted in heart, spoke to the gods and great sages:

The lord said:

2-8a. O all sages and deities having great power, listen. Ekādaśī is very meritorious and destroys all calamities. You have observed it as a day of fast in order to see Lakṣmī. Dvādaśī, dear to me, is always more meritorious than that. Since today all those men who observe a fast on the previous (i.e. Ekādaśī) day, and who, when the sun has risen on the Dvādaśī (day), worship with great faith and devotion me along with Lakṣmī and Tulasī, are freed from bondage and reach my position. Those men who do not worship me, the Highest Being, on Dvādaśī, are sinners, and are deluded by my Māyā. My Māyā, difficult to cross, throws the sinners, the most sinful ones, bound by objects of senses, averse to my worship and going (i.e. fated to go) to hell, into the continuous mundane existence.

Rudra said:

8b-11. Speaking like this, the lord, the highest soul, the ancient one, being praised by the sages, went to Lakṣmī's place. The highest lord, along with goddess Lakṣmī of large eyes, remained near (the gods) on the bed of Śeṣa in a hall resembling the sun in the Milky Ocean for appearing before the gods. Then all the hosts of gods, devoutly worshipping the ancient Tortoise-form (of the lord), praised him with delighted minds. Then lord Viṣṇu, of the form of Tortoise, was pleased.

The lord said:

12a. O best gods, ask for a boon that is in your mind.

Rudra said:

12b-13a. Then all the hosts of gods, with their minds full of joy, and joining the palms of their hands, said to Viṣṇu of the form of Tortoise:

The gods said:

13b-14a. O you very powerful one, O lord of gods, to help Śeṣa and the quarter-elephants, please sustain the earth having seven islands.

Rudra said:

14b-19. Saying, "Let it be so", the lord, the creator of the worlds, with his mind pleased, sustained the earth covered by the seven islands. Then gods with gandharvas, fiends, demons and human beings, permitted by the great sages, went to their respective world. O you of an excellent complexion, since then all gods led by Brahmā, so also siddhas, human beings, meditating saints, best sages, honouring Viṣṇu's order devoutly fasted on the Ekādaśī (day) and duly worshipped Viṣṇu on the Dvādaśī (day). O you beautiful one, I have told you all about the origin of goddess (Lakṣmī); so also about the splendour of Viṣṇu in his Tortoise-form. What else do you desire to hear?

CHAPTER TWO HUNDRED THIRTYFOUR

How to Observe the Vow of Dvādaśī

Pārvatī said:

1-2. O lord, I desire to hear about the rule about Dvādaśī, and about (how) the worship of Viṣṇu should be done on that (day). O great lord, due to your love for me (i.e. since you love me), tell me in detail the power of Ekādaśī that removes all sins of men.

Mahādeva said:

3-8. O goddess, listen. I shall tell you the rule about Dvādaśī. Merely by (one's) remembering it, Viṣṇu would be pleased. Men fasting on Ekādaśī when it has come, are freed from all sins, and reach the highest position of Viṣṇu. By worshipping Viṣṇu on Dvādaśī all the sin (of one) committed knowingly or unknowingly perishes in a moment. Thousands of horse-sacrifices and hundreds of Vājapeya sacrifices do not equal even a sixteenth part af Ekādaśī-fast. The excellent Dvādaśī (vow) gives merit, wealth, desired objects and salvation also. It fulfils all desires of men. O you of beautiful eyes, there is nothing else that saves (one) from sins like Ekādaśī. There is no other vow like that of Ekādaśī.

9-16. He who, ignoring Ekādaśī, would observe some other vow, asks for begging after abandoning great kingdom which is in his hand. O dear one, all the sin that is committed with the eleven (sensory and motor) organs would perish by means of a fast on the Ekādaśī (day). O you of an excellent face, the Purāṇas repeatedly announce: "One should not eat, one should not eat, when the day of (i.e. sacred to) Viṣṇu has come." O you of an excellent complexion, there are always certain articles of food prohibited for the castes and stages of life. The more so on the Ekādaśī of the bright half and the dark half (of a month). There is no doubt that the Ekādaśī-fast should be observed. If the anniversary day of the death of one's mother and father is on the day on which Ekādaśī falls, the presents should be given on the Dvādaśī day, but never on the Ekādaśī day. Dead ancestors and gods do not eat censured food. On an Ekādaśī day one should not eat, should never drink liquor, should not hurt a brāhmaṇa. These three (sins) are said to be equal (in gravity). Therefore, on a pure (i.e. unmixed) Ekādaśī (day), one should observe a fast. In the three conditions, with speech, body and deeds, an effort should be made (for observing a fast).

17-24. Ekādaśī mixed with Daśamī should be carefully avoided. (If Daśamī continues) at the time of dawn (on the Ekādaśī day), it (i.e. the Ekādaśī) would be mixed with Daśamī. Leaving it (i.e. that Ekādaśī day) he should, without (further) thought, observe a fast on the pure (i.e. unmixed) Dvādaśī. O goddess, if a part of Ekādaśī continues at the sunrise on the Trayodaśī day, then Dvādaśī remains on that day also. At dawn he should perform all rites. Even if a part of Dvādaśī is there, breaking the fast (on that day) is recommended. In this case one should ignore even a pure Ekādaśī. There is no doubt about it. Even if a part of the Ekādaśī continues on the Dvādaśī, when the sun has risen, one should ignore the entire Ekādaśī (on the previous day) and observe a fast on that (Dvādaśī) day. Having decided the rite like this, one should observe a fast on the day of (i.e. sacred to) Viṣṇu. Avoiding four meals, one in the evening of the first day, another in the morning of the last (i.e. the third) day, and two on the middle (i.e. the second) day, one should observe a fast. On the Daśamī day he should eat once (only), avoid (sexual) union with his wife, sleep on the ground, and should remain pure on the next day.

25-32. With his body smeared with (the pulp of) the dhātrī-fruit, he should bathe and offer the sandhyā (prayer). Intent on (observing) a fast, he should worship Viṣṇu at night. A devotee of Viṣṇu should not see, talk with or touch a heretic, one doing a prohibited act, a fallen person or a cāṇḍāla. A brāhmaṇa who is not devoted to Viṣṇu is called a heretic. One who has given up the tuft of hair on the crown of the head and the sacred thread is said to be one remaining (i.e. persisting) in (doing) prohibited acts. One having (committed) major and minor sins is said to be fallen. One belonging to the lowest caste is said to be *śvapaca*. This proper decision is taken by the Vedas. Having worshipped the lord of gods, one should keep awake. With sandal, flowers, lights, garments, ornaments, auspicious mutterings, hymns, salutations, one should devoutly worship (Viṣṇu) at night. Then in the morning having bathed according to the proper rule with water mixed with Tulasī, and having gratified the dead ancestors and deities, one should worship Viṣṇu, the lord of the world along with Lakṣmī, with tender Tulasī-leaves, and fragrant flowers. Then one hundred and eight times he should wave lights (before Viṣṇu's idol).

33-39. To both of them (i.e. Viṣṇu and Lakṣmī) he should offer a garland made of lotuses. He should also offer them incense, light, articles of food and tāmbūla. One should offer (them) charming food of rice boiled in milk along with sugar, and should offer a tāmbūla with camphor. He should devoutly salute (them) while going round them. One hundred and eight times he should offer oblations into fire with ghee, offering rice boiled in milk with the recital of every ṛc, with (the recital of) the Puruṣa-sūkta and Lakṣmī-sūkta. He should feed the brāhmaṇas, and controlled in speech he himself should also eat. He should pass that great day by the recital of the Purāṇas etc. That night he, observing celibacy, should sleep on the ground. That lord of Kamalā, being thus worshipped on the Dvādaśī day, is pleased in a moment, and the lord certainly gives all desired objects. O goddess, I have thus told you the excellent vow of Dvādaśī. What else do you desire to hear? I shall tell that to you.

CHAPTER TWO HUNDRED THIRTYFIVE

The Birth of Heretics

Śrī Pārvatī said:

1-2b. O lord, you told me that one should avoid conversation with heretics, and that it is more censurable than (talking to) a cāṇḍāla. (Tell me) of what kind they are said to be, and with what signs they are marked.

Rudra said:

2c-12a. Those who, deluded by ignorance, describe any other deity as being superior to Viṣṇu, the lord of the world, are said to be heretics. Those who use skulls, apply ash, use bones, have non-Vedic marks, have matted hair and bark-garments though they do not belong to the hermit-stage of life are (said to be) heretics. Those brāhmaṇas who are without such marks dear to Viṣṇu as conches, discs, ūrdhvapuṇḍra (upright sectarian marks on the forehead) are said to be heretics. That brāhmaṇa who does not follow the practices laid down in the holy texts and codes of laws should be known as a heretic and is condemned among all people. Those that have no devotion for the lord are said to be heretics. He who is free in all acts (i.e. performs all acts as he likes) and offers oblations into fire and gives gifts directed to deities (other than) Viṣṇu, the enjoyer of the fruit of all sacrifices and the deity of the brāhmaṇas, and who independently does all great acts laid down in the Vedas, should be known as a heretic. He who looks upon god Viṣṇu as equal to other deities like Brahmā, Rudra, would always be (called) a heretic. That brāhmaṇa who, in the three conditions, does not recognise Viṣṇu by means of speech, body and acts, would be a heretic. What is the use of saying much in this regard? Those brāhmaṇas who are not devotees of Viṣṇu, should never be asked (any question), should never be talked to and should never be seen.

Pārvatī said:

12b-15a. O lord, O best of gods, I am asking (you) a secret. Through love for me tell it. There is a great doubt. The holy texts have condemned wearing (i.e. using) skulls, (applying) ash and (wearing) hide. You wear (i.e. use) them. (Then), O god, for what purpose is it condemned? O lord of gods, O you highly intelligent one, through fickleness of (i.e. natural to) women I am asking it. It may be that due to your great power what is told ought not to be done by you. (But) you have not formerly told me in detail what ought not to be done. Therefore, O lord, please pardon me my question.

Vasiṣṭha said:

15b-17a. Thus by the goddess Śiva was asked in a lonely place, free from people. He told her the great secret, viz. whatever he did.

Śiva said:

17b-21a. O goddess, listen. I shall tell you that secret which is very wonderful. O goddess, you should not speak what I have told you among people. O you of a good vow, I shall tell it to you since your body is not separate from mine. In the age of Svāyambhuva (Manu) in olden times there were great demons like Namuci, who were very powerful, very valorous, very strong and great heroes. All of them were devoted to Viṣṇu, were pure, and free from all sins. They followed the practices (laid down) in the triad of the Vedas. All gods, being frustrated, led by Indra, and overcome by fear, approached Viṣṇu and sought his shelter.

Gods said:

21b-22a. O Keśava, you alone can conquer these great demons who cannot be conquered by all gods, and who have washed off their sins with penance.

Mahādeva said:

22b-25. Hearing these frightful words of the gods, Viṣṇu, Puruṣottama, consoled those regents of the quarters, and said to me:

The lord said:

O Rudra, O you of mighty arms, O you best god, for deluding the enemies of gods prepare a course of conduct to be followed by heretics. Narrate to them the dark Purāṇas (i.e. Purāṇas that will take them astray). O you very intelligent one, also fashion confusing holy texts. There will be brāhmaṇas and great sages who have given themselves away to me.

26-33. Approaching them through devotion for me, tell the vicious ones: Kaṇāda, Gautama, Śakti, Upamanyu, Jaimini, Kapila, Durvāsas, Mṛkaṇḍu, Bṛhaspati, Bhārgava and Jāmadagnya are the ten (?) vicious sages. Desiring to do the good of the world, approach them with your power of suggestion (bhāvaśakti?). By your power increased in viciousness infused into them they will be vicious in a moment. There is no doubt about it. Those brāhmaṇas with greater viciousness caused by you, will narrate the vicious Purāṇas and doctrines in the three worlds. O god, you yourself, wearing the marks like a skull, hide, ash, bones, fully delude the people in the three worlds. So also you, Śiva, prepare the Pāśupata order with its divisions like Kaṅkāla, Śaiva, Pāṣaṇḍa and Mahāśaiva; so also properly prepare the doctrine having no particular marks and outside the Vedic fold. All the mean men will wear ash, bones etc. and will be insensible. The vicious ones will describe you as the highest (god).

34-36a. Taking to their doctrine all the ancient demons will be averse to me in a moment. There is no doubt (about it). O very powerful Rudra, in my incarnations I too shall worship you in every age to delude the vicious ones. Having upheld this doctrine, they will undoubtedly fall.

Mahādeva said:

36b-37. O you beautiful one, having heard what Viṣṇu had said, I, though having a very large mouth (i.e. though a good speaker) became helpless then. Then having saluted the highest god, I said:

38-43. "O god, if I do what you have said on the earth, it will certainly lead to my destruction. O Viṣṇu, it is possible for me to carry out this mission. Your command is not to be disobeyed. This is very painful." O goddess, when I spoke like this, Viṣṇu, having again cheered me up, said: "Let this not lead to your destruction. Do as I order you for the good of the deities. O best god, I shall also tell you about the means for your livelihood." Then with compassion he gave me his thousand names (i.e. the hymn called *Viṣṇusahasranāma*): "Installing me in your heart, mutter my indestructible formula. The very great, six-syllabled formula is said to be Brahman, the emancipating one. Those who worship me with devotion obtain salvation. There is no doubt about this.

44-46. (Salutation to) him dark like the petal of a blue lotus, having eyes like lotus-petals, holding a conch, a disc, and the Śārṅga bow, and adorned with all ornaments. (To him) having put on a yellow garment, having four arms, the dear lord of Jānakī. 'Salutation to Śri Rāma': this excellent formula should be muttered. It removes all sins, and gives salvation even to sinners. Muttering this formula everyday you will be free from blemishes.

47-51a. All that sin produced in you due to having (applied) ash and having bones, has all become auspicious due to the auspicious utterance of my formula. O best god, being gratified I shall destroy all sin. O you of a good vow, devotion to other god than me will not come up. Worship me, the lord, the Supreme Being, mentally in your heart. Obey my order. Due to my love, all this will be auspicious for you." Having thus ordered me, O goddess, he dismissed the hosts of gods. The gods, dismissed by him went to their own abodes. Then gods, led by Indra, requested me.

Indra and others said:

51b. O god, quickly do that beneficial act as told by Viṣṇu now.

Mahādeva said:

52-56. O auspicious one, for the good of the gods, I took to the way of the heretics, and had skulls, hides, ash and bones. O auspicious one, as told by Viṣṇu, I prepared the vicious Purāṇas and the heretic Śaiva doctrines. O sinless one, having entered through my power, Gautama and other brāhmaṇas I proclaimed the texts outside the Vedic fold. Resorting to this doctrine, all the wicked demons became averse to the lord (i.e. Viṣṇu), and were enveloped in viciousness. Applying ash to their bodies, covered with (i.e. having) very severe penance, they worshipped me only with flesh, blood and sandal.

57-64. On receiving from me grants of boons, they were haughty with pride and power. They were very much attached to objects of senses, and were full of lust and anger. They, void of goodness and powerless, were then defeated by the hosts of gods. Fallen from all righteous paths, they will go to a mean position in (due) time. Those who, bereft of righteous paths, move on the earth by resorting to this doctrine of mine, always see (i.e. go to) hell. O goddess, (this) my course, that is censured, is thus (followed by me) (only) for the good of the gods. Following Viṣṇu's order I have (applied) ash and (use) bones. O goddess, this is an external mark intended for deluding the foes. In the heart however, I, always meditating upon god Viṣṇu, just mutter that emancipating formula, telling about Brahman. It is like the (hymn) Sahasranāma of Viṣṇu, Nārāyaṇa. O auspicious one, constantly muttering the great six-syllabled formula which increased the Raghu-race, we constantly obtain that Brahman which is filled with the nectar of constant joy, which is permanent happiness. O you of an auspicious face, I have told you all this that you had asked. What else do you desire to hear? Ask me that with affection.

CHAPTER TWO HUNDRED THIRTYSIX

Characterization of Various Texts and Doctrines as Sāttvika, Rājasa and Tāmasa

Pārvatī said:

1. O sinless one, tell me about the vicious texts which were composed by the brāhmaṇas bereft of devotion to the lord. O lord of gods, tell me their names in a sequence.

Rudra said:

2-4. O goddess, listen. I shall tell you about the vicious texts in a sequence. By merely remembering them even the wise ones would be deluded, First I myself proclaimed the Śaiva, Pāśupata (texts) etc. Hear about the ones which were proclaimed by the brāhmaṇas into whom my power had entered, after that: Kaṇāda proclaimed the great Vaiśeṣika text.

5-7. Similarly Gautama (proclaimed the doctrine of) Nyāya, and Kapila (proclaimed) Sāṁkhya. Dhiṣaṇa (Bṛhaspati) in the same way (proclaimed) the much censured Cārvāka (doctrine); Viṣṇu of the form of Buddha proclaimed the false Buddhist doctrine and those of the naked and wearing dark blue garments for the destruction of the demons. The doctrine of Māyā (illusion) is a wicked doctrine and said to be pseudo-Buddhist. I myself, of the form of a brāhmaṇa, proclaimed it in Kali (age).

8-12. It shows the meaninglessness of the words of the holy texts and is condemned in the world. In this (doctrine) only the giving up of one's own duties is expounded. And that is said to be religiousness by those who have fallen from all duties. I have propounded the identity of the Highest Lord and the (individual) soul. I stated this Brahman's nature to be qualityless. O goddess, I myself have conceived, for the destruction of the worlds, and for deluding the world in this Kali age, the great doctrine resembling the purport of the Vedas, (but) non-Vedic due to the principle of Māyā (illusion) (present in it). By my order formerly Jaimini propounded the great doctrine of Pūrva Mīmāṁsā, stating godlessness and making the Veda meaningless.

13-17. O Girijā, know from me the vicious doctrines. I shall also narrate the names of the vicious Purāṇas* in succession: Brāhma, Pādma, Vaiṣṇava, Śaiva, so also Bhāgavata. So also Nāradīya and Mārkaṇḍeya as the seventh. Āgneya is said to be the eighth, and Bhaviṣya to be the ninth. Brahmavaivarta is said to be the tenth, and Liṅga to be eleventh. Vārāha is said to be the twelfth and Vāmana the thirteenth. Kaurma is said to be the fourteenth and Mātsya the fifteenth. Gāruḍa is said to be the sixteenth, and Skānda to be the seventeenth. The eighteenth is Brahmāṇḍa. (These are) the Purāṇas in succession.

18-22a. Know from me that Mātsya, Kaurma, Laiṅga, Śaiva, so also Skānda and Āgneya are tāmasa (vicious). O you of

*The immediately following list is not actually that of the vicious Purāṇas but of the Purāṇas in general. The vicious six Purāṇas follow this list of eighteen Purāṇas. The word 'tāmasa' in this verse is not appropriately used. (Ed.)

an auspicious appearance, the Purāṇas, viz. Vaiṣṇava, Nāradīya, so also the auspicious Bhāgavata, similarly Gāruḍa, Pādma, Vārāha should be known to be sāttvika (or virtuous). Know from me that Brahmāṇḍa, Brahmavaivarta, Mārkaṇḍeya, Bhaviṣya, Vāmana and Brāhma are rājasa (endowed with the quality of passion). The sāttvika ones are said to give salvation and are always auspicious. Similarly, O goddess, the tāmasa are said to be the cause of (i.e. lead one to) hell.

22b-27. Similarly Smṛtis endowed with the three qualities are proclaimed by the sages. O you of an auspicious appearance, they are sāttvika, rājasa and tāmasa. Vāsiṣṭha, Hārīta, Vyāsa, Pārāśara, Bhāradvāja and Kāśyapa are said to sāttvika, giving (i.e. leading to) salvation and auspicious. Yājñavalkya Ātreya, so also Taittira, Dākṣa and Kātyāyana and Vaiṣṇava are rājasa, giving (i.e. leading to) heaven, and auspicious. Gautama, Bārhaspatya, Sāṁvarta, Yama, Sāṁkhya and Auśanasa are said to be tāmasa, and giving (i.e. leading to) hell. What is the use of talking much in the case of the Purāṇas and the Smṛtis also? The tāmasa do lead to hell. A wise one should avoid them. As the occasion has come, I have told you all the auspicious doctrines. Listen. I shall tell you about the nature of the remaining birth (i.e. of the other incarnations) of Viṣṇu.

CHAPTER TWO HUNDRED THIRTYSEVEN

The Boar Incarnation of Viṣṇu

Śrī Rudra said:

1-3. Kaśyapa's two sons, Hiraṇyaka and Hiraṇyākṣa were very powerful. They, the two sons of Diti, were great warriors and the lords of the demons. In Śvetadvīpa they were with Viṣṇu (as his doorkeepers) named Jaya and Vijaya. O goddess, (once) the two very powerful ones prevented the greatest meditating sages who were eager to see Viṣṇu. The two best, very powerful gods, the doorkeepers were cursed by them.

Sanaka and others said:

4a. O servants of the god, leave (this place) and be gone to the earth.

Rudra said:

4b-6a. Having cursed them like this, the best sages remained there. The god (Viṣṇu) having come to know the affair called them (i.e. the sages) and the two (doorkeepers) also, to whom, after they had stood, the lord, the cause of the beings, said:

The lord said:

6b-8a. O you very powerful ones, you have done a great wrong to the noble (sages). O doorkeepers, you cannot pass it over. If you desire to have seven existences, then you will be my sinless devotees. If you want to remain as my enemy, then you will have three existences.

Rudra said:

8b. Thus addressed, the very powerful Jaya and Vijaya said to the highest god:

Jaya and Vijaya said:

9-10a. O you who respect others, we can't go to (and live on) the earth for a long time. Therefore, know that we shall go to (i.e. have) those existences causing enmity (for you). O god, killed by you only, we shall come near you.

Rudra said:

10b-14. Having spoken like this, the two very powerful door-keepers were born from the womb of Diti, (the wife of) Kaśyapa. Hiraṇyakaśipu was the elder and Hiraṇyākṣa the younger. Both of them were well-known in the world. Both were very powerful and haughty due to their might. That Hiraṇyākṣa of an immeasurable body and very haughty removed, with his thousands of arms, the earth along with mountains, oceans, islands, and all living beings. Having removed it out and put it on his head he entered the lower world. Then all the hosts of gods, afflicted by fear, cried.

15-19. They sought the shelter of Nārāyaṇa, Viṣṇu. Then

knowing that wonder, he, Viṣṇu, the holder of a conch, a disc, and a mace, took up the Boar-form, existing everywhere and having no beginning, middle or end. The highest lord full of everything, having hands and feet on all sides, having large fangs and arms, struck the demon with one fang. The mean son of Diti, with his huge body pounded, died. Seeing the earth fallen (from the demon's head), he lifted it with his fang, and putting it on Śeṣa's head as before, took up the form of a Tortoise.* Seeing great Viṣṇu of the form of the hog, all deities and sages, with their bodies bowed with devotion, praised him.

The gods said:

20-25. Salutation to Yajñavarāha. Salutation to you of a hundred arms. Salutation to the god of gods. Salutation to you, the omnipresent. Salutation to you of an abiding form, to you of the form of all sacrifices. Salutation to you (of the form of the divisions of time like) kalā, kāṣṭhā and nimeṣa, to you of the form of time. Salutation to you, the soul of beings. Salutation to you having the Ṛgveda as your body. Salutation to you, the soul of the gods. Salutation to you, the Sāmaveda. Salutation to you, Oṁkāra. Salutation to you of the form of the Yajurveda, so also of the form of the ṛc and full of the four Vedas. Salutation to you of the (four) Vedas, the Vedāṅgas and the Upāṅgas. Salutation to you Govinda, having no beginning or end. Salutation to you knowing the Vedas, and having a peculiar form. Salutation to you the lord of Śrī, Bhū, Līlā and the father of the world.

Rudra said:

26-29. Having thus praised god Viṣṇu, the lord of the soul, and of the form of the boar, they worshipped him with sandal, flowers etc. He, being properly worshipped by the gods, gave them a boon desired (by them). Viṣṇu who (i.e. whose praise) was being joyfully sung by the gandharvas and celestial nymphs, and being praised by the great sages, vanished there only. A devoted man who, having got up in the morning, praises (the

*This is rather confusing. As is well known, Viṣṇu assumed the form of a tortoise in the second incarnation to give support to the mountain Mandara which served as a churning rod for gods who wanted to acquire Amṛta from the Milky Ocean. (Ed.)

lord) with these (hymns), gets a desired (piece of) land, full of corn and fruits for a long time. I have told you this splendour of the Boar (incarnation) of Viṣṇu. In the same way I shall describe (his) Nārasiṁha (incarnation). Listen, O you of an excellent face.

CHAPTER TWO HUNDRED THIRTYEIGHT

The Emergence of Nṛsiṁha

Rudra said:

1-2. Having learnt that his brother was killed, the great demon Hiraṇyakaśipu practised a penance near Meru (dedicating it) to me. O auspicious one, he, the very powerful one, eating (i.e. subsisting on) air, muttering the five-syllabled formula, worshipped me for thousands of divine years.

3. Then with a pleased mind, I said to the great demon: "O demon, ask for the boon that is in your mind." Then the demon spoke to me, who was pleased, O you of an auspicious face:

Hiraṇyakaśipu said:

4-5. Grant me exemption from death from gods, demons, human beings, gandharvas, serpents, fiends, beasts, birds, animals, noble siddhas and yakṣas, vidyādharas, so also kinnaras, so also all diseases, weapons, all principal sages.

Rudra said:

6-14. O you of a pleasing appearance, I said to the demon: "Let it be so." The very powerful demon, having got the great boon from me, conquered Indra and gods and became the lord of the three worlds; and he himself forcibly took all portions of sacrifices. Gods, vanquished by him, did not find a protector. All gandharvas, gods, demons, yakṣas, nāgas, siddhas and sādhyas were under his control. The very mighty king of the demons married, according to proper rites, Uttānapāda's daughter named Kalyāṇī. O you auspicious one, from her was born the very lustrous Prahlāda, the king of the demons. Even while (he was) in (his mother's) womb, he was attached to Viṣṇu. He, of a delighted mind, never knew anyone else except the lord of gods in all conditions and deeds (done) with his mind, speech and body. The humble and very intelligent one stayed in his preceptor's house at a (proper) time. Having studied all the Vedas and various sacred texts, the demon's son sometime came along with his preceptor to his father and saluted him with humility. The lord of the demons, having embraced his son of auspicious marks with his arms, and having put him who was much amazed, on his lap, said these (words to him):

Hiraṇyakaśipu said:

15. O Prahlāda, you stayed in your preceptor's house for a long time. O you of a good vow, tell me the knowledge given to you by your preceptor.

Rudra said:

16. Thus asked by his father, Prahlāda, a born devotee of Viṣṇu, affectionately spoke words removing sins to the lord of demons:

Prahlāda said:

17. After having saluted Viṣṇu, the Highest Being, the lord, who is the aim of all Upaniṣads, I shall tell you.

Rudra said:

18-20. The lord of demons, having thus heard Viṣṇu's praise, was amazed. He angrily said to the preceptor: "What have you taught my son? O you wicked one, why did you teach my son such praise of Viṣṇu, a stupid thing not fit to be done by a brāhmaṇa? O mean brāhmaṇa, due to your favour (only) this my son has told me the praise of my enemy, which is not fit to be heard."

21-24. Speaking like this and looking around, the demon-king, in a fit of anger, said to a demon: "Bind this mean brāhmaṇa." Hearing these words of the king, he bound (Śukra,) Bhṛgu's son. Seeing his preceptor being bound, Prahlāda, to whom brāhmaṇas were dear, said to his father: "O father, my perceptor did not teach me this. I have learnt it through the favour of Viṣṇu, the speaker, the seer. The lord is omnipresent. Viṣṇu alone is the imperishable agent, the controller of all human beings. Therefore, O lord, This brāhmaṇa, my preceptor, who is innocent, should be released."

Rudra said:

25-29. Having heard the words of his son, Hiraṇyakaśipu then let the brāhmaṇa free, and with amazement said to his son: "O son, why do you thus go astray (influenced) by the brāhmaṇa's words? Who is Viṣṇu? What is his form? Where does this Viṣṇu stay? Since I am the lord in the world, the master of the three worlds, honour me only. Abandon this Viṣṇu, our enemy, difficult to be overpowered. Or worship lord Śaṅkara, god Śiva, Rudra, the father of the worlds, the chief of gods, giving all splendour. After putting on the mark of three lines on your forehead with ash worship Mahādeva worshipped by demons, in the manner as told in the Pāśupata sect.

Rudra said:

30-32. Hearing these words of the lord of the demons, the priest of the demons said: "O glorious one, do like this only as your father tells. Abandon (our) enemy, Kaiṭabha's enemy, and worship the three-eyed (god, i.e. Śiva). There is no greater god than Śiva, who gives everything to men. Your father also became the lord (of demons) because of his favour only."

Rudra said:

33. Hearing these words of them, Prahlāda, a born devotee of Viṣṇu, said:

34-42. "O greatest ones, since the world is deluded by the Māyā of the lord, even brāhmaṇas knowing Vedānta and honoured among all the people, being proud, speak like this through fickleness. Nārāyaṇa is the highest Brahman. Nārāyaṇa is the highest truth. Nārāyaṇa is the highest meditator and the highest meditation. He is the refuge of the entire world. Acyuta is the eternal good. Eternal Vāsudeva is the sustainer, the creator of the world. The Highest Being is all this. Everything depends upon him. His body is all golden. He is eternal. His eyes are like lotuses. He is the lord of Śrī, Bhū and Līlā. He is pleasing, spotless and of an auspicious body. He alone created the two lords, Brahmā and Śiva, the two best gods. Brahmā and Śiva act by honouring (i.e. according to) his order only. The wind blows through his fear. The sun rises through his fear. Through his fear run fire, the moon and death as the fifth. The highest, divine god Nārāyaṇa Viṣṇu was alone there (in the beginning). Brahmā was not there; Indra was not there; Śiva was not there; the sun and the moon were not there. The heaven and the earth were not there; nor were the stars and the gods there. The wise men always see the highest abode of that Viṣṇu.

43-51a. O best brāhmaṇas, having ignored the significance of all Upaniṣads, why do you talk like this through attachment or greed before me? Abandoning that Viṣṇu, the god protecting all, and the god of all, how can I, resorting to heresy, worship Śiva? The noble meditating sages like Sanaka meditated upon Kṛṣṇa, the lord of Lakṣmī, the god of gods, Ananta, the Highest Being, dark like the petals of a blue lotus, having large eyes like lotus-leaves, with his chest marked with Śrīvatsa, adorned with all ornaments, always a youth, the lord of all, eternal joy, and giver of pleasures, whom the hosts of gods like Brahmā, Śiva, Indra and others worship, with half a glance of whose wife, gods like Brahmā, Indra, Rudra, Varuṇa, Yama, Soma and (Kubera) the lord of wealth, are looked at. Merely by recollecting his name, even sinful living beings quickly obtain salvation, very difficult to be secured (even) by Brahmā and others. That lord of Śrī alone is always the protector of even the gods. I shall worship only that Viṣṇu united with Lakṣmī. With great ease only I shall reach that highest place of Viṣṇu."

Rudra said:

51b. Hearing these words of him, Hiraṇyakaśipu, full of anger, burnt like another fire. Looking at the demons around him, he, in a fit of anger, spoke like this:

Hiraṇyakaśipu said:

52-54. By my order kill sinful Prahlāda highly devoted to

worshipping my enemy, with multitudes of fierce weapons. His protector Viṣṇu alone will protect him through love. Today only I would see (if) his being protected by Viṣṇu is effective.

Rudra said:

55-59. Then by the order of the lord of demons, the demons, with weapons raised, stood round the son of the lord of demons to kill him. Prahlāda too, meditating upon Viṣṇu in the lotus of his heart, and muttering the eight-syllabled formula, stood like another mountain. On all sides the heroes struck him with lances, iron clubs and śaktis. O you auspicious one, due to Viṣṇu's inviolable power, Prahlāda's body very much became adamantine due to remembering Viṣṇu. Then the great missiles of the enemies of gods, having reached his body, and being cutt off, fell down on the ground like blue lotuses, O auspicious one. The demons were not able to pierce (i.e. hurt) his body even slightly.

60-67. The soldiers, being amazed and with their faces hung down, stood near the king. Seeing his very powerful son of that kind, the demon-king being very much amazed and full of anger, wrathfully ordered all the very poisonous, fearful snakes like Vāsuki: "Eat him (up)." Then the very powerful, very fierce snakes, with their mouths blazing, ate (i.e. started eating) the very powerful (Prahlāda). They, full of poison, bit the devotee of (Viṣṇu) the Garuḍa-bannered one. The (snakes) that subsisted on air became poisonless and had their teeth cut off. With their limbs cut off by a thousand sons of Vinatā, and very much afflicted and vomiting profuse blood, they ran into all directions. Seeing the great snakes (reduced to a condition) like that, the angry lord of the demons then ordered the very much intoxicated quarter-elephants. The quarter-elephants, haughty with rut, ordered by that king, surrounded him, and struck him hard with their very large tusks. Then the tusks of the quarter-elephants, with their roots cut off, fell on the ground.

68-73. The elephants, rendered tuskless, and overcome by fear, fled. Seeing the great elephants (fleeing) the mighty lord of demons got angry. And burning a great fire, he threw it at his son. Fire, seeing Prahlāda, dear to Viṣṇu, did not burn the wise one. Fire became very cool. Seeing the boy not being burnt, the king, who was very much amazed, gave him, good to all beings, terrible poison. Due to the power of that Viṣṇu, the poison become nectar. Poison, due to one's offering (oneself) to that god, becomes nectar. Having thus deluded his son by means of such fierce and very terrible means, and seeing that he could not be killed, the king of demons, being full of amazement spoke mildly to his son:

Hiraṇyakaśipu said:

74-78. You have properly described before me Viṣṇu's greatness. He is called Viṣṇu because (he stands) pervading all worlds. He who is the omnipresent god is alone the highest god. Actually show me his omnipresence. Having carefully and properly seen the splendour of qualities like supremacy, power, lustre, knowledge, heroism, strength, excellent form of him the highest one, I shall honour Viṣṇu from among the gods. There is no match for my power among the gods. O you who honour (others), as a result of grant of a boon from Śiva I have obtained immunity from death among all living beings and invincibility for living beings. Viṣṇu would receive the title of lord after having vanquished me with power and might.

Rudra said:

79. Hearing these words of him, Prahlāda, being amazed, spoke. He, of a good vow, told about the glory of Viṣṇu to the demon.

Prahlāda said:

80-84. Since that Nārāyaṇa, the glorious one, the highest soul, the ancient one lives in all beings, he is called Vāsudeva. He, the sustainer of the world, is called Viṣṇu. Nothing other than him is the immobile and the mobile. The sentient objects everywhere are Viṣṇu only and none else. The heaven he has pervaded himself with three steps and the pervasion with one step is wonderful(?). That Viṣṇu, having a disc and a mace in his hands, and wearing a yellow garment, is seen by meditating sages through devotion and never without it. Viṣṇu cannot be seen through anger or jealousy. Having pervaded (everything) among gods, lower animals, immobile objects, living beings and among all small and great (objects), he dwells.

Rudra said:

85-87. Hearing these words of Prahlāda, that excellent demon, with his eyes red due to anger, reproaching his son repeatedly, said to him:

Hiraṇyakaśipu said:

If that Viṣṇu is omnipresent and the Highest Being, then actually show him to me. What is the use of much nonsensical talk?

Mahādeva said:

Speaking like this, Hiraṇyakaśipu struck a pillar of the palace with his hand, and said these (words) to Prahlāda:

Hiraṇyakaśipu said:

88. If Viṣṇu would be (i.e. is) omnipresent, then show him (to me) in this (pillar). Otherwise I shall kill you, uttering false words.

Rudra said:

89-93. Speaking like this, the lord of the demons, suddenly drew out his sword, and angrily threw it at Prahlāda's chest to kill him. At that moment, a great sound was heard from the pillar. The interior of the sky was as it were broken with sounds of the destructive fire. Due to that big sound, striking the ears of the demons, all fell on the ground like trees with their roots cut off. The frightened demons thought that the three worlds were inundated. Then great Viṣṇu, of a great lustre, came out of the pillar. He made a very fearful sound, resembling (the one) at the time of the destruction of the world. Due to that great sound stars fell on the ground.

94-97. Having assumed the body of Nṛsiṁha, Viṣṇu manifested (himself) there only. He was covered with the lustre of crores of suns and fires. In his face he resembled a lion, and in (the other parts of) the body he had a human figure. His mouth was fierce due to fangs, and was raised up to the sky with his throbbing tongue. The ends of his hair were surrounded by flames. The lord had eyes like burning firebrands. Covered by a thousand long arms, full of all weapons, he appeared like (mountain) Meru, with many trees having branches. He had worn a garland of divine flowers, and was decorated with divine ornaments.

98-107. To destroy all demons he remained in the form of a man-lion. Seeing very powerful, terrible-looking man-lion, the lord of demons, with his eyelashes burnt and body afflicted, fell (down). Then Prahlāda, seeing Viṣṇu like a man-lion, saluted Viṣṇu with the words 'Victory (to you).' On the limbs of that high-souled man-lion he saw worlds, seas, islands, gods, gandharvas, human beings; a thousand cosmic eggs were seen on the tip of his mane. Similarly in his eyes were seen the moon, the sun etc. In his eyes (were seen) gods Aśvinas, directions and intermediate directions. On his forehead (were seen) Brahmā and Rudra; in his nose (were seen) the sky and air. In his mouth Indra and Agni (were seen). On his tongue Sarasvatī (was seen). On his fangs (were seen) lions, tigers, śarabhas (i.e. the fabulous eight-legged animals), and great serpents. On his throat was seen Meru, and great mountains (were seen) on his shoulders. On the arms of the noble one (were seen) gods, lower animals and human beings. The atmosphere (was seen) in his navel, and the earth (was seen) on his feet. On his hair all herbs (were seen). On the rows of his nails trees (were seen). In his breaths, Vedas with Aṅgas and Upāṅgas (were seen). On all his limbs (were seen) Ādityas, Vasus, Rudras, hosts of Maruts, gandharvas and celestial nymphs.

108-114. Thus were seen the splendours of the highest soul. The son of the lord of demons, seeing Viṣṇu having Śrīvatsa and Kaustubha (worn) on his chest, adorned with a garland of wood-flowers, endowed with weapons like a conch, a disc, a mace, a sword, the Śārṅga (bow), the goal of all Upaniṣads, had his body sprinkled with tears of joy and repeatedly saluted him. The lord of demons, who was under the influence of (i.e. in the clutches of) death, seeing Viṣṇu, and raising his sword, ran to Nṛsiṁha to fight with him. Then all the very powerful demons who had regained consciousness, took their own weapons, and hurriedly struck Viṣṇu. The weapons were reduced to ash on (reaching) the body of Viṣṇu, as straws thrown into fire (are burnt) in various ways. At that time Viṣṇu, seeing the armies of the demons, burnt them with his bright mane which was arranged with lines of flames. The demons were very much burnt by the fire coming out of Nṛsiṁha's mane.

115-123. All the attendants (were thus burnt). The army had none left in it. Seeing that army, except Prahlāda with his followers, reduced to ash, the lord of demons angrily drew out his sword and moved (towards Viṣṇu). The lord of gods seized the lord of demons with a sword in his hand with one arm, and dropped him down, as a stormy wind (knocks down) a branch. Nṛsiṁha, taking the huge-bodied (demon), fallen on the ground, placed him on his lap. He saw Viṣṇu's face. At that time the sin due to censuring Viṣṇu, and due to the blemish of not being a devotee of Viṣṇu, was reduced to ash merely by Viṣṇu's touch. Then Nṛsiṁha tore off the huge body of the lord of demons with his sharp, hard nails resembling the thunderbolt. The lord of demons, with his soul purified, and with his heart torn off with the nails, actually saw the face of Viṣṇu, and being (thus) fortunate, gave up his life. Great Viṣṇu, having cut off his body into a hundred pieces, and drawn out his long entrails, put the dear ones round his neck (put them affectionately round his neck). Then all hosts of gods, sages having penance as their treasure, led by Brahmā and Rudra, slowly came there to praise (him). They were afraid to propitiate the blazing (Viṣṇu) having faces on all sides.

124-126. (Then) they brought before their mind the goddess, the mother, the supporter of the worlds, of a golden complexion, extremely beautiful (hariṇī)[1], and destroying all troubles. Having prought before their mind the auspicious Lakṣmī (wife) of Viṣṇu, always of a blameless body, with the hymns of the goddess (i.e. Lakṣmī), and devoutly saluted her, the eternal one, brought before their mind by them, that goddess, having four arms, large eyes, and adorned with all ornaments, appeared (there).

127-128. Seeing the beloved of the god of gods, who had put on silken garments, and a divine garland, all gods, with the palms of their hands joined, said to her: "Propitiate your husband. Act in such a way that the lord would give the three worlds immunity from fear."

1. Hariṇī—One of the four classes of women, also called 'Citriṇī', who is said to be a woman endowed with various talents and excellences. The four divisions into which writers on erotical science class women are: Padminī, Citriṇī, Śaṅkhinī, and Hastinī or Kariṇī.

Rudra said:

129-133. The goddess, thus addressed, suddenly went to her husband Viṣṇu and having bowed down before him and saluted him, said to him: "(Please) be pleased." Seeing his own dear wife, Viṣṇu, the lord of all, gave up his anger due to the demon's body, and in a moment became pleased. That ocean of pity, Viṣṇu, placing the goddess on his lap and embracing her, looked at the gods with eyes wet with the nectar of favour. Then there was a joyful agitation among them, praising him and saluting him, and seen by him with kind eyes. Then all the hosts of gods, with their minds full of joy, having saluted the god, the lord of the worlds, with the palms of their hands joined, said (to him):

The hosts of gods said:

134-135. O lord of the worlds, we are not able to see your very wonderful lustre, and your very wonderful form, marked with many arms and feet. We, all gods, are not able to see and put up with your very strong lustre that has filled the three worlds.

Mahādeva said:

136-146. Thus requested by the gods, the lord of gods withdrew that very fearful lustre, and became of a pleasing appearance, auspicious, resembling a crore of autumnal moons, having eyes like lotuses, resembling crores of flashes of lightning due to the mass of his mane full of nectar. The great lord was graced with four delicate, divine arms, endowed with divine armlets and bracelets full of various jewels, resembling the branches with fruits of the desire-yielding tree. The lord was decorated with lotus-like hands resembling japā-flowers. The man-lion was adorned with two raised hands holding a conch and a disc, and with other two granting boons and freedom from fear. His chest was (marked) with Śrīvatsa and Kaustubha; he was adorned with a garland of wood-flowers. He was also decorated with ear-rings resembling the rays of the rising sun. The man-lion, adorned with ornaments like necklaces, armlets, bracelets, shone with Lakṣmī sitting on the left (lap) of his body. The deities along with the great sages, seeing Lakṣmī and the man-lion, with their hearts full of joy, sprinkled them with tears of joy. They, plunged into the ocean of joy, constantly saluted them. By offering divine flowers, they worshipped the lord of souls. Having sprinkled the ancient Nṛsiṁha with the nectar from jewelled pitchers full of nectar, having worshipped him with divine offerings of lights, they praised him with divine hymns, and repeatedly saluted him.

147-155. Then the lord of Lakṣmī, who was pleased, gave them boons desired by them. Then Viṣṇu, to whom his devotees are dear, along with all hosts of gods made the imperishable Prahlāda the king of all demons. Having cheered up Prahlāda, and having, with the best gods, consecrated him, he gave him the boons desired by him and faithful devotion. Then Nṛsiṁha, being praised by all hosts of gods, and his body scattered over with beautiful flowers, vanished there only. Then all the hosts of gods went to their respective abodes. And again, they, with their minds pleased, enjoyed the portions of sacrifices. Then the gods, along with gandharvas, became free from fear. When the great demon was killed, all were delighted only. Prahlāda, Viṣṇu's devotee, then righteously ruled over the kingdom. The best devotee of viṣṇu obtained the kingdom through Viṣṇu's grace. He having worshipped Nṛsiṁha with many sacrifices and gifts etc. obtained, at (the proper) time, Viṣṇu's eternal place, obtained by meditating sages. Those who everyday listen to Prahlāda's account, are all free from sins, and will obtain the highest state. O goddess, I have told you this grandeur of Viṣṇu as Nṛsiṁha. O goddess, listen to the remaining state of grandeur in due order.

CHAPTER TWO HUNDRED THIRTYNINE

The Rise of Bali and Kaśyapa's Penance

Rudra said:

1-4. A son was born to Prahlāda, who was known as Virocana. His son, the large-armed one, was lord Bali, (like) fire. He was the best among those who knew the ways of the world; he was veracious; his senses were subdued; he was the dearest devotee of Viṣṇu; he was always engaged in pious practices, and was pure. The very mighty one, having defeated all gods with Indra and hosts of Maruts, brought the three worlds under his control, and ruled. Without being tilled, the earth grew (corn). It gave much corn and many fruits. All cows were full-milking. Trees had fruits and flowers.

5-9. All men, free from sins, were engaged in their own duties. Free from torment they constantly worshipped Viṣṇu. In this way, Bali, the lord of the demons, ruled righteously. His servants, the gods like Indra, stood by him. Removing the pride of the might (of others) he enjoyed supremacy in the three worlds. Kaśyapa, seeing his son, deprived of his kingdom, and desiring his good, practised penance, along with his wife, in honour of Viṣṇu. Along with (his wife) Aditi, the pious one, took to the vow of (drinking) water (only). He worshipped Padmanābha, Viṣṇu, the lord of gods. Then for thousands of years he worshipped Viṣṇu.

10-13. The ancient one, with the goddess (Lakṣmī) appeared there only. He saw the lotus-eyed (Viṣṇu), holding a conch, a disc, a mace, dark like the jewel sapphire, adorned with all ornaments, graced with a bright crown, armlets, necklaces, and ear-rings, with his chest brightened with Kaustubha, covered with a yellow garment, and seated on a great round seat with Lakṣmī. Seeing the lord of the worlds, the best brāhmaṇa, with his heart full of joy, and with his wife, saluted and praised him.

Kaśyapa said:

14-23. Repeated salutations to you, O lord of Lakṣmī, O omniscient one, O lord of the world, O soul of all, O lord of all gods, O creator and destroyer of the world; O you having no beginning, death or end, salutation to you having a body supporting the universe, having the body of the Vedas and the Vedāṅgas, and seeing everything; salutation to you, the soul of all; salutation to you, very subtle one, full of auspicious qualities; to you whose soul is fit to be meditated upon by the meditating sages; salutation to you the youthful boy, the lord of Śrī, Bhū, and Līlā; to you who are eternally free and the only pleasure; to you who dwell in the highest abode; salutation to you, O you of four characters; salutation to you, O you of four forms; salutation to you having five conditions, and of the nature of five. You are always worshipped by the meditating sages, devoted to the five-natured one. You remain in the five sacraments of those who know the five principles. O Viṣṇu, your form superior to the five (forms) should always be known. O you of a complete form, the wise certainly know you in four ways. Your servants purify the entire world, your creation. In a moment you cause the freedom from the bond of the mundane existence of those brāhmaṇas, full of (the knowledge of) the three Vedas, devoted to their duties, and loving (your) devotees. Salutation to the supporter of the three worlds, the self-supporting one, and the soul of all. Salutation to you the supporter, the creator, the universe, of the form of the universe; to Nārāyaṇa, Kṛṣṇa, Vāsudeva, Śārṅgin; to Viṣṇu, Jiṣṇu, of pure energy.

Mahādeva said:

24. The lord Janārdana who was thus properly being praised with such eulogies by the great sage, was pleased, and spoke with a grave voice:

The lord said:

25. O greatest brāhmaṇa, I, devoutly and properly worshipped by you, am pleased with you. Ask for a boon. Well-being to you. I shall do as desired by you.

Mahādeva said:

26. Then Kaśyapa, with his wife, thus spoke to Viṣṇu:

Kaśyapa said:

27-28. O lord of gods, being (born) as my son, do what is good to the gods. O god, Bali has forcibly conquered the three worlds. Being born as Indra's younger brother known as Upendra, and having, through your Māyā, vanquished Bali by whatever manner, give eternally the three worlds to Indra.

Mahādeva said:

29-31. Thus addressed by the brāhmaṇa (i.e. Kaśyapa), Viṣṇu said: "All right." Being praised by the gods, he vanished there only. In the meanwhile, the lord, the creator of beings, came to the womb of Aditi, (the wife) of the noble Kaśyapa. At that time Bali, with (the help of) eight great sages commenced a long sacrificial session according to the rules.

CHAPTER TWO HUNDRED FORTY

Viṣṇu Incarnates as Vāmana

Śrī Mahādeva said:

1-5a. Then at the end of a thousand years Aditi gave birth to Vāmana, Viṣṇu, Acyuta, Hari, the lord, who was the great lord of all the worlds, who had Śrīvatsa and Kaustubha on his chest, whose lustre was like that of the full moon, who was handsome, whose eyes were like lotuses, whose body was very short, who was dressed like a lad, who could be known by means of the Vedas and the Vedāṅgas, who was marked with such signs as a girdle, a (piece of) deer-hide, and a staff. Seeing him of a great vigour, all deities led by Indra, along with great sages, praised and saluted him. Then the lord who was pleased, said to the best gods:

Vāmana said:

5b. O best gods, tell me what I should do today.

Śrī Śaṅkara said:

6a. Then the gods who were delighted, spoke to that highest lord:

The gods said:

6b-7. O Madhusūdana, Bali's sacrifice is going on now. O lord, this is the time for the lord of demons not to turn down (any request). Having asked for the three worlds from him, (please) give them to us.

Śaṅkara said:

8-10. Thus addressed by all gods, Viṣṇu went to Bali, seated at the place of the sacrifice along with eight sages. Seeing him having come as a guest, the king of demons suddenly got up. Seeing (as if) Viṣṇu himself had come as a guest, he, with a smile, seated him on a seat of flowers and properly honoured him. Having bowed before him and saluted him, he said in a faltering voice:

Bali said:

11-12. I am fortunate, I am blessed. My life is fruitful. O best brāhmaṇa, having honoured you, what dear to you, should I do? O best brāhmaṇa, I shall give you that for which you have come to me. O best among those who know the Vedas, speak quickly.

Śaṅkara said:

13a. Then with a delighted mind (Viṣṇu) spoke to the king:

Vāmana said:

13b-18. O best king, listen. I shall tell you the reason for my arrival. O lord of demons, O you who remove the pride (of others, or you who respect others), give me (that much piece of) land measured by my three steps, for an enclosed place for keeping the fire-vessel. I do not desire anything else. Of all gifts, the gift of (a piece of) land is the best. That king who gives even that much piece of land measured by his thumb, to a poor brāhmaṇa, would be the lord of the world. In this world there is no other gift like that (of a piece) of land. Both of them—he who receives (a piece of) land and he who gives (a piece of) land—are meritorious and, after death, go to heaven. Therefore, O great king, give me that much piece of land measured by my three steps. O king, do not hesitate to give such a small (piece of) land. O king, that will indeed be (tantamount to) the gift of the three worlds.

Śaṅkara said:

19-20. Then the king, with his face delighted, said, "All right." He intended to make him the gift of land in the proper way. Seeing the king of demons, his priest, Uśanas, said to him (these) words, "O king, do not give him the land."

Śukra said:

21-22. O king, this is Viṣṇu, the highest lord, who was requested by the gods. He has come here to take the entire earth after deceiving you. Therefore, land should not be given to the noble one. O king, by my word, give him some other object.

Śrī Śaṅkara said:

23a. Then having laughed the king firmly said to his preceptor:

Bali said:

23b-25a. To please Viṣṇu, I have done all meritorious acts. Today I am fortunate that Viṣṇu himself has come (to me). Today I shall very happily give (even) my life to him. Therefore, I shall give him even the three worlds.

Śrī Śaṅkara said:

25b-27a. Speaking like this, the king devoutly washed his feet and first (offering him) water, gave him the land in the proper manner. Taking him round, and having saluted him he gave him wealth as a present. With his heart delighted, he again said to the brāhmaṇa:

Bali said:

27b-28a. O brāhmaṇa, I am fortunate, I am blessed having given you land. O best brāhmaṇa, take this land as desired by you.

Śrī Śaṅkara said:

28b-35. To the king Viṣṇu said: "Near you, in your presence, I shall get the land measured with my steps." Saying so, the highest lord abandoned his dwarfish form, and taking up the body of Viṣṇu, extending up to fifty crores (of yojanas) he seized the earth along with the seas and mountains, along with the oceans, islands, gods, demons and human beings. With one step of his body he crossed the entire earth. Then he said: "O best among the demon-kings, what do I do now?" It was the very powerful Trivikrama-form of the lord. It was good for the well-being of even the gods and the noble sages. It would not be possible even for Brahmā or Śiva to see it. O auspicious Girijā, having occupied the entire earth, that step became a hundred yojanas long. The ancient one gave the demon-king a divine sight. He showed him his Janārdana-form.

36-37. Seeing that universal form of the god, Bali, the lord of demons, got matchless joy, and was covered with tears of joy. Seeing the god, having saluted him, having praised him with eulogies, he, with his heart delighted, spoke in a faltering voice:

Bali said:

38. Seeing you, the highest god, I am fortunate, I am blessed. O highest lord, accept these three worlds.

Śrī Śaṅkara said:

39-48. Then Viṣṇu, Acyuta, the lord of all, spread up his other immutable foot along with stars and planets, and covering all gods, up to Brahmā's world. He was full of the foot of Acyuta, O you of an auspicious face. Then Brahmā, the grandsire, (seeing) that foot of the god of gods, which was marked with (the signs of) a disc, a lotus etc. saying, with his heart full of joy, "I am blessed," took his pot (of water), and with devotion washed the foot with the water from it. Due to Viṣṇu's majesty that water became inexhaustible. That pure holy water fell on the peak of Meru. For purifying the world it flowed in four streams: Sītā, Alakanandā, Cakṣu and Bhadrā in due order. Alakanandā is said to be (flowing) to the south of Meru in three streams; she, purifying the world, and having three streams is called Tripathagā. The auspicious river is called Mandākinī in heaven, Bhogavatī in nether world, and the speedy Gaṅgā in between (i.e. on the earth flowing) for purifying human beings. O you of an auspicious face, seeing her flowing over the Meru mountain, I held her on my head to purify myself. Having held (on my head) the auspicious water of Gaṅgā for a thousand divine years, I obtained bliss, and am adored in all worlds.

49-53. There is no doubt that he who would carry on his head the water of Gaṅgā rising from Viṣṇu's foot, or would drink it, would be respected by the world. He who would utter (the words) 'Gaṅgā, Gaṅgā' even from (a distance of) hundred yojanas, is freed from all sins, and goes to Viṣṇu's heaven. Then king Bhagīratha and Gautama having a great penance (to his credit) worshipped me with penance and asked for Gaṅgā. O goddess, then I affectionately gave that auspicious best river Gaṅgā, (rising from the foot) of Viṣṇu to them for the good of the entire world. Since she was brought by Gautama, she was called Gautamī. Since she was chosen by king (Bhagīratha), she was known as Bhāgīrathī.

54-60. I have in course (of the narration) told you the excellent greatness of Gaṅgā. Then that glorious lord Nārāyaṇa loving his devotees, gave the auspicious nether world to Bali, the lord of demons. He made Bali the king of all the demons, serpents and the aquatic animals till the (final) inundation (of the earth). In the guise of a lad the immutable Viṣṇu, the killer of demons, the son of Kaśyapa, affectionately gave the worlds to Indra. Then gods with gandharvas and the very powerful sages praised Viṣṇu with divine eulogies and worshipped him. For them to see his form, he contracted it; and being honoured by them Viṣṇu vanished. Viṣṇu, the mighty one, thus protected Indra well. The lord of the three worlds (i.e. Indra) obtained the three worlds and great affluence. I have thus told you the account of the auspicious splendour of Viṣṇu's incarnation as Vāmana. The rest of the splendour I shall narrate in due order.

CHAPTER TWO HUNDRED FORTYONE

Paraśurāma's Story

The lord said:

1-3a. Bhṛgu's son was the great, best brāhmaṇa (named) Jamadagni. He had mastered all Vedas and Vedāṅgas and had practised a severe penance. O you beautiful lady, on the auspicious sandy bank of Gaṅgā the religious-minded one practised penance (in honour) of Indra for a thousand years. Then lord Indra, being pleased, said these (words):

Indra said:

3b. O best brāhmaṇa, ask for a boon that is (i.e. that you have) in your mind.

The lord said:

4a. Then the brāhmaṇa sage spoke to Indra who was pleased:

Jamadagni said:

4b. O god, give me (the desire-yielding cow) Surabhi always fulfilling one's desires.

The lord said:

5-8. Then Indra, the lord of gods, being pleased, gave him the divine Surabhi fulfilling all desires. That Jamadagni of a great penance (to his credit), having obtained Surabhi lived with great grandeur like another Indra. Jamadagni, of a great penance (to his credit) married in the proper manner, Reṇukā, Reṇuka's daughter. The pious-minded one for many years enjoyed with her as Indra with Paulomī, his auspicious queen.

9-17a. Then the very pious one, with a desire for having a son, performed a sacrifice. With (that) sacrifice he pleased god Indra. (Indra) Śacī's husband, being pleased, (promised) him a very strong, very powerful, mighty-armed son, tormentor of all enemies. Then in course of time the best brāhmaṇa generated a very strong and powerful son with a part of a portion of Viṣṇu and having all (good) marks, on Reṇukā, O you of a bright smile. When the very powerful son (was born), his grandfather joyfully gave him a name indicating Viṣṇu's portion. He gave him a very auspicious name (Paraśu-)Rāma. Being born from Jamadagni he was called Jāmadagnya. The best brāhmaṇa of the family of Bhṛgu grew. His thread ceremony was performed; he was proficient in all sciences and arts. To practise penance he went to the Śālagrāma mountain. There he saw the brāhmaṇa-sage Kaśyapa of unlimited splendour. The brāhmaṇa, Marīci's son, was full of delight with (i.e. on seeing) him. In the proper manner he gave him the indestructible formula of Viṣṇu.

17b-23. Having received the formula from Kaśyapa, the high-souled one, (Paraśu-)Rāma, muttering day and night the great six-syllabled formula, worshipped the lord of Lakṣmī. That pious Bhārgava (i.e. Paraśurāma) meditating upon Viṣṇu having eyes like lotus-petals and the omniscient one, practised penance for many years. He, with senses subdued and speech controlled, and (practising) great penance, remained (there). The brāhmaṇa-sage Jamadagni remained on the auspicious bank of Gaṅgā. He performed pious acts according to the precepts like sacrifices and gifts. By the favour of Indra's cow his wealth was full. Sometime the king, the lord of Haihaya, surrounded by his entire army, having conquered all countries, reached the hermitage of Jamadagni, the son of Bhṛgu. Seeing the glorious, best sage, he saluted him.

24-29. The king, having asked the devout great sage about his well-being, gave him garments and ornaments. He too honoured the king that had come to his house. Having honoured according to the precept the king with *madhuparka** the sage fed the best king along with his army. The very intelligent son of Bhṛgu (i.e. Jamadagni) solicited Surabhi. She, the cow of plenty, produced food, drink etc. at that time. The best sage, of a great penance, gave the inexhaustible food, drink etc. produced by her to the king along with his army. Seeing that cow of plenty, the king was full of curiosity. The very wicked-minded (king) longed for the cow. The best king then begged Jamadagni for Surabhi.

Kārtavīrya said:

30. O brāhmaṇa, give me this tawny cow of plenty, giving all desired objects. O you of a good vow, I shall give you thousands of other cows.

The lord said:

31-32. Thus addressed by the king, Jamadagni of a great penance (to his credit) said (to him): "O king, this cow of plenty cannot be given to you by me. This one was protected by Indra, the god of gods. O king, how should the wealth of deities be given by me?"

33-36. The king, thus addressed, was then excited with

*A preparation of curd, clarified butter, water, honey and sugar offered to guests.

anger. He, surrounded by the entire army, seized the cow of plenty forcibly. Then, O you of an excellent complexion, the glorious cow of plenty became angry, and with her horns and soles of her hoofs struck his huge army. Then that goddess, the cow of plenty, having, in a short time, struck that army, vanished, and in a moment went near Indra. Then (Kārtavīrya) Arjuna, seeing his army struck, was overcome by anger. With his fist he struck Bhārgava, the best brāhmaṇa.

37-39. Being struck by him in many ways, he was weakened. The best brāhmaṇa suddenly fell on the ground and died. The lord of Haihaya, the wicked-minded one, having killed there the best sage, and surrounded by a great army entered his own city. Rāma Bhārgava worshipped the god of gods. Pleased by his worship Viṣṇu said:

God Viṣṇu said:

40-41. O child, with the penance of you of a controlled mind, I am pleased. O brāhmaṇa, I shall give you a very auspicious power. Possessed of my power, kill the wicked great kings for destroying those who cause a burden to the earth and for the good of the deities.

Mahādeva said:

42-44. Speaking like this, the god gave him an axe capable of killing the enemies, so also the great bow of Viṣṇu and many divine missiles. Lord Viṣṇu, having given (these) to Jamadagni, said: "O best brāhmaṇa, you, the killer of the enemy's soldiers, having killed many arrogant kings repeatedly, take this entire earth bound by the ocean. Full of piety and great heroism you protect it. In course of time, you will reach my position by my grace."

The lord said:

45-50a. Having said like this, and having given the brāhmaṇa a boon, the god vanished. Rāma also suddenly went to his father's hermitage. Seeing his father killed, Bhārgava (i.e. Paraśurāma) was filled with anger. He desired to make the earth, crowded with kings, clear of kṣatriyas. He went to the city of the king of Haihaya, which was full of kings. With his body burning with anger, he, with his weapons raised, stood at the gate. The citizens of his city seeing that very powerful Jāmadagnya, with a blazing body, looked upon him as the destructive fire at the end of the world. Being afflicted by fear, all ran to the king, the lord of Haihaya. They praised him of great energy and equipped with all weapons. Hearing their words, the king with an amazed mind, said:

King of Haihaya said:

50b-51. Who is that forcibly standing at the gate of my city with weapons? Even Indra, or Yama, or Rudra, or Kubera, can never stand with weapons at the gate of my city.

Mahādeva said:

52-55. Saying so, the lord of kings impelled his very strong servants to see him, and the wicked one said to them: "Arrest him." Having gone, they saw at the gate a very strong hero burning like the destructive fire at the end of the world, and difficult to be seen due to his lustre. The mighty ones were not even able to look at him. From all sides they, desirous of seizing him, often went to him. Seeing all those servants of the lord of kings with weapons, the very powerful best brāhmaṇa, Jāmadagnya, said laughing:

Paraśurāma said:

56-57. O mean men, I, Rāma, the son of Bhārgava, have come (here). I shall kill all best kings for (i.e. as a revenge of) my father's murder. To my (dead) father I shall offer Kārtavīrya's blood mixed with sesamum-seeds, and shall offer the piṇḍa with his lotus-head.

Mahādeva said:

58-62. Thus addressed, the very powerful servants of the king struck him with arrows as fire with straws. Then the very brave Rāma of genuine valour was angry, and drawing the bow of Viṣṇu made the sound of the bow-string. With that great sound the three worlds were filled. Even gods were frightened. (Such) was the great wonder. Then the very strong Paraśurāma struck the very brave, very powerful servants with arrows resembling fire. Having killed the servants of the glorious king, he stood like the destructive fire at the end of the world, deadly to all beings.

63-68. Hearing that his servants were killed in the battle by the intelligent (Paraśu-) Rāma, the brave king of Haihaya, with his eyes red with anger, went out with his army to the place where Bhārgava stood. Seeing him appearing deadly and blazing with his own lustre, all the men there, suspecting the destruction of human beings were frightened. Then a very fierce battle took place between Rāma and the kings, with fearful strokes of weapons and missiles, as between two showering clouds. Then Rāma of a great lustre easily burnt the king's army in a moment with the missile of Viṣṇu. Then Rāma of unlimited valour cut off the thousand arms of the wicked Kārtavīrya with his sharp axe. The very brave king could not fight with (Paraśu-) Rāma in the battle.

69-74. The wicked-minded one lost his valour due to his own sin. The mighty son of Reṇukā, being angry, cut off his head, as mighty Indra did the peak of a big mountain, and he who was brave and angry, killed Sahasrabāhu and all the kings with his axe in the battle. Seeing Rāma, the very fearful one, all kings on the earth, struck by fear, ran away as elephants do on seeing a lion. The angry Rāma killed the kings even though they had fled due to the resentment against his father's murder, as the angry Garuḍa killed the serpents. The valorous Rāma made the entire (world) clear of the kṣatriyas, but protected (i.e. spared) only the very great family of Ikṣvāku, due to its being the family to which his maternal grandfather was related, and due to his mother's words.

75-78. Rāma, the destroyer of the families of kings, deprived the kings of the family of his maternal grandfather of their kingdoms, but did not kill them belonging to Manu's dynasty. But the brave one destroyed the families of all (other) kings. The brāhmaṇa, the mighty son of Jamadagni, having made the earth clear of the kṣatriyas, duly performed the great horse-sacrifice. He gave the earth with the seven islands to chief brāhmaṇas. That brave son of Jamadagni, having given the earth to the brāhmaṇas, went to the hermitage of Nara-Nārāyaṇa to practise penance.

79-81. O goddess, I have told you this account of the incarnation of lord (Viṣṇu), holder of the Śārṅga bow, who had entered Rāma with his power. Due to the entrance of the power this (form) of the noble one cannot be worshipped. The chief, noble, brāhmaṇas, the devotees of the lord, should worship the incarnations of (Dāśarathi) Rāma and Kṛṣṇa, perfect with virtues, worshipped by sages, and giving salvation to human beings.

CHAPTER TWO HUNDRED FORTYTWO

The Story of Rāma

Rudra said:

1-3a. Formerly Svāyambhuva Manu muttered the great formula of twelve syllables at Naimiṣa on the pure, auspicious bank of Gomatī. For a thousand years he worshipped Lakṣmī's lord. Lord Viṣṇu said to him: "Choose a boon from me." Then Manu Svāyambhuva joyfully said to Viṣṇu:

Manu said:

3b-4a. O Viṣṇu, be born as my son in three existences, O lord of gods. I am worshipping you with a desire for a son.

Rudra said:

4b. Thus addressed, Lakṣmī's lord spoke with very good words:

Viṣṇu said:

5-7. O greatest king, whatever is desired (by you) in your mind will take place. I too have a great pleasure in being your son. O best king, when you will be born in the period having stability as its aim, I shall also be born as your son, O you of a good vow. O sinless one, in every age I shall be born of you for protecting the good, destroying the wicked and establishing righteousness.

Rudra said:

8-14. Having thus given him a boon, Viṣṇu vanished there only. From Manu Svāyambhuva he had the first birth. He was born as king Daśaratha in the Raghu-family formerly. The second birth was that of lord Vasudeva in the family of the Vṛṣṇis. He will be born as a brāhmaṇa in the town of Śambhala in the last two quarters of the Kali-age of the measure of a thousand divine years. Kausalyā was born as the wife of king Daśaratha. Devakī was known (to be born) to serve the Yadu-family. Devaprabhā was born as the wife of a brāhmaṇa Harivrata. Thus they obtained the motherhood of Viṣṇu in three existences. O you of a good vow, I shall first tell you the account of Rāma, by just remembering whom even sinners get liberation. Hiraṇyaka and Hiraṇyākṣa, taking up second birth, will be born as the very strong Kumbhakarṇa and Rāvaṇa.

15-22. O you innocent one, pious Viśravas, a brāhmaṇa, was the son of Pulastya. His wife, a demon's daughter, was Viśālākṣī. She was the daughter of Sukeśī. And the demon Sumālin's daughter Kekasī (Kaikasī?) was his (another) wife of a firm vow. Being excessively full of lust, the slim, respectful lady of a charming appearance had sexual intercourse with the great sage in the evening. Due to her desire for sexual enjoyment in the evening two very powerful demons, Rāvaṇa and Kumbhakarṇa, known in the world, were born to her. A daughter, Śūrpaṇakhā of a deformed face was also born to her. After sometime Bibhīṣaṇa was born to her. He was of a good character, devoted to God, veracious, pious and pure. Rāvaṇa and Kumbhakarṇa were greatest like the Himālaya mountain. The two very much propitiated me with very severe penance. O goddess, that wicked Rāvaṇa worshipped me with just a wicked deed with his lotus-like heads. Then, I with my mind very much pleased said to him:

23-30. "Ask for a boon that is in your mind, O child." Then the wicked one said: "With a desire (i.e. as I have a desire) to conquer all worlds, let me not be killed by gods, demons or fiends." Then, O you of a beautiful face, I gave the wicked demon immunity from death from gods, demons or fiends. The very powerful demon, proud due to the grant of the boon, troubled the three worlds, gods, demons and fiends. Gods, troubled by him, full of fear, led by Brahmā, sought the shelter of god

(Viṣṇu), the lord of Lakṣmī. Understanding their anguish, the ancient one said, in order to grant them immunity from fear, to all gods led by Brahmā and Rudra:

The lord said:

I shall be born in the family of Raghu as the son of king Daśaratha. I shall kill the wicked Rāvaṇa with his relatives. Taking to a human body I shall kill the thorn (i.e. nuisance) to the deities. You too, born as monkeys due to Nandin's curse, help me, O best gandharvas and celestial nymphs.

Rudra said:

31-32. All deities, thus addressed by Viṣṇu, god of gods, were born on the earth after being turned into (i.e. as) monkeys. Bhārgava also gave the earth girt by the ocean. It was formerly given to the very noble Raghus by great sages.

33. There was Vaivasvata Manu's son, known as Ikṣvāku, the best among kings and very powerful, best among those who knew the ways of the world.

34-38. In his family was born the very brilliant and powerful king Daśaratha, king Aja's son, truthful, pure, and of a good character. The king protected the entire earth with valour. He installed all best kings on the kingdoms (i.e. thrones). That king married Kausalyā, king Kosala's daughter, beautiful in all limbs. His second wife was Sumitrā by name, Magadha king's daughter, of a bright smile. His third wife was Kekayī, having eyes like lotus-petals, and the daughter of Kekaya king.

39-44. With these three wives the Kākutstha king (i.e. Daśaratha) enjoyed while protecting the earth. There was a city named Ayodhyā situated on the bank of Sarayū. It was full of all jewels and wealth and grains. It possessed ramparts and town-gates. It had golden ramparts. It had excellent elephants and horses as Indra's city (had). In it lived the righteous king along with best sages and the noble brāhmaṇa Vasiṣṭha, his family priest. And he ruled over the kingdom in which the thorns (i.e. sources of nuisance) were destroyed. That city of Ayodhyā also was called holy, since the revered Supreme Being would be born in it. O auspicious one, the name of that city of the abode (of Viṣṇu) was great.

45-51. That is the highest place where revered Viṣṇu dwelt. There salvation, instantly cutting off (the bonds of) all acts, would take place. When Viṣṇu was born there, O you of an auspicious face, all men were delighted. That king (Daśaratha) having protected the entire earth, and longing for a son performed a sacrifice in honour of Viṣṇu (to propitiate) Hari, Acyuta. Worshipped with the sacrifice in his honour by him, Viṣṇu, the omnipresent king, the lord of Lakṣmī, giver of boons said. In the fire Viṣṇu of the form of sacrifice then appeared. He was like pure gold. He held a conch, a disc and a mace. He had put on white garments. He was glorious, and adorned with all ornaments. On his chest were Śrīvatsa and Kaustubha; he was adorned with a garland of wood-flowers. His large eyes resembled lotus-petals, he had four arms, and was of a generous mind. The lord of Lakṣmī, with Lakṣmī seated on his left lap, appeared there. He who loved his devotees, said to the king: "I am the giver of boons (i.e. I shall grant you a boon)."

52-54a. Seeing him, the lord of all worlds, the king full of joy and with his mind full of delight, with his wife (wives?) saluted him. With the palms of his hands folded, and bowing down, he spoke words faltering due to joy. He said to Viṣṇu, the lord of gods: "Be my son." Then Viṣṇu, the lord, being pleased, said to the king:

Viṣṇu said:

54b-55. O best king, for the good of the gods and the earth, I shall be born (as your son), for the protection of the good, for killing the demons, for granting liberation to the worlds, and for establishing righteousness.

Mahādeva said:

56. Viṣṇu gave the king bright rice boiled in milk, kept in a golden pot and held in the hand of Lakṣmī.

Viṣṇu said:

57. O king, O you of a good vow, give this rice boiled in milk to your wives. On them will be born sons from my body.

Mahādeva said:

58-60. Speaking like this, Viṣṇu, being praised by all sages, presented himself, and vanished in the same way. The very calm king, seeing the eldest and the youngest queen, divided the divine rice boiled in milk, and gave it to them. In the meanwhile his beautiful-eyed middle wife, longing for a son, came near him.

61-62. Seeing her, Kausalyā and Kekayī of a beautiful waist, gave half (the portion of) their divine rice boiled in milk to her. Eating that divine rice boiled in milk all the queens with beautiful waists, conceived and they, of a bright lustre, shone.

63-68. Then Viṣṇu, the lord of gods, wearing yellow garments and holding a conch, a disc, a mace in his hands, appeared in their dreams. In this charming time, O you of a bright smile, in the month of Caitra, in the bright half of the month, on the ninth day, when the Sun was in the Puṣya constellation, in the noon, and at a time when all Planets were auspicious, Kausalyā gave birth to a son, Viṣṇu, the lord of worlds, who was dark like lotus-leaves, who resembled crores of Cupids, whose eyes were large like lotus-petals, and was adorned with all ornaments. On his chest were Śrīvatsa and Kaustubha. He was graced with all ornaments. He shone with two ear-rings (bright) like the rising sun, resembled many suns, was covered with great lustre. He, the charming one, was born from the body of the highest lord, as one lamp is produced (i.e. lighted) from another lamp.

69-70. He was the lord of all worlds, who was fit to be meditated upon by all meditating sages, was ancient, the goal of all Upaniṣads, endless and the highest god. He was Viṣṇu, the cause of the creation, maintenance and destruction of the world, the protector of all beings, the lord full of all beings.

71-75. When the lord of the world was born, in heaven divine drums were sounded; the best gods sent down showers of flowers. Gods led by Brahmā, seated in aeroplanes, and along with sages and with their entire bodies overcome by joy, praised (him). The chiefs of gandharvas sang and bevies of celestial nymphs danced. Holy, auspicious breezes blew. The sun became very bright. The fires burnt (after being) subsided; the ten quarters were clear. Then the king joyfully seeing his son, the ancient (god Viṣṇu), performed through Vasiṣṭha, the ceremony to be performed at the birth of a child. Then revered Vasiṣṭha also gave him a charming name.

76-79. "This great lord is the 'ramaṇa' or lover of Śrī, living in a lotus. Therefore, his ancient name Śrīrāma is settled." It is equal to the thousand names of Viṣṇu (i.e. the hymn Viṣṇu-sahasra-nāma) and gives salvation to human beings. Brought into existence by Viṣṇu, he is called Viṣṇu. The revered sage Vasiṣṭha, having named him, taken him round, having saluted him, having praised him with eulogies and having recited the thousand names (of Viṣṇu) for the good luck of the noble one, the very lustrous one, went from that most auspicious house.

80-82. Then the king gladly gave much wealth to chief brāhmaṇas. He also righteously caused to give the gift of a myriad of cows. The best of the Raghu dynasty gave a hundred thousand villages (to brāhmaṇas). With divine garments, and ornaments, and immeasurable wealth, he gratified the brāhmaṇas to please Viṣṇu.

83-87. Kausalyā with expanded hands saw him resembling a white lotus, having a lotus in his lotus-like hand. She saw, O you of an excellent face, (marks of) lotuses on his beautiful feet. On his body (she saw) (signs of) a conch, a disc, a mace, a lotus, a flag and garments etc.; on his chest (she saw) Śrīvatsa and Kaustubha along with a garland of wood-flowers. On his body she saw the entire world with gods, demons and human beings. The large-eyed (Kausalyā) saw the fourteen worlds on his smiling face. In the breath of the noble one she saw Vedas and Itihāsas (historical accounts). O you of an excellent complexion, on his buttocks (she saw) islands, oceans and mountains. In his navel (she saw) Brahmā and Śiva. In his ears (she saw) the bright quarters. In his eyes she saw fire and the sun and in his nose (she saw) the very speedy wind.

88. Seeing all his splendours, the goal of all the Upaniṣads, the beautiful (lady) was afraid, and having saluted him again and again, and with her eyes full of tears, she, with the palms of her hands folded, said (these) words:

Kausalyā said:

89. O lord of the god of gods, I am fortunate in having got you as my son, O master. O lord of the world, be pleased with me. Show towards me a son's affection.

The lord said:

90. Viṣṇu (i.e. Rāma), the omnipresent one, thus addressed

by his mother, obtaining illusory manhood, cried due to his being a child.

91-93. Then queen Kausalyā of a beautiful waist and auspicious characteristics, joyfully embraced her son and gave him (i.e. fed him with) milk from her breast. The eternal one drank (sucked) milk from her breast as a child; the great lord, the sustainer of the world remained on his mother's lap. Citizens and countrymen, being delighted, celebrated a festival in that auspicious, charming region, giving all desired objects of men.

94-96. Bharata produced from the Pāñcajanya (conch of Viṣṇu) was born to Kaikeyī. Sumitrā gave birth to Lakṣmaṇa of auspicious signs. The glorious one also gave birth to Śatrughna, the tormentor of his enemies. Lakṣmaṇa, the killer of the enemy's heroes, was born with a portion of (the snake) Ananta. Śatrughna, of unlimited valour, was produced from Sudarśana. They all grew there in the family of Vaivasvata Manu.

97-98. The sons were properly taught by the very vigorous Vasiṣṭha. The princes studied the Vedas and were proficient in general knowledge. They knew the essential nature of all branches of knowledge, and were skilled in archery. They were very generous and they increased the joy of people.

99. The princes Rāma and Lakṣmaṇa formed a pair. Similarly Bharata and Śatrughna formed a pair.

100-104. Then Lakṣmī, the chief goddess of the worlds, who was beautiful, who resembled a crore of young suns, whose hands were like red lotuses, who was endowed with all (good) characteristics, who was adorned with all ornaments, who, the beautiful one, had worn on her bosom a garland of fresh flowers, was born in Janaka's house, at the opening of a furrow, at an auspicious moment in an auspicious field dug up by Indra's plough. Seeing that girl, auspicious and full of all Vedas, the lord of Mithilā took her out and nourished her as (his) child. The chief goddess, dear to the lord of worlds, grew in the charming house of Janaka for the protection of the entire world.

105-110. In the meanwhile, O goddess, the great sage, Kauśika, well known in the world, commenced the performance of a sacrifice in the established hermitage on the auspicious, meritorious bank of Bhāgīrathī. When that sacrifice of the brāhmaṇa proceeded, the demons of Rāvaṇa destroyed his sacrifice. Pious Kauśika, having thought, desired to bring for the good of the world, Viṣṇu (i.e. Rāma) born in Raghu's family. Having gone to the charming city of Ayodhyā protected by (Daśaratha, the descendant of) Raghu, the best sage saw Daśaratha, the best king. The king of a great lustre too, having seen Kauśika, got up, and with the palms of his hands joined, saluted, along with his sons, the best sage.

111-112a. The descendant of Raghu, saying, "I am fortunate" honoured the best sage with proper rite after seating him on an excellent seat. Having taken himself round him, and saluted him, he said to him: "What do (i.e. should) I do?" Then Viśvāmitra, with great penance (to his credit), and with his mind delighted, said:

Viśvāmitra said:

112b-113. O king, give me Rāma for the protection of my sacrifice. In Rāma's vicinity (i.e. presence) may my sacrifice be fruitful. Therefore, O king, please give (me) Rāma for the protection of (my) sacrifice.

The lord said:

114-116. Hearing the words of the best sage, he, the best among the all-knowing ones, gave the best sage, Rāma with Lakṣmaṇa. Taking Rāma (with him), that best brāhmaṇa Viśvāmitra with great penance (to his credit), and being pleased, went to his hermitage. When the best descendant of Raghu went (with the sage), gods were delighted. The very lustrous ones sent down showers of flowers, and praised (him).

117-118. Then the very powerful Garuḍa, delighted in heart, came there unseen by beings, and having approached (the best descendant of) Raghu (i.e. Rāma), gave the two (i.e. Rāma and Lakṣmaṇa) two bows, two quivers, and two inexhaustible arrows. The bird also gave them divine missiles, weapons, and left.

119-123. The two heroes, Rāma and Lakṣmaṇa, were informed of the fierce-looking demoness moving in the forest by the noble Kauśika. O goddess, her name was Tāḍakā, and she was the wife of the demon Sunda. The two great heroes struck her with arrows discharged from their divine bows. Struck (with his arrow) by Rāma, the fierce-looking demoness gave up her fierce form, and became one of a divine form. She was glowing with her body, was adorned with all ornaments; having saluted the two (best descendants of) Raghu, she went to Viṣṇu's world. Having killed her the celebrated and very lustrous Rāma entered, with the noble Lakṣmaṇa, the auspicious hermitage of Kauśika.

124-126. Then the delighted sages, having gone forth to meet the best of Raghus, seated him, and worshipped the highest soul with materials of worship etc. The best sage Kauśika, being initiated along with the sages properly commenced the excellent sacrifice. When the great sacrifice proceeded, a demon named Mārīca, along with his brother Subāhu, came there to create an obstacle.

127-129. Seeing the two fierce demons, Rāma, killer of his enemy's heroes, killed Subāhu, the lord of demons, with one arrow. With a great wind-missile, he caused Mārīca to fall into the ocean as wind causes a dry leaf (to fall down). That best demon, seeing the great valour of Rāma, put down his weapons and went to a great hermitage to practise penance.

130-132a. Viśvāmitra, of great lustre, worshipped Rāma there with a pleased mind after the great sacrifice was over. The best sage, having embraced the noble one who had side-locks on his temples, who was dark like a lotus-leaf, whose eyes were large like lotus-leaves, and having smelt his head, praised him.

132b-141. In the meanwhile, the lord of lords, king of Mithilā commenced, with the (help of) best sages, the Vājapeya sacrifice. To see it all sages of auspicious hearts led by Viśvāmitra went along with best of the Raghus (to Mithilā). With the lotus-like foot of that Rāma who was going (to Mithilā), the land was purified, and the great stone was approached. That Ahalyā too, who was formerly cursed by her husband Gautama, became auspicious by the touch of Rāma's foot. Then the best sages having reached the city of Mithilā with the two descendants of Raghu (viz. Rāma and Lakṣmaṇa) were delighted at heart. The very powerful king of Mithilā having seen the illustrious ones to have come, went forth to meet them and honoured them. (He saw) Rāma whose eyes were large like lotuses, who resembled a lotus-leaf (in complexion), who had put on a yellow garment, was gentle, had tender limbs and was bright, who, the excellent one, had slighted Cupid with his handsomeness, who was endowed with all (good) marks, was decorated with all ornaments, who, the slender Viṣṇu, was born in the heart-lotus of the highest god, with the highest virtues like good character, as one lamp would be produced (i.e. lighted) from another. Seeing that Raghunātha, Janaka was delighted at heart.

142-145a. He looked upon Rāma, Daśaratha's son, just as the highest lord. Saying, "I am fortunate" he honoured the descendant of Kakutstha. He took that to be the favour of Viṣṇu, Vāsudeva. The lord thought to his mind to give him (in marriage) his daughter. Knowing the two to be sons from Raghu's family, the best king honoured them in accordance with Dharma with bright garments and ornaments. With honour like *madhuparka* he worshipped the sages.

145b-148. Then at the end of the sacrifice, the lotus-eyed Rāma broke the divine bow of Śiva and won Janaka's daughter. The lord of Mithilā, very much pleased with the great purchase-price in the form of (Rāma's) valour, gladly gave her (in marriage) to him, as formerly the great Ocean gave Lakṣmī to Viṣṇu. The lord of Mithilā sent a messenger to (Daśaratha) the descendant of Raghu. The pious one entered Mithilā with his two sons.

149-153. That best descendant of Raghu stayed along with the delighted Vasiṣṭha, Vāmadeva, etc. in Janaka's charming city. The king properly honoured by king Janaka got Rāma married to the Earth's daughter (i.e. Sītā) at an auspicious time. The king got Urmilā, Janaka's daughter, married to Lakṣmaṇa, and the two daughters of good figures and having all (auspicious) marks, Māṇḍavī and Śrutakīrti to Bharata and Śatrughna respectively. Then having completed the nuptial rites the powerful, happy Daśaratha surrounded by citizens and (other) subjects started for Ayodhyā.

154-156. Receiving the wedding present, and honoured by the king of Mithilā, he, along with his sons, daughters-in-law, horses, elephants and attendants (left for Ayodhyā). On their way, the very strong and valorous son of Jamadagni, the destroyer of kings, taking an axe, like an angry lion desiring to fight, ran to the descendant of Kakutstha. Reaching Rāma, and seeing him, Bhārgava spoke (these) words:

Paraśurāma said:

157-159. O Rāma, Rāma of mighty arms, listen to my words. Having killed many very brave kings in battles, and having given the land to brāhmaṇas I went to practise penance. Having heard about your valour and power, I have come to fight with you. The Ikṣvākus born in the family of my maternal grandfather are not to be killed by me. Having heard (i.e. when I hear) about the valour of a kṣatriya and his power, I cannot bear it.

160-162. O prince, you broke the fierce bow of Śiva difficult to be assailed. Therefore, O best of Raghus, O liberal one, fight with me. O you who curb your enemies, this is Viṣṇu's bow which is like that (bow of Śiva). Fix (an arrow to it). Then I am vanquished (by you) with your valour. Or abandon your weapons before me, the powerful one. If you are afraid in your heart, then submit to me, O Kākutstha.

The lord said:

163-166. Kākutstha (i.e. Rāma), the brave one, thus addressed by Paraśurāma, took his bow and the power too of him (given to him) by Viṣṇu. Deprived of that power, that brave Paraśurāma became powerless and lustreless like a brāhmaṇa deprived of (holy) acts. Seeing Paraśurāma lustreless, the best kings repeatedly praised Rāma (with the words): "Well (done), well (done)." Rāma having easily raised the bow and fixed the arrow to it, spoke to Paraśurāma, who was amazed:

Rāma said:

167. O brāhmaṇa, what should I do to you with this best arrow? Do (i.e. should) I cut off this world, the nether (world) or heaven, or should I destroy your penance?

The lord said:

168. Bhārgava, seeing that very fierce arrow of Rāma and knowing him to be the highest self, was delighted, and said to Rāma:

Paraśurāma said:

169-176. O Rāma, Rāma of mighty arms, I did not know you to be the ancient (soul). Today only I knew you by means of your virtues like valour. You are actually the first, highest soul. You are the highest Brahman. You are the highest, the immutable one. You are Ananta (the endless one), great Viṣṇu, Vāsudeva, higher than the highest. You are Nārāyaṇa. You are the lord of Śrī. You are full of the three (Vedas). You are the Time (or Death). You are the entire world. You yourself are the one called *A*. You are the creator, the supporter and the destroyer. You are the highest lord. You are inconceivable; you are of the form of a great being; you are a great hymn. You are the highest being having four, six, five qualities. You are the sacrifice. You are the vaṣaṭkāra (i.e. exclamation used on making an oblation). You are the *Oṁ* consisting of the three (Vedas). You are of a manifest and an unmanifest form. You possess qualities. You are qualityless and the highest one. I am unable to praise you who are beyond the scope of even the Vedas. O lord, you, the absolute one (should) please forgive me my rash behaviour towards you. Having conquered, due to your power, all princes and having given the earth to the brāhmaṇas, I obtain peace due to your favour only.

The lord said:

177-185. Having spoken like this, Paraśurāma of a great penance (to his credit) having gone round and saluted Rāma, the protector of the world, offered the heaven merited by having performed one hundred sacrifices to that missile. Rāma of a great lustre, then saluted the great sage. He duly worshipped him with water for washing his feet, materials of worship and water for being sipped. Paraśurāma, of a great penance (to his credit), honoured by him went to the hermitage of Nara-Nārāyaṇa, for practising penance. And the mighty king Daśaratha, along with his sons and wives, entered his own city at an auspicious moment. Rāma, Lakṣmaṇa, Bharata and Śatrughna, having approached their wives, amused themselves with their minds delighted. Rāma, the pious one amused himself with Sītā for twelve years, like Viṣṇu amusing himself with Lakṣmī. At that time only king Daśaratha affectionately desired to bestow his kingdom upon his eldest son (Rāma). His dear wife Kaikayī who was given (two) boons (by him) formerly, asked the best king for the coronation of Bharata and banishment of Rāma for fourteen years.

186-188. That king, with his mind struck by grief, (and) due to being veracious, banished his son. Rāma, the descendant of Kakutstha, though capable (of snatching the kingdom), righteously left it for him, and to (keep) the promise of his father, went, with Lakṣmaṇa and Sītā, to the forest to kill Rāvaṇa. That king (Daśaratha), afflicted by the separation from his son, died.

189-190. Pious Bharata, being appointed to the kingdom along with the ministers showing that he was a good brother, did not desire the kingdom. Having come to the forest, he requested (Rāma) his brother and the descendant of Kakutstha. Rāma who curbed his enemies, did not desire the kingdom as a result of his father's order.

191-193. He gave him his own sandals. He (i.e. Bharata) too received them with devotion. Bharata brought Rāma's auspicious sandals to the kingdom, and he, Kaikayī's son, everyday worshipped them with sandal, with flowers. And the best king, being engaged in the practice of penance, remained in it (i.e. the kingdom). Till the noble Rāma came (back to Ayodhyā) all the citizens remained engaged in vows.

194. Rāma with Sītā enjoyed himself on the mountain like Citrakūṭa, in the holy hermitage of Bharadvāja, and the holy water of Mandākinī.

195-202. Sometime the magnanimous Rāma was resting (with his head) on Sītā's lap. Indra's crow came there and went about him. He, seeing Jānakī there and being tormented by Cupid's arrow, tore her plump and raised breast with his sharp nails. King Rāma, seeing the crow, took a darbha with his hand and uniting it with the missile of Brahman, discharged it. The crow, seeing the fierce blade of grass, with its form full of flames, and crying with a distressed tone, ran away. Rāma's very fierce missile followed the crow. The crow, oppressed by fear, wandered in the three worlds. Wherever the crow, desiring shelter, went, the fearful missile of Rāma went after him. The crow, tormented by the missile and (therefore) seeking a shelter, quickly went to Brahmā, Indra, Rudra, Yama and Varuṇa. All the wise gods like Rudra and the demons, seeing the crow, said: "We are not able to protect (you)." Then Brahmā, the lord of the three worlds, said (to the crow):

Brahmā said:

203-205. O best of crows, submit yourself to him only. He, the glorious one alone, is the ocean of pity for all. He, the lord of beings, endowed with qualities like good character and affectionate to those who have sought his shelter, will certainly protect you. He is the father, the mother, the companion and the friend of the entire world. Seek the refuge of the lord of gods. O bird, there is no other refuge.

Mahādeva said:

206-208. Thus addressed by Brahmā, the crow, overcome by fear, suddenly approached Rāma and fell on the ground. Seeing the crow in peril of life, Sītā politely said to her lord, the mighty (Rāma), "Protect him, protect him." The respectable lady Sītā put the head of the crow that had fallen before her on Rāma's feet.

209-211. The virtuous Rāma, the ocean of the nectar of pity and afflicted by compassion, raised him with his hand and protected him. Rāma, the treasure of compassion, said to the crow: "Do not be afraid. I shall grant you protection from fear. Go as you please." He, protected by Rāma, repeatedly saluted Rāma and Sītā, and quickly went to heaven.

212-213. Then Rāma, along with Sītā and the intelligent Lakṣmaṇa, being praised by great sages, lived on the Citrakūṭa mountain. Rāma, the best of the Raghus, being worshipped on it by Bharadvāja, went to the very huge hermitage of Atri.

214-217. The excellent pious sage, seeing the best of the Raghus to have come, with joy went forth with his wife to greet him. Having seated him, along with Sītā, on a very auspicious and divine seat, he affectionately offered him materials of worship, water for washing his feet and for sipping, and various garments, *madhuparka*, so also ornaments and unction. His wife Anasūyā affectionately gave Sītā divine and excellent garments and bright ornaments. She fed Rāma with divine food, drink and eatables, etc.

218-219. Prince Rāma, along with Lakṣmaṇa, very devoutly honoured by him, lived there for a day. When it dawned, Rāma got up, took himself round the great sage, saluted him, and set about going.

220-221. Permitted by him the lotus-eyed Rāma went to the Daṇḍaka forest thronged by great sages. There he killed the very fierce demon named Virādha and then entered the auspicious hermitage of Śarabhaṅga.

222. He, on seeing Rāma, had his sins instantly destroyed and went, along with gandharvas and celestial nymphs to Brahmā's world.

223-224. One by one Rāma went to the hermitages of Sutīkṣṇa, of Agastya, of Agastya's brother also, and was honoured by them. Then Rāma lived very happily and for a long time in Pañcavaṭī, on the auspicious bank of Godāvarī.

225-227. On going there the greatest sages, the religious ascetics, worshipped the lotus-eyed Rāma, the lord of the souls. They acquainted him with the threat coming from the hosts of demons. Having comforted them, he gave them the gift of fearlessness. After being honoured by him they went to their own hermitages. Rāma passed thirteen happy years there.

228-229a. After sometime, the demoness, Rāvaṇa's unconquerable sister of a fierce form, entered the charming Pañcavaṭī on the auspicious bank of Godāvarī.

229b-235a. Having seen the excellent Raghu (i.e. Rāma) resembling a crore of Cupids, dark like lotus-leaves, having large, lotus-like eyes, a raised nose, large arms, a conch-like neck, and a large chin, resembling a red lotus, with his palms marked with lotuses, adorned with a row of nails like the spotless moon resembling glossy and tender dūrvā (grass), an auspicious treasure of delicacy, wearing a yellow silken garment, adorned with all ornaments, of the age of a youth, having a body deluding the world, the demoness, oppressed by Cupid's arrows, approached Rāma having lotus-like eyes, and said to him:

The demoness said:

235b-236. Who are you, dwelling in the Daṇḍaka forest in the guise of an ascetic? Why have you come to (this forest) difficult to be approached (even) by demons? Quickly tell the truth. (Please) do not tell a lie.

Maheśvara said:

237-240a. That Rāma, thus addressed, laughed and said:

Rāma said:

I am king Daśaratha's son, called Rāma. This archer is my innocent younger brother, Lakṣmaṇa. This is my dear wife Sītā, Janaka's daughter. By my father's order I have come to this forest. With a desire to do good to the sages, we are roaming in this great forest. O beautiful lady, why have you come to my hermitage? Who are you? In whose family are you born? Tell me the whole truth.

Maheśvara said:

240b. Thus addressed by Rāma, she said fearlessly:

The demoness said:

241-245a. O king, I am the daughter of Viśravas and the sister of Rāvaṇa. I am Śūrpaṇakhā by name, and am well-known in the three worlds. O lord, this Daṇḍaka forest is given to me by my brother. Eating groups of sages I roam in the great forest. Seeing you, an excellent sage, I, tormented by Cupid's arrows, and being very fearless, have come (here) with a desire to dally with you. O best king, please be my husband. O king, I desire to devour this Sītā (wife) of you. With you I shall dally in the forest with prominent mountains.

Maheśvara said:

245b-252a. Seeing the demoness, after having spoken like this, ready to devour Sītā, Śrī Rāma raised his sword and cut off her nose and ears. The demoness, with her face deformed, and weeping with fear, entered Khara's house, and told him Rāma's act. He, the killer of his enemies, surrounded by thousands of demons, and with Dūṣaṇa and Triśiras, came to fight violently with Rāma. Rāma easily killed those demons of huge bodies in the fearful forest with arrows resembling Death (i.e. with fatal arrows). With arrows resembling serpents he knocked down in the battle Khara, Triśiras and the very powerful Dūṣaṇa. Having killed all the demons living in the Daṇḍaka forest, and worshipped by hosts of gods and praised by great sages, (Rāma) lived in Daṇḍaka forest with Sītā and Lakṣmaṇa.

252b-255a. Learning about the murder of the demons, Rāvaṇa, rendered violent with anger, came along with the wicked

Mārīca to Janasthāna. That demon Rāvaṇa came to Pañcavaṭī with Mārīca of an illusory deer-form, and when Daśaratha's sons were away from the hermitage he, desiring his own murder, kidnapped Sītā, the wife of Rāma.

255b-257a. The powerful Jaṭāyu, the king of vultures, seeing her being kidnapped, fought due to his affection for Rāma with the demon. Rāvaṇa who resisted his enemies, killed him with the strength of his arms and entered the city of Laṅkā.

257b-261. Having kept Sītā in the Aśoka-grove he, desiring death by Rāma's arrow, entered his house. And Rāma having killed the demon Mārīca who had taken up the form of a deer, again came there (i.e. to his hermitage) with his brother Lakṣmaṇa. Coming to know that Sītā was kidnapped by a demon, the very intelligent son of Daśaratha, being tormented by great grief, lamented. Looking for Sītā in the forest, he, on his way seeing a very mighty vulture fallen on the ground with his feet and wings cut off and with his entire body full of blood, was amazed.

262a. The glorious Rāma asked him: "Who desired to kill you and why?"

262b. The vulture, on seeing Rāma, very gently spoke:

The vulture said:

263. O Rāma, the mighty Rāvaṇa has kidnapped your wife. He, the chief of the demons, struck me in the battle.

Maheśvara said:

264-266. Having spoken like this, he suddenly cast his life before Rāma. Rāma performed his obsequies according to the Vedic precepts. And he gave him his own eternal abode, fit to be reached by meditating saints. The best bird, the vulture, attained salvation, the final position due to the common form of Viṣṇu. Then Rāma went to Mālyavat (mountain), to the auspicious hermitage of Mataṅga.

267-270. He went to the pious, glorious Śabarī. That best among Viṣṇu's devotees, seeing Rāma and Lakṣmaṇa, went forth to greet them. Having saluted and seated them on a seat of *darbhas*, she washed their feet. With her mind full of joy she devoutly worshipped them with fragrant wild flowers. She, of a firm vow, then offered the two descendants of Raghu (viz. Rāma and Lakṣmaṇa) fragrant fruits and sweet roots. (Rāma,) the descendant of Kakutstha, gave her the highest liberation.

271-273. Then Rāma, killer of his enemies, having gone to the Pampā lake killed there the demon Kabandha of a fierce form. The very vigorous one, having killed him, burnt him. (Then) he (i.e. Kabandha) went to heaven. Then the lotus-eyed Rāma, having gone to Godāvarī, asked her, "O Gaṅgā, do you know my dear (wife) Sītā?" That Gaṅgā, covered with ignorance, did not tell him (anything).

274-275. Rāma angrily cursed her: "Be of red water." Then being dejected she through fear, led by great sages, and being helpless and with the palms of her hands joined sought Rāma's refuge. Then all great sages said to the eternal Rāma:

The sages said:

276. Gaṅgā, purifying the three worlds, has risen from your lotus-like feet. O lord of the world, you alone can free her from the curse.

Maheśvara said:

277a. Then the pious Rāma, affectionate to those who seek his shelter, said:

Rāma said:

277bc. May this Gaṅgā, destroying sins, be free from my curse merely by Śabarī's bath and united with auspicious water.

278-279. Speaking like this, the very powerful Rāma made, with the tip of his Śārṅga bow, the Śabari-tīrtha like Gaṅgā and Gayā. In its water was the holy place of great devotees of Viṣṇu. "Undoubtedly that form becomes venerable to the world."

280-282a. Speaking like this the descendant of Kakutstha went to Ṛṣyamūka mountain. Then on the bank of Pampā lake he was joined by the monkey Hanūmat. At his words (i.e. request) he came in contact with Sugrīva. At the words (i.e. request) of Sugrīva, Rāma, having bound Vālin, the lord of monkeys, consecrated Sugrīva on that kingdom.

282b-287. And the lord of monkeys desiring to find out

Sītā, sent heroes like Hanūmat. Hanūmat, the son of Wind, entered the city of Laṅkā and saw (there) the helpless Sītā emaciated due to fasting and being very much grieved, with her body smeared with dirt and mud, and wearing a dirty garment. The monkey, having shown her the token of recognition and having told her the news (about Rāma), having killed seven sons of the ministers, so also Rāvaṇa's son, after having uprooted the pillar of the gateway, and having cheered up Sītā, destroyed the grove, the garden-keepers, the servants and the chief leaders of the army.

288-291. By chance he was arrested by Rāvaṇa's son. Seeing the lord of demons and having also talked to him, the monkey burnt the city of Laṅkā with the fire from his (burning) tail. Having taken the token of recognition given by her (i.e. Sītā) he again came (back to Rāma). The very lustrous chief of monkeys, approached the lotus-eyed Rāma and reported to him that he had actually seen Sītā. Rāma, with Sugrīva, and surrounded by many monkeys, went to the shore of the great ocean, and kept his army there.

292-294. Rāvaṇa's younger brother called Bibhīṣaṇa, who was pious, veracious, and best among the great devotees of Viṣṇu, knowing Rāma to have arrived, abandoned his elder brother (Rāvaṇa), so also the kingdom, sons, wife, and submitted himself to Rāma. At the words of Hanūmat the lord accepted him, and granting protection to the gentle one, consecrated him on the kingdom (i.e. the throne) of the demons.

295-297. Then Rāma, the descendant of Kakutstha, desiring to cross the ocean, approached him, and he, the mighty one, seeing the very clean water, took up the Śārṅga bow and dried up the ocean with volleys of arrows. Then the ocean, the lord of rivers, yielded himself to the descendant of Kakutstha (i.e. Rāma), the treasure of pity. Then Rāma again filled the ocean with the Varuṇa missile.

298-299. Then on the ocean, the abode of alligators, Nala constructed a bridge with rocks brought by the monkeys. Then the great army entered the city of Laṅkā, and a great battle between the monkeys and the demons was fought.

300-306. Then Rāvaṇa's very mighty son Indrajit bound both Rāma and Lakṣmaṇa with magical nooses (literally, serpent-nooses). Garuḍa, having come (there), let loose the nooses. The very powerful monkeys killed all the demons. In the battle Rāma killed Rāvaṇa's younger brother, the very strong Kumbhakarṇa, with arrows resembling flames of fire. With the missile presided over by Brahmā the angry Indrajit knocked down the monkeys. The mountain having great herbs was brought by Hanūmat. And all got up (alive) by the touch of it that was brought. Then Rāma's brave younger brother (i.e. Lakṣmaṇa), knocked down with arrows Indra's conqueror (i.e. Indrajit) as Indra did Vṛtra. The very strong Rāvaṇa set out with his complete army and ministers to fight with Rāma on the battlefield. The battle between the monkeys and demons took place on all sides.

307-321. A battle took place between Rāma and Rāvaṇa; so also with Lakṣmaṇa. The lord of demons knocked down Lakṣmaṇa with (the missile called) Śakti. Then the angry Rāma, of great lustre and the destroyer of the demons, killed the demon soldiers with arrows resembling Yama, the god of death, and destroying eveything. Rāma very much covered the demon Rāvaṇa with thousands of blazing arrows resembling the rod of (Yama, the god of) Death. The demon, with his entire body pierced with missiles of Rāma, fled through fear from the battlefield to Laṅkā. Seeing the world full of Rāma, he entered his house through dejection. Then Hanūmat brought the great mountain with great herbs. Due to that Rāma's younger brother regained consciousness. Then with a desire for victory Rāvaṇa commenced a sacrifice. The chief monkeys then destroyed it of a magical form. Then Rāvaṇa again set out, after getting into a divine chariot and along with many demons, to fight with Rāma. Then the intelligent Indra sent to Rāma a divine chariot, yoked with bay horses and with a charioteer. The best of the Raghus, having got into the chariot brought by Mātalin (Indra's charioteer), and being praised by hosts of gods, fought with that demon. Then a great, very fierce battle, with weapons and missiles took place day and night for a week between Rāma and Rāvaṇa. All the gods, remaining in aeroplanes, witnessed the battle. The best of the Raghus cut off the heads of Rāvaṇa, which many times sprang up due to the boon of Śiva. Rāma quickly discharged a very fierce missile sacred to Brahmā and resembling the fire at the time of the deluge to kill the wicked one. That missile, discharged by Rāghava, tore Rāvaṇa's chest, pierced the earth and went to the nether world, and being honoured by serpents (again) came back to Rāma's hand. That great demon losing his life, fell down and died.

322-325. Then all the hosts of gods with their minds full of joy, dropped showers of flowers on the noble lord of the world. The chiefs of gandharvas sang (his praise) and bevies of celestial nymphs danced. So also auspicious breezes blew, and the sun was very bright. Sages, siddhas, gods and kinnaras praised (him). The best of the Raghu-family consecrated the greatest demon Bibhīṣaṇa on the throne of Laṅkā, and looked upon himself as having accomplished his object. Having consecrated Bibhīṣaṇa Rāma then said these words to Bibhīṣaṇa:

Rāma said:

326-327. As long as the moon and the sun exist, as long as the earth exists, as long as my account exists, the kingdom (of Laṅkā) will rest with Bibhīṣaṇa. Being very powerful, reach, along with the host of your sons and grandsons, my divine, ancient abode accessible to meditating saints.

The lord said:

328-330. The very mighty one, Rāma, having thus given a boon to the demon and having approached Sītā, spoke many harsh and censurable words to her in the assembly of people. The chaste lady much censured by him entered fire. Then all the hosts of gods led by Śiva, Brahmā, seeing the mother (i.e. Sītā) entering fire, were afflicted by fear, and approaching the greatest of Raghus, said, with their palms joined, to him:

Gods said:

331-339. O Rāma, Rāma, O you of large arms and of a great valour, listen. Sītā is extremely pure. She never violates your norms of conduct. You should not abandon her wrongly, as the sun does not give up his light. She is the mother of the entire world, and is support of the whole world. Rāvaṇa and Kumbhakarṇa were your former highly devoted servants. Due to the curse of Sanaka etc. they were born on the earth. For their liberation Sītā was seized (by Rāvaṇa) in the Daṇḍaka forest.

The two pre-eminent demons were killed by you. They are (now) liberated, and with their sons, grandsons and followers have gone to heaven. You are Viṣṇu; you are the highest Brahman; you are the ancient one meditated upon by the meditating saints. You alone, of all gods, are the immutable (god) without a beginning or an end. You are the glorious Nārāyaṇa. Sītā is the ancient Lakṣmī. She is the mother of all the worlds. You, O highest lord, are the father. This mother of the world is eternal and shall never abandon you. O best of the Raghus, as you are omnipresent, so also she is. Therefore, O you descendant of Kakutstha, O you gentle one, accept this chaste Sītā of a good conduct and a strong vow, as (Lakṣmī) from the Milky Ocean.

The lord said:

340. In the meanwhile Fire, the observer of the world, brought Sītā there, and handed her over to Rāma in the vicinity (i.e. the presence) of gods. Fire, present in all bodies, then said to the descendant of Kakutstha:

Fire said:

341. O lord, this Sītā is of a good conduct and is sinless. O Rāma, accept her quickly. I have told you the truth.

The lord said:

342-343. Then Rāma, the descendant of Raghu, having accepted Sītā at the words of Fire, (and) being worshipped by the best gods, was pleased. Those excellent monkeys who were killed in the battle by the demons, came back to life and got up due to the boon of the grandsire.

344-347. Then (Bibhīṣaṇa,) the lord of demons gave Rāma the aeroplane named Puṣpaka which resembled the sun, which belonged to Kubera, and which was seized (from Kubera) by his brother (Rāvaṇa). He (also) gave Rāma garments and ornaments. The brave, glorious Rāma, Daśaratha's son, honoured by him got into the excellent aeroplane along with Sītā and his brave brother Lakṣmaṇa, so also along with the hosts of bears and monkeys, the noble Sugrīva, the brave Bibhīṣaṇa, and the very mighty demons.

348-352a. All the bears, monkeys and demons got into the

aeroplane and the ever-liberated noble ones got into an aeroplane of Vaikuṇṭha. Rāma, being praised by best gods, proceeded to Ayodhyā. Rāma of a genuine valour went to Bharadvāja's hermitage, and sent Hanūmat near Bharata. The best monkey having gone to the fisherman's house, saw Guha, a devotee of Viṣṇu, and told him about Rāma's arrival. Then from there he went to Nandigrāma, saw Rāma's younger brother and told him about the joyous occasion of Rāma's arrival.

352b-357. Having learnt from the monkey (i.e. Hanūmat) about the arrival of Rāma, Bharata, along with his younger brother and friends, obtained incomparable joy. Having again come back to Rāma, Hanūmat, the son of Wind, told all that Bharata did. Rāma also along with his younger brother got down from the best aeroplane and saluted with his wife Bharadvāja, the treasure of penance. The sage honoured the descendant of Kakutstha along with his younger brother by (offering him) cooked food, fruits, roots etc. and garments and ornaments. Honoured by him, Rāma saluted the best sage, and permitted by him, again, along with his followers, and surrounded by his friends went to Nandigrāma in the Puṣpaka (aeroplane).

358-361. Kekayī's son (Bharata) with his younger brother and along with his ministers and chief citizens, so also strong best kings, gladly went forth to greet his elder brother (Rāma). Approaching the best of Raghus, he, surrounded by his followers, saluted him. Rāma, the tormentor of his enemies, got down from the Puṣpaka aeroplane, and embraced Bharata and Śatrughna. The very lustrous one, along with Sītā and Lakṣmaṇa, saluted his family priest Vasiṣṭha, and relatives like his old mothers.

362-368a. Bharata embraced Bibhīṣaṇa, Sugrīva, Jāmbavanta, so also Aṅgada, Hanūmat and Suṣeṇa. After an auspicious bath along with his brother and attendants, he, having divine flowers and garments and smeared with divine sandal and being praised by gods, Sītā and Lakṣmaṇa, got into a divine auspicious chariot occupied by Sumanta. Bharata, Sugrīva, Śatrughna and Bibhīṣaṇa, Aṅgada and Suṣeṇa, Jāmbavat, Hanūmat, Nīla, Nala, Subhaga, Śarabha, Gandhamādana and other brave monkeys, so also Guha, the lord of the Niṣādas, very brave demons and very powerful greatest kings, mounted many auspicious elephants and horses.

368b-369. The highly lustrous one entered the indestructible city of Sāketa to the accompaniment of many auspicious musical instruments, many eulogies, and along with bears, monkeys, demons and excellent warriors of Niṣādas (i.e. fishermen). Prince Rāma, on seeing the capital, and thinking only of his father king (Daśaratha) on the way, entered the house purified by the movements of the meritorious feet of Sugrīva, Māruti and Bibhīṣaṇa.

CHAPTER TWO HUNDRED FORTYTHREE

Rāma's Consecration

Śaṅkara said:

1-17a. On that auspicious day at an auspicious moment people performed auspicious acts for the consecration of the pious one. These sages—Vasiṣṭha, Vāmadeva, Jābāli, and Kaśyapa, Mārkaṇḍeya, Maudgalya, Parvata, so also Nārada, performed the auspicious consecration of the best king there with muttering of hymns and sacrifices. Having seated Rāma along with Sītā on an auspicious golden seat full of (i.e. decked with) jewels, as Viṣṇu with Lakṣmī, the sages who had fulfilled their vows, muttered the auspicious Vedic hymns in honour of Viṣṇu and consecrated the descendant of Kakutstha and the lord of the world with pure water which was purified with hymns, was (brought) from all holy places, was holy, which had auspicious substances in it, was furnished with tips of dūrvā grass, tulasī-leaves, flowers and sandal. At that most auspicious moment gods beat drums in heaven and dropped showers of flowers from all sides. With his queen (Sītā) the descendant of Raghu adorned with divine garments, ornaments, divine sandal and unguents and with various kinds of flowers looked superb in the company of the sages, the masters of the Vedas. At that time Lakṣmaṇa held the divine umbrella and chowrie. By his side(s) Bharata and Śatrughna stood brilliantly with fans. Bibhīṣaṇa, the lord of demons, gave him the mirror. Sugrīva, the lord of the monkeys, held a pitcher full (of water), and the very lustrous Jāmbavat (held) a charming garland of flowers. Vālin's son gave Rāma a tāmbūla with camphor. Hunūmat (held) many divine lamps, and Suṣeṇa (held) an auspicious flag. The ministers, surrounding the noble one, waited upon him. Sṛṣṭi, Jayanta, Vijaya, Saurāṣṭra, Rāṣṭravardhana, Akopa, Dharmapāla, and Sumantra are said to be (his) ministers. Kings, best men, lords of various countries, citizens, traders, old men waited upon the king. He was surrounded by bears, chief monkeys, ministers, kings, demons, principal brāhmaṇas and servants.

17b-23. As the lord of Lakṣmī completely united with deities in the highest heaven (shines), similarly the best glorious king then shone in Sāketa. The hosts of gods seated in aeroplanes and with their minds full of joy, so also gandharvas and hosts of the celestial nymphs, praised with shouts of victory the descendant of Kakutstha, the best of the Raghus, whose hands reached his knees, who had worn a yellow garment, whose neck was like a conch, whose chest was large, who had (put on) beautiful ornaments, who was seated with queen (Sītā), and who was consecrated. Then Rāma, consecrated by great sages like Vasiṣṭha, shone with Sītā like god Viṣṇu with Lakṣmī. Śiva afraid due to Rāma's being a great mortal, of waiting on his lotus-like feet, seeing Rāma was pleased and with delight praised him. He folded the palms of his hands, was full of joy, and had a faltering (voice). He delighted all gods, sages and monkeys also.

Mahādeva said:

24-30. Salutation to the original source, to the eternal highest soul, to the one having the nature of existence, consciousness and bliss, to the one identical with the universe, to the creator. Salutation to Viṣṇu the bulb, the root of continuous joy, to the form delighting the three worlds; salutation to the one venerable to Brahmā and Indra, to one bringing about the welfare and giving protection from fear. Salutation to the one of the form of Viṣṇu. O you of the form of everything, salutation to you. Salutation to (you) the cause of creation, sustenance and destruction (of the world), to (you) of three qualities, to you of the form having no limitation, to the great soul. (Salutation to you) causing Nescience in the form of this goddess Sītā as a limiting adjunct. Salutation to both of you, the Puruṣa (the soul) and the Prakṛti (the primordial matter), the author of the worlds. Salutation to the mother and the father of the world, to the mother (Sītā) and to Rāghava (i.e. Rāma). Salutation to you, of the form of visible world, and of the form without the visible world. Salutation to you, of the form of meditation, to the form of the Supreme Soul fit to be meditated upon by the meditating saints. Salutation to both of you devoid of change and no-change.

31-40. Salutation to you the supreme soul, of the form of the seed, to Sītā and to Rāma. Sītā is Lakṣmī; you are Viṣṇu. Sītā is Pārvatī; you are Śiva. Sītā herself is Sāvitrī; you are the four-faced Brahmā. Sītā is Indrāṇī; you are Indra. Sītā is Svāhā (the oblation made to all gods); you are Fire. Sītā is the destructive goddess; you are of the form of Yama. Sītā is all wealth; you are Kubera, O best of Raghus. Sītā is goddess Rudrāṇī; you are very strong Rudra. Sītā is goddess Rohiṇī; you are the Moon giving pleasure to the world. Sītā is Saṁjñā; you are the Sun. Sītā is the Night; you are the Day. Sītā is goddess Mahākālī. You always are Mahākāla. In the three worlds whatever is of the feminine gender is Sītā. Whatever is marked with the masculine gender is you, O lord. O lord of all gods, Sītā is the supporter everywhere. Then you are also there to protect. Her power sustains the universe. Therefore, the merit marked (acquired?) by you two is a crore-fold. Your deeds marked (described?) by Śiva and Śakti, give peace. O Rāma, we two are venerable to the world. You two are always venerable to us. Gaurī mutters your name. I mutter your formula. To one desiring to die at Maṇikarṇikā and remaining in half of its water I give your emancipating formula, giving (i.e. leading to) Brahman.

41. Therefore, O lord of Jānakī, you are certainly the highest Brahman. All deluded by you do not know you truly.

The lord said:

42-50. Thus addressed by Śambhu, Rāma who had assumed a divine form and was of a wonderful appearance, became disposed to favour. Seeing him of that form, men, monkeys and deities were not able even to see that lustrous, great, wonderful (form). The best gods, through fear saluted him devoutly. Rāma, realising that men, monkeys and deities were frightened, took up the illusory human form and again spoke to the gods:

Rāmacandra said:

O gods, listen. That man who will everyday praise me with the hymn told by Śiva, will be equal to a god. Freed from all sins he obtains my nature. In a battle he gets victory and is never repulsed. He is not tormented by ghosts, vampires and female deities to whom sacrifices are offered for destructive and magical purposes. A sonless man obtains a son. A maiden gets a husband. A poor man obtains wealth and would become virtuous and of good disposition. The glorious one has the power equal to that of the (highest) soul. There is no doubt about it. In all acts and undertakings men have no obstacle. Whatever desire, difficult to be fulfilled, is entertained by a man is satisfied within six months due to the grace of this eulogy. By means of this hymn is obtained the fruit a crore times more than the religious merit obtained in all holy places and all sacrifices.

The lord said:

51-53. Speaking like this Rāmacandra dismissed Maheśvara. He (also) dismissed all gods like Brahmā that had come there. Rāmacandra honoured all men and dismissed with affection all men, monkeys and deities full of love. All of them thus dismissed by him, went very much delighted, reciting the great hymn uttered by the lord and remembering Rāma of a universal form.

CHAPTER TWO HUNDRED FORTYFOUR

Rāma Goes to Heaven

Śaṅkara said:

1-6. Rāma enjoyed with Sītā royal pleasures as desired while protecting directions on all sides for a thousand years. All inmates of the harem, so also the citizens, censured Sītā who had stayed in the demon's house. Rāma who warded off his enemies, through fear of public scandal, and exhibiting human behaviour, abandoned the princess (Sītā) who was pregnant, in the assembly of sages in Vālmīki's holy hermitage in a large forest on the bank of Gaṅgā. Dependent upon her husband she stayed in the sage's house. Taken care of by the sage Vālmīki, she was honoured by sages' wives. There only she gave birth to twin sons named Kuśa and Lava. Educated and trained by the sage they grew there only.

7-13a. Rāma too, along with his brothers, protected the earth. He, the king, endowed with virtues like restraint, and free from all enjoyments, always worshipping Viṣṇu having no beginning or end, and highly devoted to celibacy, ruled over the earth. Śatrughna, the righteous descendant of Raghu, having killed Lavaṇa, ruled, along with his two sons, over Mathurā created by gods. Bharata, having killed gandharvas on both the sides of Sindhu, installed his two very mighty sons in that country. The very powerful Lakṣmaṇa, having killed the Madras in the western Madra country, consecrated his two brave sons, and again going back to Ayodhyā, touched Rāma's feet. (Rāma,) the descendant of Kakutstha brought back to life the son of a brāhmaṇa that had met death, and then killed a śūdra ascetic.

13b-17. Then Rāma, the killer of his enemy's heroes performed a horse-sacrifice in the Naimiṣa (forest) in the assembly of people on the bank of Gautamī. Rāghava, knowing the highest truth, fashioned a golden (image of) Jānakī, and with that the very mighty one performed many sacrifices. The lord performed various sacrifices, complete with presents, like myriads of horse-sacrifices, Vājapeya sacrifices, Agniṣṭoma, Viśvajit, Gomedha and Śatakratu. In the meanwhile, Vālmīki of a very great (i.e. severe) penance (to his credit) brought Sītā there, and said these words to Rāma:

Vālmīki said:

18. O you of a good vow, you do not deserve to abandon (i.e. please do not abandon) sinless Sītā. This chaste one is free from passion and is like light to the sun. O descendant of Kakutstha, she is identical with you. O sinless one, why did you abandon her?

Rāma said:

19-22. O brāhmaṇa, from your words I understand that Sītā is sinless. The chaste lady was formerly kidnapped by Rāvaṇa in the secluded Daṇḍaka (forest). Having killed him in battle, and having properly taken Sītā who was purified and who came out of Agni's mouth, I came to Ayodhyā (again). There was a great public scandal among the citizens. Being afraid of it I abandoned her of a good conduct, near you. Therefore, for satisfying the people, Sītā who is highly devoted to me, must convince the kings and great sages (of her innocence).

Maheśvara said:

23-24. Thus addressed the chaste Sītā put forward a proof amazing the people in the assembly of sages and kings. Showing those people her sole devotion to Rāma, the chaste Sītā, with the palms of her hands folded, said in the assembly of all (people):

Sītā said:

25-26. Since I have not thought of anyone except Rāma, may goddess Earth give me a cavity. Since I spoke the truth that I do not know anyone else but Rāma, Dharaṇī (i.e. the Earth) would at once come to her daughter Vaidehī.

Maheśvara said:

27-32. Then the lord of birds, the hero, knowing the mother (had come) from below the earth, held a seat full of jewels. Then goddess Dharaṇī, holding Sītā with both her hands, greeted her with a welcome, and seated her on the seat. Seeing her seated on the seat, the hosts of gods in heaven profusely and continuously scattered a shower of flowers on divine Sītā. She too, the ancient one, being honoured by divine damsels mounted on Garuḍa, and went to heaven by that path. On her front the goddess of the world was surrounded by hosts of maids. She reached the highest ancient abode, accessible to the meditating saints. Seeing her entering the lower world, all men shouted loudly: "Well (done), well (done), This is Sītā."

33-36. Rāma, overcome by grief, took both his sons and along with sages and best kings entered Sāketa. Then after a long time, (Rāma's) mothers who had fulfilled their vows, died and went to the heaven of their husband (i.e. to the heaven where Daśaratha had gone). Rāma who had fulfilled his vows righteously, ruled over the kingdom for ten thousand and ten hundred years. Sometime the god of death came to Rāma's abode in the guise of an ascetic and spoke (these) words:

Death (*Kāla*) *said*:

37-38. O Rāma, Rāma, O you of large arms, I am sent by the Creator. O best of Raghus, O very intelligent one, listen to what I say. We shall carry on a conversation (lit. wordy duel). He who enters in between (i.e. disturbs us) will merit death.

Maheśvara said:

39. Promising him with the words "All right" the lotus-eyed Rāma placed Lakṣmaṇa at the door. Then Death spoke (these) words: Yama (Death) spoke to Rāma, Daśaratha's son:

Kāla (*Death*) *said*:

40-42. O Rāma, listen to what led to my arrival. You descended on the mortal world, saying, after having killed the two best demons: "I would live in the mortal world for ten thousand and ten hundred years." Thus (also) told by the hosts of gods (you have stayed for that much period). Now the time for you to go (back) to heaven has come. O sinless one, let the gods today have the lord in you.

Maheśvara said:

43. To the great sage Rāma said, "Let it be so". In the meanwhile the great ascetic Durvāsas came to the gate of the royal palace and spoke (these) words to Lakṣmaṇa:

Durvāsas said:

44. O prince, O descendant of Kakutstha, go quickly and report to Rāma (about the arrival of) me.

Maheśvara said:

45. To him Lakṣmaṇa said: "O brāhmaṇa, (Rāma has ordered that) no person should be allowed near (him)." Then the best sage overcome by anger said:

Durvāsas said:

46a. I shall pronounce a curse if you do not present me to Rāma, the descendant of Kakutstha.

Maheśvara said:

46b-53. Due to the fear of the curse (Lakṣmaṇa) reported to Rāma (the arrival of) the sage. There only Death causing fear to all beings vanished. The king worshipped sage Durvāsas that had come (there). That best Raghu, Lakṣmaṇa, knowing that promise of his elder brother, gave up his human form in the water of Sarayū. Giving up the human form he entered his own body. He having a thousand hoods, and having a lustre of a crore of moons, having divine flowers and garments, smeared with divine sandal, surrounded by thousands of serpent-damsels, well-adorned, having got into a divine aeroplane, went to the abode of Viṣṇu. The best Raghu Kākutstha (i.e. Rāma) knowing Lakṣmaṇa's going to heaven, also desired to go to heaven. Then Rāma, having consecrated his sons Kuśa and Lava, having divided wealth along with chariots, elephants and horses gave it to them. The best of Raghus installed righteously on his kingdom (i.e. throne) Kuśa at Kuśavatī and Lava at Śarasvatī.

54-58. Knowing the intention of Rāma who had realised his soul all the very powerful monkeys and demons came there. (They were) Bibhīṣaṇa, Sugrīva, Jāmbavat, (Māruti) the Wind's son, Nīla, Nala, Suṣeṇa, and Guha, the lord of the Niṣādas. Śatrughna also consecrated his brave sons as kings, and all of them came to Ayodhyā protected by Rāma. Having saluted the noble one, with their palms joined they said to him:

The monkeys and others said:

O best of the Raghus, having come to know that you are ready to go to heaven, we have come (here) to follow you. O lord, O Rāma, we cannot live without you (even) for a moment. Therefore, O large-eyed one, with you we shall go to the abode of gods.

Maheśvara said:

59. Thus addressed by them the descendant of Kakutstha said: "All right." Then the very lustrous one said to Bibhīṣaṇa, the lord of demons:

Rāma said:

60. Rule over your kingdom righteously. Do not falsify your promise. Being well pleased enjoy as long as the moon, the sun and the earth remain. Then at the (proper) time come to my place.

Maheśvara said:

61-62. Speaking like this the lotus-eyed Rāma affectionately gave to him his ancient (image of) Viṣṇu, gentle and lying (on Śeṣa) and the family deity of the Ikṣvākus. To Hanūmat Rāma, the killer of his enemies, said:

Rāma said:

63. O lord of monkeys, as long as my stories go on (being narrated) on the earth, remain on the earth. At the (proper) time, O you of a good vow, go to me.

Maheśvara said:

64a. Speaking like this to him, Rāma said to Jāmbavat:

Rāma said:

64b-65. When Dvāpara (age) will come, I shall again be born on the earth in the family of Yadus for destroying the burden of the earth. O best of bears, I shall (then) fight with you.

Maheśvara said:

66-72. The very powerful Rāma, the descendant of Kakutstha, having thus spoken to him, said to all the bears and monkeys (these words): "(Please) go." Ministers, traders, Bharata, the son of Kaikayī, determined to follow Rāma, came (there). Then the celibate, wearing white garments, went to the Supreme Spirit. Holding kuśas in his hands the restrained one went to the Supreme Spirit. To Rāma's right side was Ramā (i.e. Lakṣmī) with a lotus in her hand. Similarly to the side other than the right (i.e. to the left side) was goddess Dharaṇī (i.e. the earth). O Pārvatī, in the same way Vedas with the Vedāṅgas, Purāṇas with Itihāsas, Oṁkāra, Vaṣaṭkāra, so also Sāvitrī purifying the world, followed Rāma. Missiles, weapons like bows etc., all having male bodies followed Rāma. Bharata and Śatrughna, so also all citizens with their sons, wives and attendants went after Rāma.

73-78. Ministers, hosts of attendants, servants, traders, so also monkeys, bears along with Sugrīva and with their sons, wives went after the very intelligent descendant of Kakutstha. Beasts and birds, so also all immobile and mobile objects went after the noble one. So also the best men who saw the descendant of Kakutstha going to heaven. They who thus followed Rāma, did not return. Then having gone over three yojanas he saw Sarayū on the western side. With his followers he entered Sarayū of auspicious water. Then Brahmā, the grandsire, surrounded by hosts of all gods, and along with sages praised the best among Raghus with (suitable) words. He said to Rāma who had entered the water of the Sarayū (river):

Brahmā said:

79-81. O Viṣṇu, come, prosperity to you. O you who honour (others), you have luckily come (here). With your brothers, lustrous like gods, enter your own body of Viṣṇu, which is very bright, divine and ancient. O god, you are the refuge of the world; only few do not take cognizance of you who are inconceivable, noble, immutable, and comprising everything. O you of great lustre, enter that body which you desire (to enter).

Maheśvara said:

82-91. When he was full of the sun's rays, and when showers of flowers were dropped on him, he abandoned the human form and entered his own body. Both the noble Śatrughna and Bharata, endowed with divine lustre, were with him with the conch and the disc, his portions. He, the four-armed one, who had a conch, a disc, a mace, and the Śārṅga (bow) in his hands, who was possessed of divine ornaments, who had (his body) smeared with divine sandal, who had worn divine yellow garments, whose eyes were like lotus-leaves, who was a youth, whose body was handsome, who was bright with delicate parts, whose hair was very glossy, dark and curly, who had auspicious marks, who was dark like fresh dūrvā-sprouts, whose face resembled the full moon, got along with the two goddesses into an aeroplane;

and he, the lord, of a great lustre, praised by all gods, sat on the divine throne at the root of the desire-yielding tree. Those bears, monkeys and men, just on touching the water of Sarayū, happily cast their life. Due to Rāma's grace all they were handsome and had divine forms. They had worn divine flowers and garments; they had divine, auspicious lustre. There were innumerable men. Śrī Rāma, having lotus-like eyes, surrounded by all, worshipped by hosts of gods and siddhas, praised by all gods, got into the aeroplane.

92-95. The lord came to his own eternal, divine, imperishable place. O you of a beautiful appearance, one who would recite the (full) account of Rāma, or would listen to a verse or half a verse or would devoutly remember it, would, being free from sins committed knowingly or unknowingly during crores of existences, reach, along with his sons and wife, without any effort, Viṣṇu's world, to be reached (only) through abstract meditation. O goddess, I have narrated to you this great account of Rāma. Due to the narration (of the account) of Rāma, I am blessed along with you, O goddess. O you of an excellent face, what else do you desire to know? I shall narrate all that.

CHAPTER TWO HUNDRED FORTYFIVE

The Brave Deeds of Kṛṣṇa

Śrī Pārvatī said:

1-2. O lord, you have told well the story of Rāma. Having heard it through your grace, I am happy, O great god. O lord of gods, I desire to hear the great story removing sins, of Kṛṣṇa, the son of Vasudeva.

Rudra said:

3-8a. O goddess, listen. I shall narrate (to you) the story giving all fruits to men, of the noble Kṛṣṇa, Vasudeva's son. O goddess, in the family of Yadus was born the son of Devamiḍha, called Vasudeva, the best among those knowing Dharma. The prince duly married Devakī of a divine complexion, the daughter of Devaka (Ugrasena's brother), in Mathurā. Kaṁsa was the brave and very strong son of Ugrasena. With the two (Vasudeva and Devakī?) the charioteer was driving the excellent chariot (*obscure*). When they came on a charming path bringing on auspiciousness, a divine voice gravely spoke from the air:

The heavenly voice said:

8b. O Kaṁsa, her eighth embryo (i.e. child) will take away your life.

Rudra said:

9. Having heard it, Kaṁsa set about killing his sister, Vasudeva, with presence of mind, said to him who was very much enraged:

Vasudeva said:

10. O glorious one, do not kill your legitimate sister. O very mighty king, just kill the embryos (i.e. children) that will be born.

Rudra said:

11-13. Saying "All right", Kaṁsa having arrested Vasudeva and Devakī, placed them in his charming house full of all pleasures. In the meanwhile, O goddess, goddess Dharaṇī (i.e. the Earth) very much troubled by the burden of sinners, suddenly went to Brahmā. Having gone to Brahmā, the lord of the world, Dharaṇī, the supporter of the people, said with a grave voice:

Dharaṇī said:

14-16. O Creator, O lord, I am unable to support these people. O you of a good vow, the sinful demons have put up on me. The very powerful ones destroy all good practices of the world. All men deriving their strength from unrighteousness are deluded by sin. In this world very little of religious merit is seen. O god, I have sustained (people) because of (their) religious merit, truth, purity and control. Therefore, I am unable to sustain the world springing from unrighteousness.

Rudra said:

17-18. Speaking like this goddess Dharaṇī vanished there only. Then all hosts of gods led by Brahmā and Rudra and great ascetics went to the lord of the world at the northern shore of the Milky Ocean, and praised him with divine eulogies. Then the lord who was pleased, said to all those best sages:

The lord (Viṣṇu) said:

19a. O hosts of gods,. for what purpose have you come here?

Rudra said:

19b. Then the grandsire said to Viṣṇu, the god of gods:

Brahmā said:

20-22a. O god of gods, O lord of the world, the Earth is oppressed with burden. In the world many unconquerable demons are born, like Jarāsandha, Kaṁsa, Pralamba, Dhenuka and others. The wicked ones torment all old people. You are fit to take down the burden of the Earth.

Rudra said:

22bc. Thus addressed by Brahmā, Viṣṇu, the immutable lord of the world, spoke with a grave voice:

The lord (Viṣṇu) said:

23. O very powerful gods, descending (i.e. being born) in the family of the Yadus, I shall cooly remove the burden of the Earth.

Rudra said:

24. Thus addressed, all gods, having saluted Viṣṇu, went to their respective worlds, and thought of that highest god. Then the highest lord said to the Nārāyaṇī Māyā:

The lord said:

25-28. Taking the six sons of Hiraṇyākṣa to the earth, put them into (the womb of) Devakī, the wife of Vasudeva. The seventh one, a portion of Śeṣa, has already entered (Devakī).

Do not tarry. O you of an auspicious appearance, give it to Rohiṇī, her co-wife. Then in the eighth my portion will be born on Devakī. Then Mahānidrā, your ancient portion, will be born on Yaśodā, Nanda's wife. She will go to the great mountain Vindhya, and there being worshipped by gods led by Indra would kill the very powerful demons led by the demon Śumbha.

Rudra said:

29-38. Saying, "All right" Mahāmayā put the sons of Hiraṇyākṣa as the six embryos in (the womb of) Devakī one by one. The very powerful Kaṁsa killed them as soon as they were born. The seventh embryo was infused by a portion of Śeṣa. (Mahāmayā) took the growing embryo into (the womb of) Rohiṇī. Due to drawing out (saṁkarṣaṇāt) of the embryo, the immutable Saṁkarṣaṇa was born on her. On the eighth of the dark half of Bhādrapada (he was born) at an auspicious moment. Rohiṇī gave birth to a son, the lord Saṁkarṣaṇa. Then all hosts of gods seated in aeroplanes in the sky, and with their minds full of joy, praised Devakī. Then, O Pārvatī, in the tenth month (of her pregnancy) Viṣṇu was born on her at mid-night of the eighth of the dark half of Śrāvaṇa. He was dark like the petal of a blue lotus. His eyes were large like lotus-leaves. He had four arms. His body was handsome. He was graced with divine ornaments. On his chest were Śrīvatsa and Kaustubha (marks). He was adorned with a garland of wood-flowers. This ancient Vāsudeva (i.e. Viṣṇu) was born of Vasudeva. Seeing Kṛṣṇa, the lord of the worlds, Vasudeva with his palms joined saluted him, full of the world, and said:

Vasudeva said:

39-41. O lord, O desire-yielding tree to the devotees, O lord of the world, you are born of me (i.e. as my son). You, the highest being, are the one without a beginning or an end among the gods. O you inconceivable one, you are a great son. You are thought of by the meditating saints and are ancient. O you sustainer of the earth, you have become my son on the earth. The sinful demons, seeing this your wonderful majestic form will not bear the great vigour, O highest being.

Rudra said:

42-55a. Thus requested by him the ancient Viṣṇu withdrew his form possessed of four arms. He shone as a human being only with two hands. All the demons, his bodyguards, that were there, were deluded by his Māyā, and were covered by mental darkness. In the meanwhile Vasudeva, praised by all gods, took the god, and quickly went from that city. The very strong king of serpents devoutly covered him with a thousand hoods, and accompanied him, when it was raining. At that time the town-gates were opened due to the touch of his feet. Being broken they were wide open; and those (people) that were there, became unconscious. That river Yamunā, that was full, flowed with her water knee-deep only, when the noble one entered her (water). Having crossed Yamunā, the best of the Yadus, being praised by gods, entered (Vraja—the station of cowherds) situated on her bank. There, that wife of Nanda, delivered in the auspicious cow-pen. She who was asleep was deluded by Māyā and covered with Tamas (darkness). That Yādava (i.e. Vasudeva) having placed on her bed the god (i.e. Kṛṣṇa), and taking that daughter again went (back) to Mathurā. Having given that daughter to his wife (Devakī), he remained well-composed. She who was on Devakī's bed, wept due to her being a child. Having heard the voice of the girl in the house, the bodyguards informed Kaṁsa of the auspicious delivery of Devakī. Kaṁsa quickly came there, and seized the girl, and then threw her on a stone. She too quickly went to the sky. Placing her foot on his head, she stood with her full face (visible). The goddess with eight arms said to the lord of demons:

The goddess said:

55b-56. O dull one, what is the use of having thrown me? He who will kill you, is born. He, who is the creator, the sustainer and the destroyer of the world is born in this world. He will snatch your life.

Rudra said:

57-58. Having spoken like this, the goddess filling the sky with her lustre, and being praised by gods and gandharvas, suddenly went to the Himālaya mountain. Then Kaṁsa, with his mind dejected, and oppressed by fear, called his demons led by Pralamba, Cāṇūra, and said to them:

Kaṁsa said:

59-61. All hosts of gods, through our fear, have gone to the Milky Ocean, and have told everything about the destruction of the demons to Viṣṇu. Hearing their words, the supporter of the earth, the immutable one is born on the earth as a human being. So today, all you demons, taking any form as you desire, kill, without any fear children of excessive might.

Rudra said:

62-63. Having thus ordered (them), and having comforted and freed Vasudeva and Devakī, he entered his own house. Vasudeva then went to the excellent cow-pen (Vraja) of Nanda. Honoured by him, he gladly kept his son there. The descendant of Yadu said to Yaśodā, Nanda's wife:

Vasudeva said:

64. O honoured mother, protect as your own son, this son of mine, born from Rohiṇī's womb, who has come (i.e. been brought) here through fear of Kaṁsa.

Rudra said:

65-70. Nanda's delicate wife, of a firm vow, said, "All right". And having received a son of the pair, nourished him with joy. Having kept the sons in the house of the cowherd Nanda, Vasudeva being confident, went to Mathurā protected by Kaṁsa. Then on an auspicious day, Garga, impelled by Vasudeva, went to the cow-pen (Vraja) of the cowherd Nanda. The brāhmaṇa was honoured by the (people) residing there. Having duly performed their birth-rites in Gokula of the god, he gave divine names to Vasudeva's sons. The brāhmaṇa gave the elder one such names as Saṁkarṣaṇa, Rauhiṇeya, Balabhadra, Mahābala, Rāma. (He named) the younger one as Śrīdhara, Śrīkara, Śrīmat, Kṛṣṇa, Ananta, Jagatpati, Vāsudeva, Hṛṣīkeśa etc.

71-87. "In this world they will be known by the names Rāma, Kṛṣṇa." The best brāhmaṇa, having said so, and having worshipped the dead ancestors and deities, and being honoured by the cowherds again came (back) to Mathurā. At night Kaṁsa sent Pūtanā, the killer of children. She gave her breast smeared with poison to Kṛṣṇa of unlimited lustre (for being sucked by him). Knowing her to be a demoness, Kṛṣṇa the very lustrous, the best of the Yadus, drank (i.e. sucked) her breast deeply and profusely along with the life of the demoness. She with her body afflicted, and with her sinews suddenly cut off, fell down trembling and making a loud sound died. With her loud sound the sky was filled. Then all the cowherds seeing the demoness fallen on the ground, and Kṛṣṇa playing on her large breasts, were frightened. Being dejected, they quickly took the boy, and due to the fear of the demon, sprinkled with the cow's tail cowdung on his head. O you beautiful lady, the cowherd Nanda came and took the son. Having sprinkled (water) on all the limbs of his body to the accompaniment of (the utterance of) the names of the lord, put that wicked, fearful (demoness) out of Vraja. The group of cowherds who were frightened burnt her in that Vraja. Once Madhusūdana, Viṣṇu, lying under a cart, and having spread out his feet wept. With the stroke of his foot, he turned over the cart. With the pitchers and pots scattered about, it fell upside down. Then the cowherds and cowherdesses, seeing that great cart, were very much amazed, being apprehensive of what it was. The amazed Yaśodā quickly took the boy. Within just a short time only the two boys, the best Yadus, nourished with Yaśodā's milk, and growing, shone while crawling on their knees and hands. A fraudulent demon, disguised as a lad, set out to kill Kṛṣṇa, moved on the earth. Kṛṣṇa, knowing him to be a demon, struck him with his foot. In the form of the demon only he fell down and died. Then Kṛṣṇa roamed in the entire cowshed.

88-94. In every house of the cowherdesses, he took away butter. Then Yaśodā who was angry, tied him with a rope to a mortar and went to sell milk etc. Kṛṣṇa, the supporter of the earth, tied to the mortar with a rope, dragged it, and went between two arjuna trees. With the mortar Kṛṣṇa knocked down the two trees. With their trunks broken, they fell on the ground making a sound. Due to (i.e. on hearing) that loud sound, old, very vigorous cowherds went there, and seeing it were very much amazed. Yaśodā also being dejected freed the lord of the earth and taking him who was amazed gave the noble one her breast (i.e. breast-fed him). Since the lord of the world was tied with a rope (dāmnā) by his mother, therefore, he was called, *Dāmodara* by all the great sages. The two arjuna trees reached the status of kinnaras.

95-100. Then all the old cowherds, led by the cowherd Nanda, regarding it to be a great portent, went to another place. In the charming Vṛndāvana on the auspicious bank of Yamunā, they made an abode for the cows and the cowherdesses. Then the growing, very strong Rāma and Kṛṣṇa, accompanied by keepers of calves, looked after the calves. A great demon, named Baka, endeavoured in the form of a crane to kill Kṛṣṇa, the best of the Yadus, who was with the cows and the calves. Seeing him, Viṣṇu also easily raised a clod and struck on his wing. The great demon fell on the earth. Then after a few days, he, looking after the cows and calves in the forest, slept on the earth on sprouts under the shade of a jambū tree.

101-107. In the meanwhile god Brahmā surrounded by hosts of gods came to see Kṛṣṇa, and seeing the two best Yadus (i.e. Balarāma and Kṛṣṇa) asleep, snatched the calves and the children of the cowherds, and again went (back) to heaven. When they got up they saw that the children and the calves were lost. They were amazed as to where the cows, calves, and children of the cowherds had gone. Knowing that it was the act done by the Creator, Kṛṣṇa, the ancient one, created the children, the cows and the calves just like that. Madhusūdana, the protector and the lord of the worlds, quickly created the calves and the cowherds of the same form. In the evening the cows—the mothers—seeing their own calves having come (back) behaved as before. When thus the period of a year was passed by the noble one, the creator again gave him (back) the calves and the children. Brahmā, the lord of the three worlds, with his palms joined, taking himself round and saluting Govinda, spoke through fear:

Brahmā said:

108-113. Salutation to you, the soul of all; to you of the nature of true knowledge, of the nature of eternal joy; to the noble one, of a loving soul. You are minute, are of a big, gross form. You are omnipresent, immutable. O you, the beginning, the middle and the end, salutation to you. Salutation to you of eternal knowledge, power and supremacy; to you full of valour and lustre; to you, O you of a great power; to you of the form of six qualities. O brahman, you are the Supreme Being (described) of the Vedas; you are the great Puruṣa; you are the embodied Supreme Being; you are the Supreme Being of the sacred texts. You are the four (great) men; you are the best ancient man. O Brahman, the earth, fire, air are your powers. Due to your words the earth and fire sprang up, O lord of the world. With your life, O lord, the atmosphere and air were created.

114-118. O you immutable one, in the same way, from your eyes were created the sky and the sun; and O sinless one, from your ears were created the quarters and the moon. From your mind, O great god, were created the flow of water and Varuṇa. That Brahman which is manifested in the Mīmāṁsā that is proclaimed, is also (manifested) in sacrifices or in a great vow, in the hymns that are sung, in the sky, in the heaven. It is also the air. It is also in the sky, so also in the herbs. It is also in the stars, all planets, and the sun also. In the same way it is in the beings. The holy texts call it 'Brahman'. That also is the highest Brahman, well known and immortal all round.

119-122. *Hiraṇmaya*, *Avyaya* (Immutable), *Yajña*, *Śuci* (Pure), *Śucipād* (of pure feet)—these are his epithets in the Vedas. Nowhere is his (likeness found). The holy text describes him as *Cakṣurmaya* (consisting of eyes), *Śrotramaya* (consisting of ears), *Chandomaya* (consisting of Vedas), *Manomaya* (consisting of mind), *Vāṅmaya* (consisting of speech), the highest soul, the highest god. O you lotus-eyed one, thus you are the (sole) aim of the Upaniṣads. This one is not able to praise you, who has mastered the entire Vedānta. It was a great offence that I snatched your calves. O you who are affectionate to those who seek your shelter, forgive me.

Maheśvara said:

123-130. The Creator, having thus praised Viṣṇu, and having repeatedly saluted him, gave him (back) the calves, and went home. He, delighted, nourished, and practising severe penance, always keeping in his mind Viṣṇu in the form of a child, lived with the gods, O goddess. Kṛṣṇa created the calves and children as before. They became one with him, when the gods were observing (i.e. in the presence of gods). With the keepers of the calves Kṛṣṇa went to Nandagokula. Then after a few days the best of Yadus, Acyuta, Madhusūdana, went with the cowherds to the pool of Yamunā, and there having injured easily with his one foot the thousand hoods of the very strong serpent, made him face the risk to his life. That Kāliya, regaining consciousness, sought his shelter. Then revered Kṛṣṇa protected the serpent who had given up his poison. Having made marks with his foot on the hoods of him who was afraid of Garuḍa, the best of the Yadus banished him from the pool of Yamunā.

131-137. Then that Kāliya, along with his sons and wife, quickly left that pool. Having saluted Govinda he went (elsewhere). The trees on the bank that were formerly scorched by (Kāliya's) poison, on being seen by Kṛṣṇa quickly bore flowers and fruits. Madhusūdana, the lord, full of all gods, after having attained youth in (due) time, looked after the herd of cows. The best Yadu, with cowherds of his age and with Balarāma, moved in the charming Vṛndāvana. There having killed a very fierce demon of a huge body and of the form of a serpent and as big as Meru and Mandāra (mountains), he reached the forest of Dhenuka having the arbours of palm trees like tāla and hintāla; he entered that charming forest, full of fruits and having arbours of palm trees, and having lifted Dhenuka, of the size of a mountain, and always having the form of an ass (or a cruel form), by seizing his feet, he struck him against a palm tree. At that moment only his keepers rejoiced near him.

138-143. Quickly moving out from that forest they came to the Bhāṇḍīra forest. There they played children's sports with Rāma and Kṛṣṇa. A demon named Pralamba came there in the guise of a cowherd. Putting Rāma on his back he quickly went to the sky. Knowing him to be a demon Rāma angrily struck his head with his fist; then he, with his body afflicted, fell (down). Roaring with a loud voice in his demonish form only, he, with his head and body broken, and smeared with blood, died. Then Nanda's son (Kṛṣṇa) remained, in the evening, in Govraja (cow-pen), with the young cowherdesses, sporting in

Kaumodavarcasa. The best demon Ariṣṭa went there in the form of a bull; as he had come to kill Kṛṣṇa, he roared loudly.

144–149. Seeing him, all cowherds, oppressed by fear, ran away. Kṛṣṇa too, seeing the chief of demons to have come, uprooted a palm tree and hurt him with it between his horns. He, with his head and horns broken, and vomiting profuse blood, died while roaring. Thus having killed Ariṣṭa, the chief demon of a huge body, he called the young cowherds, and lived there only in Govraja (cow-pen). Then after a few days a great demon named Keśin came to Vraja taking up the body of a horse, to kill Govinda. Having gone to that charming Govraja, he neighed loudly. Due to that neighing all the three worlds were filled. All the hosts of gods, thinking it to be the end of the age, were frightened.

150-154. All the cowherds and cowherdesses living there were confounded and disturbed. Coming to senses they all ran on all sides. Saying "Protect (us)", the cowherdesses sought Kṛṣṇa's shelter. He who loved his devotees, said, "Do not be afraid, do not be afraid." Then he, the younger brother of Indra, having comforted them, easily and quickly struck with his fist on the head of the demon. With his teeth and eyes broken, he roared very loudly. He (i.e. Kṛṣṇa) lifting a great rock, dropped it on his body. The great demon with his entire body crushed, and roaring with a fierce sound, suddenly dropped on the ground and died.

155-156. Seeing Keśin killed, the hosts of gods in heaven profusely dropped showers of flowers and said, "Well (done), well (done)." Viṣṇu (i.e. Kṛṣṇa) having thus killed in his childhood very powerful demons, just happily rejoiced with Balarāma.

157-162. He was dark like the petals of a blue lotus. His eyes resembled lotus-petals. He wore a yellow garment. He had put on a garland. He was graced with a garland of wood-flowers. His chest shone with the Kaustubha (gem). He had a chaplet on his head, and smearing (of sandal etc.). He was (adorned) with lovely ornaments. He was graced with earrings. He had worn a tulasī-garland. He had put on the mark of musk. His very glossy, dark, curly hair was tied into a braid. He had the head ornaments of a peacock's plumage with various kinds of flowers tied; the palms of his hands, the soles of his feet and his lips resembled red lotus. Between the sides (shone) his face with the eyebrows resembling the spot on the moon. He shone with necklaces, anklets, armlets and bracelets. The descendant of Yadu, sweetly playing upon the flute remained in the very charming Vṛndāvana, graced with fruits and flowers.

163-167. Seeing Viṣṇu who had despised the beauty of crores of Cupids, all the cowherdesses were tormented by Cupid's missile. Formerly all sages living in Daṇḍaka forest, seeing Rāma desired to enjoy Rāma of a beautiful body. All of them, turned into women, were born in Gokula. Having approached Viṣṇu with love, they were then freed from the ocean of the mundane existence. Since the demons angrily came to Kṛṣṇa, and met with death in the battle, they after being killed, obtained liberation. In the world lust and anger of people are the cause of (their falling into) hell. The cowherdesses, haters of gods (in their former existence), having devoutly approached him, were liberated.

168-173. Those who betake themselves to Viṣṇu (even) through lust, fear or hatred reach Vaikuṇṭha. Then what to say of those who do so through devotion! Having heard the sound of his flute at night the wives of the cowherds all got up from their beds with their garments and hair dishevelled. Tormented by Cupid's arrows, they left their husbands, sons, relatives, so also sense of shame and their own family; they came to the lord of the world. All the cowherdesses, having approached Govinda, embraced him with their arms, and enjoyed (i.e. kissed) his lower lip as the gods enjoy nectar. With all those, the lord of the self sported in Govraja. All those fearless women also sported with him in Vraja. Thus day after day they sported with Keśava in the charming Vṛndāvana and the bank of Yamunā.

Pārvatī said:

174. How would he, Janārdana, who had descended on the earth for the protection of Dharma, approach others' wives?

Rudra said:

175-177. O you of an auspicious face, he does not differentiate between his own body and those of others. The entire world is his body. There is nothing different from it. Due to his naturally being the lord, the master of the soul and the lord of the world, the noble one does not recognise the difference between a male and a female. So also due to his power of removing sins the (all-) pervading lord, the highest soul, the god, is not at a fault, O fortunate one.

Vasiṣṭha said:

178. Having thus spoken to Pārvatī, Rudra, the destroyer of Śrī Tripura, commenced telling the whole life of Kṛṣṇa.

Rudra said:

179-183. When autumn arrived, the cowherds led by the cowherd Nanda started celebrating the festival of the lord of gods (i.e. Indra). But Kṛṣṇa stopped that festival of Indra, and he, the powerful one, got celebrated the festival of Govardhana, the lord of mountains. Then the angry Indra, continuously poured down very heavy showers for seven nights in Govraja of Nanda. Kṛṣṇa, having uprooted the great mountain Govardhana, easily held it for the protection of the cows. O you of a good vow, having got the protection of the mountain, the cowherds and cowherdesses lived happily only as if they were in a mansion.

184-186. Then the thousand-eyed Indra who was afraid, with his mind confounded, stopped that shower, and went to that Vraja of Nanda. Kṛṣṇa too put the great mountain as before. All those old cowherds, led by the cowherd Nanda, worshipped Govinda (i.e. Kṛṣṇa) and were very much amazed. Then god Indra, having approached Kṛṣṇa, with his palms joined praised him with a voice faltering due to joy.

Indra said:

187-195. O lotus-eyed one, O omniscient one, O superior Viṣṇu, salutation to you. I salute you, O you who are beyond the three constituent qualities (of sattva, rajas and tamas), O lord of all, and the soul of the universe. You yourself are the sacrifice, the formula used on making an oblation to a deity; you are Oṁkāra, sacrifice (or power), oblation. O Keśava, you are the father and the mother of all gods. Before the creation you, Hiraṇyagarbha, existed. You alone are the lord, the Supreme Being, the Brahman. O god, you alone have supported this earth and heaven. O lord of the world, you thus give yourself (to your devotees) and give fruits (of devotion). O you, the lord of the worlds, gods have obtained light. O ancient one, your shadow is nectar as well as death. To that god, to you, we offer an oblation. From him these golden ones have come up. O Keśava, of him the oceans and the earth are the carrier. O you immutable one, these directions, intermediate directions and the air (Vāyu) belong to you. To that god, to you, who growing (in size) again got on the earth, we offer an oblation. O Brahman, O great lord, you supported heaven. In the atmosphere you remain in a mote of the sun-beam. You are omnipresent and immutable.

196-204. To that god we offer our oblation, to whom, shining, of a hot lustre and full of qualities, you cry.* Śrī would always necessarily see him mentally. In the highest place (i.e. in him) the sun, that has risen, shines. To you, that god, we offer an oblation. Your great water conceiving at the time of creation create the streams of water. Who, the immutable lord of gods (but you) stood before the demon? To you, that god, we offer our oblation. The water saw Dakṣa Prajāpati. Having a sacrifice they first produce the oblation. You are, among the gods, the superior god, the greatest of the great. To you, that god, we offer an oblation. You the immutable Man, the creator of the world, (please) do not harm us. He, the lord, of a pious act, created heaven. He created the moon, profuse water and the entire world. To you, that god, we offer our oblation. O lord, all these created objects have been around you.

205-211. O lord, beings have sprung from you. You are Acyuta. The future and the past are due to you. Let that, desiring which we offer a sacrifice, come to us wholly. Due to your kind gaze, may we be the lords of the three (worlds). You are the Supreme Being called Hiraṇmaya, having golden beard and moustache. From the point of the nail everything is gold. The sun shares gold. This is omnipresent Brahman that has settled as

*Vv. 196, 198, 199, 200, 201 etc. are not clear.

the sun. That is the excellent, best lustre of god Savitṛ. May we always think of the form of you who always illumine our minds. O you lotus-eyed one, O you lord of Śrī, O you lord of all, O Keśava, salutation to you. O you fit to be known through Vedānta, O lord of sacrifices, O you of the form of sacrifice, salutation to you. Salutation to you, to Vāsudeva, dressed as a cowherd. I have offended (you) by destroying all that. Forgive it, O lord of the world, O you ocean of compassion, O Supreme Being. In a short time kill Kaṁsa who is unassailable. Having done good to the gods, live in happiness, settling on the earth.

Mahādeva said:

212-221. Indra, the lord of all gods, having thus praised Kṛṣṇa, crowned him with nectar and divine garments and ornaments. Having worshipped the lord of gods, he went (back) to heaven. The old cowherds and cowherdesses saw Indra there. And being honoured by him, they were very much delighted. The very brave Rāma and Kṛṣṇa adorned with divine ornaments, remained happily in Nanda's Govraja. O goddess, in the meanwhile, the best sage Nārada suddenly went to Mathurā, and entered Kaṁsa's vicinity. Being honoured by the king there, he was seated on an auspicious seat. He informed him of the acts of Viṣṇu, the active exertion of the deities and the birth of Viṣṇu (as Kṛṣṇa). So also (he told him about) Vasudeva's having put his son in Vraja, the death of the demons, and the expulsion of the king of the serpents; so also about (Kṛṣṇa's) holding up the best mountain (i.e. Govardhana) and the meeting with Indra. Having told Kaṁsa everything fully he, honoured by the demon, went to Brahmā's abode. Kaṁsa, with his mind dejected and surrounded by his ministers, deliberated with them about his death. There the very powerful lord of demons, Kaṁsa, told about the mission for his good to Akrūra, the best among the intelligent ones and loving Dharma.

Kaṁsa said:

222-228. Due to my fear all gods led by Indra, overcome by fear, approached Viṣṇu and sought his shelter. He, Madhusūdana, the revered creator of the beings, granted them exemption from fear and was born from Devakī's womb. The wicked-hearted Vasudeva also deceived me and at night he, the very wicked one, put his son in Nanda's house. Even as a child he killed the unassailable great demons. There is no doubt that he is also ready to kill me. But even gods and demons along with Indra cannot kill him. So having brought him here, I must kill him with (some) stratagem. Through intoxicated elephants, wrestlers, or excellent horses—with this or that means he can be killed here. Therefore, O best of the Yadus, having gone to Govraja, fetch here to enjoy the ceremony of arrows, Kṛṣṇa, Rāma, so also all old cowherds led by Nanda, O descendant of Yadu.

Mahādeva said:

229-242. Saying "All right", the best of the Yadus, the powerful one, eager to see Kṛṣṇa, got into a chariot and went to the charming Gokula. Akrūra, the best among the great devotees of Viṣṇu possessed of politeness, saw the unafflicted Kṛṣṇa settled among the cows. (He was) like a dark cloud; (he was) adorned with all ornaments; his eyes (were large) like lotus-leaves; (he had) long arms, and (was) healthy. (He had) covered himself with a yellow garment; (he was) handsome in all limbs; (his) chest (was) shining with the Kaustubha; (he was) graced with jewelled earrings. (He possessed) the garland of tulasī (-leaves) and wood-flowers; (he had put on) ear-ornaments of wood-flowers. Seeing Kṛṣṇa surrounded by young cowherdesses, he, the descendant of Yadu, with his entire body horripilated and his eyes full of tears of joy, got down from the chariot and saluted him. Joyfully approaching Kṛṣṇa, taking himself round him, and saluting him, he put on his head (Kṛṣṇa's) feet resembling red lotuses and marked with the signs of Vajra, and repeatedly saluted him. That descendant of Yadu then saw Balarāma resembling the full autumnal moon and decorated with pearl-necklaces, and saluted him. The two heroes, best of the Yadus, raised him with joy, and having embraced him, came home with that Akrūra, a descendant of Vṛṣṇi. The cowherd Nanda, of a great lustre, seeing the best of the Yadus to have arrived (there), approached him, and having seated him on an excellent seat, gladly, duly and devoutly honoured him with materials of worship, water for washing his feet, divine garments and adorations. Akrūra, a descendant of Yadu, gave garments and ornaments to Rāma, Kṛṣṇa, to the cowherd Nanda, and to Yaśodā. The intelligent one seated on a kuśa-seat asked the cool one about his well-being, and asked about all the stateaffairs, said to him:

Akrūra said:

243-251. This Kṛṣṇa of great lustre, actually the immutable Viṣṇu, requested by the hosts of gods and magnanimous sages for the good of the deities and the protection of the good, so also for the destruction of those who were a burden to the earth, and for establishing righteousness, was born in (i.e. from) the belly (i.e. womb) of Devakī at midnight in rainy season. Through Kaṁsa's fear Vasudeva brought the lord of gods, Viṣṇu, his son, and put him in your house in that night. At that time only, the glorious Yaśodā gave birth to a daughter of an auspicious face born from a portion of Māyā (of the lord). She had deluded this entire auspicious Vraja. (Vasudeva) having put the best Yadu (i.e. Kṛṣṇa) on the bed of unconscious Yaśodā took the daughter and went home. Having put her on Devakī's bed, he came out. She (i.e. the daughter), remaining in Devakī's bed then quickly cried. O you of a good vow, having heard it (i.e. her crying), Kaṁsa suddenly took the girl and the powerful one, having whirled her, dropped her on a stone. That girl, (then) got up; and she having eight hands and weapons, and remaining in the sky, angrily spoke to Kaṁsa in a grave voice:

The girl said:

252. O you mean demon, he who is the Supreme Being, the lord of all gods, the eternal one, has gone to Vraja (is born) to kill you.

Akrūra said:

253-261. Speaking like this that Mahāmayā (the Great Illusion) went to the Himālaya (mountain). Since then the wicked one, with his mind dejected through fear, sent demons to kill the noble (Kṛṣṇa). This intelligent boy alone easily killed them all. The highest god performed very wonderful acts. Having heard about (these acts like) holding the Govardhana (mountain), expulsion of the king of serpents, meeting with Indra, death of all demons, which were told to him by the divine sage (Nārada), he, tormented by fear is eager to take from here the unassailable Rāma and Kṛṣṇa of mighty arms and to get them killed by intoxicated great elephants or by wrestlers. He has sent me here to fetch Kṛṣṇa. The wicked one has imprisoned Vasudeva. (I have) told you all these acts of that very wicked one. To enjoy the ceremony of arrows all you cowherds, inhabitants of Vraja please go tomorrow, taking with you curd, ghee etc., and with Rāma and Kṛṣṇa to him. There is no doubt that Kaṁsa will be killed by Kṛṣṇa. Therefore, giving up your fear go (to Mathurā) by the order of the king.

The lord said:

262-272. Speaking like this, that very intelligent Akrūra became silent. Hearing those fierce and awe-inspiring words of him all old cowherds led by the cowherd Nanda, stupefied by grief, were in an indescribable ocean of sorrow. Seeing them (like that) the lotus-eyed Kṛṣṇa cheered them. The powerful one said: "Do not entertain any fear from the demon. Accompanied by Rāma and you, I shall go to Mathurā to destroy this wicked Kaṁsa. Having killed there that wicked Kaṁsa, the chief of demons, so also having killed all demons, I shall protect the earth. Therefore, giving up your grief, go to Mathurā." The cowherds led by the cowherd Nanda, who were thus addressed by Kṛṣṇa, repeatedly embraced him, and smelt his head. Having thought over the immeasurable acts of the very noble one, and on Akrūra's words, all the cowherds, were free from affliction. Yaśodā gave Akrūra many pure cooked foods—tasty, savoury, and sweet—so also sumptuous, agreeable meals. The best of the Yadus (i.e. Akrūra) enjoyed, along with Rāma, Kṛṣṇa, the best cowherds like Nanda, so also the young and the old people, the food given by Yaśodā, which was tasteful, removed foulness, diseases, which was good, in her (house) that was well decorated.

273-279. Having properly fed them and having given them water to rinse their mouths with, she of a firm vow, gave him a tāmbūla with camphor. When the sun had set, the Yādava, having offered the evening prayer, and having, along with Rāma and Kṛṣṇa, enjoyed the excellent food of sweetened milk, went to sleep with them. Kṛṣṇa slept as Viṣṇu on the Śeṣa, in that best mansion that was charming, illumined with lamps, beautiful, that had lovely beds, and that was graced with various flowers. Seeing him, the excellent bliss, Akrūra, marked with tears of joy and horripilation, gave up his sleep of ignorance, and the best devotee of Viṣṇu shampooed the feet of Viṣṇu (i.e. Kṛṣṇa). "By (doing) this much my life is fruitful; I have lived well. This is the prosperity in the three worlds; this is the best happiness, this is the righteous kingdom; this is the best joy of liberation.

280-284. It is not possible to recollect it mentally by deities like Śiva, Brahmā, best sages like Sanaka, and great sages like Vasiṣṭha. That couple of feet of the lord of Śrī, bright like the autumnal lotuses, and touched by Indirā, Lakṣmī with her hands, gives great pleasure. Fortunately I have secured this auspicious lotus-like couple of feet of Viṣṇu." Due to that great joy of (having secured) Brahman, the night passed as a moment. Then when the morning dawned Viṣṇu, being praised in heaven by the best hosts of gods, got up from the bed. Having properly rinsed his mouth, the intelligent one, along with Rāma, fell at the feet of his mother and made the departure agreeable.

285-287. Having raised them, Yaśodā, full of grief and joy, and with her face full of tears, affectionately embraced her sons. The respectable lady of a firm vow conferred a blessing (on them) and after repeatedly embracing the great heroes, she allowed them to go. Akrūra also saluted Yaśodā and with his palms joined, said:

Akrūra said:

288-289. O glorious one, I shall (now) leave. O sinless one, favour me. This Kṛṣṇa of great arms will, after killing the very powerful Kaṁsa, be the king of the entire world. There is no doubt about it. Therefore, O you of an excellent face, give up sorrow and be happy.

The lord said:

290-297. Thus addressed she allowed Akrūra, the best of Yadus, to go. With Rāma and Kṛṣṇa he got into an excellent chariot. Being praised by groups of celestial nymphs he quickly went to Mathurā. All old cowherds led by the cowherd Nanda, followed him. Seeing that Kṛṣṇa going the cowherdesses again took curd, ghee, various fruits, and followed Kṛṣṇa going out, seated in a chariot. Kṛṣṇa sent back all the cowherdesses. With their minds tormented by grief, they wept for the lotus-eyed one. They repeatedly wept saying, "O Kṛṣṇa, O Kṛṣṇa, O Kṛṣṇa, O Govinda." The helpless ones with their eyes full of tears, remained there weeping. Then Akrūra, the Yādava, along with Rāma and Kṛṣṇa drove that chariot from Govraja to Mathurā. Having quickly crossed Yamunā, and having placed the excellent chariot on the bank, having got down from the divine chariot, he set about to bathe there. Then to do the necessary (rites) he plunged in the auspicious water.

298-304. Muttering the expiatory hymn the best devotee of Viṣṇu saw in the water the bright Rāma and Kṛṣṇa. He saw Rāma like a crore of autumnal moons, the lord wearing a dark garment, with his body smeared with divine sandal, and having beauty due to ornaments of pearls, having eyes like red lotuses, and having ear-ornaments of white lotuses; and saw Kṛṣṇa like a dark cloud and wearing a divine yellow garment, having large lotus-like eyes with his body smeared with yellow sandal, and graced with various gems. Seeing (them) there the best Yadu was very much amazed. Getting up he saw the two very mighty ones in the chariot. Again plunging (in the water) and muttering the couple of hymns, he saw Viṣṇu in the ocean of nectar along with Lakṣmī being praised by Sanaka and others and waited upon by all gods. Seeing the god in the water there, he was highly amazed. The best of the Yadus praised the omnipresent god Viṣṇu.

Akrūra said:

305-315. Salutation to you of the nature of Kāla (time or death), to you without a beginning or an end; salutation to you who are unmanifest and unchanging. Salutation to you, the lord of beings; repeated salutations to you, O best being. Salutation to you, the controller of all beings and the highest soul. Salutation to you, the changing and the unchanging, the actual Highest Being; to the lord of qualities and to the restraining (one). Salutation to you who are without such differences as of place and time. Salutation to you, the endless one, and the unfalling one. Salutation to you, to Govinda, to the lord of the three (Vedas), to the holder of the Śārṅga bow, to Nārāyaṇa, Viśva and Vāsudeva. Salutation to you, to Viṣṇu, of many forms; repeated salutation to you, the eternal one; to you, having lotus-like eyes, to the eternal one, to the holder of the conch and the disc. Repeated salutations to you whose brilliance is graced with ornaments resembling crores of rising suns; to Hari; to the lord of all worlds. Salutations to Savitṛ (the generator), to the seed of the worlds, to the highest soul, to Saṁkarṣaṇa, Kṛṣṇa, Pradyumna. Salutation to you, Aniruddha, the supporter, the creator, the origin of everything, having a thousand forms, and having many heads, feet and hands. Salutation to you, having a thousand names, to the eternal one, to the Highest Being. Salutation to you shining on the bed of the serpent, to you of a pleasing form. Salutation to you, to Keśava, having put on a yellow garment, having a bright lustre while pressing in embrace the hard breasts of Lakṣmī, to you Śrīdhara, to the lord of Śrī, and to you having innumerable forms.

The lord said:

316-319. A man who at the time of bathing, meditating upon the ancient god, devoutly recites this hymn, is free from all sins. Having got the fruit of (visiting) all holy places, he would secure absorption in Viṣṇu. That best devotee of Viṣṇu thus praised the god (while remaining) in water and he, Akrūra, worshipped him with water and fragrant flowers. Being blessed, Akrūra then came out of the water of Yamunā and full of auspiciousness approached and saluted Rāma and Kṛṣṇa. Seeing him polite and amazed, Viṣṇu said to him:

Śrī Kṛṣṇa said:

320a. O Yādava, what wonder did you see in the water?

The lord said:

320b. Akrūra spoke to the greatest of the Yadus, Kṛṣṇa, of great lustre:

321-326. "What wonder is there, O lord, of the greatness of you, the omnipresent lord of the world? O Hṛṣīkeśa, you yourself are the entire world. You are the water, the sky, the fire, the earth and the wind. You are this entire world of four kinds, the immobile and the mobile. O Vāsudeva, there is none other than you, as water from cloud only. You are the sacrifice, you are the exclamation on offering an oblation to a deity; you are the Oṁkāra; you are the oblation also. O lord of gods, you have taken up the form to protect righteousness. You obtained the grandeur (of the forms) of the Fish, the Tortoise, the Boar. O lord, you alone protect this entire world, full of you."

The lord said:

327-330. Having thus praised Govinda, and having saluted him, the best of the Yadus got into the divine chariot along with them. Then having quickly reached Mathurā created by gods, he, having kept Rāma and Kṛṣṇa at the city-gate, went into the harem. Then having informed the king of their arrival, he, honoured by the king, entered his own house. Then in the evening Rāma and Kṛṣṇa, holding each other's hands went into Mathurā.

331-335. The two very powerful, noble, best Yadus, while passing along the royal path, saw a washerman dyeing garments. Kṛṣṇa, the powerful one, along with Rāma, seeing him wearing divine garments and coming to the palace, asked for those garments. The washerman did not give them to him, and remaining there on the path spoke to him many caustic words. With the palm of his hand only Kṛṣṇa beat him. On the way itself, he, vomiting much blood, was struck down. Rāma and Kṛṣṇa, the two heroes, along with their relatives, put on those charming garments.

336-342a. The two best Yadus reached the house of a garland-maker. Seeing them he honoured them with fragrant flowers. Being delighted, the two best Yadus granted him his desired boon. Then they came to the path. There they saw a humpbacked lady of a happy face, whose body and back were crooked, and who had held a pot containing sandal. Seeing her they asked for the sandal. She, smiling, gave them excellent sandal. They took that divine sandal, and smeared (their bodies) as they liked. Giving her a beautiful form, they came to the path. Being observed by ladies, the two delicate noble ones of charming faces entered the sacrificial chamber with their followers. Keśava, Madhusūdana, seeing there a decorated, divine bow, easily took it and broke it.

342b-343. Kaṁsa, the chief of demons, seeing that bow being broken, was very much perturbed, called the principal, pre-eminent wrestlers and charioteers, and having deliberated with his ministers said to Cāṇūra:

Kaṁsa said:

344-345. Rāma and Kṛṣṇa, the destroyers of all demons, have come. In the morning kill them in wrestling without hesitation. With this or that means the two, proud of their strength, should be killed with endeavour by intoxicated elephants or chief wrestlers.

The lord said:

346-350. Having directed like this, the king with his younger brother and ministers, mounted, through fear, on the top of his divine palace. He put at all gates and on all paths intoxicated elephants. Everywhere he put wrestlers and intoxicated elephants. Knowing all that the intelligent Kṛṣṇa also, along with Rāma, stayed, with his followers, in the sacrificial chamber in the night. When at the end of the night, the day broke, Rāma and Kṛṣṇa got up from the bed, offered water, were well adorned, and having eaten (something) were eager and ready to fight. They went out of the house as two lions from a cave.

351-354. Kṛṣṇa saw at the gate of Kaṁsa's palace his elephant named Kuvalayāpīḍa who resembled the peak of the Himālaya mountain, bestowed prosperity on Kaṁsa, removed the pride of the elephant of god (Indra), whose body was huge, who was intoxicated. Seeing that great elephant, Kṛṣṇa the supporter of the earth, held his trunk with his hand, and jumping properly, easily whirled him round and threw him on the ground. That great elephant, with his entire body crushed, and crying with a fierce sound, suddenly fell on the ground, and died.

355-361. Having killed him, Rāma and Kṛṣṇa drew out his tusks, seized them and then entered the arena to fight with the wrestlers. The demons that were there, on seeing the valour of Kṛṣṇa were frightened; they fled and came to the harem. Having very securely closed the doors they remained there in thousands. Seeing the doors firmly closed, the mighty Kṛṣṇa easily struck them with his foot and caused them to fall down. The two being broken were knocked down. The army and the troop were arranged. All remaining there were killed with bodies and necks crushed. O you noble one, then the two very strong, magnanimous fleshy ones, eager to fight, whirling the tusks, saw the wrestlers, Cāṇūra and Muṣṭika. Kaṁsa also, seeing the very strong Kṛṣṇa and Rāma, was frightened, and then said to his best wrestler, Cāṇūra:

Kaṁsa said:

362. O wrestler, kill the two young cowherds at this time (i.e. now). Dividing my kingdom I shall readily give you half of it.

The lord said:

363-370. At that time Kṛṣṇa appeared to be great to the wrestlers, like another great Meru mountain in the house and the battle. He, Acyuta, was another fire of destruction in the eyes of Kaṁsa. To women he actually appeared like Cupid, and to his parents like a child. He appeared like Viṣṇu to the gods, and to cowherds like their friend. They there saw the omnipresent Viṣṇu in many forms. Vasudeva, Akrūra, so also the very intelligent cowherd Nanda climbed upon another palace, and saw the great destruction. Devakī, along with ladies staying in the harem, remained there; and all the auspicious ones with their eyes full of tears saw the boy's face. The queen consoled by them entered the house. Then all the hosts of gods, seated in aeroplanes in the sky, praised the lotus-eyed Kṛṣṇa with shouts of victory. The gods, and hosts of Maruts loudly said, "Kill Kaṁsa." In the meanwhile, when the musical instruments were sounded, the very strong, best Yadus attacked the two great wrestlers.

371-376. The magnanimous ones, resembling dark and white mountains fought with them—Kṛṣṇa with Cāṇūra, and Balarāma with Muṣṭika. Due to the fight between the wrestlers, so also to (strokes of) fists and kicks, there was a great havoc, causing fear (even) to gods. Kṛṣṇa, having sported with Cāṇūra for a long time, having crushed the body of the wrestler, easily knocked him down. That great wrestler who caused great unhappiness to gods and demons, vomiting profuse blood, fell on the ground and died. Similarly Rāma fought with Muṣṭika for a long time. The powerful one struck him on his chest with fists. With his bones and sinews broken he fell on the ground. Then all the wrestlers seeing the valour (of Balarāma) ran away.

377-387. Kaṁsa suffering from agony, was very much frightened. In the meanwhile the invincible, magnanimous heroes, Rāma and Kṛṣṇa got upon the high palatial seat. Kṛṣṇa, Hari, striking with one foot Kaṁsa on his head knocked him down on the ground from the top of the palace. He, with all his limbs broken, (fell) dead on the ground. When Kṛṣṇa had killed Kaṁsa, very strong Rāma also struck his (Kaṁsa's) younger brother Sunāman with the fist only. The supporter of the earth (i.e. Balarāma) knocked him down on the ground. Rāma and Kṛṣṇa, having killed the wicked Kaṁsa along with his younger brother, approached their parents, and saluted them devoutly. Devakī and Vasudeva repeatedly embraced them and longing for sons, smelled the two affectionately on their heads. Over them the breasts of Devakī showered milk. Then having cheered up their parents, Rāma and Kṛṣṇa went out. O goddess, in the meanwhile divine drums were beaten, and the chief gods dropped showers of flowers. The divine hosts of gods having praised and saluted Kṛṣṇa, and being very highly pleased, went to their respective worlds. Kṛṣṇa, the pious one, along with Rāma saluted the cowherd Nanda and the old cowherds, and joyfully embraced them. He gladly gave them wealth with many gems.

388-392. Kṛṣṇa honoured all those old cowherds with garments, ornaments etc. and with much wealth and corn. Dismissed by that Kṛṣṇa, they, led by the cowherd Nanda, and full of joy and sorrow, went to the divine Vraja. Having approached their maternal grandfather, the invincible Rāma and Kṛṣṇa freed him from imprisonment, and having repeatedly consoled him, Kṛṣṇa consecrated him on the kingdom (i.e. as the king). Through best brāhmaṇas he got performed the obsequies of Kaṁsa. Having installed the chief Yadus like Akrūra on the kingdom (i.e. as kings) he made Ugrasena the (chief) king, and Kṛṣṇa, Vasudeva's pious son, ruled the kingdom righteously.